Th
I Dreame

February 2014

To Ellen —

About your fabulous friend

Bill Ehrhart

From a friend to you both!

Love,
Gato

The Last Time I Dreamed About the War

Essays on the Life and Writing of W.D. Ehrhart

Edited by JEAN-JACQUES MALO

McFarland & Company, Inc., Publishers
Jefferson, North Carolina

ALSO OF INTEREST:
Edited by Jean-Jacques Malo *and* Tony Williams: *Vietnam War Films: More Than 600 Feature, Made-for-TV, Pilot and Short Movies, 1939–1992, from the United States, Vietnam, France, Belgium, Australia, Hong Kong, South Africa, Great Britain and Other Countries* (1994; paperback 2012)

W. D. Ehrhart's *Vietnam–Perkasie* and *Passing Time* are also available as ebooks.

Poems and excerpts of poems by W. D. Ehrhart are published here by permission of W. D. Ehrhart, who wishes to express gratitude to all of the publishers over the years who have taken his work seriously enough to publish it, McFarland included.

LIBRARY OF CONGRESS CATALOGUING-IN-PUBLICATION DATA

The Last Time I Dreamed About the War : Essays on the Life and Writing of W. D. Ehrhart / edited by Jean-Jacques Malo.
    p.   cm.
Includes bibliographical references and index.

ISBN 978-0-7864-7699-2 (softcover : acid free paper) ∞
ISBN 978-1-4766-1653-7 (ebook)

1. Ehrhart, W. D. (William Daniel), 1948– I. Malo, Jean-Jacques, 1958– editor of compilation.
PS3555.H67Z73 2014
811'.54—dc23
[B]   2014005445

BRITISH LIBRARY CATALOGUING DATA ARE AVAILABLE

© 2014 Jean-Jacques Malo. All rights reserved

No part of this book may be reproduced or transmitted in any form or by any means, electronic or mechanical, including photocopying or recording, or by any information storage and retrieval system, without permission in writing from the publisher.

Front cover image of soldiers © iStock/Thinkstock

Printed in the United States of America

McFarland & Company, Inc., Publishers
  Box 611, Jefferson, North Carolina 28640
    www.mcfarlandpub.com

Acknowledgments

I wish to thank W. D. Ehrhart for his graciousness in answering all the queries from contributors, including myself, and making material available for the research of this book. All poems printed and quoted herein are used with the permission of the author, for which I am grateful.

I want to express gratitude to John S. Baky, the curator of the Imaginative Representations of the Vietnam War Collection at La Salle University in Philadelphia. His active support and help were essential in the creation of this volume. This Vietnam War Collection is the most important research center in the field for scholarly research into the literature of the Vietnam War and its aftermath. The W. D. Ehrhart Archive, in its entirety, resides in that Collection at La Salle University. The Ehrhart Archive includes 32 linear feet of manuscript and holograph material, personal correspondence, editorial material and variant editions, marketing correspondence, reviews, editorials, and visual material and ephemera. These archives constitute the entire literary biography of one of the most important and early literary figures of the era. There are no other collections of material by or about W. D. Ehrhart that compare with this archive. The Imaginative Representations of the Vietnam War Collection is the largest collection in the world of novels, short stories, poetry, film, graphic art, and ephemera related to the Vietnam War and its aftermath.

I extend my sincere thanks to all the people who showed interest in this project and who supported me, particularly Kirstie Le Poul in the last stages of the preparation of the manuscript.

Table of Contents

Acknowledgments v
Preface 1

Part One. The Prose Writer of Memoirs and Essays 13
    "*Making the Children Behave*"—*W. D. Ehrhart*

Darkness Carried: W. D. Ehrhart's Memoirs 14
    DONALD ANDERSON

"The Chameleon War": *Passing Time* and the Remembrance
    of the Vietnam War 22
    SUBARNO CHATTARJI

W. D. Ehrhart, Essayist: Musings of a Librarian and Friend 31
    DAVID A. WILLSON

Part Two. The Poet as an Artist 49
    "*The Farmer*"—*W. D. Ehrhart*

Relieving the National Debt: W. D. Ehrhart and the Wages
    of Memory 50
    AMMIEL ALCALAY

"We are the ones you sent": Moral Responsibility and War
    in the Poetry of W. D. Ehrhart 59
    ADAM GILBERT

W. D. Ehrhart at the Vietnam Veterans Memorial 77
    DIEDERIK OOSTDIJK

From Patriot to Poet to Peacenik 88
    NICOLE GOLLNER

Poetry and the Art of Resistance: The Literature
    of W. D. Ehrhart, in Context 99
    DALE RITTERBUSCH

W. D. Ehrhart and Chimei Hamada: War Memories of a Poet
and of a Print Artist 109
    Yoko Shirai

The Poetry of W. D. Ehrhart: A Bibliographic Essay 120
    N. Bradley Christie

The Art of Writing Poetry: An Interview with W. D. Ehrhart 139
    Jean-Jacques Malo

Part Three. The Influential Writer 155
    "The Heart of the Poem"—W. D. Ehrhart

Ehrhart Effect 156
    Jan Barry

The Importance of Being Earnest: A Veteran's Eye View
of W. D. Ehrhart's Vietnam War Poetry and Prose 167
    Edward F. Palm

Authentic Voices: Echoes of Bill Ehrhart and Me 178
    Robert C. Doyle

W. D. Ehrhart and Adastra Press: A Publisher's Perspective 187
    Gary Metras

**Part Four. The Educator Who Knows Things
Worth Knowing** 197
    "The Teacher"—W. D. Ehrhart

Bill Ehrhart as Educator 199
    Martin Novelli

W. D. Ehrhart: Teacher-Poet 207
    Charles L. Yates

W. D. Ehrhart: Transformational Teacher 219
    Joseph Cox

"I have learned by now where such thoughts lead":
W. D. Ehrhart's Poetry and Rethinking How We Study
and Teach History 228
    Matthew K. Irwin

Making the Wreckage Beautiful 241
    Clint Van Winkle

Appendix A: Ehrhart's Military History 247
Appendix B: Ehrhart Poems Selected by Contributors 249
An Ehrhart Bibliography 267
Selected Works About Ehrhart 269
About the Contributors 271
Index 275

*If you need a reason to care,
consider this feather I've found,
consider the sweetness of bare
young arms in sunlight, or the round
perfection of a ripe pear.*
　　　　　　　—W. D. Ehrhart*

---

*"Nothing Profound," *Beautiful Wreckage: New & Selected Poems* (Easthampton, MA: Adastra Press, 1999), 222.

Preface

W. D. Ehrhart has been writing since he was a teenager, even before he joined the Marines straight out of high school in 1966. He has been publishing for a bit less time—four decades. *A Generation of Peace*, his first book of poetry, appeared in 1975—only three years after he was first anthologized in *Winning Hearts & Minds: War Poems by Vietnam Veterans*.[1] His twentieth opus, *Dead on a High Hill: Essays on War, Literature and Living, 2002–2012*,[2] came out in 2012. In addition he has also published ten chapbooks of verse. He is therefore a prolific writer who has dealt with a variety of genres: poetry, memoir, and essays. His prose and poetry have appeared in hundreds of publications.

Ehrhart is renowned as one of the major Vietnam War authors, for having penned a trilogy of memoirs about his war experience, both in Southeast Asia and upon his return home. He is one of the first veteran poets to have put down his feelings about the war into verse and publish it in magazines, journals and anthologies. In 1996, Kalí Tal was one of the first to point out that most of Ehrhart's writings were tinted by his war experience.[3] However, in 1991, when Ehrhart had already been labeled a "Vietnam writer"—which he never meant to be—he admitted that his "entire life has been lived in the shadow of Vietnam."[4] He reiterated this statement in 2002: "That experience has haunted my days. It has troubled my nights. It has shaped my identity and colored the way I see the world and everything in it."[5] By then only a third of his essays dealt directly with the war; it had been three-quarters in 1991. In *Dead on a High Hill* (2012), again just a third of his essays are Vietnam War related. Therefore, even without a close examination of his writings, one can readily remark that Southeast Asia is not Ehrhart's sole concern. Each of his three essay collections—published between 1991 and 2012—contains chapters about various aspects of his war and its consequences on him and the U.S.A., but also pieces which deal with topics including South Africa, early Soviet Russia, Central America, tugboats on the Delaware, education, and poetry, to name a few. They all reflect one aspect or another of Ehrhart's life. The same goes for his poetry. During the first fifteen years he published verse, Ehrhart dealt regularly with the war, but as early as 1984, his poetry collection *The Outer*

Banks & Other Poems[6] showed the wide variety of interests expressed in his verse. In 1990, *Just for Laughs*[7] proved it again, as did subsequent poetry books and chapbooks. Thus Ehrhart is not really a "Vietnam writer," but an author whose life was profoundly altered and influenced by the Vietnam War.[8]

    W.D. Ehrhart's writings are extensive and they have been discussed and analyzed in scores of journal articles, master's theses or Ph.D. dissertations, as well as in papers at conferences in the United States and other parts of the world where he has been regularly invited. He has spoken at universities, colleges, cultural centers and other public venues in England (Manchester, Leicester, Oxford), Wales (Swansea, Aberystwyth), the Netherlands (Amsterdam), Spain (Seville), Germany (Freiburg, Heidelberg, Munich), Austria (Graz, Innsbruck, Klagenfurt, Salzburg), Slovenia (Ljubljana), Japan (Amakusa) and Vietnam (Hanoi), as well as 30 of the 50 states in the U.S.[9] However he does not have the reputation of Vietnam War fiction novelists such as National Book Awards recipients Tim O'Brien (1979)[10] or Larry Heinemann (1987).[11] This is partly due to the fact that Ehrhart does not write fiction, that poetry is read by a minority of people, that memoirs interest a small readership, just like essays. Hence, he does not conform to the canons of what a Vietnam War author is for the general public as well as for commercial publishers—without taking into account the fact that he often tackles themes not related to Southeast Asia. Moreover, since Ehrhart came back from the war, he has voiced his opinions about the government positions he disapproves of, as well as all sorts of other topics, in documentary films and articles. For decades he has been fighting revisionism and American foundational myths, and his regular denunciations do not fare well with common thinking obscured by historical rewriting.[12] For many he does not tell the "right" story, the one which would look good. But Ehrhart is not interested in just looking good; he wants to tell the truth. He has been doing it in poetry readings since 1976, and in talks and lectures since 1982. He has spoken before hundreds of audiences including all three U.S. service academies.[13] He is sometimes thought of as being polemical—which he rightfully resents—especially when it comes to his poetry. If critics have not read *The Outer Banks* and *Just for Laughs*, and if they concentrate only on his war verse, they cannot have a complete picture of the poet he is. Ehrhart does not mean to be a polemicist, but he wants to question, confront reality, and make people think. Therefore Ehrhart sits on the edge of fame—although he is revered in academia.

    Logically W.D. Ehrhart holds a strong position as a man of letters, and that is why a collection of essays on his writings has been long overdue. This is what I propose in this volume, a critical look at the whole of his work, from poetry to essays, from memoirs to anthologies. However, that is not really sufficient to get a fully rounded picture of the man who has also been an educator since he first started to speak out against the Vietnam War in the spring of 1970, in the wake of the murders at Kent State University. He started teaching as an instructor of undergraduate composition while he was a graduate student at the University of Illinois Chicago Circle, from January 1977 to June 1978.[14] He then had other such positions in other schools, and since 2001 has been teaching English and history at The Haverford School in Pennsylvania. Many high school teachers and college professors use Ehrhart's writings to teach the Vietnam War, and he has been invited numerous times to talk to classes in many parts of the U.S. This activity is also a significant aspect of Ehrhart's oeuvre: he does not remain in his ivory tower. He interacts with people, he argues, he debates so as to open minds and get people thinking. This aspect is a major part of this book: the influence of W. D. Ehrhart as an educator viewed from multiple angles.

Contributors to this volume come from a wide variety of avenues: college professors, historians, graduate students, publishers, poets, former military personnel (some of whom served in Vietnam or in Iraq; some of whom were Marines, or were in the Navy or the Army). Some of the essayists fill several of these capacities at the same time. One feature of this collection is that it includes essays not only by Americans but also by writers from other parts of the world: Europe, with England, the Netherlands, Austria and France, as well as Asia, with contributions from India and Japan. This international perspective broadens the critical approach to the work of one of the worthiest American writers of today. Consequently this collection is deliberately varied and pluralist, as it intends to have readers make connections for themselves. Thus critical methodology and perspectives differ, but this collection of essays addresses the complete body of Ehrhart's oeuvre. The organization of this volume encourages the reader to register the interactions between the chapters. The diverse essays assembled herein demonstrate an effort to present a range of perspectives and to draw attention to the multiple facets of W. D. Ehrhart.

W. D. Ehrhart came to a wider attention when he published *Vietnam–Perkasie: A Combat Marine Memoir*,[15] the first volume of his memoir trilogy. Tired of hearing a lot of nonsense about the Vietnam War, he wanted to set the record straight. It took him another two volumes to say it all, over a period of twelve years in *Passing Time: Memoir of a Vietnam Veteran Against the War* and *Busted: A Vietnam Veteran in Nixon's America*.[16] Donald Anderson read this trilogy in reverse chronological order, so his perspective on this much-talked-about and written-about series offers a new angle. In the first part of this volume, he tells us why he believes *Busted*, the third opus, is actually the most stylish one, born out of *Vietnam–Perkasie* and *Passing Time*. As he refers to the texts with precision, we understand better Ehrhart's goals in his memoirs.

Subarno Chattarji narrows down his study of the memoirs more precisely on *Passing Time* recalling that when he first read this book in Delhi in the early 1990s, he had not yet heard of W. D. Ehrhart. The impression it made on the young man from India was powerful and has remained so to this day. Hence he discusses the contradiction of what he calls "radical awakening" and the relative lack of light shining on Ehrhart publicly. The naïveté and the disillusion of the young veteran gave way to an understanding of the wider picture and consequently to a transformation of his person from which he did not absolve himself regarding his participation in the war. Chattarji reflects on how the memoirist regularly defies the "system" and how his condemnations of American founding myths and policies place "him outside widely accepted discursive frames," and how his search for the truth dictates the writing of the memoir.

Another trilogy by Ehrhart is made up of his essay collections, all published by McFarland between 1991 and 2012. They have not been analyzed as often as his memoirs, although reviews have appeared over the years—for example by Edward F. Palm or by David A. Willson.[17] The latter takes a long look at these three volumes, not only from the perspective of a reader, but also that of a Vietnam veteran and a college reference librarian and Vietnam War bibliographer. As someone who has known W. D. Ehrhart for a long time, this hindsight helps us understand even better and appreciate these three opuses even more. Willson looks at Ehrhart's thinking and essays not only from the writing angle but also from the performance viewpoint, reminding us that the essayist has been giving talks, lectures and keynote addresses in a multitude of venues—about 250—over the last thirty years.[18] How does delivering an address to a live audience influence essay writing? Willson gives us the answer, while pinpointing a number of articles on a great variety of subjects at the same time.

Let us remember that between 1975 and today, W. D. Ehrhart has published eight poetry collections as well as ten chapbooks of verse. He is also the editor of two poetry anthologies and the co-editor of another two compilations. He wrote his first verse as a class assignment in 9th grade when he was 14, and he has not stopped writing poetry since.[19] For forty years, his poems have been published in scores of magazines, journals and anthologies.[20] His verse has also been translated and published in at least seven languages as diverse as German, Vietnamese and French (the latter by myself). Hence it is essential to scrutinize this fundamental aspect of Ehrhart's writing. This is precisely the object of the second part of this volume.

To begin with, Ammiel Alcalay confronts the "wages of memory" with W. D. Ehrhart's poetry, examining the early poems based on his war years and his memoirs, and later pieces which become more lyrical and have an even stronger emotional charge. Alcalay warns us not to relegate Ehrhart's poetry "to a particular historical event or experience." He sees this writing as central to literary and cultural history, not only because the poet is a veteran—and therefore an authentic voice—but because he uses his personal experience as well, and he has the courage to reveal aspects of his life that the vast majority of us would not dare to offer to any audience.

Adam Gilbert is concerned with morals. How do we define this notion? Is what seems black and white actually real? Or do we have shades of grey? Hence he examines moral responsibility and war, and precisely how it applies to W. D. Ehrhart's poetry. Is it one-sided? Does it relate only to politicians and the military in times of armed conflict? Can we also refer to a national responsibility? Or should we include generational accountability, too, when we are discussing such issues? What's more, are soldiers devoid of responsibility because they obey orders? It is well known that since he came back from the war, W. D. Ehrhart has been bearing witness in his writings, so how do we connect them to all the aspects of responsibility? In his chapter Gilbert analyzes all these issues through the scope of Ehrhart's poetry, from his very early published pieces.

Quite a number of poets have written about the Vietnam Veterans Memorial in Washington, D.C., since its inauguration in 1982. Diederik Oostdijk has noted that almost two dozen poems have already been published which focus on the Wall. Hence for three decades the monument designed by Maya Lin has been the source of inspiration for many a writer—this, of course, without referring to cinema, novels and essays. Nevertheless very few poets have written more than one piece on the subject. Such is the case of Yusef Komunyakaa and W. D. Ehrhart. Oostdijk provides a close examination of these pieces along with Doug Anderson's "The Wall." The essayist refers to war memorials and looks at the relationship of these three poets to the granite tribute to Vietnam veterans, and he compares their visions, how the symbolism of the big, black, shining wall affects these writers in their verse.

W. D. Ehrhart volunteered to join the U.S. Marines Corps at a very early age, barely out of high school. He had to get his parents' permission to do so. He was obeying Uncle Sam, who asked him to go to Southeast Asia to defend freedom and prevent dominoes falling, and thus stop the spread of communism to his beloved country. Being a decorated combat soldier, wounded in action in Hué City during Tet in 1968, there is no denying that Ehrhart is a patriot. However, even while he was in Vietnam, he started questioning the validity of the American presence and their purpose in this faraway land. Upon returning home, after being discharged honorably from the U.S.M.C., he put down on paper, in poetic form, his powerful feelings about his war, about the war, and about what it was doing to his country. After reading *The Pentagon Papers* in June 1971, he joined Vietnam Veterans Against the War, which was founded in 1967 by Jan Barry and several others. He has been a member of VVAW ever since.[21] Therefore there was a dramatic change in his position. Nicole Gollner looks at this evolution by focusing on Ehrhart's poetry.

Can poetry be synonymous with resistance? Can it be political? Or even polemical? Anthologies tend to present soft versions of war poems, and not the ones which clearly express the horror of armed hostility and its consequences. Some see verse as adornment which does not present troubling images nor raise questions. This is the case for many poets who prefer to romanticize visions of wars and dramatic events. Thus, Dale Ritterbusch argues that when writers are ignorant of historical events, and even war literature, their attempts at describing history directly are frequently as poor as some World War II examples show, or as has been the case for 9/11. These instances of mediocre verse might well develop a warlike frame of mind. Ritterbusch insists that this does not concern W. D. Ehrhart, whose writing—and particularly his poetry—is unwavering in telling the truth. This places him outside the conventional avenues as he does not hide his purpose, whether it brings about upsetting deductions or not. Therefore Ritterbusch analyzes Ehrhart's work in the context of resistance within the framework of poetry.

Across continents and time, artists have expressed their reaction to war in diverse ways. Maya Lin's design of the Wall in Washington was the illustration of her vision of the U.S. military personnel who died in Vietnam. Frederick Hart's "The Three Soldiers," the statue that makes up part of the Vietnam Veterans Memorial, is another perception of the sacrifice G.I.s made in Southeast Asia. Scores of novels and films gave their renditions of the conflict—but whether they are all artistic is debatable. Vietnam War paintings are also to be found, combined occasionally with narrative.[22] Since 2000, Philadelphia painter Jane Irish's work has been influenced by the disastrous American experience in Southeast Asia. She sometimes blends verse—including that of W. D. Ehrhart—with her pictures and with the ceramics she makes, in order to evoke powerful images.[23] It is no surprise that in another country, Japan, a veteran from a different era presented his vision of the ravages of war in much the same way. Chimei Hamada is a famous print artist who fought in China in the early 1940s. While she was visiting a Hamada exhibition, three prints reminded Yoko Shirai of W. D. Ehrhart's poem "Making the Children Behave." She analyzes how war memories can occasionally govern the creativity of both an American veteran-poet and a Japanese veteran print artist, how art is transcended by different approaches and techniques to render intense feelings.

As previously mentioned, W. D. Ehrhart's poetic writing is immense, both in terms of quantity and quality. As I am putting my pen to paper for this introduction, "Patrick," one of his most recent poems, has been published by *The Veteran*.[24] It is symptomatic that this piece can be read on different levels.

It has now become important to be directed to better appreciate the expanse of Ehrhart's verse. N. Bradley Christie provides a bibliographic essay in which he scrutinizes the poet's publishing career, in his own books, chapbooks and the anthologies in which he appears. Not only does Christie analyze the readily available books but he considers rarer chapbooks too. He looks at changes—sometimes minor—in poems in different publications, and offers his view on such emendations. He thus allows the reader to see and understand the evolution of Ehrhart's work, both in terms of creativity and inspiration, as well as from a publishing perspective.

Through the years W. D. Ehrhart has publicly voiced his opinions on various issues, whether it be in talks (during conferences, keynote addresses or lectures) or in writing, as he did recently regarding the Vietnam War Commemoration.[25] He has also given some interviews, of which "A Conversation" at the U.S. Air Force Academy is particularly famous and often quoted. It was published in 1996 in *War, Literature & the Arts*.[26] In August 2012, Ehrhart was questioned on the radio with his Vietnam buddy Ken Takenaga.[27] However, few of these interviews have appeared in print. Such unpublished interviews do exist. For instance, Subarno Chattarji recorded a long conversation in 1996 when he was preparing his book on poetry and the Vietnam War.[28] So did Stephen McVeigh when Ehrhart was working on his Ph.D. at the University of Wales in Swansea in 2000. While working on his own Ph.D., in March 2010, English historian Adam Gilbert came to Philadelphia to study in the most important research center in the field, La Salle University's Imaginative Representations of the Vietnam War Collection curated by John S. Baky. He took the opportunity of getting Ehrhart's words on tape. Readers of Italian can actually enjoy the 1997 conversation between Ehrhart, Baky and Stefano Rosso of the University of Bergamo in Italy.[29] But these words in print are too few. Therefore I thought it was time to give readers an opportunity to peruse Ehrhart's answers to questions at their own leisure. From a very long interview, I have selected questions which relate directly to poetry, including inspiration, technique and other issues.[30]

Part Three of this volume means to show how influential W. D. Ehrhart has been in the last forty years on people who met him, read his work, and the nature of the lasting effect he has had on some folks. This is the case for several Vietnam veterans featured in this part. One of them, Jan Barry, is also an author, editor, journalist and journalism teacher. He is a poet as well. In 1972 he co-edited the famous *Winning Hearts & Minds: War Poems by Vietnam Veterans*, in which eight Ehrhart poems are included. In 1976, with W. D. Ehrhart, he co-edited *Demilitarized Zones: Veterans after Vietnam*.[31] It goes without saying that these two veterans have known each other for a very long time. They have developed a close relationship as well as a complicity, due in part to both of them writing verse. In his essay, Barry gives the viewpoint of a poet on another poet, he reflects on the nature of the influence of their own writing on the other's writing. He also recounts how seminal books like *WHAM* and *DMZ* were born and takes us into the very womb of creation.

Edward F. Palm is a former enlisted Marine, a Vietnam veteran, and a retired Marine officer. He then became an academic who attended conferences on the Vietnam War, and wrote about it. He looks at Ehrhart's "limited success" in the commercial world and what may be the reason for that. He argues that it is the poet and memoirist's determination for truth-telling, telling it like it was, which has kept him from popular success. For Palm, W.D. Ehrhart is committed to bearing witness to the trauma he—and his generation—had to endure, and how he does not want his experience to be earmarked, and included in myths which do not mirror his life. This attitude accorded fully for Palm, who recognized the "process of individual and collective disillusionment," as he puts it. He sees it clearly in some poems by Ehrhart as well as in his memoirs, the latter being important books which allow the general public to understand the Vietnam experience well.

Robert C. Doyle is another Vietnam veteran turned academic. He did not serve in the Marine Corps but in the Navy. His war started shortly after W.D. Ehrhart left Southeast Asia. When, in 1987, Doyle discovered Ehrhart's writings, he saw parallels between their lives as young men and soldiers of Uncle Sam, which he then reflected upon. When he entered academia, Doyle started about teaching the Vietnam War as this had become popular at the time in the mid–1980s. To describe the full and authentic experience, Doyle used *Vietnam–Perkasie*. However, he was not content with only using the text for his students, so—as many others did—he got W.D. Ehrhart to come to his class at Penn State for an in-person event with the writer. To this day some students still remember that very visit. Doyle also taught in colleges in a couple of countries in Europe. He first went to Münster in Germany, then to Strasbourg in France. In these two European universities he again used Ehrhart's first volume of memoirs. He was thus able to perceive the universality of the book, which moved German and French students the way it did Americans. Doyle demonstrates the parallels between these episodes—whether they be military, personal or professional—with Ehrhart's writings.

As mentioned earlier, for over forty years W.D. Ehrhart and Jan Barry have developed a strong and special relationship, both from a personal point of view and in the field of poetry. A similar rapport has grown between Ehrhart and publisher Gary Metras since the late 1970s. Adastra Press has put out eight Ehrhart titles—including four poetry collections and four chapbooks, as well as some broadsheets. Through Metras's voice we get into the heart of writing, editing and publishing poetry. We understand how a collection of verse is created, what is included and what is not, how discussions can go back and forth about whether to include a particular piece. The publisher also gives us insight into why selected poem collections get the approbation of readers, and why this very poet gets the approval of audiences at readings. It is fascinating to understand that their "poetry" relationship is not just about publishing, but very much about writing, with echoes of Jan Barry.

Robert C. Doyle already helped us understand the interest and the importance of W. D. Ehrhart's writing in teaching as well as the benefits of his presence in front of students. But there is more to say about that, and this is precisely what Part Four intends to do. Martin Novelli is another college professor who has been teaching the Vietnam War for many years. To that effect he has been using *Vietnam-Perkasie* and *Passing Time*, the first two volumes of Ehrhart's memoirs. However, this was not enough for Novelli, as he also wanted his students to interact with the author for long—even very long—sessions. In three different colleges where he has been teaching, Novelli has profited from the memoirist and poet's "tireless willingness to speak to and with students about the folly he lived through and the folly he has been observing for the last four decades." Thus, referring regularly to texts, Novelli reflects on the impact Ehrhart has had on students for years, and how as a writer, storyteller and truth-teller, Ehrhart is an educator through his books and also in front of the college classes he visits.

Charles L. Yates is one more Vietnam veteran (he served in the U.S. Navy) who knew of W. D. Ehrhart before he actually met him in 2001. For a long time he had known of the writer through television documentaries from 1983 and 1991[32] in which he would repeatedly tell viewers about the lives of Vietnam veterans, how they had been transformed and had become who they were then. Yates became a college professor too. Much like Robert C. Doyle, Yates sees many parallels between his personal and military experience and Ehrhart's. When Doyle used the memoirs, Yates used *Carrying the Darkness*, the poetry anthology, to teach about the Vietnam War.[33] Like Doyle and Martin Novelli, it was important for Yates that his students meet the author—which was thus organized. A "renewed sense of moral clarity" resulted from this encounter in which Ehrhart demonstrated again that he wanted people to understand the world the way it is, even if some of his arguments displease members of the audience, even if he takes them to "unfamiliar, unsettling places." He revealed how much he passionately wants to educate people in order for them to open their eyes and their minds, and also how much poetry can teach people.

It is obvious that W. D. Ehrhart's writings have had a great influence on teachings on the Vietnam War—but not only; they've had great influence on life as well. It is evident that in his many talks, lectures, visits to numerous venues in the last three decades throughout the U.S. and in Europe he has inspired his audiences through his educational approach. But let us not forget Ehrhart's direct involvement at various times in his life as a university instructor, or as a high school teacher. He has been teaching English and history full time at The Haverford School, a boys' high school in Pennsylvania, since 2001. Joseph Cox had a 30-year Army career before becoming the headmaster of that school. He had met Ehrhart at a 1993 conference. Years later he got him to visit his class on "The Art of War" at West Point since this officer believed Ehrhart was the "best Vietnam veteran poet." Cox understood how well Ehrhart could connect with students through his authenticity, hence a few years later he convinced him to come and work with him. Through the headmaster's account and his references to poetry, we are able to see an unfamiliar feature of the writer-memoirist-poet: how he is able to share his life-long experience with younger generations in the classroom, and how humane he is in the transfer of knowledge to youths.

The substance of teaching is not just a matter of people or of a mere topic. It is also a question of how one, as an educator, mediates knowledge, helps students understand the finality of the field. The methods and tools used are then essential to this mediation. Matthew K. Irwin contends that the majority of American academics who study and teach history use out-of-date means and methodologies. Facts and figures—however useful they may be—do not convey the intricacy of human interaction which forms one of the bases of history. Irwin argues that today methodologies ought to be re-examined, particularly when it comes to teaching Vietnam War history. So, can poetry, such as W. D. Ehrhart's, be used as a primary source to that effect? Can it serve to recount real life experiences? Can it chronicle not only some of the most resonant moments of soldiers' lives, but voice the hearts and minds of countless Americans and Vietnamese as well? Irwin analyses how the classroom discussions on Vietnam War history can benefit from the use of verse.

It is fitting that an essay collection on an ex–Marine (as he refers to himself), Vietnam veteran and writer ends with a chapter by another former Marine, a war veteran, too, but from a different and much more recent conflict. Clint Van Winkle is an Iraq War veteran, he is the author of *Soft Spots: A Marine's Memoir of Combat and Post-Traumatic Stress Disorder*.[34] He is also the director of *The Guilt*, a 2010 documentary film about combat veterans, a follow-up to his book. Both titles are explicit enough for readers to understand the direct connection between two generations of former soldiers turned memoirists who give accounts of their wars. Once back in civilian life and studying at Arizona State University, Van Winkle discovered W. D. Ehrhart under the guidance of Professor Eric Wertheimer. As it happened for other Vietnam veterans, Ehrhart's memoirs and poetry resonated for Van Winkle, who was looking for a way to fight PTSD and grasp the homecoming experience. The impact

Ehrhart's prose and verse had on Van Winkle pushed him to start a correspondence with his literary elder. It eventually encouraged him to write *Soft Spots*. Thus, he recounts the influence of a war veteran on another combatant from a younger generation, both from personal and literary points of view.

The last section of this volume consists of poems by W.D. Ehrhart selected by contributors as an appreciation of his work.

Notes

1. Rottmann, Larry, Jan Barry, and Basil T. Paquet, eds., *Winning Hearts & Minds: War Poems by Vietnam Veterans* (Brooklyn, NY: First Casualty Press/McGraw-Hill, 1972).

2. Ehrhart, W.D., *Dead on a High Hill: Essays on War, Literature and Living, 2002–2012* (Jefferson, NC: McFarland, 2012).

3. Tal, Kalí, *Worlds of Hurt: Reading the Literatures of Trauma* (Cambridge: Cambridge University Press, 1996), 77–114.

4. Ehrhart, W.D., *In the Shadow of Vietnam: Essays 1977–1991* (Jefferson, NC: McFarland, 1991), ix.

5. Ehrhart, W.D., *The Madness of It All: Essays on War, Literature, and American Life* (Jefferson, NC: McFarland, 2002), 1.

6. Ehrhart, W.D., *The Outer Banks & Other Poems* (Easthampton, MA: Adastra Press, 1984).

7. Ehrhart, W.D., *Just for Laughs* (Silver Spring, MD: Viet Nam Generation & Burning Cities Press, 1990).

8. Ehrhart, *Dead on a High Hill*, 1.

9. Ehrhart, email to Malo, 3 December 2012.

10. O'Brien, Tim, *Going After Cacciato* (New York: Delacorte, 1978); *The Things They Carried* (Boston: Houghton Mifflin, 1990).

11. Heinemann, Larry, *Paco's Story* (New York: Farrar, Strauss, Giroux, 1986); *Close Quarters* (New York: Farrar, Strauss, Giroux, 1977).

12. See for example Bill Ehrhart, "Thank You for Your Service," *The Veteran*, 42:2 (Fall 2012), 16, on the decade-long Vietnam War Commemoration.

13. "I participated in several group readings with other students at Swarthmore College in 1971, 1972, and 1973. The first reading I did on my own was at Sandy Spring Friends School, Sandy Spring, Maryland, in March 1976. The first lecture or talk that I gave was at the Interlocking Curriculum School in Colesville, Maryland, in April 1982." Email from Ehrhart to Malo, 21 October 2012.

14. Email from Ehrhart to Malo, 13 December 2012.

15. Ehrhart, W.D., *Vietnam–Perkasie: A Combat Marine Memoir* (Jefferson, NC: McFarland, 1983).

16. Ehrhart, W.D., *Passing Time: Memoir of a Vietnam Veteran Against the War* (Jefferson, NC: McFarland, 1989). *Busted: A Vietnam Veteran in Nixon's America* (Amherst: University of Massachusetts Press, 1995).

17. See Edward F. Palm, "Perkasie Lost: W.D. Ehrhart's Vietnam Saga," *Marine Corps Gazette*. Apr. 1996: 65–67. Or David A. Willson in "Books in Brief," posted on 25 June 2012 on the website of *The Veteran*, http://vvabooks.wordpress.com/2012/06/25/dead-on-a-high-hill-by-w-d-ehrhart/, accessed 27 June 2012.

18. See Ehrhart's website, http://www.wdehrhart.com/readings-lectures.html, accessed 15 November 2011.

19. See J.-J. Malo's interview of W. D. Ehrhart in this volume.

20. As early as 1972, eight Ehrhart poems were included in *Winning Hearts and Minds: War Poems by Vietnam Veterans*, co-edited by Larry Rottmann, Jan Barry, and Basil T. Paquet (New York: McGraw-Hill Book Company, 1972).

21. Email from Ehrhart to Malo, 16 October 2012.

22. See for example *Vietnam War Paintings*, art by James Davis Nelson; narratives by participants (Clinton, LA: St. John's Press, 2003).

23. See Jane Irish's art exhibit, "War Is Not What You Think," a collaborative exhibition at Philadelphia's La Salle University Art Museum and Connelly Library, curated by John S. Baky, director of the Imaginative Representations of the Vietnam War Collection, and Vietnam veteran. http://www.youtube.com/watch?v=kBuB_H3qwXQ. Accessed 5 December 2012.

24. Ehrhart, Bill, "Patrick," *The Veteran*, 42:2 (Fall 2012), 18. Also http://www.vvaw.org/veteran/article/?id=2150&hilite=&print=yes. Accessed 5 December 2012.

25. See Bill Ehrhart, "Thank You for Your Service," *The Veteran*, 42:2 (Fall 2012), 16.

26. Anderson, Donald, and Thomas G. Bowie, Jr., interviewers, "A Conversation with W. D. Ehrhart," *War, Literature & the Arts: An International Journal of the Humanities*, 8:2 (Fall/Winter 1996), 149–157.

27. "Radio Times," host Marty Moss-Coane, NPR affiliate WHYY-FM, 6 August 2012. They talked about their trip to Japan and Vietnam in 2011. See W. D. Ehrhart, "Ken and Bill's Excellent Adventure," in *Dead on a High Hill* (Jefferson, NC: McFarland, 2012), 163–185. Ehrhart has also been featured on other local and regional radio programs, as well as on national radio, e.g. on NPR's "All Things Considered" and "Morning Edition." Email from Ehrhart to Malo, 13 December 2012.

28. Chattarji, Subarno, *Memories of a Lost War: American Poetic Responses to the Vietnam War* (Oxford: Oxford University Press, 2001).

29. Rosso, Stefano, "Conversazione con William D. Ehrhart e John S. Baky, Philadelphia, ottobre 1997," *Ácoma* (no. 19, Primavera-Estate, 2000, anno VII), 40–47. Republished in Stefano Rosso, *Musi gialli e Berretti Verdi: Narrazioni Usa sulla Guerra del Vietnam* (Bergamo: Bergamo University Press, 2003), 233–249.

30. Hopefully the long version will eventually be published.

31. Barry, Jan, and W. D. Ehrhart, eds., *Demilitarized Zones: Veterans After Vietnam* (Perkasie: PA, East River Anthology, 1976).

32. *Vietnam, A Television History* (13 episodes, 1983; series director: Bruce Palling) and *Making Sense of the Sixties* (6 episodes, 1991; director: David Hoffman).

33. Ehrhart, W. D., ed., *Carrying the Darkness: The Poetry of the Vietnam War* (Lubbock: Texas Tech University Press, 1985).

34. Van Winkle, *Soft Spots: A Marine's Memoir of Combat and Post-Traumatic Stress Disorder* (New York: St. Martin's Griffin, 2009).

PART ONE.
The Prose Writer of Memoirs and Essays

Making the Children Behave

Do they think of me now
in those strange Asian villages
where nothing ever seemed
quite human
but myself
and my few grim friends
moving through them
hunched
in lines?

When they tell stories to their children
of the evil
that awaits misbehavior,
is it me they conjure?

—W. D. Ehrhart*

**A Generation of Peace (Revised)*, 29; *To Those Who Have Gone Home Tired*, 20; *Beautiful Wreckage*, 15.

Darkness Carried: W. D. Ehrhart's Memoirs

Donald Anderson

The 1995 publication of *Busted: A Vietnam Veteran in Nixon's America* completed Bill Ehrhart's autobiographical trilogy. Twelve years earlier, *Vietnam–Perkasie: A Combat Marine Memoir* initiated the work, followed in 1989 by *Passing Time: Memoir of a Vietnam Veteran against the War*. My reading of the trilogy was reversed. I read *Busted*, then worked my way backwards to *Vietnam–Perkasie*, an account that is, by my lights, the best single, unadorned, gut-felt account of one American's route into and out of America's then longest war. That is not to say that the route out brought cure. Like the country he fronted, Bill Ehrhart was poisoned by the experience. Throughout my reading of the trilogy, I kept hearkening to Tim O'Brien's actual and metaphorical caution: "If you don't care for obscenity, you don't care for the truth; if you don't care for the truth, watch how you vote. Send guys to war, they come home talking dirty."[1]

In the first pages of *Vietnam–Perkasie*, Ehrhart recounts his uneventful, earnest, and normal youth. He read books about John Paul Jones, Pecos Bill, collected money for UNICEF, heard the dinnertime admonishments about starving Chinamen, respected Ike, and began each school day with the Lord's Prayer and the Pledge of Allegiance. On Memorial Days, he rode his decorated bicycle in his town's parades. Like a nineteenth-century student, he could quote by heart the Twenty-third Psalm and the Gettysburg Address. But like a twentieth-century child, he suffered nightmares about *Sputnik*. His favorite game was war, and favorite toy, a Christmas-delivered, battery-powered .30 caliber machine-gun mounted on a tripod stand, with simulated sound and flashing barrel: "I mowed down thousands with it. Everybody wanted to be on my side, until I broke my plastic miracle hitting the dirt too realistically. For a long time afterwards, I was regularly appointed a dirty Commie. It was almost unbearable."[2]

In tenth grade when Kennedy was shot, Ehrhart traveled to Washington to stand in line to view the casket. He took fully to heart the dead President's mild reproof, "Ask not what your country can do for you; ask what you can do for your country" (Inaugural Address, January 20, 1961). He followed the Cuban Missile Crisis and worried about the hectoring Khrushchev. As Ehrhart's senior year in high school neared its finish, he had lettered in track and been elected a member of the National Honor Society. He had been granted admission by four universities. Then teachers began to stop Ehrhart in the school halls to congratulate him, for Ehrhart's photograph had appeared in the local weekly, standing beside a Marine Corps recruiter in front of the school. Still seventeen, Ehrhart had needed his parents' signatures.

For the next 300-odd pages, Ehrhart carries us to boot camp, to Vietnam, and, as the short-time and returning vets termed it, "back to the World" again. The concluding scene in *Vietnam–Perkasie* brings us to a boy at a dance-bar in a town near the Marine Corps Air Station at Cherry Point, North Carolina. After thirteen months in Vietnam, he's still underage, too young to legally drink, to vote, or to buy and title a car (with his war-earned money) without signed parental permission. He's drunk and sad. None of the women will dance with him.

> I thought of the young woman with the AK-47, the one in the photograph I'd taken off the dead Vietcong. I thought of the woman in the gun pit in Hue. After a while the beer made thought impossible. My stomach heaved up and down. I went to the men's room and threw up. I left the bar. I called Jenny [his high school sweetheart] from a pay phone and begged her and begged her to love me, running out of change about the time I realized I was talking to Jenny's dorm counselor. I went back to the base and masturbated in the shower, passing out beneath the warm stream of water before I finished.[3]

Here is enough impotence, forlornness, and shame for us all. And earlier—in-country—this:

> "Anyone wanna get laid tonight?" asked Wally, grinning.
> "Where?" asked Seagrave. "Here? In Hue?"
> "Yeh," said Wally. "We found a whore over at the University. She'll take us all on and it won't cost us a single piaster. All she wants is food."
> "A fuck for a box of C-rations," added Mogerty.
> "A case?"
> "No. One box. One meal per fuck."
> "Count me in," said Hoffy.
> "Why not?" said Seagrave.
> "All right!" Wally whooped. "Get some!"
> "Where's all this gonna happen?" asked Seagrave.
> "I got a buddy in the 60-mike-mike platoon by the river," said Mogerty. "It's all set up. He'll let us use his gun pit if we cut him in on it."

"Someone's got to stay here on radio watch," said Seagrave.

I thought about volunteering. I wasn't sure I wanted in on a gang-bang. But I wasn't sure I wanted out either. The idea repelled me, but it aroused my curiosity, too, and I didn't want the others to think I wasn't game.

"I'll keep an eye on the radio," said Morgan. "You guys go on."

The rest of us slipped into the darkness, moving cautiously in single file as though we were on any ordinary patrol. It was raining. Mogerty led us to the river, found his friend, and the two of them muscled the little 60-millimeter mortar out of the gun pit. "I hope to hell we don't get a fire mission," said the friend. Wally arrived a short time later with a Vietnamese woman wearing dark silk trousers and a light silk blouse. It was too dark to see how old she was or what she looked like. Wally and Mogerty counted heads—six—and paid for all of us: one-half a case. We sat in the rain, smoking and listening to the gunfire coming from the other side of the river, while each of us took his turn. No one said much.

When my turn came, I jumped down into the pit. The woman was sitting up on some cardboard, protecting her body from the mud. She was naked from the waist down. I didn't know what to say or where to begin. "Chow Co," I said. "Hello." She just grunted softly and fumbled for my belt buckle. Her hands were cold. I undid the buckle myself and dropped my trousers. Cold air and rain bit at my buttocks and tightened my thighs. I hadn't had much experience at this sort of thing but even I knew that the woman's awkwardness and stiff body suggested either inexperience or deep hatred. "Probably both," I thought. My stomach felt sick. I finished quickly, pulled up my trousers, and climbed out of the pit.

"I don't think she was a whore," I said to Hoffy as we sneaked back through the rain toward the MACV compound. Hoffy said something that I couldn't hear. "What?" I asked.

Hoffy leaned into my ear. "So what?" he said.[4]

Busted, the trilogy's final volume is, to my mind, more sophisticated in both its structure and politics, but *Vietnam–Perkasie* is its source, and *Passing Time* the bridge. And if *Passing Time* traces the political development of a Vietnam vet attending college, then *Busted* brings us an Ehrhart to whom the only sensible escape is escape. Having survived both war and college, his goal is to ship out as a merchant marine, to clear the mainland of the nation he'd killed for. In a sweep aboard ship, he is "busted" for a vial of marijuana. All the while we are moving towards Ehrhart's on-and-off again federal trial, Nixon is sinking forever deeper into the murk of Vietnam and Watergate. In an embarrassing argument with his mother, Ehrhart comes to a simplified but telling postulate: "So marijuana is illegal, but it's okay to drop napalm on gooks."[5] Later, following his acquittal from the drug charge, Ehrhart responds to his mother's query if he wasn't happy when the "system" worked to his benefit? As always, Ehrhart's honesty as a person and writer is full-face, up front, and clear:

No, I wasn't happy about it. They made up the game. They made up the rules. They said, "Play or else." They could have sent me to prison, Mom. To prison. For smoking pot. You know what it says on the back of my Purple Heart medal? "For Military Merit." I'm guilty, all right. I'm guilty of murder, attempted murder, arson, assault and battery, aggravated assault, assault with a deadly weapon, robbery, burglary, larceny, disorderly conduct, you name it, I've done it. And according to our so-called system, it was all perfectly legal. They gave me a medal for it. Am I relieved about the way the trial turned out? Yes. Am I happy about it? Not hardly.[6]

But if Ehrhart is honest about his own history, he is honest, too, about his nation's:

The fire hoses and police dogs unleashed against Negroes singing hymns and offering prayers on a bridge in Birmingham, Alabama, had shown Americans something they had not wanted to see. Beefy police officers swinging their black polished nightsticks like so many Splendid Splinters in the streets of Chicago, their badge numbers taped to prevent identification, had shown Americans something they had not wanted to see. The bodies of men, women, and children strewn hugger-mugger in thick piles in a ditch at My Lai, gunned down by American boys like Jews in a Nazi concentration camp, had shown Americans something they had not wanted to see.[7]

And:

In 1968, the Reverend Doctor Martin Luther King, Jr., was shot dead and America's cities, already tinderboxes of Black frustration, caught fire and burned. Robert Kennedy ruthlessly stole Eugene McCarthy's thunder, only to be ruthlessly murdered for his trouble, plunging the Democratic party into the hands of Lyndon Johnson's lapdog and the country's yearning for peace into the hands of Richard Nixon. In 1971, broken-hearted veterans hurled their medals back at the Congress in whose name they had been given while Congress cowered behind a cyclone fence it had erected to keep its members safe from the unclean rabble that had done its bidding. The Pentagon Papers, commissioned by McNamara himself though never intended for public consumption, finally revealed what any dumb grunt could have told you after ninety days in Vietnam, that the war was madness. And none of it had mattered. The war went on like a ballpeen hammer in the hands of a steady workman.[8]

Then:

"Four Students Killed at Kent State," read the headline. I sat down on the curb and read for a while. Then I got up and went to my room.
  It isn't enough to send us halfway around the world to die, I thought. It isn't enough to turn us loose on Asians. Now you are turning the soldiers loose on your own children. Now you are killing your own children in the streets of America. My throat constricted into a tight knot. I could hardly breathe.[9]

Long-respected as a poet and editor of Vietnam War poetry, Ehrhart's nonfiction autobiographies have not found the larger audience they so clearly deserve. H. Bruce Franklin queries the undersize of Ehrhart's following in his foreword to *Busted*:

> Part of the problem may be in Ehrhart himself. Some of the very qualities that make him such a potent writer—his passion, his searing honesty, and scorn for greed, duplicity, pettifogging, selfishness, bureaucracy, and the self-serving ethos of the corporate world—make him an inept businessman particularly unsuited for success in these tough times for serious authors in the U.S. publishing industry.[10]

Of course, what Ehrhart reports *is* unpleasant:

> Around mid-morning, we came onto a small cluster of houses—or rather, what was left of them. The hooches had been blown to splinters, probably the night before. There was no one around but a middle-aged woman sitting amid the rubble in a dark pool of coagulated blood. She was holding a small child who had only one leg and half a head, and she had a tremendous gaping chest wound that ripped open both of her breasts. Flies swarmed loudly around mother and child. The woman was in a kind of trance, keening softly and gently rocking her baby....
> "Holy Christ, what hit this place?" said Pelinski.
> "Artillery," I said, trying to hold my voice steady, "or naval gunfire. The VC got nothing big enough to do this kind of damage." One of the corpsmen came over and looked at the woman, then gave her a shot of morphine.[11]

Swallow the casual factuality of:

> I rubbed the sleep out of my eyes and stood up. Gerry was pointing toward the east. "What?" I asked.
> "That red streak," he said. It was gone, but I could see the lights of an airplane circling in the sky far out over the dunes, maybe six or seven miles, out near the ocean. I was awake now.
> "Keep watching," I said. The lights continued to circle over the same spot. The aircraft was too far to hear the engines. Suddenly a brilliant red streak silently began to descend toward the earth until it connected the flashing lights to the ground below with a solid bar of color. Many seconds later, as the flashing lights and red bar continued to move like a spotlight sweeping the sky from a fixed point on the ground, a sound like the dull buzz of a dentist's slow-speed drill came floating lazily through the humid night air, sound and visual image appeared to be synchronized for awhile. Then the red streak slowly fell away from the circling lights and disappeared into the earth, leaving the thick sound humming alone in a black vacuum. Finally, long after the lights had stopped circling and begun to move off in a straight line toward the south, the sound abruptly stopped.
> "That's Puff the Magic Dragon," I said. "The gunship."
> "What's that?"
> "Air Force C-47 with Vulcan cannons." I explained that the old transporter plane, a military version of the DC-3, had been converted into a flying battleship by mounting three Vulcan cannons along one side of the fuselage. The Vulcan

worked like a Gatling gun; it had six barrels that rotated as the gun was fired, so that each barrel fired only once every six shots. Each of the three cannons could fire 6,000 bullets per minute. Since the guns were in fixed mounts they could only be aimed by tilting the entire aircraft toward the ground and circling around and around over the target.

"That's 18,000 rounds a minute, my man," I said, "300 bullets per second. Chops up anything and everything like mincemeat: fields, forests, mangroves, water buffalo, hooches, people. Everything. Take a patch of redwood forest and turn it into matchsticks before you can hitch up the horses. I've seen places where Puff's left his calling card. Unbelievable. Looks like a freshly plowed field ready for planting. I saw a body once, got chopped up by Puff. You wouldn't have known it had ever been a human being. Just a pile of pulp stuck to little pieces of cement and straw that used to be the guy's hooch—or her hooch, absolutely no way to tell the difference. It was so gross, it wasn't even sickening. It was just there, like litter or something."[12]

In a 1996 interview, Ehrhart said,

The Vietnam War changed my life forever. And in ways that are not particularly good. I can't overemphasize the degree of idealism I possessed. When I enlisted, I thought I was doing a good thing—a *cosmically* good thing. To come to terms with the truth of so many things about myself and my country and about the world in which we live at such a young age—well, the impact was immeasurable. And that's what you see in the books, my trying to come to terms with what all that meant. And I have come to terms somewhat—clumsily and awkwardly and with a great deal of damage to myself and to lots of people who care about me. I have a wife who loves me, a daughter who loves me. I am fortunate.[13]

In the same interview, Ehrhart makes a telling point about being categorized as a "war" writer:

I wish that the writing I've done, primarily in poetry that's not about Vietnam, would receive more attention. And really the bulk of my public poetry does not deal with the Vietnam War or any war. But most people who have any knowledge of me at all don't know that. All they know is the Vietnam stuff. That bothers, even irritates, me. I feel uncomfortable about basically making what modest reputation and living I have out of an experience that I think was irredeemably repugnant. So that makes me uncomfortable. On the other hand, as I get older, I recognize that most writers never get identified with any form. They live and die in obscurity. So, if people did not identify me as a Vietnam War writer, they probably wouldn't see me as anything. So I have to be grateful for that. You can see it is hard for me to even get those words out of my mouth, but it's a reality. I don't get invited to the Pueblo's Writer's conference. I don't get invited to the North Poetry Festival which is only thirty miles from where I live. I get invited to the Vietnam War conferences. I'm beginning to realize that I shouldn't complain about that too much, because most writers don't get invited to anything. It's something I've come to terms with, but I don't like it very much.[14]

It's typical of Bill Ehrhart that in a 2012 email exchange, he described *Vietnam–Perkasie* as just an "okay" book—this notion despite the fact that the book has remained in print for thirty years and is, in fact, a gift. Between the opening and closing paragraph of *Vietnam–Perkasie*, the text breathes— a living thing—a memory, confession, and cry against our or any nation that ignores the links among its ordinary citizens and the geopolitical decisions and ambitions of its leaders. *Watch how you vote.*

Over the years, Ehrhart has taught courses in Vietnam War literature and it must dawn on him that students today were born as far from the start of the Vietnam War as Bill was from World War I. No wonder that conflict seems so ancient to them. But as Bill has written, "That's okay."

> I want them to imagine, however imperfectly, the dilemma of a boy with a fresh draft notice in his hand, the weight of a rucksack after ten hours of humping the boonies, the damage high speed steel does to human flesh, the terrible anguish that is so benignly pigeonholed as Post Traumatic Stress disorder.... Human lives, our own or anyone else's, ought not to be squandered. A little imagination might have saved the world a whole lot of trouble. It might still. And there is nothing to stimulate the imagination like a good book.[15]

I have long believed that if it seems to fall to the historian to make distinctions among wars, each war's larger means and ends, the trajectory for the artist, regardless of culture or time, seems to fall towards an individual's disillusionment, the means and ends of war played out in the personal. For the individual soldier, the sweeping facts of history are accurately written not in the omniscient, third-person plural, but in the singular first. We live in a culture that values the individual. Our works of art about war mirror this welcome bias. At their best, war memoirs—*stories*—testify to the power of word and image and for the human craving for meaning. Whose very earliest recollections don't include the request, Tell Me a Story? Bill Ehrhart has told his. The human race needs stories. We need all the experience we can get.

Notes

1. O'Brien, Tim. "How to Tell a True War Story." *The Things They Carried* (New York: Broadway Books, 1998).
2. Ehrhart, W.D., *Vietnam–Perkasie: A Combat Marine Memoir* (Jefferson, NC: McFarland, 1983; New York: Zebra, 1985; Amherst: University of Massachusetts, 1995), 7–8
3. Ehrhart, *Vietnam–Perkasie*, 311.
4. Ehrhart, *Vietnam–Perkasie*, 263–4.
5. Ehrhart, W.D., *Busted: A Vietnam Veteran in Nixon's America* (Amherst: University of Massachusetts, 1995), 21
6. Ehrhart, *Busted*, 141.
7. Ehrhart, *Busted*, 27.

8. Ehrhart, *Busted*, 61.
9. Ehrhart, W.D., *Passing Time: Memoir of a Vietnam Veteran Against the War* (New York: Avon, 1986 [as *Marking Time*]; Jefferson, NC: McFarland, 1989; Amherst: University of Massachusetts, 1995), 88.
10. Ehrhart, *Busted*, xi.
11. Ehrhart, *Vietnam–Perkasie*, 115.
12. Ehrhart, *Vietnam–Perkasie*, 63.
13. Anderson, Donald, and Thomas G. Bowie, Jr., interviewers, "A Conversation with W.D. Ehrhart," *War, Literature & the Arts: an International Journal of the Humanities*, 8:2 (Fall/Winter 1996), 149–157.
14. Ibid.
15. Ehrhart, W.D., "Teaching the Vietnam War," *In the Shadow of Vietnam: Essays, 1977–1991* (Jefferson, NC: McFarland, 1991), 147–148.

"The Chameleon War":
Passing Time and the Remembrance of the Vietnam War

SUBARNO CHATTARJI

"Memories are acts of commemoration, of testimony, of confession, of accusation."[1]
—For Phil Melling, Vietnam scholar, mentor, and friend

W. D. Ehrhart occupies a pivotal and unique niche in the writings that have emerged from the Vietnam era. He is a preeminent anthologist, poet, commentator, and memoirist of the period and while he is acknowledged as such in specialist circles he remains relatively unknown. When I first read *Passing Time* as a student in Delhi in the early 1990s I had no idea who Ehrhart was, and can still recollect the impact his searing narrative had on a mind largely innocent of the Vietnam War and its academic study. This essay while speculating on the paradox of radical awakening (the memoirists' in particular) and comparative obscurity, will through a discussion of *Passing Time* examine the ways in which the Vietnam War has been experienced, memorialized, and critiqued.

Ehrhart's authority to narrate and the authenticity of his criticism arise from his status as a war veteran and he is ironically aware of his "unique" status while a student at Swarthmore—"I was Swarthmore's real live Vietnam veteran. I was a specimen. A curiosity. I was a freak in a carnival sideshow."[2] The memoir traces a trajectory from "innocent" patriotism to disillusionment, anger, and dissent—a trajectory available in other narratives, such as Ron Kovic's *Born on the Fourth of July*—and one which replicates the frustrations and disillusion of First World War writers.[3] The repeated references to military desire and innocence create the foundation of "a direct confrontation with one's own false consciousness."[4] "[...] I figured I owed it to my country. [...] This place ain't perfect, but it's still worth something to be an American. [...] The day I'd graduated from Marine boot camp had been the proudest moment of my life [...]."[5] As in the trenches of World War I so too combat experience in the "alien" topography of Vietnam leads to the unraveling of the self centered on patriotic blandishments. "I want it to have been worth something, and I can't make myself believe that it was. [...] The war was a horrible mistake, and my beloved country was dying because of it. [...] Vietnam a mistake? My God, it had been a calculated, deliberate attempt to hammer the world by brute force into the shape perceived by vain, duplicitous power brokers."[6] The narrative crescendo precipitated by the revelations of *The Pentagon Papers* is emblematic of the memoir as epistemic journey from innocence to experience and disillusion. To "know" Vietnam and the war is to "know" oneself, one's nation and its political, ideological moorings and that "knowledge" is accompanied by a "heightened sense of morality."[7] Underlying *Passing Time* is not just experiential authority but a transformational messianic authority—the "messiah complex" that Pam perceives in his obsessive pursuit of Vietnam.[8] These revelations of the "truth" about U.S. involvement in Vietnam create a kind of narrative excess as "knowledge" leads to an exaggerated negation of American values and policies: "Trapped like a cornered rat, I knew at last that nothing I had ever done in Vietnam would ever carry with it anything but shame and disgrace and dishonor; that I would never be able to recall Vietnam with anything but pain and anger and bitterness; that I would never again be able to take pride in being American."[9]

The narrative progression can possibly be explicated within varying paradigms. One is "the locus of loss felt by the narrator,"[10] the fact that familiar social and political moorings have been dislodged, which in turn leads to a sense of betrayal. "[...] when I'd gotten back to the States, I discovered that in my absence America had become an alien place in which and to which I no longer seemed to belong. [...] We *believed* in this country, and we were betrayed."[11] The trope of betrayal is an oft repeated one in Vietnam War narrations and predicated on the stability of ideological networks that constitute and sustain America—what Roger Bastide "calls networks of complimentarity," a belief in which the system sets itself up for inevitable disappointment when the instability and corruption of these structures reveals itself.[12] The naivety to disillusion journey is devastating and problematic because it assumes an originary "innocence"—whether of American ideals or of belief in those ideals ("America where have you gone?").

Naivety can perhaps be understood in terms of a second paradigm inherent in the writing of memoirs and the autobiographical gaze that by its nature looks back upon events and in that backward glance reconstructs memories and lives. Memories as Benjamin observed are "endless interpolations into what has been,"[13] a continuous process of reforming and reconstituting both the narrating self and the narrated self. Ehrhart posits an "earlier" naive self gradually transmuted by war and its aftermath into a confused, alienated, angry, and finally wise-alienated self drifting outside the literal and psychic boundaries of the nation and its beliefs. The contrast is located in "knowledge" or lack thereof, a trope Nicola King associates with trauma narratives of the Holocaust. "Autobiographical narratives reconstruct the events of a life in the light of 'what wasn't known then,' highlighting the events which are now, with hindsight, seen to be significant."[14] This then-now frame underpins Ehrhart's narrative progression: "If only I had known when it had mattered. [...] I'd been a fool, ignorant and naive. A sucker. For such men, I had forfeited my honor, my self-respect, and my humanity. For such men, I had been willing to lay down my life."[15] What distinguishes Ehrhart's account from other veteran memoirs is its seeming refusal to exculpate the self that participated in Vietnam and is now tainted by that encounter. Ehrhart's indictment of American myths and policies is extremely valuable especially within contexts of revisionist historiography of the Vietnam War and contribute perhaps to his relative obscurity. The trilogy of which *Passing Time* is the second volume offers unrelenting insights of not just the Vietnam era but wide swathes of U.S. depredations in continental North America and beyond. Ehrhart's narratives do not sit comfortably with American founding myths and this places him outside widely accepted discursive frames. As Samuel Hynes notes: "In the process of myth-making, personal narratives both share in the creation and preserve it. Not all of them, to be sure: most narratives of any war, sit dustily on library shelves, unread because they are ill-written and dull, no doubt, but partly because they tell the wrong story, because they don't conform to the myth. Those that *are* read tend to confirm each other—Sassoon supports Graves supports Blunden supports Frederic Manning supports Guy Chapman; Caputo supports O'Brien supports William Merritt supports Tobias Wolff."[16] Ehrhart's memoir is powerfully written and compelling but it tells "the wrong story" and does not have the ideological backing that some of his fellow-veterans' writings do.

 The experiential and moral value of Ehrhart's criticisms of U.S. policies in Vietnam are intertwined, however, with the partial positioning of his postwar self as victim. The participation in a myth of victimhood is a potential third paradigm explicating narrative progressions in *Passing Time*. Drawing on René Girard's "logic of sacrifice" in World War I narratives Evelyn Cobley argues that while "First World War writers rationalize their participation in acts of aggression by constructing the soldier as a sacrificial victim of forces beyond his power. In Vietnam narratives, [...] the soldier is constructed as a crazed killer [...]."[17] While Cobley's distinction is applicable to narratives she analyzes such as *The 13th Valley, The Short-Timers,* or *A Rumor of War,* they along with Ehrhart retrieve spaces of the soldier-as-victim. This construction allows the soldier to ostensibly separate himself from "the system," often represented by the "men" for whom Ehrhart had forfeited his "honor" and "self-respect." Simultaneously, however, he is aware of the ways in which power and disciplinary networks circulate and the difficulty of challenging normative structures: "'How do you change a system like this? Money, power, property—and all of it so deeply entrenched that even the people getting screwed every day think it's the greatest system in the universe. [...] The system's got a life of its own, man. You can't kill it, you can't beat it, and you can't change it.'"[18] This imbrication with power creates a discomfiting yet powerful paradox, one that haunts Ehrhart's poetry as well. While the "system" is seemingly impregnable Ehrhart feels impelled to challenge it at every possible turn, even though his modes of resistance are inadequate in their very expression of oppositions that majority discourses marginalize as unacceptable. As he wrote in an essay "Stealing Hubcaps": "Nothing I do will make any difference, but to do nothing requires a kind of amnesia I have yet to discover a means of inducing."[19] Between the larger cultural and political amnesia over and revisions of the Vietnam War and insistent memorializations lies the specter not just of (ir)relevance but also of a quietist victimhood that seems to erase responsibility. "As a victim," Cobley writes of First World War combat narrations, "the soldier epitomized human suffering; as a killer he was a cog in an impersonal machine over which he had no control."[20] Ehrhart's memoir is precariously poised between victim and killer and although he accepts his role in the war he occasionally projects that role as being part of a "system" of which he was ignorant: "If only I had known when it had mattered." The memoir is both a belated recognition of the "system" and a retrospective justification for individual actions in their location within ignorance.[21]

The individual-system relation brings me to the fourth aspect of narrative development: the idea of agency or choice. In so far as narrative is a means of giving "shape to one's suffering"[22] *Passing Time* delineates through its innocence-experience trajectory the specificities of combat, its aftermath, its personal and social implications. The memoir indicates clearly that going to Vietnam was a deliberate choice and that decision reflects immersion in prevalent belief systems: "I consider it a blessing and a privilege to be an American citizen, [...] Freedom doesn't come cheap [...] If you want it, you have to fight for it."[23] Quite clearly the chasm between idealized patriotic verities and the realities of war are hugely destabilizing and the narrative, while indicating "personal" choice, becomes increasingly cognizant of ideological coercion that determines seemingly free choices such as going to Vietnam. While agency is highlighted, it can and does morph into victimhood in its strident and often justified critiques of war policies and its generative "systems," and the moral criticisms of the "system" sometimes elides and erases individual decision making.

Questions of choice figure in Vietnam War narratives and Tim O'Brien's *The Things They Carried* is one valuable instance. In an interview with Steven Kaplan in 1991 O'Brien expressed his belief that all great fiction explores moral quandaries and portrays characters who are confronted with difficult choices: "The reason choice seems to me important as a word and as a way for me to think about stories is that it involves values. It's most interesting when the choices involve things of equally compelling value."[24] The pivotal scene in "On the Rainy River" ends with a damning summation: "I was a coward. I went to war."[25] In a different narrative mode Ehrhart too arrives at a similar conclusion but *after* his war experiences. Pre-war agency in *Passing Time* is represented not so much as a moral quandary but as a set of certitudes and that might explain the anger and bitterness that permeates the text as it "searches for [post-war] ontological stability."[26] The idea of choice has important implications not only within frames of autobiographical retrieval but also, as Kendrick Oliver points out, in creating a moral historiography of the Vietnam War:

> Indeed, as James Axtell has suggested one of the benefits of retaining a place for moral critique in historical scholarship is that it forces us to remain sensible to the opportunities for choice that usually exist in the environments within which our subjects operate, and not to assume without close interrogation of those environments that the choices they made were the only ones possible.[27]

Oliver's sophisticated critique refers to studies of Vietnam which are "reluctant to render moral judgement," focusing instead on "notions of the tragic, in which the ration of individual culpability becomes impossible to disentangle from the structuring contingencies of ideology, precedent, human fallibility, and History conceived in the grandest scale."[28] The soldier-as-victim narrative coupled with innocence tends to minimize "individual culpability" while at the same time offering indictments of the "system" from a point of seeming moral vantage "outside" historical contingency. The veteran writer's authority resides within this duality and allows him to straddle worlds of innocence and experience that are denied to men such as politicians, military planners, and other morally dubious beings.

Oliver's essay disentangles the complex networks of contingency, choice, and context that make definitive either-or historical judgments of the Vietnam War naive at best and suspect at worst. That definite historiographical narrations—on both sides of the ideological divide—proliferate is unsurprising given the manner in which the conflict and its aftermath have been commemorated in the U.S. The now commonplace circulation of the idea of Vietnam as a "noble cause" and of veterans who were victimized first by the war and then on their return home was most recently on display in the 50th anniversary commemorative events. President Obama in a speech at the Vietnam Veterans Memorial in Washington, D.C., declared:

> You were often blamed for a war you didn't start, when you should have been commended for serving your country with valor.... You came home and sometimes were denigrated, when you should have been celebrated. It was a national shame, a disgrace that should have never happened. And that's why here today we resolve that it will not happen again.[29]

The rhetorical contrast between blame, denigration, "shame," and "disgrace" on the one hand and "valor" and commendation on the other is obvious and indicative of a normative, bipartisan, culturally constructed and acceptable reinterring of the Vietnam War and rehabilitation of its sadly neglected warriors.

It is within these inhibitive, amnesiac spheres that *Passing Time* circulates and continues to offer insights, however much it is itself imbricated in narratives of innocence and victimhood. If "The moral function of memory is to compel us to confront what we—and all around us—wish to leave behind,"[30] then Ehrhart succeeds admirably and it is that success that damns him to the margins of contingent memorial spaces within the U.S. Like all memorial landscapes Ehrhart's conceals as well as reveals and to say that he yearns for a pre-war America or pre-war self as he does is not necessarily to offer a moral criticism. The fractures, contradictions, nostalgia are symptomatic, as Martin Jay points out in an essay on Benjamin and mourning, of a more fundamental disruption of the arc of history:

> Whereas historicists assumed a smooth continuity between past and present, based on an Olympian distance from an allegedly objective story, he [Walter Benjamin] assumed the guise of the "destructive character" who wanted to blast open the seemingly progressive continuum of history, reconstellating the debris in patterns that would somehow provide flashes of insight into the redemptive potential hidden behind the official narrative.[31]

Benjamin's "destructive character" seems as much a part of the narrative self in *Passing Time* at the same moment that that self, unlike Benjamin, mourns the loss of an earlier self. Within the memoir's economy of representation that pre-war self is too precious, it haunts the narrative even (especially?) as it forges "flashes of insight into the redemptive potential hidden behind the official narrative." As Ehrhart tells his friend Gerry: "'We've got to find a way to get back to what this country's supposed to be, Gerry. That's the one good thing that just might come out of all this.'"[32] "The one good thing" is continually frustrated and deferred in the memoir, an impossible touchstone of redemption and arrival, yet in the insistence of its criticism *Passing Time* refuses to give up on "redemptive potential[s]."

Reading and re-reading *Passing Time* I am struck by the kind of earnest, insistent quest for truth and lies that dominates the narrated self. This is a quality that is also evident in Ehrhart's poetry—a patient refusal, a type of bloody mindedness in the midst of cultural rewritings and continuous wars post–Vietnam, a type of integrity with all its corruptions and fallibilities. Perhaps it is a moral orientation that Michael Lambek, citing Charles Taylor, perceives as intrinsic to life writing:

> If, as Charles Taylor argues, our life narration and our sense of self are inextricably linked to our sense of the good, the chronotope of memory must be a moral space. Taylor posits three axes of moral thinking, namely respect for others, understanding of what makes a full life, and dignity, i.e. "the characteristics by which we think of ourselves as commanding (or failing to command) the respect of those around us."[33]

The experience of Vietnam marks an abrupt departure from Taylor's "axes of moral thinking," it leads to a loss of "respect," "a full life, and dignity" and the writing is an attempt to recover "a moral space," however problematic it might be. *Passing Time* in its desires for originary goodness even within the moral bankruptcy of post–Vietnam America and the complex interplay between memory, history, nostalgia, and the self attempts to memorialize the contraries within which "moral space[s]" may be created, inhabited, posited and that seems to me its singular achievement.

This essay is a token and inadequate acknowledgement of the value not only of just one of Bill Ehrhart's works for me, but also a mode of expressing my gratitude and thanks to Bill for his writings, friendship, and example.

Notes

1. Antze, Paul & Michael Lambek, ed., "Introduction: Forecasting Memory," *Tense Past: Cultural Essays in Trauma and Memory* (New York, London: Routledge, 1996), xxiv–xxv.
2. Ehrhart, W. D., *Passing Time: Memoir of a Vietnam Veteran Against the War* (Jefferson, NC: McFarland, 1989), 10.
3. As Siegfried Sassoon put it "[...] the war was a dirty trick which had been played on me and my generation," *Sherston's Progress* (London: Faber & Faber, 1936), 278.
4. Franklin, Bruce H., "Can Vietnam Awaken Us Again? Teaching the Literature of the Vietnam War," *The Radical Teacher* 66 (Spring 2003), 29 (28–31).
5. Ehrhart, *Passing Time*, 16, 162.
6. Ehrhart, *Passing Time*, 18, 88, 172.
7. Loeb, Jeff, "Childhood's End: Self Recovery in the Autobiography of the Vietnam War," *American Studies* 37:1 (1996), 106 (95–116).
8. Some of Ehrhart's poetry is imbued with the idea of the poet-prophet preaching

in the wilderness. See Subarno Chattarji, *Memories of a Lost War. American Poetic Responses to the Vietnam War* (Oxford: Oxford University Press, 2001), 184–191.

9. Ehrhart, *Passing Time*, 233.
10. Loeb, 96.
11. Ehrhart, *Passing Time*, 55, 216. Italics in original.
12. Bastide, Roger, "Setting the framework," in Jay Winter and Emmanuel Sivan, eds., *War and Remembrance in the Twentieth Century* (Cambridge: Cambridge University Press, 1999), 27.
13. Benjamin, Walter, "A Berlin Chronicle," *One Way Street and Other Writings*, trans. Edmund Jephcott and Kingsley Shorter (London: New Left Books, 1932 [1979]), 321.
14. King, Nicola, *Memory, Narrative, Identity: Remembering the Self* (Edinburgh: Edinburgh University Press, 2000), 22.
15. Ehrhart, *Passing Time*, 173, 175.
16. Hynes, Samuel, "Personal narratives and commemoration," *War and Remembrance in the Twentieth Century*, ed. Jay Winter and Emmanuel Sivan (Cambridge: Cambridge University Press, 1999), 207. Italics in original.
17. Cobley, Evelyn. "Violence and Sacrifice in Modern War Narratives," *SubStance* 23:3 (1994), 75 (75–99).
18. Ehrhart, *Passing Time*, 42, 271.
19. Ehrhart W.D., *In the Shadow of Vietnam: Essays 1977–1991* (Jefferson, NC: McFarland, 1991), 126.
20. Cobley, 88.
21. In its recurrent returns to "innocent" pasts *Passing Time* is unable to resist what Paul Ricoeur calls "the retrospective illusion of fatality," *Time and Narrative*, vols. 1–3. Trans. Kathleen McLaughlin and David Pellauer (Chicago: Chicago University Press, 1984/5), 188.
22. Kirmayer, Laurence J. "Landscapes of Memory: Trauma, Narrative, and Dissociation," *Tense Past: Cultural Essays in Trauma and Memory*, eds. Paul Antze & Michael Lambek (New York, London: Routledge, 1996), 185.
23. Ehrhart, *Passing Time*, 125.
24. Kaplan, Steven, "An Interview with Tim O'Brien," *Missouri Review* 14:3 (1991) 108.
25. "[…] O'Brien has noted on several occasions, *Things* is intended to be read as a memoir, a writer's memoir." Herzog, Tobey C. *Tim O'Brien* (New York: Twayne Publishers, 1997), 61. Throughout *The Things They Carried* O'Brien explores the complex interplay between autobiography and fiction.
26. Ringnalda, Donald, "Fighting and Writing: America's Vietnam War Literature," *Journal of American Studies* 22:1 (1988) 30 (25–42).
27. Oliver, Kendrick, "Towards a New Moral History of the Vietnam War?" *The Historical Journal* 47:3 (2004), 759 (757–774).
28. Ibid., 758.
29. Mason, Jeff and Laura MacInnis, 2012. "Obama calls treatment of Vietnam War veterans 'a disgrace,'" http://in.news.yahoo.com/obama-pledges-no-more-wars-unless-absolutely-necessary–165101186.html (Accessed 29 May 2012).
30. Kirmayer, Laurence J., "Landscapes of Memory: Trauma, Narrative, and Dissociation," *Tense Past: Cultural Essays in Trauma and Memory*, eds. Paul Antze & Michael Lambek (New York, London: Routledge, 1996), 193.

31. Jay, Martin, "Against consolation: Walter Benjamin and the refusal to mourn," *War and Remembrance in the Twentieth Century*, ed. Jay Winter and Emmanuel Sivan. (Cambridge: Cambridge University Press, 1999), 230.

32. Ehrhart, *Passing Time*, 201.

33. Lambek, Michael, "The Past Imperfect: Remembering as Moral Practice," *Tense Past: Cultural Essays in Trauma and Memory*, eds. Paul Antze & Michael Lambek (New York, London: Routledge, 1996), 249.

W. D. Ehrhart, Essayist: Musings of a Librarian and Friend

David A. Willson

W. D. "Bill" Ehrhart is a poet who writes essays. His essays are as carefully crafted as his poems, which are minutely and precisely designed. I started to count the number of poems Bill has written, but quickly gave that up as a lost cause. I was going to make a comparison in numbers and type between Bill's poems and his essays. Some of Bill's poems do seem essay-like and his essays contain many bits and pieces that are more poetry than prose.

For this essay, I retrieved his three collections of essays from my shelves and spent weeks reading and rereading them. I started with Bill's most recent collection, *Dead on a High Hill: Essays on War, Literature and Living, 2002–2012*, published by McFarland, 2012. Next I went to his middle collection, *The Madness of It All: Essays on War, Literature and American Life*, also published by McFarland, 2002. These essays were originally published 1991–2002, as the acknowledgments attest. His first book of essays, *In the Shadow of Vietnam: Essays, 1977–1991*, was published by McFarland, 1991. On the title page of this green hardcover book are these words, written in black ink, "For David Willson, Ever your loving friend, Bill Ehrhart, WCSC, 11-4-94." This 196 page book contains twenty-three essays. Bill's middle book, *The Madness of It All*, presents forty-three essays in a 273 page book. *Dead on a High Hill* provides the reader twenty-five essays in 194 pages. That's a total of 94 essays in three books if you count the three prefaces, all written by Bill.

As a student of book covers, the first thing I notice about a book is what it looks like. Bill's first book looks to this reader, who spent thirty years as a college reference librarian, like a sturdy, green buckram bound library-destined book. There are no illustrations of any kind in this book. On the spine and on the title page there is a tiny logo of a lamp of some primitive sort, perhaps meant to give the reader subliminally the notion this book will bring the light of knowledge to that reader.

Bill's middle book, *The Madness of It All*, is a handsome paperback volume, with a shiny purple-red cover dominated by the convergence of two great Vietnam War icons—the helicopter and the Black Wall in Washington. The helicopter displays the number "33" and is hovering so two armed troopers can leap from it, rifles in their right hands, so they can take their place in the roll call of the dead on the Wall. If a viewer squints or uses a magnifying glass, a third ghostly figure is visible, overlapping the middle trooper. Or are my eyes playing tricks on me? The sense I get is of death, death awaiting these young men. With my magnifying glass I could read some of the names on this piece of the wall, but I won't go there. I was interested that in Bill's essay in this book, "Who's Responsible?" he writes, "And the Wall has become an awful cliché. Photographs of the Wall adorn the jackets of dozens of books about the Vietnam War."[1] Barrie Maguire is credited as the artist of this cover which is entitled, "Forever Gone."

There are many fine illustrations in this middle book, including three I especially like of Bill Ehrhart, author (p. 267). The one that accompanies Bill's "About the Author" note shows Bill as I have known him, casual in a plaid sweater vest, over a white shirt, aviator glasses, moustache, ears showing under moderately shaggy hair, bemused expression on his kindly face. The second photo (p. 201) is of "Corporal William D. Ehrhart, 1st Battalion, 1st Marines, Vietnam, 1967. (Photography provided by W.D. Ehrhart.)" Most of a tank is in this photo. Bill is standing in front of the tank, touching the frame of the front of the tank above the tread, with his right hand. He's wearing no head cover. He is not smiling. He has a wrist watch on his left wrist. There are two, perhaps three other troopers, ghostly Marines, on top of the tank, pale, faded, not individually identifiable. Bill is in jungle fatigues, loaded down with stuff. I spotted no M-16, no .45, even with my magnifying glass. Two pages earlier (p. 198) is a great photo of Bill, class of 1966, a callow youth, not that he isn't still, even posed with a tank in Vietnam.

Bill's third book, *Dead on a High Hill*, is a light green glossy paperback, with a color photo dominating the cover, of Bill and his friend Ken Takanega filling sandbags. More about that later. I commented that the first book was marketed as a library book. I deduce from the packaging of the second and third books that there were higher and broader hopes of an audience of readers interested in war books. *Madness* is obviously aimed at a readership looking for a Vietnam War book. Nothing about the cover of *Dead on a High Hill* shouts "Vietnam War" to this reader. There are subtle clues, but not the smack between the eyes that is the icon dominated cover of *Madness*. Bill and his buddy, Ken, could almost be two troopers from any modern American war, assigned the task of making empty bags into full ones. There is no author photo accompanying the "About the author" note.

If a curious reader gleans through this book, many fine photos are found, accompanying and informing the text, including one (Preface, p. 2) of Bill and his wife Anne, kissing their beloved daughter (and only child) Leela, on the cheeks, on the occasion of her graduating from high school, 2005. There is a fine recent photo of Bill (p. 30) Fall, 2011, with his high school English teacher Bob Hollenbach. Bill looks about ten to twelve years older here than his author photo in *Madness*, but he still sports his moustache, aviator glasses and his full head of hair, now seeming grayer. The photo of Bill with the tank appears again (p. 119), but this time the caption tells us more, adding, "Operation Pike." And the word "Regiment" to First Marine. No "s" on Marine this time. My favorite photo of Bill in this book (p. 168) shows him with General Vo Nguyen Giap and an unnamed Foreign Ministry interpreter. The caption comments that later Bill learned that General Giap "understands, reads and speaks English flawlessly." No wonder they won the war. This caused me to think two other things. I am sure that General Westmoreland knew little or no Vietnamese. Also, there is no photo of Bill in any of his books with General Westmoreland.

All three essay collections share a feature that I as a college reference librarian and Vietnam War bibliographer much appreciated and enjoyed. When I don't find this feature in a book of this sort I am disgruntled and out of sorts—Acknowledgments. When I looked for this feature in *In the Shadows of Vietnam*, I missed it the first time through, even though it is listed in the excellent table of contents. It's presented in such small print, I had to get out my magnifying glass to read it. But I was rewarded with the information that Bill had published these essays in such places as the *Philadelphia Inquirer* and the *Virginia Quarterly Review*, as well as many other notable publications.

The acknowledgments in *Madness* were much easier to read. Bill continued to publish in the *Philadelphia Inquirer* and the *Virginia Quarterly Review*. He also published in the *VVA Veteran*, the *Washington Post*, the *Swarthmore College Bulletin*, *American Poetry Review*, *Marine Corps Gazette* and *Poetry Wales*. A study of the acknowledgments in *Dead on a High Hill* shows us that Bill published in the *Seattle Post-Intelligencer*, *War, Literature & the Arts*, the *New Hampshire Gazette* and many others. These acknowledgments hedge a bit, with "some of these essays first appeared in the following publications." Okay.

After this librarian/bibliographer scrutinizes the "Acknowledgments" the next stop is the index. If a book of this sort lacks an index, I've been known to toss it against yonder wall. I don't do that anymore, thanks to a couple of anger management classes and ten years of Vietnam veteran counseling. I consulted the index in *In the Shadow*, first. I looked for familiar names first—names of friends and colleagues or Big Guns. I found plenty of both. John

Balaban, David Connolly, Larry Heinemann, Lynda Van Devanter and Bruce Weigl in the first group. In the second group I found Spiro T. Agnew, William P. Bundy, Gerald Ford, Barry Goldwater, Ho Chi Minh, Adolf Hitler, Robert McNamara, Karl Marx, Pol Pot and Ronald Reagan. I was amused, when I got to the "W" section to find not one, but two double "L" Willsons. Brian and me. I'm glad I didn't have to lose my two legs (as Brian did) to make it into the index.

The index of *Madness* takes up all of five pages. A lot of the same folks pop up, including Hitler and Ho Chi Minh. Brian Willson doesn't make it this time, but I get three page references. All the folks I identified as friends or colleagues listed in the index of Bill's first book appear again, most with more references. Bob Dylan shows up this time.

The index in *Dead on a High Hill* takes up three and one half pages. No Bob Dylan reference this time, No Hitler either. But Jane Fonda does appear. President Obama pops up once. I predict that in Bill's next book of essays the name of our next president will appear in the index. I look forward to that reference and the essay that will feature Bill skewering the president and whatever new war he or she has propelled us into, perhaps with Mexico or Canada so we won't have to ship the cannon fodder so far.

Now I'll deal with each of the three collections, in reverse order of publication. That puts *Dead on a High Hill: Essays on War, Literature and Living, 2002–2012*, first. That's the green shiny one, with Bill and Ken filling sandbags with the reddish laterite soil of South Vietnam. The last and longest essay in this book is "Ken and Bill's Excellent Adventure" so it makes design sense to feature Ken and Bill on the cover having a small and maybe not excellent adventure filling sandbags. Bill has a grimace on his face, perhaps from the exertion of filling the sandbag with the short handled entrenching tool he is wielding or perhaps he is mugging for the camera. Bill is shirtless, his dog tags dangling down, his arm muscles bulge. He's still wearing a wrist watch. Bill's head and Ken's are covered with soft Marine Corps caps, so they might have been in a secure area, or thought or hoped they were. There is a body of water in the background. I would advise them to not go for a dip in it, as seductive as that might be, as it is probably tainted by Agent Orange, mentioned on page 101 of this book.

Did I mention that Ken is sitting, wearing his shirt and fiddling with something on his knee, perhaps a sandbag he is preparing for Bill to fill. There are a lot of empty sandbags in the foreground, so the young Marines have just begun this task. Ken will get his turn, perhaps, unless Bill wants to hog all the glory. When I received this book in the mail, the cover made me eager to read it, as I immediately shared a common history with these two men. When I was young and green, I too was in Vietnam, filling sandbags with that reddish soil. We were not allowed to remove our green t-shirts, because the sergeant in charge of this detail informed us, "We don't want you damaging government property, do we?" No, sarge, we can't have that. Our sunburn did qualify as damaged government property. This cover motivated me to open and read this book much more than the green buckram binding of the first of Bill's books, which offered me zero encouragement, except for the huge one that Bill Ehrhart's name was on the cover. The cover on the second book let me know that it would be about death, which anyone who remembers the Vietnam War will know already. Enough about the covers.

Oh, one more thing before I begin a discussion of *Dead on a High Hill*. One of the things that readers expect from an essay of this sort is that they be provided quotations from the essays under discussion, quotations that will illustrate how fine the essays are. I've always felt great trepidation in doing that while at the same time realizing that without examples the reader has to take your assertions on faith—until the reader reads the essays, that is.

But I do feel that presenting the reader with a sentence or two from an essay of Bill's is akin to sharing a beautiful bird with a friend by killing and dismembering the bird. Then you carry the bird's feet or its left elbow (if birds have elbows) around in your pocket. Whenever the subject of the bird comes up, you remove the feet or its left elbow from your pocket, and display them to your friend and ask, "Wasn't it a beautiful bird?' Your friend stares bug-eyed at the feet or the left elbow of the dead bird and says, "Well, yeah, I guess so. The feet are nice. The left elbow has a nice curve to it." But the friend is just humoring you, taking your assertion on faith. You have to have seen the bird fly. You have to read Bill's essays with your own eyes.

Another aspect of Bill's essays that needs to be discussed before I get to discussing each collection of essays separately, is that many of the essays in these books were written for performance or to be delivered to a special group. I suspect that Bill rehearsed these essays meant for this special purpose by reading them aloud, perhaps many times before he performs or delivers them. Once when Bill and I were in Emporia, Kansas, to address a college English class, he and I had a lot of time on our hands at the bed and breakfast we were staying in. Yusef Komanyakaa had left to go visit family who lived nearby, so Bill and I discussed how to spend our time. Should we rent a cab and have the cabby drive us around the town of Emporia to see the sights? No, our host, Chris, had already shown us some of the local countryside, so we were good with that. We decided to walk up to the nearby liquor store and buy a bottle of Evan Williams and spend the time in one of our rooms consuming the contents of that bottle and discussing life and how we live it. We walked to the liquor store, and were waited on by a woman I knew from Auburn, Washington, where I was currently living. She worked in the liquor store there. I asked her what was up. She had just that week moved to Emporia and was now going to work in this liquor store. She had tired of seeing the same old faces day in and day out. But here was one of them in Emporia. She asked what we were doing there. We told here we were there to lecture to an English class. Her eyes glazed over.

We bought the bottle of Evan Williams and walked the two blocks back to our rooms in the bed and breakfast. I don't remember which room we drank in, but I'll bet that Bill does remember. One of the things we talked about was the nature of lecturing and whether our being old hands at it dispelled all fears. I remember Bill saying that when he was going to perform or deliver a lecture, it did end up being written somewhat differently than a piece that would appear in the newspaper. I had no experience with that sort of thing at all, being published in a newspaper or in a magazine, but I had spent a lot of time in front of classes. I never could figure out how to adapt a presentation I made to a live group for publication. I did it once or twice, but with unsatisfactory results. I think that the essays in these three books that were given as speeches, are amongst Bill's best essays. Because Bill is a fine, disciplined poet, and that carries over to his essays, whether written to be published only or to be performed, he does not waste a word. Each word tells.

I practiced reading some of Bill's published speeches aloud, to test them out. I discovered that these speeches, written to be spoken and delivered to a particular audience with his voice, have a rhythm, a cadence, almost hypnotic. I thought it unlikely that those other essays, those not written to be spoken would be less like this, so I picked out a few of those and read them aloud. Some of them read like the ones designed to be spoken, and others did not. Were they clunky and awkward? No, Bill writes nothing like that, but they were less euphonious. So what did I determine? Not much I guess. I do know from having heard Bill lecture and speak many times that his voice and delivery become integral to his words. In every case, the speeches written for a particular audience, even, or especially, if that audience is a young one, such as "The Origins of Passion" which he gave as Senior Dinner Remarks to The Haverford School on June 10th, 2010 spoke to me. Bill proves he can have it both ways. I counted fourteen essays in these three books that were originally prepared for a live audience. Many of them are my favorite essays in these three volumes.

Dead on a High Hill. We are told that Bill served as a U.S. Marine in Vietnam with the First Marine Battalion, First Marine Regiment in 1967, first as an intelligence assistant, and later as an assistant intelligence chief. He participated in several combat operations including Con Thien and Hue City. Ehrhart was awarded the Purple Heart for wounds received in action in Hue City.

Ehrhart's new book proves once again that he is the finest poet/memoirist/

essayist of the Vietnam Generation. The truths he tells in these essays are often sad and always powerful. The book is a classy production, well-edited and contains more than two dozen excellent essays. The cover alone is worth the price of admission. It shows the author and a buddy, Corporal Takenaga, filling sandbags near Quang Tri, Vietnam, October 1967. This information is given near the bottom of the print on the back cover. Don't believe what you are told on the verso of the title page. This is the only glitch I found in this superb book of essays.

My favorite essay in the book, is "Carrying the Ghost of Ray Catina."[2] Ray Catina is really Alan Catlin who was anthologized as "Ray Catina" in Ehrhart's book *Carrying the Darkness*. The first thing I did after reading this essay, was to dig out my copy of *Carrying the Darkness* to read the two poems by one more guy who pretended to be a Vietnam veteran for obscure reasons of his own.[3] I didn't remember the poems from a few months ago when I most recently reread this anthology, in search of best overlooked poets of the Vietnam War. Did I like the poems? Does it matter that he is a fake and phony? The proof of the pudding is in the eating, my grandpa always told me. So I read the poems again. They are not gems, but perhaps my appreciation of them was colored by my knowing the poet faked his Vietnam service. The poems are good enough and specific enough that when I read them without inside information, no red flags went up.

What this fine little essay brings up for the reader is the question, what constitutes a Vietnam veteran? There is a great debate about that. Some folks believe that a Marine Corps combat veteran is the ultimate Vietnam Veteran. Others make the case that that common experience for most Vietnam veterans was in the rear with the beer and gear, so that means that REMFs are the ultimate Vietnam veterans. Most folks seem to agree that if a poet was never in Vietnam in any capacity at all, he/she is stretching the truth to claim to be a Vietnam veteran. But I read somewhere in a classic Vietnam War book that "Vietnam, Vietnam, Vietnam ... we've all been there." So where does that leave us? One of the great beauties of Ehrhart's book is that it provokes the reader to think, to contemplate, to re-examine long-held beliefs and prejudices.

My second favorite essay is "Good Fences Make Good Neighbors"[4] which I wish every American man, woman and child would read or hear. This piece was delivered as a speech at Clarion College. I have no idea how it was received at Clarion, but I know that if he delivered it at our local community college near Maple Valley, Washington, he would be lucky to not be tarred, feathered and rode out of town on a rail. This speech claims that historical facts are more important than patriotic myth, superstition and legend.

The third essay I recommend highly is "They Want Enough Rice."[5] This is the essay that, if read, should shut up every die-hard Vietnam veteran I've ever argued with when I've heard them claim, "I don't know what happened in Vietnam after I left. When I came home we were winning that war. The media and Jane Fonda sold us down the river." Ehrhart explains what really went wrong with that dirty little war and why.

To me the most exciting essays in the book are those about Korean War poetry. Bill is my favorite scholar of Korean War poets and poetry out of all of them. His three essays, "Hell's Music: A Neglected poem from a Neglected War," "James Magner, Jr., William Meredith and Reg Saner: Reluctant Poets of the Korean War," and "Dead on a High Hill: Poetry of the Korean War" are eye-openers.[6] Bill goes where no scholar has gone before, not in such detail and with such authority. He explores the reasons for the Korean War being such a forgotten war, and why that war produced such a small body of poetry, especially compared to the Vietnam War. Several Korean War poets are introduced to us: Rolando Hinojosa, William Childress and Keith Wilson, among others. Bill has done a great thing to retrieve these men from differing degrees of obscurity. Quoted fragments of their poems justifies their being brought to our attention.

The last essay in the book, mentioned by me earlier, because the main characters in it are pictured on the cover, is "Ken and Bill's Excellent Adventure."[7] Ken and Bill go back to Vietnam, where they first met, decades ago. This long, moving and fascinating essay motivated me to make a serious effort to get together with my closest friend in Vietnam, Charles Bryant. Due to my health, we could not journey to Vietnam, as Bill and his friend, Ken Takenaga, but we did meet in Maple Valley and spent a few hours together chatting about our lives. This is the great thing about Bill and his essays. He has the power to inspire action. Whether it is to seek out and buy a book of Korean War poetry or to reunite with an old Vietnam War buddy, Bill's prose is action-oriented and can provoke action in the reader.

I've only sampled the essays in this book, as the length of this chapter cannot allow me to review each essay in the book. The problem with that approach is that I find myself writing an essay about essays that speak best for themselves. I just want you to find the books and read them. I don't want to try to make you think that this short essay in any way substitutes for the voice of Bill as you'll find it yourselves when you read his essays. Bill is a much better essayist than I am, especially when he is writing about his chosen subjects.

Buy and read this book if you are up for being provoked to think, and perhaps abandon some of your closely held preconceptions.

The middle book is next for this treatment. *The Madness of It All*. When I first got this book in the mail I scanned the index and there in the "W's" I spotted William Wantling's name. Major entries with lots of page numbers compared to the passing references on three pages devoted to other Korean

War writers. The large numbers of page number references and the discovery of two complete essays about William Wantling transfixed me. "I Want to Try It All Before I go: The Life and Poetry of William Wantling,"[8] and the second essay, "Setting the Record Straight: An Addendum to the Life and Poetry of William Wantling."[9] The first essay is nine pages and the second is five pages. I'd been wondering about William Wantling since the early 1960s when an English professor at the University of Washington, Dr. Burns, introduced me to Wantling's love poetry. Was the poem that caught my eye in those long gone days, "Lemonade 2 Cents?" Perhaps. I even looked for a chapbook of Wantling's poems up and down the Ave in Seattle's University District and found a tiny pink one, jammed on the shelf reserved for tiny poetry chapbooks. Magus, I believe, was the name of the shop. The book I had was a tiny, dog-eared book. I only remember love poetry in it. I have no idea where that tiny book went, or if it contained war and prison poetry. But thanks to Bill, I now know a lot about Wantling, more than I ever thought likely I would know.

One of the things I love about Bill is that if he gets something wrong, he revisits it and sets the record straight. He does that in his second essay on Wantling. Bill writes in his second essay, "a good deal of what little we thought we knew about Wantling turns out to not be true." Later Bill writes of Wantling that "'Poetry' is one of the best prison poems ever written by anyone." Still, after I went on-line and read Wantling's prison poetry and his war poetry, I still preferred his few love poems. Many of the on-line entries credit Bill as the one who brought out what accurate information can be found about Wantling. I still wish I could lay my hands on that small, pink, dog-eared Wantling chapbook that I once owned, but it is missing, and I admit that is due to my messy life, and it is likely gone from me forever. I need to quit obsessing about it.

As much as I loved the Wantling essays, the ones that captured my attention most easily, were those that mentioned my name. Here is my chance to set the record straight. In Bill's fine essay, "Who's Responsible?" written to be presented to the Freshman Forum at La Salle University, Philadelphia, Pennsylvania, October 15th, 1991, my name is connected to a collection of "several hundred pornographic novels using the Vietnam War as a backdrop" (p. 25). It amazes me that that conference was 22 years ago. My twenty-year-old daughter, Alice, had not been born yet. Only in the sense that war itself is pornographic did I ever have such a collection. I had a dozen or so sleazy novels that were marketed in porn shops and would be perceived generally as pornographic novels. They had covers that signaled that content, and there were barely clad warriors on most of the covers, accompanied by SE Asian lovelies in various stages of disrobement. But not several hundred. I apologize for that being a matter of record and take the blame for that being communicated to Bill. I do not remember how I said it, but probably I was indulging in a flight of hyperbole.

Bill's other essay which mentions me is "The Vietnam War and the Academy,"[10] and it was pure fun for me to read. It's about the Vietnam War conferences that both Bill and I attended, but unlike Bill, I took no notes and never wrote a thing anywhere about the conferences. When I attended the first conference he writes about in this essay, the 1986 conference at Manchester Polytechnical Institute, "Cultural Effects of Vietnam (EVAC)," like Bill, I'd never heard the word "hegemony" before. I had no idea what the word meant. I suppose that Bill and I might have been the only two at the conference who didn't know. Unlike Bill, I had to pay my own way to the conference. I had published nothing, as *REMF Diary* was still in the future, 1988. My wife Michele was pregnant with our first child, Joaquin, who was born later that year, and I hated to leave her in Auburn while I went traipsing off to England, but I figured that this conference was likely the only international conference on this subject that I'd ever get invited to, so I went.

The two and one half pages of this essay that Bill devotes to EVAC bring back my memories powerfully. There's even a photo of John Clark Pratt, the first person I encountered when I got to the Institute from my flight and went in search of a drink. I was parched and jet lagged and needed something to tide me over and boost me up. I had dragged a huge duffle bag which contained dozens of Vietnam War novels with me to Manchester, mostly mass market paperbacks, but some hardcovers, too, and I was pooped.

I found Professor Pratt in a tiny dorm kitchen making himself a drink, and he invited me to join him, which I did. Thanks to Bill for evoking that memory of John Clark Pratt and his generous and compassionate treatment of a clueless guy who had never been to England before and who was baffled by their customs. I had been invited there to give my slide presentation, "Sex, Death and Military Might," which was a chronological series showing the covers of mass market paperbacks and what visual motifs they used to market their product. When I was very near the beginning of my slide show, in a darkened amphitheater room, with steeply pitched rows of seats, a tall guy about my age stumbled into the room, found a seat while making a great fuss, and after he'd been there in the room for a minute or two, spoke up in a loud voice, a British voice, one of those upper class voices, "This presentation doesn't make much sense, and would be a lot more interesting if the dates were given to us." What everyone already in the room knew was that I had a large red and black slide every few slides, showing the year transition for the clump of slides I was about to show. It so happened that the very next slide was one of those date slides. 1966. I flicked my control mechanism and the huge red and black date appeared on the screen. 1966.

I had not replied to his criticism, figuring I would bide my time. As I continued my lecture to the group, I said, "Those of you who have your eyes open, can see that now I am going to show you the slides of mass market paperback covers for the year 1966. We just saw the slides of the covers for 1965 and after these slides of the 1966 covers, we will view those for 1967. I apologize for the complexity of this presentation, but will try to clarify when necessary. Are you all with me now?" The newcomer to the room said not another word. Bill Ehrhart's laughter was the loudest in the room. This laughter made my trip to England worth the trouble. Bill came up to me after the slide show, and we talked and that was the beginning of our friendship.

Later someone told me that latecomer was an important graphic arts professor at Berkeley who had a new and important book out on the political subtext of comic strips. I forget his name. Bill covers this event within an event in two and a half lines in his "Academy" essay in his book, *Madness*. Here they are. "College librarian, novelist and Vietnam Veteran David A. Willson gave a hilarious and brilliant paper on the cover art of the Vietnam War paperback books" (p. 60). If we had not been fast friends already, that generous and succinct comment would have gone a long way to making that happen. Thanks, Bill, for mentioning me in an essay which includes the names of many of the scholarly and creative luminaries of our Dirty Little War: Some of them being, John Clark Pratt, John Balaban, Don Luce, Larry Heinemann, Adi Wimmer, and Pilar Marin.

1986 is a long time ago, 26 years and counting, but such is the power of Bill's prose, that it acted like a time machine and reminded me of that long gone time and of the fools, foreigners and fast friends I met there in Manchester, England, and I found myself thinking that the Vietnam War was not an entirely bad thing, after all, to propel me to leave Auburn, Washington, to meet such a variety of people, all of them with a huge interest in what I'd thought of as my war, a war that nobody close to me, my parents, or their friends, wanted to hear a word about. But here there were big rooms full of people who couldn't shut up about it. When I am awake at 3:00 in the morning, jolted from my sleep by bone pain due to the multiple myeloma that America's faith in science brought down on me while I was showering at Long Binh or drinking Jell-O punch in the messhall, I have the memories of these adventures with friends to keep me company in these dark hours. Thank you, Bill, for evoking those times with your magic words.

Bill's "Academy" essay also treats a 1990 conference in Toronto, and Professor Robert Slabey's Notre Dame Conference, which it seems as though everyone was at. I won't list the names of all those who were there, as it would almost be easier to list those who missed it. Everyone interested in how the Vietnam War and "the Academy" intersected must read this essay of Bill's. He gives Slabey's Notre Dame Conference his highest accolade. "I wouldn't mind my kid taking a course or two with folks like that."

I scanned the table of contents to find an essay that on the face of it would hold little interest for me and have nothing to do with the Vietnam War. I picked out "Tugboats on the Delaware."[11] It was originally published in two parts in *New Jersey Waterways*, September 1996 and March/April 1997, I never really cared much about boats of any kind, especially tugboats, but Bill writes about those boats and their people in such a way that I found that essay almost as interesting as the one on the Vietnam War and the Academy or the ones on William Wantling. Such is Bill's gift or talent or the result of hard work at the writing desk. Listen to Bill communicate his joy at being aboard the *Teresa McAllister*. "It's the kind of cozy, oddball niche that little kids go nuts over, and it's all mine." That's Bill's comment on the cabin he'll be staying in. "Tugboats" reads like a sublime and beautiful industrial poetry. Bill writes of the engine. "Surrounded by various generators, pumps, gizmos and all manner of pipes, and valves and whatnot, the engine itself—think of your car's engine block without all the paraphernalia attached to it—is about the size of my Subaru Legacy station wagon, not quite so wide but longer and taller." It didn't make me want to go aboard the *Teresa McAllister*, but it made me feel that I had been aboard in some cerebral sense, and it made me glad Bill had and that he had the gifts and experience to write this essay. There was nothing in this essay about the Vietnam War, although the Korean War gets a name check, and Musto, the mate, "got her first ship out of Bahrain out of the Gulf War, a voyage that included mines in the Persian Gulf, machete-wielding pirates in the Philippines, a blown engine in the South China Sea, and two months in a Singapore drydock." It's a tough assignment to read an essay of Bill's and not find war of some sort in there somewhere. It's not Bill, though, it is the world we inhabit. No one writes more poetically of that world.

In the Shadow of Vietnam: Essays, 1977–1991 is Bill's first book of essays and the only one to mention the Vietnam War in the title. The other two say "war," but this one says it straight out, Vietnam. It is a country, not just a war, of course. We've been told that for a long time, to shame us into giving that little country more of an identity than what relates to our time there. I've read what seems like a million memoirs and novels by guys who were there and the thing they always obsess about is the "smell," as though it was something the people who lived there created and didn't notice because they were somehow not human the way we were. It didn't seem to occur to any of those authors that we brought that smell with us. That Saigon smelled that way (and Binh Hoa) because the garbage was no longer being picked up because the garbage men were gone, for reasons related to our American War in Vietnam. Long Binh smelled foul because of our shit being burned. I ought to know that, as

I was in charge of plenty of shit burning details. I've read several books recently by Americans who have returned to Vietnam, and they comment on how the "smell" is gone. Right. They say things smell normal now, no worse than things smell in Honolulu. Right, again.

In an essay in this book, "Waiting for the Fire,"[12] Bill writes, "For a long time—in fact—longer than I care to admit, I really believed that you couldn't write about Vietnam unless you'd been there. " Bill goes on to say, and I love how he says it, "It was the credo of a sore loser, both as veteran and poet, but I clung to it tenaciously." "Credo of a sore loser." Those words cry out to be a title. There are many essays in this book that I love, especially "The United States Screw and Bolt Company," but let's go to the essay that I went to first when I was given the book, "Teaching the Vietnam War."[13] I taught classes that dealt with that war for most of thirty years, both in the classroom and on-line after I retired from being a librarian at Green River Community College in Auburn, WA. Bill tells us why he teaches about that war. "I think it is important. I think people ought to know what happened and why." No teacher is better at teaching these things about that war. I have sat in a room filled with young people when Bill explained what happened and why. I was dazzled and I learned plenty, even though I had been teaching about that war for years myself. Bill has a way of coming at things from different angles and surprising you. He surprised me. My advice to anyone who is a co-lecturer with Bill, is avoid following him. Following him is like going on stage back in the '50s and following Jerry Lee Lewis who played "Great Balls of Fire," and left the stage with the piano actually on fire, due to his application of lighter fluid and a match. Bill doesn't need the lighter fluid and the match, but the next one up might.

Bill writes in his essay how the public image of the Vietnam veteran during the '80s somehow transformed from that of "drug-crazed psychopath to cultural icon." I remember the first part of that stereotype directly from the treatment I got from my family and their friends in November of 1967 which was sort of the depths of that image, but the icon part has eluded me. I have seen it in the *Rambo* movies, of course, as portrayed by the mumbling but noble Sylvester Stallone who I am told spent some of that war in Switzerland. I don't begrudge him that, unlike some. I wish I'd spent the war there, too, and I don't even ski or care much about time pieces. Good for him. As Bill points out in one of his essays in a later book, most young men of our era neither went to the war nor protested it. They just somehow shrugged it off and went on with their normal lives. It must take some kind of a dummy to not manage to do that, when most of his cohorts did that. All my closest high school buddies in Yakima did just that, shrugged and went on with their lives. The funny thing is that at least two of them are long since dead, and one is gone and most probably dead, too. And here I am, as big and loud and obstreperous as ever, reading and reviewing Bill's essay books, and proud and happy to be doing it, even though I was told I would most likely be dead by October 2011, due to the Agent Orange that gets just a brief mention in Bill's essays.

Deep into Bill's essay on teaching the Vietnam War, I ran into the name of Lynda Van Devanter and the title of her book, *Home Before Morning*.[14] Suddenly a flood of tears went down my face. Not so unusual for me these days. One of the meds I take for my multiple myeloma is said to cause "excess of emotion." But is it excess of emotion to tear up when reading Lynda's name, dead ten years now, aged 55, from exposure in Vietnam to chemical agents such as Agent Orange? I remember her hugging me goodbye in an airport, I have no idea which one, after a long ago conference, the last time I saw her alive. I am not much of a hugger, having been raised a Norwegian Lutheran, but I gladly hugged Lynda, one of the sweetest and best people I ever knew and the author of one of the best and most honest books ever written about the Vietnam War and its impact on a young woman.

Bill's essay, "The United States Screw & Bolt Company"[15] uses a point-counterpoint presentation. On the one hand we have the Big Political Guns of the time and on the other hand we have the mostly ordinary young men, nobodies, who served and died or worse. It starts with McGeorge Bundy, and next is Michael Pacek. All these years later, I suspect that most young readers are so ignorant of American history that they won't likely know which is the Big Gun and which is the nobody. There is no introduction to prepare the reader, just the sudden stark shock. It starts right off and proceeds for thirteen pages, with no conclusion. It just stops.

The power of this essay as a list, is the interaction and juxtapositions of items and how they resonate with each other and with the reader. After it starts with Bundy and Pacek, it deals with 64 more men, by my count. I admit that I counted several times and got a different total each time. These days, counting is not my best thing. I blame it on the oxycodone. The list ends many pages later with a biographical entry of sorts of Robert L. Schlosser, whom I have known for decades.

One of the main points I get from this essay is that it was better to be an older man in a position of power during the Vietnam War, than to be a young man with no power and influence. Good things happened to the older guys. It could be a very bad thing to be a young man during that war. Some of the options made clear in this essay were: service in Vietnam, death, wounds, loss of limbs, PTSD, exposure to Agent Orange, being involved in things shameful or dishonorable, prison, flight to Canada.

A larger point could be that it was always better to be an older man, preferably a white man, as all of these older men are, as old men rarely get near a war zone, and if they do they are usually not there long enough to be seriously in harm's way. Most of the old white men in Bill's essay list were in the position of placing young men at risk in a war zone and they seemed not at all reluctant to do it. As Mendal Rivers is quoted by Bill, when he supports a three year Federal prison sentence for a young man who damaged his draft card, "This is the least we can do for our men in South Vietnam fighting to preserve freedom." Whose freedom, he does not say. Not the young man who got sent to prison for tearing a small piece of paper.

"Screw and Bolt" is a brilliant piece of work that operates on its own with no need for explication, only footnotes that explain the origins of the information that accompanies each of the over sixty names. It's not necessary for the reader to know the people on the list or to know of them as the information in a few lines, barebones as it is, tells the tale. But, and this is a big but, my knowing a couple of the people listed here, does add power and punch to the point that Bill is making, which is made clear in the great title Bill came up with. The list is all about the "military industrial complex" that President Eisenhower warned us about in his Farewell Address. The list alternates between those the system, the MIC, screws and those who do the screwing, and receive the benefits of this system, which are large and which seem to continue until the Big Guns expire, covered with riches and glory and rewarding book publishing deals.

Robert L. Schlosser is the last entry in this essay, and seeing his name struck me like a hammer blow when I first read this article. Not long ago, he drove out from Seattle, where he lives a quiet life, retired from the over thirty years he spent working for the Washington State Liquor Control Board, to see me. I am not easily able to get into Seattle, now without a lot of effort, as my Agent Orange caused multiple myeloma has cursed me with considerable bone pain, which is provoked by every bump and pothole on the badly maintained I-5 Highway that we travel to get to Seattle. The other day I heard that to properly upgrade that highway would cost more than a billion dollars. That is not going to happen. The money is there for wars, not for infrastructure such as highways and bridges.

We talked about war, current events, Vietnam poetry and about the state of America's roads and bridges. You name it, and we discussed it. Bob is the proprietor and informing intelligence of an enterprise named Friday's Egg Calendar, the most amazing calendar I am aware of. Some years I am honored by having a short work of mine published in this calendar which showcases art, poetry, short prose and photographs. Bill Ehrhart's poetry sometimes appears in Friday's Egg, too. This is one way Bob keeps busy in his retirement years.

Bob Schlosser is the one person on this long list/essay who I know for sure is doing well. I figure many or most on this list are dead. But Bob is alive and lively and traveling in Europe with his wife Nancy. Good for him. He got his revenge. Like all of us, he has had his ups and downs since his tour in Southeast Asia, but he is currently happy and healthy. There is life after the Vietnam War for some of us, even if Bill included you in his "Nuts and Bolts" piece. I will quote here the entry that Bill composed for Bob.

> Robert L. Schlosser. Formerly U.S. Army. Indochina veteran, 1969–70. He spent his time in Thailand "surrounded by U.S. Air Force bases that sent bombers over Laos, Cambodia, every day of every one of those fourteen months I spent guarding bombs and picking up stoned and drunk soldiers out of alleys. So what do we have now? Winnebagos, McDonald's hamburgers. Was Vietnam real? Is television real? Or the state of contemporary America? Ah, hell, it don't mean nothing, man" (p. 43).

Bob was the perfect choice to end this list, and it was equally perfect to place Henry Kissinger immediately prior to Bob. I will now quote Kissinger's entry.

> Henry A. Kissinger. Director of the National Security Council, 1969–75, Secretary of State, 1973–77. October 1972: "Peace is at hand." Became a professor at Georgetown University, consultant to NBC, and Goldman Sachs and Company, and a bestselling author [p. 43].

The wages of sin are death, but not immediately enough in some cases. See the difference? Get the point? I am sure you all do.

In his Preface to this book, *Shadows*, Bill tells us the purpose of this essay better than I did above, so I'll quote what he says here:

> Thus, The United States Screw and Bolt Company is an opportunity to consider why Ronald Reagan who made movies in Hollywood during World War II, who staunchly supported the war in Vietnam while his own sons avoided military service, so willingly sent the Marines to Lebanon; why George Bush, whose sons did not serve in Vietnam or anywhere else that I know of, has twice put young Americans in harm's way in the space of less than a year; why Danforth Quayle who spent the Vietnam War safe and snug in the National Guard, is now vice president of the United States [pp. ix–x].

For readers who wish to know more about McGeorge Bundy, they need go no further than this book, for on page 135 is Bill's essay, "A Letter to McGeorge Bundy."[16] He wrote Bundy quite a good letter about asking for him to apologize for all the mistakes he had made related to the Vietnam War. Bill never got an answer. I am not surprised. Those Big Guns of the American War in Vietnam are too busy with their successful lives to pay any attention to any lowly Vietnam veteran. I think we are nothing to them, not even as annoying as a mosquito that buzzes in their ears when they are on their yachts.

Thank you, Bill. Bill is very good at all the things he does: teacher, poet, memoirist, essayist. After spending so much time with his essays, I am tempted to say he is best at that, but I know that if I spent the same amount of time reading his memoirs, then he'd get my vote as a memoirist. And it would work that way for the poetry, too. I've read and reread Bill's essays, trying to figure how he does it, what is his secret. Somehow he manages to get the fire of his in-person performances onto the page. Bill has a singular voice that is heard in the mind's ear when we read his essays.

The last few weeks, when I've found myself awake at 3:00 A.M. I've thought of the great times with Bill in Manchester, South Bend, Indiana, Emporia, Kansas and Auburn, Washington, and counted myself lucky to know him. I scribbled a lot of notes for this essay at 3:00 A. M. while thinking the above thoughts. What have I come up with? Bill is a master of writing American idiomatic English in all its ragged glory and perfection. His sentences can leave a reader breathless and flummoxed. Not a bad gift.

It has amused me and bemused me to spend these many days writing an essay about the essays of a master essayist who writes better essays than I do, and a lot more of them, too. But I was asked to do my best to do this job, and I was honored to be asked. Anything that amuses me at this stage of my life is a good thing. While reading Bill's essays, I have chuckled a lot, but I've also shed some tears and sworn vile oaths, such is the wide range of emotions evoked by Bill's essays. His prose motivates the reader to discovery and rediscovery. His excitement is contagious through the power of his words.

Was it arrogant or hubristic of me to write this essay on Bill Ehrhart, master essayist? Nobody has written better on Bill than Bill. Both in his Prefaces to these books of essays, and in his memoirs, Bill has addressed the subject of his life and work, and that is the place I advise the reader to go next. And then to his poetry. That is what I intend to do myself.

Notes

1. Ehrhart, "Who's Responsible?" in *Madness*, 21–31.
2. Ehrhart, "Carrying the Ghost of Ray Catina," in *Dead on a High Hill*, 73–74.
3. Catina, Ray, in W.D. Ehrhart, ed., *Carrying the Darkness: American Indochina. The Poetry of the Vietnam War* (New York: Avon Books, 1985), "Negotiations," 69; "Philosophy," 70.
4. Ehrhart, "Good fences Make Good Neighbors: A Brief History of National Myopia" in *Dead on a High Hill*, 75–80.
5. Ehrhart, "'They Want Enough Rice': Reflections on the Late American War in Vietnam," in *Dead on a High Hill*, 112–125.
6. Ehrhart, in *Dead on a High Hill*, respectively 32–40; 42–66; 147–162.
7. Ehrhart, "Ken and Bill's Excellent Adventure," in *Dead on a High Hill*, 163–185.
8. Ehrhart, "'I want to Try It All Before I Go': The Life and Poetry of William Wantling" in *Madness*, 173–182.

9. Ehrhart, "Setting the Record Straight: An Addendum to the Life and Poetry of William Wantling," in *Madness*, 217–222.
10. Ehrhart, "The Vietnam War and the Academy," in *Madness*, 59–64.
11. Ehrhart, "Tugboats on the Delaware." in *Madness*, 105–116.
12. Ehrhart, "Waiting for the Fire," in *Shadow*, 53–57.
13. Ehrhart, "Teaching the Vietnam War," in *Shadow*, 143–148.
14. Van Devanter, Lynda, with Christopher Morgan, *Home Before Morning. The True Story of an Army Nurse in Vietnam* (New York: Warner Books, 1984).
15. Ehrhart, "The United States Screw & Bolt Company," in *Shadow*, 30–45.
16. Ehrhart, "A Letter to McGeorge Bundy," in *Shadow*, 135–138.

Part Two.
The Poet as an Artist

The Farmer

Each day I go into the fields
to see what is growing
and what remains to be done.
It is always the same thing: nothing
is growing, everything needs to be done.
Plow, harrow, disc, water, pray
till my bones ache and hands rub
blood-raw with honest labor—
all that grows is the slow
intransigent intensity of need.
I have sown my seed on soil
guaranteed by poverty to fail.

But I don't complain—except
to passersby who ask me why
I work such barren earth.
They would not understand me
if I stooped to lift a rock
and hold it like a child, or laughed,
or told them it is their poverty
I labor to relieve. For them,
I complain. A farmer of dreams
knows how to pretend. A farmer of dreams
knows what it means to be patient.
Each day I go into the fields.

—W.D. Ehrhart[*]

---

[*]*The Outer Banks & Other Poems*, 17; *Beautiful Wreckage: New & Selected Poems*, 79.

Relieving the National Debt: W. D. Ehrhart and the Wages of Memory

AMMIEL ALCALAY

Few things are as determined as the time and place of your birth, the circumstances into which you might be born, and the relative distances you might need or want to move from those points. I was born in Boston in 1956, to parents who had come to the United States as refugee/immigrants just 5 years before, in 1951, having survived the wars of Europe. They came with great excitement, eager to be involved in new ways of life, to participate in the cultural renaissance that exploded in the 1950s, finding form in abstract painting, jazz, modern dance, and poetry. As opposed to my older brother, my age made me ineligible for the draft, which ended in January 1973, just a month before I would turn 17. Paradoxically, my brother's lethal allergy to eggs—something that nearly killed him several times—insured his 4F status, and the lucky privilege of not having to face the kind of momentous decision put before most 18 year olds then.

The open political and cultural turbulence of those years, the constant activity evident everywhere in a city like Boston—from the underground press, the music you could hear, the clothes you wore, the demonstrations you might go to or just stumble into—was impossible to ignore and I already found myself immersed in and receptive to everything taking place around me at an early age, starting in my last years of grade school: 1968 and 1969. My father was an artist and the atmosphere around the house or the studio very often included family friends who were also artists or writers. There were plenty of books around, and most of them were very far from anything that might be construed as "mainstream."

The still obscure little magazines of the 1950s and '60s—*Origin, Black Mountain Review, Yugen, The Floating Bear, Big Table, Evergreen,* and so many others—populated the bookshelves through which I freely wandered, as did the work of the so-called Beat generation or those closely identified with them.

I remember coming back again and again to a very short essay I encountered by the poet Charles Olson, most well known for his epic *The Maximus Poems* and his ground-breaking work on Melville, *Call Me Ishmael*; it was a review of a book on Billy the Kid, and opened like this:

> It's this way. Here's this country with what accumulation it has—so many people having lived here millennia. Which ought to mean (people being active, more or less) an amount, you'd figure, of things done, and said, more or less as in other lands. And with some proportion of misery—for which read "reality," if you will wait a minute and not take "misery" as anything more than a characterization of unrelieved action or words.
>
> That is: what strikes one about the history of sd [said] States both as it has been converted into story and as there are those who are always looking for it to reappear as art—what has hit me is, that it does stay, unrelieved. And thus loses what it was before it damn well was history, what urgency or laziness or misery it was to those who said and did what they did. Any transposition which doesn't have in it an expenditure at least the equal of what was spent, diminishes what was spent. And this is loss, loss in the present, which is the only place history has context.[1]

I was caught by this, haunted then, over 40 years ago, and it remains a quote that I keep coming back to the truth of, as, to paraphrase Olson, it stands "more revealed." What I still find unique about it is the concept of "misery" being a state of "unrelieved" reality, and that, in order for history to become meaningful, to integrate itself into one's very consciousness (not to mention a more collective consciousness), there must be as great an effort in its presentation as there was in its very unfolding.

It is in the crux of this conundrum—between the burden of history, the burden of memory, and its coming to consciousness—that W.D. Ehrhart's enormous achievement as a poet, memoirist, essayist, and creator of essential anthologies should be located. Within a literary culture that tends to follow the trends of technology (always looking for the latest formal innovation or theory), it is very difficult to find critical terms for the kind of historical burden and seemingly straightforward forms that characterize Ehrhart's work. Moreover, because he has established the context of his own history, through the early poems drawing on his war experiences and his memoirs, when we come to later, lyric poems, we are presented with an increased emotional charge precisely because of what we already know about how difficult a journey it was to achieve the clarity of such moments, as in this poem, "Nothing Profound":

> If you need a reason to care,
> consider this feather I've found,
> consider the sweetness of bare
> young arms in sunlight, or the round
> perfection of a ripe pear.[2]

Thus, what might appear trite in another context suddenly forces us to reconsider the title: for most people, the feather or the pear is "nothing profound," but for Ehrhart, who has had the courage to explore the depths of self-loathing and human horror, these simple things are, indeed, most profound.

In our consumer culture, where we have stopped manufacturing almost everything, and have come to rely on labor that isn't ours, I would even say that our own history has taken on the character of our economy: we print and we print and we print, but there is so very little behind what a devious character on the Powderpuff Girls calls our "happy paper." How did we get to this state? As early as the 1940s, poet Muriel Rukeyser wrote, "We are a people tending toward democracy at the level of hope; on another level, the economy of the nation, the empire of business within the republic, both include in their basic premise, the concept of perpetual warfare."[3]

Not being a small country with borders to defend or under intermittent siege or attack, the method through which perpetual warfare becomes naturalized in the United States must include both perverting the aspirations of youth, and their actual physical displacement. Given that getting the populace to want to send their children overseas to kill people they never even met isn't the easiest feat for a government to accomplish, we have to be cognizant of the enormous overt and covert machineries and mechanisms put into place in order to actually make this happen, something that has certainly been true since the First World War, and has only grown in intensity since then.

Until, of course, the American war in Southeast Asia. Until the enormous resistance mounted, first and foremost, by soldiers, but aided and abetted by parents, students, urban uprisers, and so many others. In a book of essays dedicated to the heroic work of W. D. Ehrhart, one would hope that some or most of this would be self-evident. But in a country in which Ehrhart is not a household name, or even considered among the leading literary voices, one is better off not assuming anything. Having taught his work in a variety of contexts over the years—from seminars on contemporary American Poetry or Global Decolonization to Introduction to American Studies—it has become increasingly clear that his work resonates across many different subjects and approaches. More importantly, it both calls into question and illuminates—through the integrity of his experience and the force of his expression—both received knowledge and true blank spots. When students never exposed to such images see the very short surviving film clips of Dewey Canyon III (which took place in April 1971), that extraordinary action in which veterans of the war in Vietnam chose, as a last resort, to liberate themselves by throwing their medals at the Capitol, and connect it to readings of Ehrhart's poems, essays, and memoirs, a whole new world opens up for them, a world they can hardly imagine actually existed.

I want to turn here to the role of poetry, that obvious catalyst for everything Ehrhart has written. During the American Civil War, for example, poetry was common currency. From the now more famous—Walt Whitman, Herman Melville, Emily Dickinson, Henry Wadsworth Longfellow, Bret Harte, William Cullen Bryant, Ralph Waldo Emerson, or Julia Ward Howe, to the countless unknown soldiers, their friends and families—poems were freely and constantly exchanged by letter, published in newspapers, and set to inspirational music. In Faith Barrett and Cristanne Miller's brilliant anthology *Words for the Hour,* they write that in the 19th century "Americans not only heard poems at many civic events, but they also read poetry in broadsides, pamphlets, daily newspapers, and magazines, as well as in books and anthologies ... poetry was seen as an integral part of American political culture."[4] This "explosion" of poetry is something Ehrhart himself notes about poetry from the era of the war in Vietnam; in the preface to *Unaccustomed Mercies: Soldier-Poets of the Vietnam War,* one of the ground-breaking anthologies that he has edited, Ehrhart writes: "This vast body of poetry is a phenomenon unparalleled in American literature. No previous American war, with the possible exception of the American Civil War, has produced anything like it."[5]

There is no doubt that the more political minded poets of the 1930s—someone like Langston Hughes, for example—strove to create an idiom that could function as a means of public communication, a form both containing and transmitting political, cultural, and social memory. But the advent of the Cold War pushed poetry underground or into the academy, creating what essayist, critic, and translator Eliot Weinberger has called "official verse culture." From that point on poetry became divided and institutionalized into what Robert Lowell called the "raw" and the "cooked" schools.[6] In an extraordinary series of lectures, delivered in the 1940s and eventually published as *The Life of Poetry,* Muriel Rukeyser talks about the "fear" of poetry. What I would call a pedagogy of distrust in our own common sense, in the witness of our intuitions, experiences, emotions, and consciousness, must begin early in order for the war mechanism to take root and operate. As Rukeyser wrote:

> The fear that cuts off poetry is profound: it plunges us deep. Far back to the edge of childhood.... Little children do not have this fear, they trust their emotions. But on the threshold of adolescence the walls are built.... Against the assaults of puberty, and in those silvery delicate seasons when all feeling casts

about for confirmation. Then for the first time, you wonder "What should I be feeling?" instead of the true "What do you feel?"[7]

Rukeyser goes on to speak about "repressive codes" that strike "deep at our emotional life." Breaking through these repressive codes was no easy feat. Certainly a key component in the persistence and re-emergence of cultural transmission and its historical consciousness had to do with poets of the 1950s seeking models in those who had lived through the 1930s, as younger poets looked to the example of Langston Hughes, Kenneth Patchen, Muriel Rukeyser, William Carlos Williams, and many others. Charlie Parker invented a new post-atomic language through Bebop, captivating the writers who were listening: in his "History of Bop," Jack Kerouac spoke of "America's inevitable Africa," something that could easily be related to the worldwide decolonization movement, and the return of an indigenous consciousness. In the Beat movement, so often written off as apolitical, human experience returns to the forefront, with a distinct and deeply subversive intent. Michael McClure, one of the readers at the famous Six Gallery reading where Allen Ginsberg first read *Howl* in public, describes the times:

> We were locked in the Cold War and the first Asian debacle—the Korean War. My self-image of those years was of finding myself—young, high, a little crazed, needing a haircut, in an elevator with burly, crew-cutted, square-jawed eminences, staring at me like I was misplaced cannon fodder. We hated the war and the inhumanity and the coldness. The country had the feeling of martial law.[8]

But after the collective experience undergone through the public reading of *Howl*, McClure writes of "knowing at the deepest level that a barrier had been broken, that a human voice and body had been hurled against the harsh wall of America and its supporting armies and navies and academies and institutions and ownership systems and power-support bases."[9] Wally Hedrick, one of the organizers of the Six Gallery reading, had been an infantryman in Korea, and began a series of black paintings protesting the French and encroaching American involvements in Indochina. What McClure describes, of course, becomes greatly amplified in the unprecedented role that poetry takes on among the American poet-soldiers of the Vietnam war era, but these connections are seldom articulated or traced. And, to return to the subject at hand, we must also consider the extraordinary ways in which W.D. Ehrhart has overcome this "fear of poetry" precisely through the exposure of both his own history, his coming to consciousness about that history, and his willingness to explore the most difficult emotional aspects of that process.

I am mapping this circuitous route—from my own personal background to Charles Olson, Muriel Rukeyser, the American Civil War, the Beats, and the work of poet-soldiers—to make the point that our history has been atomized, made illegible, as if there were neither connection nor consequence between one era or another, between one phenomenon and another. We have been made to think that the work of W. D. Ehrhart can somehow be relegated to a particular historical event or experience, to the war in Vietnam as a discrete event, detaching it from the collective burden of that war and all its myriad personal and political consequences that have rippled throughout our society and the world ever since. This would be like saying that Melville's *Moby-Dick* is only about whaling, and since we no longer whale, there is really no need to consider what else that book might mean. But there is another literary and cultural history that it is up to us to map and describe, a history in which Ehrhart's work would be as central as the *Autobiography of Frederick Douglass*, as central as the slave narratives and the writings of the abolitionists, as central as the massive legacy of this continent's indigenous peoples or the *Autobiography of Malcolm X*. And it is central because, by personally taking on the burden of the nation's history, a history for which he actually volunteered, Ehrhart has provided those who didn't or won't take it up with some relief.

In the new foreword to the licensed reprint of *Vietnam–Perkasie: A Combat Marine Memoir*, one of Ehrhart's most deceptive and important works, H. Bruce Franklin pinpoints one of the truly important qualities of Ehrhart's work, his "potent combination of personal experience and historical understanding." As, or even more importantly, Franklin emphasizes the profundity of Ehrhart's courage, and its relationship to historical understanding:

> *Vietnam–Perkasie* features one characteristic of Ehrhart's writing that distinguishes it from most, though not all, literature by Vietnam veterans (or anybody else): he reveals things about his own actions that very few of us are brave enough to disclose. As he relentlessly probes the moral significance of these actions in Vietnam, he begins to display their historical significance. This leads to what is most distinctive about *Vietnam–Perkasie*, Ehrhart's ability to shape the autobiographical memoir into his own special vehicle for exploring history through personal experience.[10]

By making his own experience exemplary, and daring to disclose the things most of us would do almost anything to never reveal, Ehrhart provides a vehicle—through the narrative imagination, through the story of his own experiences—that can offload some of that compressed volatility, some of that impacted and self or outwardly directed violence that continues to erupt "randomly" throughout our society.

Ehrhart's transformative abilities in this regard, in both prose and poetry, are remarkable. One text that I teach whenever I have the opportunity, and that I return to again and again as a true masterpiece is his "forensic" essay "The United States Screw & Bolt Company."[11] In the space of 15 pages, including footnotes, Ehrhart presents a series of juxtaposed biographical facts, moving between policy makers and those forced to carry out those policies, the soldiers whose lives—if they survived—would always be marked by their participation as bearers of messages created in Washington and written on paper or exclaimed in speeches, but delivered via bombs, bayonets, Zippo lighters, Agent Orange, and myriad other means of destruction. Without resorting to any commentary, any historical, political, economic, sociological, anthropological, critical-theoretical or other disciplinary source, Ehrhart lays out as accurate a picture of power relations in the United States as we have.

What comes across loud and clear in this text, and in so much of Ehrhart's work, is something expressed by another former comrade in arms, Tom Hawkins, one of the veterans included in Ehrhart and Jan Barry's anthology *Demilitarized Zones: Veterans After Vietnam*, when Hawkins writes of "the unprecedented magnitude of betrayal—the common disowning and dissociation of responsibility."[12] This sense of betrayal and dissociation has, indeed, become one of the things we hold most in common as citizens of this republic, and it remains unrelieved, unspoken, unexpressed, left to seethe like Langston Hughes's "dream deferred." For Ehrhart, and many others whose writing emerged as poet-soldiers, poetry provided a path, a way back into what Charles Olson called "the human universe." In his landmark anthology, *The Vietnam War in American Stories, Songs, and Poems*, H. Bruce Franklin writes:

> When Jan Barry, one of the earliest of these veteran poets and a leading figure in promulgating veteran poetry, speaks to students in Vietnam courses, he describes his working-class youth in upstate New York when "the last thing I would ever think of being was a poet." What he wanted to be was a career man in the U.S. Army, and as for poetry, that was something just for "sissies." But what he, along with many others, discovered in Vietnam was that "poetry saved my life."[13]

In this context, the function of poetry—first and foremost—is to reopen lines of recognition to oneself, and then to form the basis of resistance rooted in the integrity of one's own experience—personal, intuitive, emotional, imaginative, historical, economic, and political—even as that experience becomes exemplary, and neither a commodity nor a possession. In a literary culture largely built on the nepotism of prizes, awards, fashion, the professional life, and a turbo-charged will towards pyrotechnical innovation, this is, indeed, a bitter pill to swallow. More difficult in fact, is the idea that readers might not need to search for ever more obscure critical or theoretical terms to obfuscate meaning but, rather, reach ever deeper into the recesses of their own experiences and consciousness to see just how near or far they might be from the poem in front of them.

By looking at Ehrhart's most powerful work, we might also be confronted with the horrors of looking at ourselves as others might see us, others whom we have tried to obliterate from the face of the earth. Here, as in his landmark poem "Making the Children Behave," all the poet can offer is the fact of his own realization, that he comes not to bear culture or civilization but to wreak havoc, wanton destruction, and death:

> Do they think of me now
> in those strange Asian villages
> where nothing ever seemed
> quite human
> but myself
> and my few grim friends
> moving through them
> hunched
> in lines?
>
> When they tell stories to their children
> of the evil
> that awaits misbehavior,
> is it me they conjure?[14]

By displacing himself into the specters of fear projected at children whose parents or grandparents he once tried to kill, Ehrhart is displacing the power he once wielded, and handing it in trust to the emotional imagination of children who recognize in him an enemy. In this act, Ehrhart resists and refuses the stories we have been told and insists on his own experiences, and the emotional and political truths behind those experiences. At the same time, he faces head on "the fear that cuts off poetry," and the "repressive codes" that Rukeyser wrote strike "deep at our emotional life." The courage of this transposition is a triumph of imagination. In some sense, it is finally ourselves that we must imagine and imagine away, since, as poet Diane di Prima writes:

> the war that matters is the war against the imagination
> all other wars are subsumed in it[15]

Like the poets of the 1950s who turned to those who had lived through the 1930s, who had seen and responded to the oncoming wave of fascism, we too are at a crossroads. The work of W.D. Ehrhart, in all its facets, must be juxtaposed with other writers both more and less familiar on the cultural terrain, placed like litmus paper to see what colors turn up, and what the wages of memory reveal. It is high time for writers now, and the culture in general, to turn back to Ehrhart and the unprecedented explosion of writing emerging from and through the experience of the poet-soldiers in and after the Vietnam war era, to find some relief in the misery that our political reality has become, to engage in the lessons that taking on historical burdens can deliver. Otherwise, our debt cannot be transferred and we will, literally, drown in the bad paper on which there will be nothing left to draw.

Notes

1. Olson, Charles, *The Collected Prose*, Donald Allen and Benjamin Friedlander, eds. (Berkeley: University of California Press, 1997), 311.

2. Ehrhart, W.D., *Beautiful Wreckage: New & Selected Poems* (Easthampton, MA: Adastra Press, 1999), 222.

3. Rukeyser, Muriel, *The Life of Poetry* (Ashfield, MA: Paris Press, 1996), 61.

4. Barrett, Faith, and Cristanne Miller, eds., *Words for the Hour: A New Anthology of American Civil War Poetry* (Amherst, MA: University of Massachusetts Press, 2005), 2.

5. Ehrhart, W.D., ed., *Unaccustomed Mercy: Soldier-Poets of the Vietnam War* (Lubbock: Texas Tech University Press, 1989), 1.

6. The best comprehensive guide to some of these thorny issues can be found in Jed Rasula's extraordinary and encyclopedic *The American Poetry Wax Museum: Reality Effects, 1940–1990* (Urbana: National Council of Teachers of English, 1996).

7. Rukeyser, Muriel, *The Life of Poetry* (Ashfield, MA: Paris Press, 1996), 15–16.

8. McClure, Michael, *Scratching the Beat Surface: Essays on New Vision from Blake to Kerouac* (New York: Penguin, 1994), 12.

9. See McClure: 15.

10. Franklin, H. Bruce, in W.D. Ehrhart, *Vietnam-Perkasie: A Combat Marine Memoir* (reprint edition; Amherst, MA: University of Massachusetts Press, 1995), x.

11. Ehrhart, W.D., *In the Shadow of Vietnam: Essays, 1977–1991* (Jefferson, NC: McFarland, 1991), 30–45.

12. Barry, Jan, and W.D. Ehrhart, eds., *Demilitarized Zones: Veterans After Vietnam* (Perkasie, PA: East River Anthology, 1976), ix.

13. Franklin, H. Bruce, ed., *The Vietnam War in American Stories, Songs, and Poems* (Boston: Bedford Books of St. Martin's Press, 1996), 222.

14. Ehrhart, W.D., *Beautiful Wreckage: New & Selected Poems* (Easthampton, MA: Adastra Press, 1999), 15.

15. di Prima, Diane, *Revolutionary Letters* (San Francisco: Last Gasp, 2007), 104.

"We are the ones you sent": Moral Responsibility and War in the Poetry of W. D. Ehrhart

Adam Gilbert

With an impressive body of work spanning four decades, an ability and a willingness to ask difficult but necessary questions, and a desire to bear unsanitized witness to a troubled world, W. D. Ehrhart has been, and remains, one of the most insightful and compelling commentators on the long sequence of modern American wars. It is his poetry that provides the central foundation for this perspicacious voice; it is at the heart of his writing and thinking. Threaded throughout his poetry is a concern and engagement with the idea of moral responsibility, especially as it applies to war, and this essay, which focuses primarily on Ehrhart's poetic works, begins with a brief delineation of this concept. Subsequently, it is suggested that through his poetry Ehrhart offers a perceptive account of moral responsibility and war that identifies a number of interconnected accomplices. Political and military leaders are the most obvious candidates for culpability, and Ehrhart certainly recognizes them as perennial perpetrators, but he also offers a nuanced and extensive examination of national responsibility that includes explicit and implicit factors as well as a concern with generational responsibility. Moreover, he does not exculpate himself or his fellow soldiers, and his depiction of soldier responsibility is particularly interesting and insightful, especially when considered in the light of recent significant developments in moral philosophy.[1] It is also suggested that by bearing witness to war through his poetry, Ehrhart fulfils his duty as both a veteran and a poet. Finally, it is important not to overlook Ehrhart's notion, indicated throughout his entire body of poetry, that wars occur within a vast interconnected network of other moral failures, as well as his insistence that readers should consider their own role in this entangled ethical web. Although Ehrhart tries "to avoid making moral judgements" and does not necessarily write poems in order "to teach a moral lesson," his poetry nonetheless presents a variety of valuable opportunities for increasing our understanding of moral responsibility and war.[2] Additionally, a greater awareness of these moral issues can also add to our appreciation of Ehrhart's keen and penetrating poetic vision.

The modifier "moral" in the term moral responsibility alters both the focus and the scope of attributions of accountability. Put simply, the focal concern here is centered on virtues and values, on distinctions between right and wrong, good and bad, just and unjust. The emphasis is on whether certain acts or omissions are worthy of praise or blame rather than, for instance, whether they are legal or illegal, although there may be varying degrees of overlap between morality and legality. Yet, despite this focus on moral distinctions, it is vital to stress that issues of morality are rarely unambiguous, especially those connected to something as complex and contentious as war. As the philosopher Simon Blackburn suggests, a moral landscape that appears to be "black and white may be an illusion. It may be the result of a moral lens that imposes its black and white on a landscape of different shades of grey."[3] We might feel that certain values are fundamental to morality, as Ehrhart says: "I do believe, have always believed, that there are things that are inherently right and wrong."[4] Nonetheless, there is a difficulty in application, "because those who think they have a corner on morality tend to start making judgments about other persons, and that gets tricky."[5] Moreover, the process of discernment itself can be problematic. "Funny," Ehrhart writes in one poem, "how the good seems nebulous as fog."[6] Still, if we are considerate in application and careful in discernment then an exploration of the contours of moral landscapes, however murky they may be, can offer revealing insights into responsibility.

With regard to the scope of accountability, moral responsibility covers a much broader territory than that of simply direct or immediate causal connections. Certainly, such primary causal chains are helpful in identifying certain persons who are morally responsible for particular acts or omissions, but they may not always indicate, and perhaps at times can even obscure, other agents and issues that are also involved. To give an example from the war in which Ehrhart fought: despite repeated assurances during the 1964 campaign that he was not "about to send American boys ... to do what Asian boys ought to be doing for themselves," President Johnson nonetheless decided to send vast numbers of Americans to fight, kill, and die in Vietnam.[7] As the historian Fredrik Logevall argues, Johnson chose war.[8] His selection of escalation, buttressed by his advisors including "the big three of McNamara, Bundy, and Rusk," was an act that directly and immediately caused a significant expansion and intensification of American military involvement in Vietnam.[9] Certainly,

Johnson and his advisors were also morally responsible for that decision, yet to identify them as the only persons worthy of blame—if, indeed, we believe that such a choice should be condemned rather than commended—would be to overlook a wide variety of other moral agents and issues that enabled this decision to be made in the first place. Rather than looking solely at a direct or immediate causal thread, then, a broader conception of moral responsibility maps instead the large web of interwoven and interdependent threads that supported the weight of such a choice. In particular, a comprehensive account of moral responsibility and war will explore how the deeply entangled acts and omissions of all moral agents—not just those at the end of the causal chain who make the final decisions—and the value systems they build up and live by contribute to situations and structures in which war is possible and, seemingly, perpetual. It is just such a complex and multilayered picture that emerges from a reading of Ehrhart's poetry.

Ehrhart's poetic vision of moral responsibility and war highlights this multiplicity of interconnected factors, but that does not mean he neglects or exculpates the most obvious culprits. Indeed, the usual suspects in positions of power, especially political and military leaders, feature prominently as persistent perpetrators of war in his poetry. For example, in "High Country," Ehrhart writes of the American war in Vietnam:

> Our Asian war staggered on; calculating
> men in three-piece suits and uniforms
> with stars called firestorms down upon
> the heads of people with conical hats
> and spoke of Peace with Honor.

A decade later in the next verse of the poem, which appears in his 1984 collection *To Those Who Have Gone Home Tired*, the same set of people execute war again: "Calculating men in three-piece suits / and uniforms with stars are calling down / firestorms upon the heads of peasants / in Central America now."[10] It is possible to imagine a repetition of these lines for each of the following decades, as a series of men in three-piece suits and uniforms with stars continue to choose war, with the only differences being the particular place where and the people who these masters of war call firestorms down upon. In a recent essay, Ehrhart lists the locations where Americans have killed and died since Vietnam: "Cambodia, Iran, Lebanon, Grenada, El Salvador, Panama, Kuwait, Iraq, Somalia, Yemen, Afghanistan, and now Iraq again."[11] In each case, a significant proportion of the moral responsibility, Ehrhart intimates throughout his body of poetry, should be shouldered by those "in quiet rooms / pouring over maps and plotting fire."[12] Nevertheless, as accurate and important as it is to identify the politics and "the posturing of presidents / and statesmen who have never heard the sound / of teenaged soldiers crying for their mothers" as playing a decisive and reprehensible role in America's succession of wars, Ehrhart indicates that other factors should be taken into consideration as well.[13] He refuses to either soothe the conscience of the reader or evade his own complicity by only indicting political and military decision-makers. Instead, his poetry suggests that war is also dependent upon and perpetuated by nations that support war, generations that fail their own children, and the soldiers who fight.

A war cannot be fought unless the people of a nation support it. "Americans are desperate to believe they do not share in the complicity of the acts committed by their sons and their leaders," assert the editors of the seminal poetry anthology *Winning Hearts and Minds: War Poems by Vietnam Veterans*.[14] Yet, for the editors and for Ehrhart, who has eight pieces included in that collection, the American people do share in this complicity, and Ehrhart's poetry portrays an understanding of national responsibility in which both the explicit and implicit acts and omissions of the public contribute considerably to war. For example, as members of an ostensibly democratic country, American citizens exert some influence over which politicians are elected and what they do once they are put in the path of power, including the military decisions they might make. Hence, during the war in Vietnam, Ehrhart writes, American soldiers acted as "Democracy on Zippo raids, / Burning hooches to the ground."[15] Additionally, since wars are primarily funded by the public purse, there is an element of taxpayer responsibility for the perpetration of war. Ehrhart examines this aspect of complicity in his poem entitled "Responsibility," which begins with an appropriate epigraph from the United States Constitution: "The Congress shall have power to lay and collect taxes ... to ... provide for the common defense and general welfare of the United States." The final lines refer specifically to the American involvement in El Salvador, but could apply equally to all of America's military machinations:

> Friday, payday, security:
> money in my pocket for the weekend;
> money for my government;
> money for the soldiers of El Salvador,
> fifty bullets to the box.[16]

Beyond democratic responsibility, taxpayer responsibility, and, of course, direct and vocalized public support for war, Ehrhart also considers more implicit forms of national responsibility. "The climate of opinion conditions everything," the moral philosopher Jonathan Glover argues. "We need to look at the mental climate of the time: at what James Joll called 'the unspoken assumptions.'"[17] These "networks of rules or 'norms' that sustain our lives" play a crucial role in when, where, why, and how nations go to war.[18] Uncritical patriotic beliefs, for instance, are often an integral part of a belligerent moral climate. For Ehrhart, this common cause of mass killing is almost inexplicable: "How explain a world where men / kill other men deliberately / and call it love of country?"[19] Ehrhart eschews such jingoism: "You can just keep your rockets' red glare."[20] For him, the American flag symbolizes "blood, stars, an ocean of ignorance."[21] Climates marked by a suspicion of questioning and distrust of dissent can also aggrandize pro-war voices, or at least undermine anti-war activity and opinion. Ehrhart's poem about the Kent State massacre reveals just such an atmosphere during the American war in Vietnam:

> The girl kneels in the parking lot,
> her face uplifted, mouth so twisted
> she appears to be hysterical.
> ...
> She doesn't understand
> the gray-haired men who've done this
> or the millions more who think
> the dead boy at her feet has gotten
> just what he has asked for and deserves.[22]

These societal attitudes seem to stem from a self-righteousness and certainty that devalues dissent in favor of unreflective conformity, as in the town where Ehrhart grew up: "so smug it was, so self-content, / its point of view so narrow one could / get a better field of vision peering / through the barrel of a shotgun."[23] Furthermore, values can be transmitted through culture, such as in the movies Ehrhart grew up with, so that during military training, he remembers, he was "talking tough, eating from cans, / wearing my helmet John Wayne style."[24] It should be noted that national responsibility for war is as much about omissions as it is about acts—what people fail to do matters: "silence to injustice / large or small is simply cowardice."[25] Indeed, the apparent apathy of the American people, and their seeming lack of desire or effort to check their country's military ventures or curb its imperial enthusiasm, is a continual source of frustration and disappointment for Ehrhart: "Behind me lies a continent asleep, / drunk with martial glory and an empire's pride, / though each is transient as sand."[26] Viewed from this perspective, Nixon's famous phrase "the great silent majority" can be reconsidered as a particularly precise identification of the passivity and apathy responsible, in part, for the American war in Vietnam, and for many other wars as well.[27] As Karl Jaspers, in his discussion of German guilt in the aftermath of the Second World War, declares: "each one of us is guilty insofar as he remained inactive.... [P]assivity knows itself morally guilty of every failure, every neglect to act whenever possible, to shield the imperiled, to relieve wrong, to countervail."[28]

Generational responsibility is another aspect of accountability that frequently appears in Ehrhart's poetry. "What shall we give our children?" is a question he often asks.[29] Unfortunately, what people commonly give their children is war, a seemingly perpetual phenomenon in which each generation is betrayed by the one before. Ehrhart's account of the belated "Welcome Home" parade for American veterans who fought in Vietnam, which was held in New York City on 7 May 1985, "ten years after the last rooftop / chopper out of Saigon," examines this failure of generational responsibility:

> I saw one man in camouflaged utilities;
> a boy, his son, dressed like dad;
> both proudly marching.
>
> How many wounded generations,
> touched with fire, have offered up
> their children to the gods of fire?
> Even now, new flames are burning,
> and the gods of fire call for more,
> and the new recruits keep coming.
>
> What fire will burn that small
> boy marching with his father?
> What parade will heal
> his father's wounds?[30]

Thus, even though a generation may itself have been wounded by war and failed by its own parent generation, it is nonetheless still willing to offer up its own children to be wounded by war, who may, in turn, offer up their children, in a seemingly endless chain of war perpetuated by each generation's failure of responsibility. A particularly disturbing image in this poem is that of the son as he marches by his veteran father's side, only a child yet already dressed as a soldier, another sacrifice prepared for "the gods of fire," another Isaac bound by another Abraham. Given their own personal wounding by war, it might be assumed that veterans would—should, perhaps—wish for their children to avoid the same fiery fate. "You'd think that any self-respecting / vet would give the middle finger / to the folks who thought of it," Ehrhart suggests.[31]

The poem also offers an insight into the importance of memory and memorialization with regard to war. Events such as this parade promote a simplified and sanitized version of history that distorts and censors the past in order to make war seem honorable, necessary, and justified, and thus make war in the future more acceptable and more probable. Yet, Ehrhart's poetry is itself proof that a different story can be told, one that refuses to glorify war, one that refrains from an abdication of generational responsibility, one that hopes for a more peaceful future however futile that hope may be. "Above all," Lorrie Smith argues, "Ehrhart's poems warn, we are accountable to future generations; we have a choice about which values we will pass on and which stories we will tell."³² An important part of this, to return to national responsibility, is supporting and contributing to a climate in which questioning and critical thinking are encouraged and not denigrated. Ehrhart effectuates this through his poetry, and also in his job as a teacher. In "Coaching Winter Track in Time of War," from his most recent collection of poems, he wonders how he can ensure that his students are aware of the need to engage in a critical examination of the world, especially when it comes to war:

> How do you tell them it's not that simple?
> How do you tell them: question it all.
> Question everything. Even a coach.
> Even a president. How do you tell them:
> ask the young dead soldiers coming home
> each night in aluminum boxes
> none of us is allowed to see,
> an army of shades.³³

Through his concern with warning and teaching the next generation, Ehrhart accepts and enacts the generational responsibility that failed him and that continues to be neglected by so many.

A particularly powerful statement of Ehrhart's perception of national, generational, and also soldier responsibility can be found in one of his earliest poems, "A Relative Thing." He begins with an angry accusation: "We are the ones you sent to fight a war / You didn't know a thing about." But it is Ehrhart and his fellow veterans "who have to live / With the memory that we were the instruments / Of your pigeon-breasted fantasies." He continues with an admittance of soldier responsibility: "We are inextricable accomplices / In this travesty of dreams; / But we are not alone." There is an ambiguity in this last line, in which Ehrhart could be referring to a sense of solidarity among veterans or the complicity of the people to whom the poem is addressed. Either way, in the tone and direction of the poem, and in its final verse, it is clear that Ehrhart is speaking to and indicting the nation and the generation that failed him and his fellow veterans and subsequently ignored and disowned them in the war's aftermath: "We are your sons, America, / And you cannot change that. / When you awake, / We will still be here."³⁴ Of course, it is not only Americans who have failed in their responsibilities. Rather, it is a moral problem of all wars, as a view from the Soviet war in Afghanistan, which could equally apply to the American war in Vietnam or, indeed, Afghanistan or any number of other wars, demonstrates:

> It is not true that the public didn't know what was going on. Everyone could see parents opening their doors to those zinc coffins or having their sons returned to them broken and crippled.... What kind of people are we, and what right have we to ask our children to do the things they had to do there? How can we, who

stayed at home, claim that our hands are cleaner than theirs? ... The machine-gunned and abandoned villages and ruined land are not on their consciences but on ours. We were the real murderers, not they, and we murdered our own children as well as others.[35]

Nonetheless, although wars might or should be on the consciences of the public, as well as political and military leaders, they cannot be fought without the soldiers who fight them, without the "triggermen."[36] They are tied together in complicity with those whose actions and inactions delivered them to "the gods of fire": "*We* are the ones *you* sent."

Soldier responsibility is a concept currently undergoing a significant shift within the realm of moral philosophy. "Can a soldier be held responsible for fighting in a war that is illegal or unjust?," David Rodin and Henry Shue ask in *Just and Unjust Warriors: The Moral and Legal Status of Soldiers*, a recent groundbreaking collection of essays on this issue.[37] It is a question that is "at the heart of a new debate that has the potential to profoundly change our understanding of the moral and legal status of warriors, wars, and indeed of moral agency itself."[38] The "widely shared and legally endorsed conviction about war" is that soldiers "have equal rights and responsibilities irrespective of whether they are fighting in a war that is just or unjust."[39] This "moral equality of soldiers" is expounded and endorsed by Michael Walzer in his seminal work *Just and Unjust Wars*, and is a position that "is rooted in the shared experience of soldiers as victims, compelled to fight by the actions of their enemy and the coercive instruments of their own state."[40] As a result of this mutual victimhood, a combatant senses "that the enemy soldier, though his war may well be criminal, is nevertheless as blameless as oneself."[41] Hence, Walzer posits "a separation between the rules governing the justice of going to war (the *jus ad bellum*) and the rules governing what combatants can do in war (the *jus in bello*)," thus drawing "a line between the war itself, for which soldiers are not responsible, and the conduct of the war, for which they are responsible, at least within their own sphere of activity."[42] Two important consequences follow from this viewpoint. Firstly, "soldiers have an equal right to kill" each other, and so a combatant who kills an enemy soldier "does not wrong him or violate his rights, even if the soldier killed was fighting a legitimate war of self-defence."[43] Secondly, those outside of the category of soldier, that is noncombatants, "retain their title to life and liberty and may not be attacked."[44] Yet, whilst this collection of moral beliefs is "widely accepted and legally sanctioned" and forms "the 'common sense' ethics of war," it is one that has recently been challenged and criticized.[45]

Recent debates in moral philosophy have suggested that *jus ad bellum* and *jus in bello* could indeed be connected and, consequently, "many aspects of just war theory and laws of war would have to be rethought and perhaps reformed."[46] Of particular relevance here, this coupling could alter our understanding of the moral responsibility of "unjust warriors"—those soldiers who fight in unjust wars—with potential ramifications for American soldiers who fought in Vietnam, and in the long list of American wars since then. To take a key moral question of war: why, given that killing is usually deemed to be immoral, is it justifiable to kill a person in a time of war? Walzer's argument, and the orthodox just war explanation, is that since enemy soldiers pose a threat to the self and others it is permissible to kill them, an idea often seen as analogous to the right of self- and other-defense. Yet, this position "seems false by the standards of normal morality and individual self-defence," as Jeff McMahan explains:

> It is not true, for example, that one makes oneself liable to defensive attack simply by posing a threat to another. If that were true, those who engage in justified self-defence against a culpable attacker would then lose their right not to be attacked by him or her. And police would forfeit their right not to be attacked by criminals they justifiably threatened. The correct criterion of liability to attack in these cases is not posing a threat, nor even posing an unjust threat, but moral responsibility for an unjust threat. According to this criterion, just combatants cannot be liable to attack by their unjust adversaries. As in the case of an individual who engages in justified self-defence, a combatant who takes up arms in self-defence or in defence of other innocent people against an unjust threat does nothing to lose his or her moral right not to be attacked or to make himself or herself liable to attack.[47]

The American war in Vietnam might not fit this scenario perfectly but, whatever one thinks of the Vietnamese revolutionaries, it seems clear that the American military intervention failed on almost every possible just war criteria. Indeed, throughout Ehrhart's writings it is apparent that he believes the American war in Vietnam to have been immoral and unjust, and even though the idea of the "unjust warrior" has only started to gain traction relatively recently in moral philosophy, it is a concept that Ehrhart, as a soldier who fought in a professedly unjust war, has been exploring since his earliest poetic production.

In his poetic examination of his own role in the war, what he calls "my tiny piece of that / obscenity," Ehrhart reflects upon what it means to be a soldier and, more specifically, what it means to be an "unjust warrior."[48] "When I enlisted, I thought I was doing a good thing—a *cosmically* good thing," Ehrhart says, but after the war he reflects: "What I saw and did in Asia in thirteen months was unspeakably evil and immoral."[49] This idea of both the war and himself as evil is expressed in one of his earliest and most often quoted poems, "Making the Children Behave":

> Do they think of me now
> in those strange Asian villages
> where nothing ever seemed
> quite human
> but myself
> and my few grim friends
> moving through them
> hunched
> in lines?
>
> When they tell stories to their children
> of the evil
> that awaits misbehavior,
> is it me they conjure?[50]

This is a poem that, as Matthew Hill suggests, "is at once a deeply personal confession and a scathing political indictment."[51] As in all of Ehrhart's poetry, the personal and the political are inseparable. Similarly, by acknowledging his own culpability, Ehrhart refuses to draw the line that separates responsibility for the war itself from the soldier's personal responsibility for his own role in the war. Soldiers, Ehrhart suggests throughout his poetic works, are certainly victims of war but, crucially, they are also perpetrators. This dual moral status is succinctly captured in Ehrhart's "What I Know About Myself," a poem dedicated to Gloria Emerson. A friend of Ehrhart's, possibly Emerson herself, picks up "a book of photographs / from Vietnam," and says: "'Look how young / you are. How innocent. How evil.'" Ehrhart agrees with her assessment of these youthful American soldiers as both innocent and evil, victims of a war they perpetrated: "She knew I knew what she meant, / and she was right."[52] In this admission and understanding, Ehrhart both signals his acceptance of his own soldier responsibility and, despite his understandable reluctance to make moral judgments about other persons, hints that the position of perpetrator is one that could apply to all "unjust warriors."

Another way in which Ehrhart addresses the issue of soldier responsibility in his poetry is through his rejection of the violence and killing of war. Implicitly, this moral stance is displayed in all of his stark and unflinching portrayals of the horrific devastation, destruction, and death of war: "that mutilated child in its mother's arms" or those "kids not twenty / years old and dead in ricefields; / brain-dead, soul-dead, half-dead / in wheelchairs."[53] Explicitly, it is evidenced by his expressions of regret, as in, for example, "A Warning to My Students":

> If I were young again,
> I could do it all
> differently: go to college,
> go to Canada, live underground

> on the lam in basement apartments
> in strange cities—anything
> but kill
> somebody else's enemies
> for somebody else's reasons.[54]

This declaration of regret operates as a moral intervention into the past, in which the suggestion that he "could do it all / differently" implies that he *should* have done it all differently. Furthermore, it is also a moral exhortation in the present—and an act of generational responsibility—since the poem functions as a warning to his students, who may one day have to face a similar choice themselves. "The next time they come looking / for soldiers, they'll come looking / for you," he cautions them.[55] This regret is also tinged with a profound sense of sorrow for his participation in war: "once I dreamed a man / with a rifle refused to take aim; / I awoke to a sadness / deeper than dreams."[56] In one of his poems that reflects upon his postwar returns to Vietnam, Ehrhart distances himself from the process of violence that he, and his adversaries, participated in during the war. He meets a young Vietnamese soldier, and ponders: "Years ago in another life, / I had killed young men like him / and they had tried to kill me. / But not today. I'm tired of fighting."[57] In poems such as these, Ehrhart firmly rejects the primary instrument of war—killing. He acknowledges his own prior position as a perpetrator whilst simultaneously denouncing the act of killing in war and, in doing so, demonstrates a strong sense of postwar soldier responsibility. It is important to note here that Ehrhart's rejection of killing is not purely unconditional, for he is not an absolute pacifist: "I think there are legitimate wars."[58] And if there can be just wars it follows that there can be "just warriors," but for Ehrhart it is vital that the soldier fights for justifications that are his own and not simply some cause that is deemed just by the decision-makers in power: "if I'm ordered to kill anybody, I'm going to kill my enemies for my reasons and not because someone in Washington, D.C. says kill them."[59] Hence, Ehrhart's poetry presents an understanding of moral responsibility and war which suggests that soldiers are not only responsible for their own conduct within the warzone, but that they are also, to a certain extent, responsible for the war itself.

Yet, for those who fight in wars and survive, their responsibilities do not end once they leave the warzone or even after the war ends. Rather, as veterans they face an additional aspect of moral responsibility linked to war: to bear witness. As witnesses to war, they have two key obligations: the responsibility of remembering a past that is often in danger of being forgotten, distorted, or sanitized; and the responsibility of warning, of sounding a cautionary alarm to both the present and the future. However, as Janis Haswell highlights, although American soldiers are glorified as heroes, as veterans they are frequently "marginalized insofar as they are witnesses to a reality the public cannot face and war-makers deny."[60] This is a great moral loss, for it is precisely those who have been to war who "are in a position to articulate the need for a higher morality ... that determines *when* their country goes to war and *how* war is conducted."[61] In other words, veterans can offer significant insights into both *jus ad bellum* and *jus in bello*, for those willing to listen. As Ehrhart writes in "The Teacher": "I know things / worth knowing."[62]

Veterans can bear witness in a number of ways. Most obviously, they can tell others about their war, speak about their own experiences, as with Ehrhart who came "back home from Vietnam insisting it was / all just bullshit, just a lethal scam / that only proves how gullible / each generation's cannon fodder is."[63] They can resist attempts to distort or sanitize the memory of their war, such as the abovementioned parade, by challenging this state-sanctioned narrative and telling instead an uncensored version of the past. They can engage in political activism, as with those who joined the Vietnam Veterans Against the War:

> We harnessed our terrible knowledge
> And we joined the demonstrations
> And became the soldiers
> For peace
>
> And we marched
> And we prayed
> And we marched
> And we marched
>
> Till the din subsided
> In one small corner of the world[64]

And, of course, one possibility for veterans is to bear witness through artistic commitment, by writing, for example, plays, memoirs, novels, or poems. Indeed, poetry written by veterans is often classified as "poetry of witness."[65] Moreover, bearing witness to the world is also an important aspect of poetic responsibility, as Denise Levertov explains: "One of the obligations of the writer, and perhaps especially of the poet, is to say or sing *all* that he or she can, to deal with as much of the world as becomes possible to him or her in language."[66] Throughout Ehrhart's writings, he produces works in which these elements of personal, political, and poetic responsibility are inseparable, as he bears witness to the world and to the war. And he does so even though people do not always want to hear what he has to say. "You don't want me to tell you about death, / but I'm going to tell you anyway," he writes in "All About Death."[67] In the twin poem "All About Love," he begins: "Everybody loves to hear about love, / but I don't feel like talking about that. / Gimme a break. You seen the news lately?"[68] In Ehrhart's insistence on speaking out, and in his emphasis on an uncensored poetics, he fulfils his duty as both a veteran and a poet. Furthermore, being a poetic witness is a way of living with the conflict of having been both a victim and a perpetrator; it is an embodiment of what Viktor Frankl describes as "the human capacity to creatively turn life's negative aspects into something positive or constructive."[69] As Ehrhart states: "my poetry is an ongoing attempt to atone for the unethical, for my loss of a moral compass when I was a young man."[70]

Still, as suggested above, Ehrhart's poetry highlights how it was not only he or his fellow soldiers who entered into the unethical during the American war in Vietnam—the people of the nation, as well as political and military leaders, also participated in this moral failure. His poems that address the wars that have occurred since then suggest that this multiplicity of interconnected factors morally responsible for war is a recurring pattern. Moreover, from his very earliest through to his most recent poetic explorations, Ehrhart indicates that wars occur within a vast network of other moral failures. Perhaps the best example from his early work in the 1970s is "To Those Who Have Gone Home Tired," in which he connects "his evolving perception of American misjudgment and wrongdoing in Vietnam to larger political issues."[71] As Kalí Tal, one of the most perceptive explicators of Ehrhart's poetry, summarizes, this poem locates war within "a context which includes the Kent State massacre, the My Lai massacre, the dropping of the atomic bomb on Hiroshima, police brutality, capitalism, the destruction of Native American culture, repression in South Korea, and damage to the environment."[72] In the final lines of the poem, Ehrhart asks readers to consider their own role of responsibility within this entangled web of moral failures, as he wonders what excuses and explanations we will offer to the next generation for our acts and omissions that contribute to such a world: "What answers will you find / What armor will protect you / When your children ask you / Why?"[73] In doing so, he emphasizes the complicity of all of us whilst simultaneously stressing "the responsibility of the individual to resist such evils."[74]

In his more recent works, such as "On the Eve of Destruction," Ehrhart continues to map these moral connections and complicities. He remembers that "weekend Watts went up in flames," and recalls his teenage reflections:

> What did riots in a Negro ghetto
> have to do with me? What could cause
> such savage rage? I didn't know
> and didn't think about it much.
> The Eve of Destruction was just a song.
> Surf was up at Pendleton. The war in Vietnam
> was still a sideshow half a world away,
> a world that hadn't heard of Ia Drang or Tet,

> James Earl Ray, Sirhan Sirhan, Black Panthers,
> Spiro Agnew, Sandy Scheuer, Watergate.[75]

Here, violence, politics, domestic discord, and international conflict are all entangled. The Watts Riots prefigure the violence that would soon unfold in Vietnam, and, in turn, the war in Vietnam is connected to: assassinations in America; racial problems in American society; corrupt and criminal politicians; the violent crushing of dissent and killing of students; and yet more corrupt and criminal politicians. These are all part of the same network of moral failure, and as Ehrhart traces these linkages it appears as though America is as much at war with itself as it is with the Vietnamese revolutionaries. The title of the poem and the allusion to the song "Eve of Destruction" is particularly revealing, for it underlines the apocalyptic quality of these connections. Yet, Ehrhart, in his youthful naivety, and the apathetic and silent majority of Americans, seem unaware of the impending maelstrom of violence. Indeed, perhaps such a lack of awareness is also an integral part of this interconnected web, and one that persists to this day. Thus, a common answer to the question that concludes "To Those Who Have Gone Home Tired" might be Ehrhart's own explanation—understandable for a teenager, maybe less so for an adult—that "I didn't know / and didn't think about it much."

Ehrhart's poetic portrayal of moral responsibility and war is extensive and uncompromising, and leaves few untouched by complicity, including himself, his fellow soldiers and veterans, political and military leaders, the public, and his readers. Yet, just as Ehrhart accepts his veteran and poetic responsibility to speak, we must accept our responsibility to listen. Writing about Henri Barbusse's classic First World War novel *Under Fire*, the historian Jay Winter suggests that Barbusse felt as though he "had blood on his hands" and "had to find some way to escape from the moral quicksand of war. Telling the story was his way. Reading it may be ours."[76] The same is true of Ehrhart's poetry. Furthermore, although there are hints of hope in some of Ehrhart's work—"I want to think we'll be okay / if only we can touch the best / in others and ourselves"—a strong sense of tragic inevitability concerning our failure of moral responsibility runs throughout his poetry, especially with regard to war.[77] Nonetheless, for Ehrhart, who has "no use for comfortable hypocrisies / or delicate interpretations / meant to keep the world the way it is," this does not preclude an acceptance of responsibility nor prevent us from attempting to alter the way of the world and the way of war.[78] Ehrhart's friend, who identified those young American soldiers in Vietnam as a combination of innocent and evil, perfectly encapsulates his attitude towards moral responsibility:

> "Our hands will never be clean,"
> she said, "but we must try."
>
> And so I do....[79]

Notes

1. The term "soldier" throughout this essay is used to simply identify all combatants within the military, regardless of branch of service.
2. Ehrhart, W.D., interview with author, Philadelphia, Pennsylvania, 2 March 2010.
3. Blackburn, Simon, *Being Good: A Short Introduction to Ethics* (Oxford: Oxford University Press, 2001), 59.
4. Anderson, Donald and Thomas G. Bowie, Jr., interviewers, "A Conversation with W.D. Ehrhart," *War, Literature & the Arts: an International Journal of the Humanities*, 8:2 (Fall/Winter 1996), 150.
5. Ibid.
6. Ehrhart, W.D., "Fog," *Matters of the Heart* (Easthampton, MA: Adastra Press, 1981), 14.
7. Johnson, Lyndon B., "Remarks in Memorial Hall, Akron University," 21 October 1964, *The American Presidency Project*, http://www.presidency.ucsb.edu/ws/?pid=26635 (accessed 6 June 2012).
8. Logevall, Fredrik, *Choosing War: The Lost Chance for Peace and the Escalation of War in Vietnam* (Berkeley and Los Angeles: University of California Press, 1999).
9. Logevall, Fredrik, "'There Ain't No Daylight': Lyndon Johnson and the Politics of Escalation," in Mark Philip Bradley and Marilyn B. Young, eds., *Making Sense of the Vietnam Wars: Local, National, and Transnational Perspectives* (Oxford: Oxford University Press, 2008), 106.
10. Ehrhart, W.D., "High Country," *To Those Who Have Gone Home Tired: New and Selected Poems* (New York: Thunder's Mouth Press, 1984), 72.
11. Ehrhart, W.D., "Concerning Memorial Day," *Dead on a High Hill: Essays on War, Literature and Living, 2002–2012* (Jefferson, NC: McFarland, 2012), 87–88.
12. Ehrhart, W.D., "Who Did What to Whom," *Just for Laughs* (Silver Spring, MD: Vietnam Generation, Inc. & Burning Cities Press, 1990), 29.
13. Ehrhart, W.D., "Home Before Morning," *Sleeping with the Dead* (Easthampton, MA: Adastra Press, 2006), 17.
14. Rottmann, Larry, Jan Barry, and Basil T. Paquet, eds., "Introduction," *Winning Hearts and Minds: War Poems by Vietnam Veterans* (New York: McGraw-Hill Book Company, 1972), v.
15. Ehrhart, W.D., "A Relative Thing," *A Generation of Peace* (New York: New Voices Publishing Company, 1975), 27. Here, and in other early versions of the poem, the full line reads: "We have seen Democracy on Zippo raids." But when the poem was included in his 1984 collection *To Those Who Have Gone Home Tired*, and in versions reprinted since then, this line became: 'We have been Democracy on Zippo raids.' Typographically, it is a small difference; just one letter changes just one word. Morally, especially when considered in the context of soldier responsibility, it is a significant alteration; Ehrhart and his fellow soldiers are now represented as perpetrators rather than witnesses, as agents of American violence rather than mere observers of it.
16. Ehrhart, W.D., "Responsibility," *The Outer Banks & Other Poems* (Easthampton, MA: Adastra Press, 1984), 34–35.
17. Glover, Jonathan, *Humanity: A Moral History of the Twentieth Century* (New Haven and London: Yale University Press, 2001), 229, 194.
18. Blackburn, *Being Good*, 5.

19. Ehrhart, W.D., "Guns," *The Distance We Travel* (Easthampton, MA: Adastra Press, 1993), 42.

20. Ehrhart, W.D., "What Better Way to Begin," *The Bodies Beneath the Table* (Easthampton, MA: Adastra Press, 2010), 11.

21. Ehrhart, "For a Coming Extinction," *The Distance We Travel*, 33.

22. Ehrhart, "Governor Rhodes Keeps His Word," *The Distance We Travel*, 19.

23. Ehrhart, W.D., "Visiting My Parents' Grave," *Beautiful Wreckage: New & Selected Poems* (Easthampton, MA: Adastra Press, 1999), 219.

24. Ehrhart, "'... the light that cannot fade ...,'" *The Outer Banks*, 92.

25. Ehrhart, "Visiting My Parents' Grave," *Beautiful Wreckage*, 220.

26. Ehrhart, "After the Latest Victory," *The Distance We Travel*, 34. Only the date the poem was published and one reference to the Middle East establishes this "victory" as the war in the Persian Gulf, and as with "High Country" it is possible to imagine that such sentiments could be applied to any number of American wars.

27. Nixon, Richard, "Address to the Nation on the War in Vietnam," 3 November 1969, *The American Presidency Project*, http://www.presidency.ucsb.edu/ws/?pid=2303 (accessed 6 June 2012). My thanks to David Connolly for calling my attention to this link between American apathy and the silent majority.

28. Jaspers, Karl, *The Question of German Guilt*, trans. E. B. Ashton (1947; repr. New York: Fordham University Press, 2001), 63.

29. Ehrhart, "Unaccustomed Mercies," *Just for Laughs*, 84.

30. Ehrhart, W.D., "Parade Rest," *Winter Bells* (Easthampton, MA: Adastra Press, 1988), 11.

31. Ibid., 10. For another important poem on generational responsibility, see Ehrhart, "Guns," *The Distance We Travel*, 42–43.

32. Smith, Lorrie, "Resistance and Revision in Poetry by Vietnam War Veterans," in Philip K. Jason, ed., *Fourteen Landing Zones: Approaches to Vietnam War Literature* (Iowa City: University of Iowa Press, 1991), 54.

33. Ehrhart, "Coaching Winter Track in Time of War," *The Bodies Beneath the Table*, 74.

34. Ehrhart, "A Relative Thing," *A Generation of Peace*, 27–28. For a description of Ehrhart's first reading of this poem, see his memoir *Passing Time: Memoir of a Vietnam Veteran Against the War* (Jefferson, NC: McFarland, 1989), 247–248.

35. Golubnichaya, A., in Svetlana Alexievich, *Zinky Boys: Soviet Voices from the Afghanistan War*, trans. Julia Whitby and Robin Whitby (New York: W.W. Norton, 1992); quoted in Glover, *Humanity*, 165.

36. Ehrhart, "What War Does," *The Distance We Travel*, 40.

37. Rodin, David and Henry Shue, "Introduction" in David Rodin and Henry Shue, eds., *Just and Unjust Warriors: The Moral and Legal Status of Soldiers* (Oxford: Oxford University Press, 2008), 1.

38. Ibid.

39. Ibid.

40. Ibid., 2.

41. Walzer, Michael, *Just and Unjust Wars: A Moral Argument with Historical Illustrations* (1977; 4th, ed., New York: Basic Books, 2006), 36; Rodin and Shue, "Introduction," 2.

42. Rodin and Shue, "Introduction," 1; Walzer, *Just and Unjust Wars*, 38–39.

43. Walzer, *Just and Unjust Wars*, 41; Rodin and Shue, "Introduction," 2.

44. Rodin and Shue, "Introduction," 2.
45. Ibid., 2.
46. Ibid., 1.
47. Ibid., 3; Jeff McMahan, "The Morality of War and the Law of War," in Rodin and Shue, eds., *Just and Unjust Warriors*, 21–22. A common objection here is that moral considerations differ in the context of war. For more on this, and a strong rebuttal, see Jeff McMahan, *Killing in War* (Oxford: Oxford University Press, 2009), 14–15.
48. Ehrhart, W.D., *Mostly Nothing Happens: A Poem* (Easthampton, Massachusetts, Adastra Press, 1996), without page numbers.
49. "A Conversation with W.D. Ehrhart," 151; Ehrhart quoted in Timothy J. Lomperis, *"Reading the Wind": The Literature of the Vietnam War: An Interpretative Critique* (Durham: Duke University Press, 1987), 20; emphasis in original.
50. "Making the Children Behave" appears in the revised edition of *A Generation of Peace* (San Jose, Calif.: Samisdat, 1977). The version quoted here is from *Beautiful Wreckage*, 15.
51. Hill, Matthew, "America, Viet Nam, and the Poetics of Guilt," in Mark Heberle, ed., *Thirty Years After: New Essays on Vietnam War Literature, Film, and Art* (Newcastle upon Tyne: Cambridge Scholars Publishing, 2009), 95.
52. Ehrhart, "What I Know About Myself," *Beautiful Wreckage*, 196–197.
53. Ehrhart, "Chasing Locomotives," *Just for Laughs*, 69; Ehrhart, "Parade Rest," *Winter Bells*, 10.
54. Ehrhart, "A Warning to My Students," *The Outer Banks*, 23.
55. Ibid., 24.
56. Ehrhart, "Some Other World," *Just for Laughs*, 40.
57. Ehrhart, "Sleeping with General Chi," *The Distance We Travel*, 31–32.
58. "A Conversation with W.D. Ehrhart," 157.
59. Ibid.
60. Haswell, Janis, "The Lesson Unlearned: Moral Trauma in Andrew Jolly's *A Time of Soldiers*," in Heberle, ed., *Thirty Years After*, 445.
61. Ibid.; emphasis in original.
62. Ehrhart, W.D., "The Teacher," *The Samisdat Poems* (Richford: VT, Samisdat, 1980), 65.
63. Ehrhart, "What Makes a Man," *The Bodies Beneath the Table*, 32.
64. Ehrhart, W.D., "Vietnam Veterans, After All," in Jan Barry and W.D. Ehrhart, eds., *Demilitarized Zones: Veterans After Vietnam* (Perkasie: PA, East River Anthology, 1976), 126.
65. For an overview of poetry of witness, and a wide range of examples, see Carolyn Forché, ed. and introduction, *Against Forgetting: Twentieth-Century Poetry of Witness* (New York and London: W.W. Norton, 1993).
66. Levertov, Denise, "Statement for a Television Program," *The Poet in the World* (New York: New Directions, 1973), 123; emphasis in original.
67. Ehrhart, "All About Death," *Sleeping with the Dead*, 10.
68. Ehrhart, "All About Love," *Sleeping with the Dead*, 12.
69. Frankl, Viktor E., *Man's Search for Meaning*, trans. Ilse Lasch (1946; repr. London: Rider, 2004), 139.
70. Ehrhart, W.D., in "War, Poetry, & Ethics: A Symposium," *War, Literature & the Arts*, 10:2 (Fall/Winter 1998), 31.

71. Tal, Kalí, *Worlds of Hurt: Reading the Literatures of Trauma* (Cambridge: Cambridge University Press, 1996), 88.
72. Ibid., 89.
73. Ehrhart, "To Those Who Have Gone Home Tired," in Barry and Ehrhart, eds., *Demilitarized Zones*, 177.
74. Tal, *Worlds of Hurt*, 89.
75. Ehrhart, "On the Eve of Destruction," *The Bodies Beneath the Table*, 65.
76. Winter, Jay, "Introduction: Henri Barbusse and the Birth of the Moral Witness," in Henri Barbusse, *Under Fire*, trans. Robin Buss (1916; London: Penguin Books, 2003), xviii.
77. Ehrhart, *Mostly Nothing Happens*, without page numbers.
78. Ehrhart, "Visiting My Parents' Grave," *Beautiful Wreckage*, 220.
79. Ehrhart, "What I Know About Myself," *Beautiful Wreckage*, 197.

W. D. Ehrhart at the Vietnam Veterans Memorial

Diederik Oostdijk

It is remarkable that W. D. Ehrhart wrote not one but two poems about the Vietnam Veterans Memorial: "Midnight at the Vietnam Veterans Memorial"[1] and "The Invasion of Grenada."[2] It is testimony to Ehrhart's prolonged preoccupation with Maya Lin's monument on the Mall in Washington, D.C. By analyzing these two poems in the context of the controversy surrounding the monument and by comparing and contrasting them to other poems by veterans on the Wall, this chapter seeks to understand Ehrhart's concern regarding this monument. While Yusef Komunyakaa's "Facing It"[3] and "The Wall"[4] and Doug Anderson's "The Wall"[5] see the monument as an opportunity to come to terms with a traumatic past, Ehrhart is more skeptical about the monument's ability to heal the nation. Ehrhart sides neither with the small but vocal group of veterans who found the monument offensive, nor with the increasing majority of Americans who saw in Maya Lin's design a perfect symbol of a troubled war. By stating that what he "wanted was an end to monuments," as he does at the end of "The Invasion of Grenada," Ehrhart acknowledges his sorrow that war monuments exist, in the first place, and he also warns that monuments are able to make us forget unpleasant facts. As such, his two poems about the Vietnam Veterans Memorial mirror Ehrhart's uncompromising and enduring reading of the Vietnam War and its aftermath, and his recalcitrant position as a war poet.

No war memorial has been more popular to American poets than Maya Lin's Vietnam Veterans Memorial. Almost two dozen poems have been published that focus on the Wall since its consecration in 1982, including several by the principal soldier-poets of the Vietnam War and excluding the hundreds of poems that are left at the Wall every year by ordinary visitors.[6] War monuments have often functioned as inspiration for poems, and they can be regarded as a subgenre of the war poem, although they are rarely studied as such. Ralph Waldo Emerson wrote his "Concord Hymn" containing the infamous line—"the shot heard round the world"—about the beginning of the American Revolution, when an obelisk was unveiled in his hometown in 1837. Augustus St. Gaudens' more inventive bas relief sculpture to Robert Gould Shaw and the 54th Massachusetts Volunteer Infantry, which is situated opposite the Massachusetts State Capital in Boston, gave rise to a slew of poems. Written more than half a century after William James unveiled St. Gaudens' monument, Robert Lowell's "For the Union Dead"[7] must be counted as the most famous example. Considering that Maya Lin's Vietnam Veterans Memorial has been around for exactly thirty years, it is safe to predict that many more will be written and published about the enigmatic black Wall on the Mall in the years to come.

What exactly intrigues poets so much about the Vietnam Veterans Memorial is not self evident, although several typical reasons can be given to explain its attractiveness. Firstly, the originality of the design must have contributed to the many poetic responses. Lin's design was markedly different from other American war memorials at the time. Neither a classical design like the Revolutionary War obelisk in Concord and many other monuments on the Mall nor the lifelike representation of Civil War soldiers in Boston, the Vietnam Veterans memorial is strikingly modernist. It was also "a dark memorial in a city full of white monuments," as Patrick Hagopian indicated.[8] The twenty-one-year-old Yale student, Maya Ying Lin, who won the competition, designed a large V consisting of a black granite panel that cut into the ground. The names of the American casualties were carved onto the panels in the order in which they died. From the few inches listing the casualties in 1956, the V cuts deeper in the ground till one reaches the apex which visitors reach after walking down a slightly sloping hill. After the visitor walks up a similar hill to the last panels listing the last victim who died in 1975. The experience makes an acute impression on many visitors. As Kirsten Ann Hass explains:

> At the center you are half buried in a mass of names; pulled toward the black granite, you see yourself and the open lawns of the mall behind you reflected in the memorial. The center of the monument is a strangely private, buffered public space. Literally six feet into the hillside you are confronted simultaneously with the names and with yourself. The black granite is so highly reflective that even at night visitors see their own faces as they look at the Wall. The Wall manages to capture the unlikely simultaneous experiences of reflection and burial. This brilliant element of the design asks for a personal, thoughtful response.[9]

The second reason that the Vietnam Veterans Memorial is so popular among poets is related to the reflective nature of the monument. To have one's own reflection stare back at oneself through the wall confronts the viewer with himself or herself, extracting a personal response. The most anthologized poem about the Vietnam Veterans Memorial, Yusef Komunyakaa's "Facing It," revolves precisely around the reflective quality that Hass mentions. The poem is full of imagery connotations about mirrors and windows. "My black face fades, / hiding inside the black granite," Komunyakaa writes in the opening lines.[10] Since the speaker is black his face disappears into the wall as opposed to the faces of white people which are reflected: "A white vet's image floats / closer to me, then his pale eyes / look through mine. I'm a window."[11] The verb to "look through" may indicate that Komunyakaa's speaker is like Ralph Ellison's *Invisible Man*,[12] but it may also mean that the fellow vet is seeing what the speaker is seeing. Throughout the poem there is a nervous anxiety that plagues the speaker. He swears to himself and tells himself not to lose his nerve. He wants to be in control, like the wall itself, "stone," but he is "flesh."[13] Komunyakaa uses the Vietnam Veterans Wall to reflect (quite literally) on race, and also on gender.

The anxiety that the speaker has seems to also be connected to women. Komunyakaa's speaker twice eyes women suspiciously. The first time he is surprised that the names stay on the black granite wall despite the fact that the woman walks away. The second time it appears to the speaker that "a woman's trying to erase names."[14] Could there be a larger significance to this suspicion of women? Is Komunyakaa subconsciously afraid that women will rub away the memory of the war? Although Komunyakaa is apprehensive about the woman, she only turns out to be "brushing a boy's hair."[15] The former Marine corpsman Doug Anderson's "The Wall" also reflects on race and gender albeit in a more complex way in comparison to Komunyakaa's poem. Dedicated to Maya Lin, "The Wall" suggests that the monument has a feminine kind of healing power. It "draws us in, embraces," Anderson suggests early on, like "the crook of an arm to cradle the head."[16] Besides being able to hold a veteran like a baby in a mother's arms, the V-shaped monument is also a "labial gesture of stone."[17] The wall's shape is similar to that of lips, but in the context of the poem the word "labial" also suggests a vagina, especially since the poem ends with an image of the "womb of Kali."[18] Kali is a Hindu goddess who symbolized various and even conflicting qualities. She is considered the Goddess of Death and a murderous warrior, and also as a sexual partner and a devoted, compassionate mother. Anderson especially uses the connotations of the loving, considerate mother as he and the other veterans "wander in becoming whole."[19] The "womb of Kali" can be connected to Sigmund Freud's theory in his essay on "The Uncanny"[20] which suggests that human beings long to return to the womb since it symbolizes home.

It is important to note, though, that the Vietnam Veterans Memorial is neither intrinsically about gender nor about race, but that these themes are projected to the monument by Komunyakaa and Anderson. They are spurred by the minimalism of the design in order to relate a narrative that is essentially personal. The critic W.J.T. Mitchell astutely suggested that the more abstract a painting or sculpture is and, thus devoid of a narrative, "the more demand for the spectator to fill the void with language."[21] The Vietnam Veterans Memorial is a case in point, Mitchell noted: "Its legibility is not that of narrative: no heroic episode such as the planting of the American flag on Iwo Jima is memorialized, only the mind-numbing and undifferentiated chronology of violence and death catalogued by the 58,000 names inscribed on the black marble walls."[22] While Komunyakaa picks up on the monument's reflective quality and connects it to the blackness of his skin, Anderson dwells on the form of the monument and sees in it female shapes that he subsequently connects with motherhood and sexuality. It is the absence of narrative in the monument itself that evokes these strongly suggestive and personal narratives.

A third reason that helps explain the popularity of the Vietnam Veterans Memorial among poets is the list of names of those 58,000 plus Americans who died. "War and onomastics"—the study of names—"are closely connected," Kate McLoughlin reminds us.[23] After all counting and remembering names means marking the lives that were lost. Each name is capable of conjuring up memories or associations for a poet. Both Komunyakaa's "Facing It" and Anderson's "The Wall" show this. "I touch the name Andrew Johnson; / I see the booby trap's white flash," Komunyakaa writes.[24] At the moment Anderson recognizes the first name in the telephone book-like list of names at the entrance of the monument, he can see, smell, hear, and taste the memory of war:

> I move my finger down the index, find the name of the first man
> I could not help, and for a moment, the tree splintering
> in front of me, smell of blood and cordite, his lips turning blue,
> the gasp of a lung filling with blood.[25]

George Bilgere's "At the Vietnam Memorial"[26] relates how the speaker's confrontation with the name "Paul Castle" engraved on the Wall prompts a memory of the last time he read that name. Castle's name "was printed in gold on the wall / above the showers in the boys' / locker room, next to the school / record for the mile." Castle was the fastest middle distance runner in their school's history. With the memory of his name in golden letters came flooding back other memories, for instance seeing Castle at speed outrunning the other boys in school. From "the infield / of memory"—the area enclosed by the running track—Bilgere sees Castle "on the track, / legs flashing, body bending slightly / beyond the pack of runners at his back."[27] The assonance and triple rhyme make this a tightly knit image evoking the memory of this talented athlete.

Bilgere's speaker owns up that Castle did not deem him worthy enough to speak to. Castle was the prototype of a popular jock who did not associate with boys younger than him. "He owned the hallways, a cool blonde / at his side," Bilgere writes.[28] The enjambment after "blonde" suggests that he also "owned" the fair-haired girl as well. The final line of the second stanza states that Castle "aimed his interests / further down the line than we could guess."[29] While his peers toe the line, Castle continually wants to push the line. So far ahead of the rest of his fellow students, on the mile and in his ambitions, the others cannot keep up with him. Triumph in sports was not enough for this alpha male, as Castle was compelled to prevail in warfare as well. More specifically than Komunyakaa's and Anderson's, Bilgere's poem suggests how powerfully evocative the list of names is on the Vietnam Veterans Memorial. It functions as "an intense counter-urge to recuperate, catalogue and enunciate lost names," as McLoughlin argues.[30]

The uniqueness of the black V in the memorial landscape of the Mall, its reflective mirror-like nature, and the seemingly endless list of names that conjure up multiple memories, all contribute to the remarkably personal way in which visitors relate to the Vietnam Veterans Memorial. This has resulted in those almost two dozen poems, but also in the many objects that are left at the monument each day. Talking to high school students at La Salle University in 1991, Ehrhart was also struck by these "little offerings—the flowers, the handwritten notes, the high school yearbook photos.[31] Kirsten Ann Hass has defined five categories of objects: The great majority of objects mark specific individual memories, some speak to the problems of patriotism or community, some are negotiations between the living and the dead, some work to establish a community of veterans, and some make explicit political speech."[32]

Komunyakaa's second poem about the Vietnam Veterans Memorial, "The Wall" investigates this urge to deposit items at the memorial. It starts with an epigraph from William Shakespeare's sonnet 55—"Not Marble Nor the Guilded Monuments," followed by a catalog of typical items left at the monument, ranging from "a bra. lipstick / kisses on a postcard" to "a fifth of Beefeaters."[33] Komunyakaa's "The Wall" engages in a complex dialogue with Shakespeare's classic poem. In "Not Marble Nor the Guilded Monuments," Shakespeare argues that his sonnet and his love are more enduring than all monuments. After all marble will eventually be destroyed in wars, while Shakespeare's love will continue to exist as long as people can read, as he discloses in the final couplet: "So, till the judgment that yourself arise, / You live in this, and dwell in lovers' eyes." Maya Lin's monument and Yusef Komunyakaa's poem are ironic reversals of Shakespeare's sonnet in one sense. Shakespeare takes the destroyed monuments through war as a starting point for his poem and suggests that his poem is more powerful and longer-lasting. In Lin and

Komunyakaa's case, it was a war that inspired the monument, and its effectiveness in evoking memories of loved ones inspired the poem.

When comparing W. D. Ehrhart's two poems about the Vietnam Veterans War Memorial to Komunyakaa's and Anderson's poems, it is immediately clear how Ehrhart differs as a Vietnam War poet. Despite his genuine admiration of his two colleagues, Ehrhart would probably find Komunyakaa's metaperspective on memorialization and his dialogue with Shakespeare in "The Wall" a bit pretentious, and the intricate Freudian imagery of Anderson's "The Wall" is also anathema to Ehrhart's unaffected and direct style of communicating how the war impacted on him and others. Much closer to Ehrhart in style and convictions is Gerald McCarthy's "The Hooded Legion," which Ehrhart included in his anthology *Carrying the Darkness: The Poetry of the Vietnam War*,[34] unlike those by Anderson and Komunyakaa. McCarthy's poem takes its title from a desolate image of a group of veterans at the Vietnam Veterans Memorial whom the speaker sees reflected in the black granite. The steady showers bring back "memories of rain" from the Vietnam War, setting the tone for this somber reflection.[35]

The poem's four stanzas reflect four independent thoughts rather than a coherent narrative. They are not obviously related, except that they revolve around a group of soldiers who visit the monument in D.C. Joseph Brodsky's epigraph—"*Let us put up a monument to the lie*"—sets the negative and conspiratorial tone of the poem, but the tone gradually shifts to a more melancholy one, as reflected in the image of the title, of the soldiers in raingear confronting the Vietnam memorial. McCarthy's veterans are not as pitiful as Wilfred Owen's soldiers in "Dulce et Decorum Est" who were "[b]ent double, like old beggars under sacks, / Knock-kneed, coughing like hags,"[36] but these soldiers do evoke compassion as they "wander weaponless and cold / along this shore of the Potomac" in the pouring rain.[37] McCarthy opens with a bang rather than with a whimper, charging that the memorial expresses "no words here / to witness why we fought, / who sent us or what we hoped to gain."[38] McCarthy's poem oozes a sense of disappointment that the monument is politically mute and therefore concomitant to the lies that were told by the Johnson and Nixon administrations. Gradually McCarthy's tone turns more melancholy, though, when the speaker realizes that they were not the first legion to go off to war. In fact, more than a hundred years before, during the Civil War, "other soldiers" were gathered in the capital, "who camped here / looking over the smoldering fires into the night."[39] Like Ehrhart, McCarthy avoids heavy-handed metaphors, in order to get his message across as transparently as possible. The only obvious metaphors that McCarthy uses are contained in the final lines of the questioning final stanza: "What leaf did not go silver / in the last night? / What hand did not turn us aside?" The metaphor "silver" seems to connote wisdom and ageing, and the synecdoche "hand" suggests guidance by elders, which remained absent for these soldiers.[40] McCarthy subtly indicates that this generation of soldiers was not warned about the dangers of wars.

Ehrhart's "Midnight at the Vietnam Veterans Memorial" reflects on similar themes of youthful naiveté and aged wisdom in a similar tone, with anger and cynicism turning into melancholy contemplation. It focuses on "[f]ifty-eight thousand American dead" whose "average age" was "nineteen years, six months," as Ehrhart factually and unsentimentally says in the opening lines. Trying to evoke what this means for an individual person beyond the cold facts, Ehrhart bluntly adds: "Get a driver's license, / graduate from high school, / die." The full-stopped line after the word "school" followed by the single word "die" in the next line emphasizes these soldiers' cruel ending. This opening resembles Randall Jarrell's "Losses" when dead young airmen in World War II communally say: "We died like aunts or pets or foreigners. / (When we left high school nothing else had died / For us to figure we had died like.) from beyond the grave."[41] It baffles the reader that these recent high school graduates are old enough to die. Like Gerald McCarthy in "The Hooded Legion," Ehrhart feels that the Vietnam Veterans Memorial, or any monument for that matter, cannot do complete justice to the war dead, as is captured by the lines: "All that's left of them / we've turned to stone." The word "stone" here connotes coldness and hardness.

Whereas the first stanza is in parts glum, accusatory, and bitterly angry at the stupidity of a nation that sends off its young to battle, the second defiantly questions the justification that these soldiers' lives are wasted. Conceived at midnight "when no one's here," Ehrhart fantasizes how "the names rise up, step down / and start the long procession home." Ehrhart in a sense presents an alternative Judgment Day when the dead start wandering to the place they ought to belong. They march towards the lives they had but never got to finish. They wander:

> to what they left undone,
> to what they loved, to anywhere
> that's not this silent
> wall of kids, this
> smell of rotting dreams.

The ending of "Midnight at the Vietnam Veterans Memorial" provides a characteristically bold, powerful, and shocking image that has become the trademark of Ehrhart's most powerful poems. Ehrhart's image of the Vietnam Memorial as "a silent wall of kids" is different from the more respectful tone that the poems by Anderson and Komunyakaa take. Ehrhart finds the quietude of the monument oppressive, as the words on the wall are all that remain of the promising lives these people were supposed to still be living. The phrase also suggests that Ehrhart does not see the soldiers who died as men who died for their country, but as children who did not know what they were doing. The final phrase—about the "smell of rotting dreams" is seemingly incongruous. The Vietnam Memorial is an interactive sight because it cannot only be seen, but it also can be touched and perhaps—if the wind is right—heard. Metaphorically, however, the monument smells, because all monuments smell fishy, according to Ehrhart, covering up unpleasant truths.

"The Invasion of Grenada" drives home that same point more subtly but also more effectively. Its purposely misleading title suggests something that very few people realized at the time, but which seems unequivocal in hindsight: the consecration of the Vietnam Veterans Memorial in 1982 is related to American foreign policy in Central America at the time. Somehow there is a link, but Ehrhart does not spell this out for his readers as he wants his readers to investigate themselves. So how is the monument commemorating a war in Southeast Asia connected to American forces entering that small, Central American country on October 25, 1983? Despite heavy criticism from the United Kingdom, Canada, and the United Nations General Assembly, the United States invaded the island and quickly deposed the Grenadian Prime Minister Maurice Bishop, who was subsequently executed by the Grenadian army. There was great general support for the invasion among the Grenadian and American populations, but Ehrhart was not one of them. The Vietnam Monument was supposed to "make no political statement,"[42] but paradoxically by "disavowing politics in pursuit of 'healing,'" the Vietnam Veterans Memorial "pursued an irreducibly political objective, the reforging of national unity damaged by the war," as Patrick Hagopian has recently argued.[43] In the 1970s the memory of the Vietnam War "threatened to divide Americans into hostile camps and undermine Americans' willingness to stomach future wars."[44] Yet "America's political leaders," including Ronald Reagan, saw the apolitical monument as an opportunity to cement "identification with the nation and reconstructing pride in military service,"[45] as Hagopian successfully shows after a meticulous study of the archives: "Reagan's advisers judged the costs and benefits of the administration's decision about Central America policy and its stance regarding the Vietnam Veterans Memorial within the terms of a common political calculus."[46]

Ehrhart already suspected this in the early 1980s, as the clever title of his poem suggests. Ehrhart does not mention the events in Central America elsewhere in his poem, but the title is suggesting enough. Ehrhart visited Nicaragua around that time and understood well how Reagan was waging the Cold War in America's backyard, as his essay "Los Norteamericanos y Centroamérica" shows.[47] As Subarno Chattarji has argued, "The Invasion of Grenada" questions the "politically desired healing process."[48] Almost a decade after the monument was unveiled, Ehrhart confirmed this, arguing that what was problematic about the Vietnam Veterans Memorial was that it "precludes discussion or critique or wisdom, as though its dark polished face is all we will ever need to know, or ought to know, about the Vietnam War."[49] It fails to ask essential questions, such as:

> Why did all those people die? Who offered them up for slaughter? What was accomplished for the price of so much blood? How was it permitted to go on for so long? Where are the names of the three million dead of Indochina?[50]

"The Invasion of Grenada" is an ostensibly simple poem as it is in essence a list of what he does and does not want. In the first stanza, Ehrhart states that he "didn't want a monument," and in the second stanza he states "What I wanted," a phrase that occurs twice in the second stanza of six lines.[51] The poem culminates in the third stanza of just two lines that makes Ehrhart's wish unequivocal: "What I wanted / was an end to monuments."[52]

"The Invasion of Grenada" is about Grenada as well as about Vietnam. In both cases, the United States imposed its "will on others." His dislike of the Vietnam Veterans Memorial, which was consecrated in 1982, a year before the Invasion of Grenada, is not because he disapproved of Maya Lin's design of the monument as some of his fellow veterans did. In fact, Ehrhart praises Lin's "sober" style.[53] Yet Ehrhart wants "an end to monuments," as he powerfully claims at the end of the second stanza. Not only the Wall but also "a road beside the Delaware / River" that is dubbed "Vietnam Veterans Memorial Highway" are empty gestures of a nation that has not really learned from the Vietnam War, as Ehrhart argues.[54] To Ehrhart, the Vietnam Memorial represents a "vast black wall of broken lives," connecting the theme of this poem to "Midnight at the Vietnam Veterans Memorial."[55]

Yet Ehrhart also saw how the Wall quickly became "an awful cliché."[56] Everyone was so easily "moved by the terrible beauty of your own reflection in the silent, smooth granite" that it became a "substitute for substance and fact, as if the Wall says it all when in truth it tells us only what each of us chooses to hear," as he stated in 1991.[57] In other words, the reason the Vietnam Veterans Memorial has inspired so many different poems—its self-reflective quality and the fact that everyone recognizes his or her own truth in it—is also why it is a dangerous monument, as it makes a real dialogue about what happened in Vietnam impossible. After all, everyone can have an opinion about the Vietnam War which is as good as any other, but if they are devoid of historical accuracy, the monument is dangerous indeed. It is insights such as these combined with Ehrhart's suspicion of politicians, his interest in history, and his stubborn insistence that people should face the facts and be more critical, that make his poems so valuable. It is also why W. D. Ehrhart ought to be a monument of twentieth-century American literature and culture.

Notes

1. Ehrhart, W.D., *The Distance We Travel* (Easthampton, MA: Adastra Press, 1993), 21.
2. Ehrhart, W.D., *To Those Who Have Gone Home Tired* (New York: Thunder Mouth's Press, 1984), 71.
3. Komunyakaa, Yusef, *Dien Cai Dau* (Hanover: Wesleyan University Press, 1988), 63.
4. Komunyakaa, Yusef, *Thieves of Paradise* (Hanover: Wesleyan University Press, 1998), 122.
5. Anderson, Doug, *The Moon Reflected Fire: Poems* (Farmington, ME: Alice James Books, 1994), 62.
6. Other poems about the Vietnam Veterans Memorial not mentioned elsewhere in this chapter include Bill Bauer's "A Vietnam Veteran's Memorial Day," Fran Castan's "Unveiling the Vietnam Memorial," Robert Dana's "At the Vietnam War Memorial, D.C.," Eugene E. Grollmes' "At the Vietnam Veterans Memorial, Washington D.C.: Chrissie," David Jauss' "Vietnam Veterans Memorial," Maurice Lindsay's "The Vietnam Memorial, Washington DC," Alberto Ríos' "The Vietnam Wall," Karl Shapiro's "Vietnam Memorial," and Duong Tuong's "At the Vietnam Wall."
7. Robert Lowell, *Life Studies and For the Union Dead* (New York: Noonday Press, 1964).
8. Hagopian, Patrick, *The Vietnam War in American Memory: Veterans, Memorials, and the Politics of Healing* (Amherst, MA: University of Massachusetts Press, 2009), 98.
9. Hass, Kirstin Ann, *Carried to the Wall: American Memory and the Vietnam Veterans Memorial* (Berkeley: University of California Press, 1998), 14.
10. Komunyakaa, *Dien Cai Dau*, 63.
11. Ibid.
12. Ellison, Ralph, *Invisible Man* (New York: Random House, 1952).
13. Komunyakaa, *Dien Cai Dau*, 63.
14. Ibid.
15. Ibid.
16. Anderson, 62.
17. Ibid.
18. Ibid.
19. Ibid.
20. Freud, Sigmund. "The Uncanny," in *The Standard Edition of the Complete Psychological Works of Sigmund Freud*, Vol. 17 (London: Hogarth Press, 1986), 226–256.
21. Mitchell, W.J.T, *Picture Theory* (Chicago: University of Chicago Press, 1994), 219.
22. Ibid., 380–381.
23. McLoughlin, Kate, *Authoring War: The Literary Representation of War from the Iliad to Iraq* (Cambridge: Cambridge University Press, 2011), 58.
24. Komunyakaa, *Dien Cai Dau*, 63.
25. Anderson, 62.
26. Bilgere, George, "At the Vietnam Memorial." In Philip Mahony, ed., *From Both Sides Now: The Poetry of the Vietnam War and Its Aftermath* (New York: Scribner, 1998), 234.

27. Ibid.
28. Ibid.
29. Ibid.
30. McLoughlin, 62.
31. Ehrhart, W.D., *The Madness of It All: Essays on War, Literature, and American Life.* (Jefferson, NC: McFarland, 2002), 24.
32. Hass, 95.
33. Komunyakaa, *Thieves of Paradise*, 122.
34. McCarthy, Gerald, "The Hooded Legion," *Carrying the Darkness: The Poetry of the Vietnam War*, edited by W.D. Ehrhart (Lubbock: Texas Tech University Press, 1985), 182–183.
35. McCarthy, 182.
36. Owen, Wilfred, *The Collected Poems* (New York: New Directions, 1963), 55.
37. McCarthy, 182.
38. Ibid.
39. Ibid.
40. McCarthy, 183.
41. Jarrell, Randall, *The Complete Poems* (New York: Farrar, Straus and Giroux, 1969), 145.
42. Hagopian, 10.
43. Hagopian, 16.
44. Hagopian, 201.
45. Hagopian, 155.
46. Hagopian, 112.
47. Ehrhart, W.D., "Los Norteamericanos Y Centroamérica," *In the Shadow of Vietnam: Essays, 1977–1991* (Jefferson, NC: McFarland, 1991), 100–118.
48. Chattarji, Subarno, *Memories of a Lost War: American Poetic Responses to the Vietnam War* (Oxford: Oxford University Press, 2001), 101.
49. Ehrhart, *Madness of It All*, 24.
50. Ibid.
51. Ehrhart, W.D., *To Those Who Have Gone Home Tired*, 71.
52. Ibid.
53. Ibid.
54. Ibid.
55. Ibid.
56. Ehrhart, *Madness of It All*, 24.
57. Ibid.

From Patriot to Poet to Peacenik

Nicole Gollner

In my master's thesis on W. D. Ehrhart,[1] I thoroughly investigated how a convinced patriot changed into a passionate peacenik. The highly decorated American Vietnam veteran, author and teacher Bill Ehrhart has not only used pen and paper as cathartic vehicles. In fact, with his works he substantially contributes to making Vietnam War literature and poetry fully-fledged and accredited literary genres. By coming to terms with the past, his own wartime experiences and traumas suffered he gains an entirely new perspective on life and the importance of it. To understand how deeply influencing and life-altering the war experience was for Ehrhart, one has to briefly recapitulate the war and its consequences for the people who were a part of it—the veterans as well as the civilians, in order to understand authors like Ehrhart, why they feel such an urge to put what they have experienced and gone through into words.

Even many years after the war, the intervention of the U.S. government and its failure have become a taboo in the United States of America. The so-called conflict (Washington has never officially declared it a war) divided the American people more than any other military venture since the Civil War. For 15 years, under four presidents, millions of dollars were spent, millions of people died. Despite their military superiority, the Americans failed to defeat the Viet Cong who were often only equipped with simple weapons. The American people had to learn a bitter lesson from the experience. The bitterest pill, however, had to be swallowed by the war veterans.

In the first years after the war, collective suppression of this shameful defeat and constant avoidance of seriously discussing the issue inevitably led to a massive rejection of the Vietnam veterans. Soldiers returning home from World War II were venerated as heroes and liberators. Korean War vets mostly came home to deafening silence. The majority of the post-war soldiers from Vietnam were seen as losers and even labeled as the evil incarnate. They were called murderers, thieves or drug possessed butchers, who had unjustly invaded a foreign country. This way of thinking was triggered by increasingly loud voices, especially from home but also from abroad. In consequence, the veterans were increasingly marginalized. Before they went to war they had apparently been manipulated and lied to by their own government. They were sent to fight in a dubious conflict in a country—totally different culturally and geographically from their own—from which it was very difficult to return home safely and above all healthy mentally.

Many of the veterans ended up doing drugs because they were not able to cope with their traumas, others ended up in the gutter or in psychiatric facilities. Ehrhart, too, sought refuge in drugs for a while before he came to terms with his traumatic experiences. Yet, a lot of the veterans managed to reintegrate in society after a while—some sooner than later—and lead a seemingly "normal" life—including Ehrhart.

At this point it is necessary to again underline the fact that most of the veterans had serious psychological problems after returning home. So, it was not only about dealing with one's own inner conflicts but also dealing with the difficulties of readjusting at home. Ehrhart depicts it in *Tell Me Lies About Vietnam*. Those who had been sent "to pull the trigger were left alone to carry the weight of the entire disaster that was America's war in Indo-China."[2]

On the one hand the returnees were disappointed with their government who had not only abused them but then had matter of factly let them down mentally and financially after their homecoming and on the other hand they found themselves at the mercy of the hostility of society.

The more or less successful vets who were able to reintegrate found their own personal peace within their families, above all, because they did tell their stories, were able to get it off their chests, wrote their stories down or expressed themselves in other artistic ways. To Ehrhart it seems only logical that "so many former soldiers have turned to the solitude of pen and paper." He then goes on to quote Kennedy who said in a speech in 1963: "When power corrupts, poetry cleanses."[3]

Shortly after the war the perception of "the" Vietnam War veteran was rather one-sided. This image has only changed in the past few decades. This results from the increasing interest in the unsuccessful war, not least of all because of the numerous other military interventions of the American Government. Due to that, it is important to mention that a more realistic understanding of the former fighters and a broader view of the matter have arisen. As a consequence, the market has been flooded more than previously with Vietnam relevant literature. This ranges from historical, psychological and sociological studies to personal diaries, poetry and (semi) fictitious stories. Many well-known literary and cultural people have picked up the subject-matter and thereby taken the first steps to opening up a new field of literary research. The media have also increasingly dealt with the "issue" of Vietnam and produced serials or even entire program series about it.

Previously fought wars have not received so much media attention. The Vietnam War, however, has been called the first "television war" since television had increasingly found its way into American households. As already noted, soldiers from other wars were able to deal with their war experiences more easily because they had been welcomed as heroes; consequently, they had undergone a social, almost "ritual" purification through society's well-intentioned approval. Therefore there had been less interest in their experiences. The Vietnam conflict, however, was different from all the other wars that America had ever waged. It was above all the first war that the great nation of America had lost. The individual trauma of each Vietnam fighter was also reflected in the population. The debacle in Indochina became a national trauma. The defeat in the once honorable fight against oppression through communism became an internal fiasco. This was mainly the reason why the blame was laid upon the veterans.

Primarily in the media, the Vietnam veteran was initially generalized and presented as socially excluded misfit, drug addict, criminal or even psychopath. Not until the late seventies did the image of veterans begin to slowly change. He was no longer represented only as a war loser or war criminal, but also as a man who was trying to come to terms with his past and to manage the reintegration into society. In the course of the following decades the former "loser" even managed to become the "hero." Subsequently, with this "other" perception it became much easier for the veterans to bear witness to their experiences and to draw attention to their (quite often miserable) situation. Hollywood showed increasing interest in Vietnam, which thus resulted in a greater demand for Vietnam oriented literature. Apart from well-known Vietnam writers such as Bruce Weigl or John Balaban, W.D. Ehrhart particularly took a stand for the veterans and made every effort to gain attention for their concerns.

However, this is not Ehrhart's only important reason; he also wanted— and still wants—to warn future generations. Through his writing W.D. Ehrhart wanted "[...] to pull the entire Vietnam experience out of history and connect it to the world we live in today. There is little value to history if one cannot demonstrate its relevance to the present and the future [...]."[4] He and many others were deeply affected by the war. So, it can be said that writing for veterans and non-veterans is not only a way of gaining catharsis or apologizing but also a way of making people, nowadays and in the future, aware of what it means to fight a war. His experiences especially enable the recipient to learn and understand how fast it can happen how young people are almost "blindly" urged into a situation that they cannot evaluate appropriately.

As a young man, not yet 18 years old, Ehrhart was still firmly convinced that there is no more honorable thing than to fight for the freedom of an oppressed people. Before he came of age, he enlisted as a volunteer for Vietnam. However, his patriotic conviction soon gave way to the realization that that war was neither just and reasonable nor an honorable endeavor. The war was, and still is, a distinctive impetus for Ehrhart to look at himself, his country and its people in an absolutely different light. It can be said that his entire conception of the world changed due to his war experiences. However, his work does not deal exclusively with the topic of Vietnam. Even if he deals with other topics, such as love, friendship or nature, he says that everything he writes is more or less "filtered" through the war. Nevertheless, the criticism expressed through his literature is not only aimed at the Vietnam experience. His criticism and warnings also apply to other military interventions of the U.S. government, which took place after Vietnam.

By putting his experiences on paper, passing them on to his readers and students, he fulfills the necessary duty of making history experienceable and understandable by literary means. However, he does not only create a clearer understanding, it is crucial for him to try to create at least something positive out of his war service. Thus, his negative experiences are meant to be a vigorous admonition to the government and his compatriots. He is particularly concerned about young people. This is why he wants to teach them to think more critically about governmental activities, war and violence in general. He achieves this through his prose as well as through his poetry.

In *Going Back: An Ex-Marine Returns to Vietnam*[5] Ehrhart describes his experiences and feelings on returning to Vietnam in 1985—18 years after his initial war experience as a Marine. Together with his "soldier-poet" colleagues, the veterans Bruce Weigl and John Balaban, he accepted an invitation to Vietnam to do an official tour of inspection. For all three, it was crucial to see the once embattled country in times of peace. With high hopes and expectations they wanted to find answers to some essential questions. The reader can follow the travelers' journey into their past and furthermore realize that they gained a new perspective of the former fiercely fought-over war zone.

Initially, Ehrhart is very disappointed that he cannot return to the original scenes of his youth. However, in the course of his visit he becomes increasingly aware that this is not really important, but rather the fact that he can, at least, replace some terrible memories with new, peaceful experiences is significant. As in his other works, the reader learns what deep respect Ehrhart has gained for the Vietnamese people over the years. He admires the stoicism and kindness with which he and his comrades were welcomed, especially by the civilian population. The government officials also tried to make the stay for the three Americans as pleasant as possible. Despite all the new acquaintances and experiences Ehrhart does not close his mind to the negative aspects of this return.

Right at the beginning, his initial disappointment yields to deep embarrassment. Meeting elderly Mrs. Na, who gives vent to her emotions because she is still mourning her five sons killed in the war, makes Ehrhart realize that he should not overestimate his own expectations. The real misery is that he can neither soothe the old lady's suffering, nor find forgiveness. After all, the only thing he can do is ask the still grieving mother for forgiveness. This is the point where the journey can really begin. It is important not to walk along the already familiar tracks again but to find new paths—experiencing the country and its people and its culture in new, peaceful circumstances. The essential questions that run like a golden thread through the whole work are: "Why has he always wanted to go back there so badly?" "Is he able to approach the people he meets on his trip as warmheartedly as they approach him?" "What can he gain from these encounters, which lessons can be drawn from them?"

Although the journey is not always pleasant, sometimes it is even quite demanding, it seems to serve its purpose. With his realistic and very personal descriptions, Ehrhart succeeds in leaving room for the readers' own considerations. He does not intend to impose his own opinion on anybody; he rather wants to promote understanding for the veterans, the Vietnamese people and for himself. This is one of the foremost concerns of his whole oeuvre:

> [T]he Vietnamese have no corner on the market for hardship, and the world is full of governments I can't begin to approve of—many of them among the staunchest allies and clients of the United States of America. At least in Vietnam today, no one is dropping bombs or burning villages or defoliating forests, and what is taking place is not being done in my name or with my tax dollars, and no one is asking me to participate. It is their country, finally, and it is their business what they do with it. The Vietnamese have burdens of their own to bear; they have no need and no use for my anguish or my guilt. My war is over. It ended long ago.[6]

In the preface of his essay collection *In the Shadow of Vietnam: 1977–1991* Ehrhart describes why he finally chose not to forget his experiences, moreover, why he chose to turn from warrior into an anti-war advocate. This collection of essays is "an uncompromising desire to tell the truth [...] to expose the untruthful flaws behind any literary creation of warfare, and uphold the currently unfashionable banner of that most complex of terms: realism."[7] However, it was not only linked to the war in Vietnam. Ehrhart also comments on other conflicts in which the United States has been involved in politically, economically or militarily—whether it is directly or indirectly.

By taking up various issues he wants to generate awareness regarding American foreign policy. Nevertheless, he does not look at it in a wider sense. In this work that covers a period of fourteen years he focuses on personal retrospection. Additionally, the full range of human emotion is presented to the reader: Love, hate, friendship, nature, violence and death. Yet, these themes and motifs have always been influenced by his experiences in the war—as the title (*In the Shadow of Vietnam: Essays, 1977–1991*) suggests. Like in the previously discussed work, Ehrhart repeatedly uses the device of questioning in order to galvanize people into action, to encourage the reader to stay alert and thoughtful. His focus is clearly on the emphatic refusal of non-reflective thinking, of blind obedience. He does not want to belong to a "nation of sheep and followers." "The Vietnam war was for me, finally, only a starting point, the door that opened into my own soul and pointed the way to a new understanding of myself, my country, and the community of nations."[8]

The third piece of prose that I used in my previous study to illustrate why and how Ehrhart turned into an anti-warrior is a fictional short story, "The Dream," which despite its brevity is no less expressive. The author does not even need three full pages to create a short story that depicts the horrors of Vietnam experiences. Kalí Tal even calls it a "prose poem"[9] in her book *Worlds of Hurt: Reading the Literatures of Trauma*. As is usual in short stories the reader is put directly into the heart of the action, to give him/her the chance of immediately knowing in which setting the writer is going to place the story. With first person narration, the author creates authenticity. He goes on to describe what is going on at a party where the main protagonist (Ehrhart) and his friends are having a great time. This suggestive realism sets the atmosphere of the story. However, the reader soon realizes that the narrator feels increasingly uncomfortable. Although the guests around him are, in a way, "strange," he does not think that there is anything wrong with them. Yet, he is very confused. His confusion is caused by the fact that there are friends at the party he has known from different periods of his life; however, they seem to know one other. He calms himself by thinking that it is probably a party in his honor.

In the third paragraph there is an obvious turning point which works as a catalyst. Ten heavily armed soldiers storm the party and slaughter the guests there. In dramatic pictures the narrator describes how everything becomes more hectic and gets crueler. The title, but especially the depiction of those nightmarish atrocities, indicates that Ehrhart wants to address the so-called PTSD—Post Traumatic Stress Disorder—which many of the veterans suffered from. Furthermore, this nightmare can also represent a synonym for the war itself. A remarkable device Ehrhart uses to display the violent process of de-individualizing human beings in a war is that the narrator cannot see the soldiers' faces. "I can't see the faces of the Marines. I keep trying to but I can't see their faces."[10] This is a symbol that there are no individuals in a war, but only "the soldier," together with "the enemy" as a collective. In the sixth paragraph it comes to a dramatic climax. When frantically running down the corridor the narrator gets a glimpse of his reflection. Suddenly he is dressed in combat gear and carrying a gun in his hand, the barrel still smoking. The surprise ending suggests a clear message on a very personal level. One could never know on which side one could end up. Kalí Tal also concludes her analysis of "The Dream" by mentioning Ehrhart's worst anxieties: "After over a decade of writing poetry, Ehrhart is still obsessed by the notion that he is the embodiment of his worst fear. Even this volume [*The Outer Banks*—explanatory note], dedicated to his wife, he places the first poem that must alert us all that he is capable of destroying that which he most loves."[11] One can either be the perpetrator or the victim. This picture also shows the ambiguous situations the soldiers had found themselves in. On the one hand they had to execute the orders they were given, therefore they are perpetrators, on the other hand they did not have a choice other than acting on orders. Nevertheless, following military rules should never include war crimes. Ehrhart shows with "The Dream," in a very direct and precise way, how he changed, and had been turned, from a civilian into an anonymous de-individualized recipient of military orders. Ehrhart's way of coming to terms with his traumatic experiences is mainly through writing different types of literature. The personal investment is highly important—especially for combat veterans. "Literature of trauma is written from the need to tell and retell the story of the traumatic experience, to make it 'real' both to the victim and to the community. Such writing serves both as validation and cathartic vehicle for the traumatized author."[12]

In the following part of this essay it will be explained why poetry is a suitable literary genre for describing Vietnam War experiences. Ehrhart is convinced that poetry is essential when it comes to teaching about the Vietnam War. This is because poetry about Vietnam is "plainspoken" and "eloquent."

> Long before they reach college, most students are convinced that poetry is either boring or inaccessible or both. But I can't teach a Vietnam course without resorting to poetry. The poetry written about Vietnam is both plainspoken and eloquent. If students think they don't like poetry, or can't understand it, have them read some of this stuff, it'll blow their socks off.[13]

Particularly in his poems, he manages to create a better understanding and appreciation of the worries and problems of all those affected by the war— for the soldiers on both sides, as well as for the Vietnamese civilian population. However, it is not only the didactic aspect that the poet is interested in. As mentioned before, the Vietnam veteran acquires a modified perception of the world and the things going on in it. The "soldier-poet" Ehrhart displays his altered point of view in carefully considered and expressive, but by no means exuberant, imagery. His poetic diction varies, but the language can be described as straightforward. So, by not only taking up various topics and themes regarding the war, but also by conveying them through "realistic" and authentic language, Ehrhart manages to de-mystify the soldier and the veteran. On top of this, it is more expedient for the "teacher" Ehrhart to initially equip his students with knowledge about the war by using short lyric texts rather than with longer ones. He achieves this not least because of his clear, direct but never too simplistic style. Some critics may argue that Ehrhart's poetry is too didactic and polemical but

> in truth, unlike other veteran's poetry which rightfully enumerates the horrors they witnessed, Ehrhart's work engages in a dialogue with the power structure, forcing the reader to see the connection between imperialism, capitalism and war. And as an educator, Ehrhart knows too well the fascination young people have with war.[14]

Pratt distinguishes three different categories within Vietnam War poetry as follows:

> Poetry about Vietnam falls into three general categories: political protest poems, usually written by established poets who had not been to Vietnam; verse novels, in which chronologically linked poems depict one person's experiences at war; and the hundreds of usually short, personal lyrics that present individual scenes, character sketches, or events.[15]

In the analytical, practical part of my master's thesis the main focus was on W.D. Ehrhart's personal view of the war. In this respect I divided the selected poems into four main sections that I found by analyzing Ehrhart's poetic work:

- Actual combat experiences, the soldier's life with his colleagues in the jungle is described.
- Depicting Vietnamese people, their surroundings, and their living conditions during the war.
- Feeling guilt about what was done during the war, taking responsibility for the things soldiers did to their enemies. Poems that incorporate the question of personal guilt and guilt seen on a broader scale.
- Retelling, reliving and re-experiencing the trauma, the war that always will be there broodingly present.

The first section describes how comrades managed to get along with one other. That is to say: the difficulties of surviving in the jungle, as well as their "everyday worries." In addition, consequences of combat are displayed—on both sides of the war zone.

The second section deals with the situation of the South Vietnamese population in more detail. It is a dilemma the civilians found themselves in, due to the fact that they were treated disgracefully by the American as well as the Vietcong in many cases. As the Vietcong were extremely well trained for waging a guerrilla war, it was difficult, and often impossible, for the American soldiers to distinguish the VC from neutral peasants.

The third section tells of the poet's personal guilt he felt for the Vietnamese people, as well as the deceased, comrades "left behind." Furthermore, it points out the collective guilt of the American government. Moreover, sharp criticism is imparted, and more specifically, the poet issues clear warnings to future generations.

In conclusion, one can see that the poet is repeatedly challenged to deal with his tragic experiences by looking back at them. He will scrutinize them for the rest of his life, tell and relive them at various stages of his life—time after time, albeit in an alternate form. He may not be the most famous "Vietnam man of letters," but in my opinion he can be considered as one of the most dedicated. Despite Ehrhart having no clear answers to numerous questions raised regarding the war, he tries to make peace with himself, with the people and the country he fought against and with his homeland as well, although he can never think of his country the way he did before the war. He tries to deal with the dual conflict that the veterans are faced with. Moreover, he has to accept the emotions and implications of what he has done and has been a part of and, therefore, can only find his peace through love, friendship, forgiveness and awareness.

Ehrhart is aware of the prominent and privileged position he holds as a contemporary witness. For him, literature serves as a useful tool to warn not only the American, but also other governments and people. If the next generation can be saved from making the same mistakes it can also be saved from being victimized by another atrocious war. Therefore he demands political awareness from both his writers (as an anthologist) and his readers. In his poem "What Keeps Me Going" one can see what has already been underlined earlier in this essay. The war will always be with him but largely thanks to his beloved wife and daughter, his poems have attained richness and reached wider horizons; he definitely needs to be able to be a part of a "normal," peaceful world without the Vietnam War. However, he is always aware that there are many other conflicts on this earth that threaten present and future generations; we read Vietnam War literature in order to learn what not to do next time. Tal sums it up like this: "'What Keeps Me Going,' [...] represents the transfer of his hope from an amorphous 'next generation' to his own daughter, Leela, and his ambivalence about her chances of happiness."[16]

Pressed down by the weight
of despair, I could sit for hours
idly searching the ashes
from my cigarette, the darkness
of silos, the convoluted paths
we have followed into this morass
of disasters just waiting to happen,

but my daughter needs to sleep
and wants me near. She knows
nothing of my thoughts. Not one
missile mars her questioning
inspection of my eyes; she wants
only the assurance of my smile,
the familiar placed just so:

Brown Bear, Thumper Bunny, Clown.
These are the circumference
of her world. She sucks her thumb,
rubs her face hard against the mattress,
and begins again
the long night dreaming
darkness into light.[17]

Notes

1. Am Institut für Amerikanistik, Karl Franzens-Universität Graz, Graz, Austria, 2005.

2. See: W.D. Ehrhart in: Alf Louvre and Jeffrey Walsh, eds., *Tell Me Lies About Vietnam* (Philadelphia: Open University Press, 1988), 161ff.

3. Ibid., 163.

4. Ehrhart, W.D., *In the Shadow of Vietnam: Essays, 1977–1991* (Jefferson, NC: McFarland, 1991), 147.

5. Ehrhart, W.D., *Going Back: An Ex-Marine Returns to Vietnam* (Jefferson, NC: McFarland, 1987).

6. Ehrhart, *Going Back*, 180.

7. Williams, Tony. In reviewing *The James Jones Reader*, James R. Giles and J. Michael Lennon, eds. (Birch Lane Press, New York, 1991), with W.D. Ehrhart, *Going Back: An Ex-Marine Returns to Vietnam* (Jefferson, NC: McFarland, 1987, and W.D. Ehrhart, *In the Shadow of Vietnam: Essays, 1977–1991* (Jefferson, NC: McFarland, 1991), Tony Williams finds that "despite their different backgrounds, James Jones and W.D. Ehrhart have several common characteristics, a desire to honestly tell the truth as they experience it, and a belief in the possibility of peace no matter how impossible it may appear. See http://www2.iath.virginia.edu/sixties/HTML_docs/Texts/Reviews/Williams_Jones_Ehrhart.html.

8. Ehrhart, W.D., *In the Shadow of Vietnam: Essays, 1977–1991* (Jefferson, NC: McFarland, 1991). Preface, ix.

9. Tal, Kalí, *Worlds of Hurt: Reading the Literatures of Trauma* (Cambridge: Cambridge University Press, 1996), 95.

10. Ehrhart, W.D., *The Outer Banks & Other Poems* (Easthampton, MA: Adastra Press, 1984), 12

11. Tal, Kalí, *Worlds of Hurt*, 96.

12. Ibid., 21.

13. Ehrhart, *In The Shadow of Vietnam*, 146.

14. Jaffe, Maggie (1996) "Worlds of Hurt: Reading the Literatures of Trauma by Kalí Tal." *War, Literature & the* Arts. [online] http://www.kalital.com/Text/Worlds/Jaffe Rev.html, accessed 29 May 2001.

15. Pratt, John Clark (1999). "Poetry and Vietnam." *Modern American Poetry* [online]. http://www.english.uiuc.edu/maps/vietnam/poetryandvietnam.htm, accessed 19 March 2003. 2001.

16. Tal, Kalí, *Worlds of Hurt*, 112.

17. Ehrhart, W.D., *Just for Laughs* (Silver Spring, MD: Vietnam Generation Inc. & Burning Cities Press, 1990), 79.

Poetry and the Art of Resistance: The Literature of W. D. Ehrhart in Context

Dale Ritterbusch

It is a given in our culture that poetry and politics do not mix. For example, when Billy Collins was asked what the poet's response should be to 9/11, he said the solution was to bus all the poet laureates into Washington, and, after they'd mucked things up, to bus them out again. Such disdain for the role of the poet and the practice of writing substantive and consequential poetry that deals with real world issues is so common that poets themselves believe it as if it were the very foundation of modern poetry. Robert Duncan's attacks on Denise Levertov over her poems written in response to the Vietnam War, despite his own polemical poetry, destroyed their long, endearing friendship. And if one were to do a quantitative analysis of literary anthologies selected for use in the college classroom, one would find few selections of war poetry. Most anthologies would include Wilfred Owen's "Dulce et Decorum Est"[1] as the representative poem from World War I and Randall Jarrell's "Death of the Ball Turret Gunner"[2] representing World War II. Otherwise the selections are scant: in one anthology chosen for use by my department (Languages & Literatures at the University of Wisconsin-Whitewater) the representative Pablo Neruda poem was "Ode to My Socks,"[3] not the haunting "I'm Explaining a Few Things"[4] which the poet had written against fascism, a poem that details the responsibilities of the poet when faced with political evils; if you think otherwise, "come and see the blood in the streets."

It is against this backdrop that W. D. Ehrhart is seen as troublesome; his constant reminders that poetry matters, that it exposes our hypocrisy, that war, Vietnam or otherwise, is always with us, rankles the sensibilities of those who believe poetry should be mere ornamentation. Ehrhart's work insists on intellectual honesty and therefore rests outside the traditional canon. But his repertoire is tied to the literary history of Western Civilization which has, since *The Iliad*, diligently and brilliantly dealt with war and its attendant issues. We have no king, but *Henry V* still resonates and will until such fury shall abate.

In America, W.H. Auden observed, poets practice a harmless hobby like playing with model trains or building bird houses, and this perception is reinforced by the educational experience which is designed to protect students from knowledge necessary to grapple with substantive concerns. Even the Veterans of Foreign Wars (VFW) wants nothing truthful to be told in the history books if that truth conflicts with an ideological vision of the American experience. Better to provide a poem which captures a romantic but disingenuous sentiment as is found in Alan Seeger's "I Have a Rendezvous with Death."[5] The poem sanitizes the story in the way the VFW wishes history books to be written. Few Americans, for example, know much if anything of our own war in the Philippines, a war I knew next to nothing about until I saw a romanticized painting of it hanging on the walls of a classroom at the Infantry School at Fort Benning. Ehrhart's work, his poetry, memoirs, and historical studies are all wrought in that knowledge vacuum: there is much to redress in a climate that values sanitization over acute understanding.

When our gifted writers are the product of historical and literary ignorance, their attempts at responding to the immediate history and the wars that inform them are often foolish, like many of the poems written in response to 9/11. Going back to World War II, Marianne Moore's poem "In Distrust of Merits" contains the lines, "If these great patient / Dyings—all these agonies / And woundbearings and bloodshed / Can teach us how to live, these dyings were not wasted (lines 66–70)."[6] Such banality reflects an ignorance of both the history of war and the literature of war. Randall Jarrell is quite correct in condemning these lines. To defend Moore's poem, regarded by many as the greatest of World War II poems, is to buy into an argument that perpetuates a mindset which ensures further wars; it contributes to a warrior mentality that infuses American culture. One can learn little if anything from her elementary response; her lines are infused with simplistic comprehension. Had she not read *The Iliad* (and not the children's version)? Was she unfamiliar with Owen and Sassoon, Li Po, John Donne, or William Shakespeare? Since writing had become a practiced art, war has been its subject, and no poet should be unversed in the richness of this literary history.

John Balaban wrote, "Poets are not nice people."[7] His assertion may be literally true, but figuratively it may be used to describe the responsibility of the poet to serve as provocateur, as someone to prick the consciences of the populace: art is subversive and the artist is the agent of this subversion. Consider, for example, Robert Frost's poem "Mending Wall"[8] where the line "Good fences make good neighbors" (27 & 45) is spoken by a man who appears to be a savage armed as he is with the stones needed to repair the wall. Frost disguises the line in such a way as to make it seem a positive and responsible aphorism. Surely the Israelis think so as do the Americans who support the construction of a wall separating the United States from Mexico. Frost's method is game playing, a posture alien to Ehrhart. Frost, representing the baseline of American poetry, creates a similar subterfuge in "The Road Not Taken" where we learn both paths are *equal* and *just as fair* (lines 6 & 15): there is then little, if any, difference (20) between them, both paths leading largely to the same end. But there has to be a significant difference if one has control over one's personal destiny. Such control is mythical, but we prefer otherwise, embracing an enculturated belief that we are the masters of our fate, the captains of our souls, as if deterministic forces of various sorts were not in constant operation. Contrary to Frost's method of engagement, Ehrhart refuses to disguise his intent. There is no attempt at obfuscation, no kowtowing to conventional wisdom, no fence straddling or pandering to the rules of political correctness. He refuses ambiguity for the sake of ambiguity and insists on avoiding simple bumper sticker assessments in favor of critical assessments that yield disturbing conclusions. Put a magnetic sticker on the car that reads *Support the Troops*, tie a yellow ribbon around that tree in the front yard and be done with it. Ehrhart refuses such simple-minded assessments, although they inform the understanding of so many. Instead he insists on an honest and direct line of inquiry, reflective but concretely expressed. He repudiates both muddled thinking and that which is overly simplistic. His writing, both prose and poetry, insists on an aesthetic clarity such that there is no room, no place, for obfuscation that masks deception.

As much as Ehrhart is interested in laying bare the political and experiential facts for a public to readily comprehend, he also knows of its reluctance and willful intransigence to do so. It is not uncommon for veterans to have disdain for the population that refuses to know or learn the lessons of their war experience. A student of mine, an Iraq War vet, a Marine with multiple tours, told me he could not stand those *COEXIST* bumper stickers formed of all the symbols of the major religions. Such blind simplification does nothing to create a cogent political and historical insight. That Marine's disgust at sloppy thinking reminded me of returning to college after my time in the Army, sitting behind a student who doodled a flowery *LOVE* at the top of the page before each class. I wanted to hit him with an upper butt swing from an M-14, thinking that might eliminate some of his blind obedience to sophomoric prescriptions. Nothing has changed from Vietnam to Iraq: the bumper sticker mentality still infects the general population, and even the nicest, most decent people refuse to see any further than the local Wal-Mart.

Ehrhart's prose poem, "What War Does,"⁹ is a particularly good example of his disdain for the willful ignorance of civilians: turning his wrath on those who refuse to know echoes the sentiment of Siegfried Sassoon expressed in his poem "Blighters."¹⁰ There the poet proposes the idea that the only way to make the public understand what it so blindly supports is to turn the tanks on them as they celebrate their militaristic impulses in a music hall. Even the absurdly romantic chauvinist Alan Seeger wrote contemptuously of the civilians back home, those people the soldiers "scorn yet die to shield / That world of cowards, hypocrites, and fools" (Sonnet XI, "On Returning to the Front After Leave," lines 13–14). If one so willing to sacrifice himself for the cause feels such disdain, then others more realistically attuned are likely to feel an even greater contempt. As Balaban said, "Poets are not nice people," but war poets can hardly be expected to be nice when facing such cultural blindness.

All of Bill's effrontery is for our own good: he insists on not letting go, on requiring those with a discerning intelligence to confront crucial historical and contemporary issues. He knows how the past interpenetrates the present, how the word Iraq could easily be exchanged for Vietnam in official documents. Largely he refuses to accept revisionist interpretations that are nearly always self-serving. He knows, for example, that General Westmoreland's autobiography is the same as General Tommy Franks' autobiography, both defenses of the indefensible. In an address given at Illinois College, Ehrhart spoke of "history filled with arrogance, ignorance, half-truths, obfuscations, falsehoods, deceptions, and lies (Oct. 2009)."¹¹ His poems and memoirs have represented the opposite, and his scathing assessment of disingenuous histories extends to our culture's gullible acceptance of preposterous propositions in virtually every area of contemporary concern. His acute awareness of our cognitive dissonance, our sleazy use of euphemistic language and doublespeak, our inability to see the truth because we do not want to see it, causes considerable discomfort in most audiences, most readers of his work. As a general principle, our species prefers pleasure to painful insights. Most of us see the gossamer gold cloth of the emperor; when told otherwise we look away. As Francis Bacon observed, "Man prefers to believe what he prefers to be true." Ehrhart will have none of that.

His moral compass has been redirected as a result of his tour in Vietnam. When called to jury duty, he was asked by the judge if he could accept the judge's instructions even if they conflicted with the dictates of the juror's conscience. Ehrhart said no, and in his essay on jury duty he enumerates a litany of all the times he had been lied to and told to accept those lies as the truth. That piece in *The Madness of It All*¹² serves as an exemplar of the ethos expressed in his poetry; in one sense it is an exposition of Philip Larkin's admonition, "Never such innocence again (MCMXIV, line 32)."¹³

If we think of Ehrhart's work in terms of the *good,* a category that has informed our philosophical understanding since antiquity, then there is a particular concern that must be explicated. Given the political realities, content is not to be sacrificed to the god of form; in effect, his poetry serves as a form of moral and philosophical discourse in which he wants his poems to act upon the reader such that a category of goodness will result. This is not to turn Ehrhart's work into some sort of didactical sermon. Instead the goodness and grace that result from contending with a descent into hellish nightmare, the knowledge of what one has done and how one has been manipulated and used as an instrument of bankrupt policy, are a manifested transcendence that attains the power of decency and rectitude in the face of so much hurt. The value of Ehrhart's literature lies in this transcendence, an acceptance of the *horror* as Kurtz defined it and the courage to confront that horror and not embrace it as an expression of real politick astuteness.

The category of the good which is a graceful decency is conjoined with a dismissal of the category of power. Ehrhart is contemptuous of its application, refusing even to possess a firearm, but more insistently rejecting the appeals of those who orchestrate the transmission of power such that the willing and willfully ignorant are persuaded to support its application as would a schoolyard bully.

The above reference to Kurtz is not whimsical; in fact Conrad's *Heart of Darkness* (1899) parallels Ehrhart's life and work. *And this also has been one of the dark places on this earth* is literally and figuratively true—literally, of course, because one can throw a dart almost anywhere on a world map and find, upon exploring its history, that terrible things have been done as that land has been *civilized* with all the virtues consigned to the nobility of our human character. But figuratively Marlow's statement works to explain the very nature of our being, the deceit and hypocrisy that allow us to behave holding onto the lies we tell ourselves while our conduct wouldn't be tolerated in the darkest regions of hell.

Ehrhart is not a sympathetic figure any more than say, Henry V, or anyone else whose prime directives are not motivated by the Sermon on the Mount. Ehrhart did not question John Fitzgerald Kennedy's *ask not* command. Nor did he read Bernard Fall's *Street Without Joy*[14] or any other work that might have intervened, causing him to question his naïve belief in the legitimacy of the Vietnam War. He was then the perfect product of a socialization process that each generation produces. Any honest, critical appraisal of American history, any history for that matter, was counter to the aims of those in power. A positive spin is mandated to keep the subordinate classes subservient and obsequious.

The virtue of Ehrhart, the good, involves his transcendence, his ability to learn from his experience and his subsequent reading of history: accordingly, his triumph over institutionalized ignorance makes him admirable and deserving of the attention of readers who don't wish to embrace the hokum and bafflegab they are fed on a daily basis.

Consistent with Jarrell's point that "a real war poet is always a war poet, peace or anytime," Ehrhart makes connections between one war and the next, one failed policy and the next, so that the whole pattern unfolds. Ehrhart, then, is not merely a Vietnam War poet, but a poet that contends with the overlay of political and historical principles. Such knowledge, however, leads to a high degree of intransigence, an unwillingness to compromise when one has learned where such compromises lead. Whereas others may offer acceptance and obsequiousness, Ehrhart's resistance is Thoreauvian. Like St. Thomas More who was executed not for his refusal to sign the succession act but for his refusal to bend to a higher secular authority, Ehrhart's refusal to acquiesce to the unconscionable is admirable but problematic as he notes in his poem "Sound Advice": injustice is a *natural thing,* an incontrovertible law that cannot be changed.[15] Ehrhart's inability to accept this makes others *uncomfortable,* but the resistance which is in evidence everywhere in his work defines that work and gives it a higher measure of value.

One night late, during the summer of 1999, Bill and I were sitting on the porch of a bed and breakfast on the Jersey shore talking of the usual things, and he mentioned the story of Lance Corporal so and so, and I didn't recall that Marine's story recorded in *Ordinary Lives: Platoon 1005 and the Vietnam War.*[16] Ehrhart had tracked down and interviewed most of his boot camp platoon and recorded their stories in that book. He then mentioned a corporal so and so, and I didn't recall his story either, and Bill exclaimed, "Geez Ritterbusch, didn't you bother to read the book?" "Bill," I replied, "you know I've read everything you've ever written." And I had read that book not long before. So when I returned to the Midwest after our visit, I reread the interviews, wondering why the stories hadn't resonated such that I'd remember them. I realized that many of those Marines whose lives Bill had faithfully recorded had little to say about their military experience, that the year and more they'd spent in Vietnam had not created the revelatory insights that defined Bill's work. It was as if going to Vietnam were the equivalent of taking a trip to the hardware store. It had not resonated any more than that.

The irony of the title *Ordinary Lives* is not lost on the reader; certainly many of those lives were extraordinary, but in one respect there is an ordinariness that is disturbing: the assessments of the war voiced by many of the Marines in the book are startlingly similar as if some process of deindividualization governed them all, preventing any real critical and insightful assessment or scrutiny of their experience in Vietnam or of American foreign policy or of Vietnamese political and cultural history. Many voiced the same ideas on how the war should have been conducted, why it was lost and so forth: for example, several veterans thought the proper strategy should have been to take the war North; "We should have invaded North Vietnam," one veteran said,[17] and another stated, "We just didn't have the right people making decisions—take ground and hold it. We should have invaded North Vietnam."[18] Those are simplistic and superficial understandings of policy and overall strategic planning. Others projected a naiveté that has not been superintended by the passage of time. One former Marine said, "I didn't have any idea what the politics of the war were.... I never really thought about it. I did my time. I did my work."[19] Another stated, "Politically, I had no opinion on the war, not then. Now I just think it was a bad idea.... But I don't question the government. What difference does it make? There are things that we're not privy to."[20] What they should have learned and confronted and understood is contained in Ehrhart's work. These Marines, like the nation as a whole, have been unwilling to reflect on the important ramifications of America's foreign policy; they refuse to recognize that there are limits to the principle of American exceptionalism. Contrary to the experience of most members of Platoon 1005 Ehrhart has devoted his life to an acute examination of our history, shredding our mythical constructs in favor of honest and enlightened inquiry. And, of course, that is dangerous ground: no one wants his beliefs refuted by contrary evidence, no matter how overwhelming that evidence might be.

Goethe noted that for many practitioners of the art, an accomplished technical mastery yields a simplistic triteness. That offense is not present in Ehrhart's poetry, as evidenced by his poem "Guatemala." In that poem a woman "runs a kitchen and school" for the poor. She is of little consequence in the world of geopolitical values. A general explains:

> "There will always be poor," he says.
> "The ones in the dump would find you.
> Your embassy would send me a letter.
> Nothing more would be done."[21]

This poem is indicative of Ehrhart's aesthetic which demands answers to disturbing questions involving the ethical nature of our foreign entanglements. If we are the Beacon on the Hill then why do we ignore the Sermon on the Mount? That question may be rephrased any way one wishes, but the result would still be the same. We do not want answers that tell us what we do not want to know. To dismiss "Guatemala" as a political poem ignores its quest for the reimposition of decent and humane values.

It is a matter of balance, a balance that is generally ignored by critics who concentrate on the more sensationalistic poems such as "What War Does" or the early poems that are unreflective and unrepentant in their honest engagement with the war. Unlike other writers who have hedged their bets waiting for the weight of history to decide the proper stance, and unlike those who either straddle the political fence, in effect embracing a mode of political correctness, Ehrhart builds on the experience and assessment of the war to provide a progression of understanding applicable to the increased militarism that defines American culture and character. If, as he says, war destroys one's humanity, then his work serves to explicate that destruction and to resurrect a more humane and just life that does not disguise the lingering after effects.

On the other side of the equation, the counter balance that makes his work worth reading, worth taking to heart, are the poems devoted to his wife and daughter. Just as Balaban wrote in his title poem "Words For My Daughter," "I want you to know the worst and be free from it. / I want you to know the worst and still find good (lines 70–71)."[22] Ehrhart projects a life for his daughter that will withstand the impact of terrible events and their pernicious consequences. In "Some Other World" Ehrhart is holding his sleeping daughter in his arms; he addresses her as follows:

> Once, before you were born,
> I watched for a moment
> an egret ascend from a pond
> with the grace of a whisper.
> And once I dreamed a man
> with a rifle refused to take aim;
> I awoke to a sadness
> deeper than dreams.
>
> And I'm wishing this moment
> could last forever; I'm wishing
> the things that trouble my dreams
> could be kept outside like the wind.[23]

Similarly in his poem "Why I Don't Mind Rocking Leela to Sleep," Ehrhart reflects on "the plodding sameness of cruelty" in a "world impervious to change"; he expresses the wishes for his daughter in these lines:

> What I want for my daughter
> she shall never have:
> a world without war, a life
> untouched by bigotry or hate,
> a mind free to carry a thought
> up to the light of pure possibility.
>
> She should be young forever.
> I could hold her here in my arms
> and offer her comfort,

>   a place to rest,
>   the illusion, at least, of shelter.
>   I don't want her
>   ever to be alone in a world
>   with the Gentle Shepherd
>   frozen in glass and the voice
>   of a pitiless, idiot god
>   chasing her down the years.[24]

These poems by Balaban and Ehrhart express a wish that their daughters will not know what their fathers know, and the desire for daughters, not sons, is to have a child not drawn into the mire of war. The idea may seem antiquated in light of a voluntary military that provides women with opportunities virtually unavailable elsewhere, the feminist movement pushing for equality for women in the military even to the point of serving in the combat arms, but the thought still lingers that one might, as a woman, remain largely untouched by the terrible and debilitating experience of war and thus fulfill a more just and humane life. There is both a sense of hopeful realism and fanciful ideality in this. Ehrhart's emphasis on wife, daughter and family is a quiet insistence on the primacy of values inimical to the practice of war. The argument is ongoing as Kayla Williams, author of *Love My Rifle More Than You*, proposes the idea that the best way to achieve equality in the military and by extension in the rest of the world as well, is for women to be allowed to serve in combat and not be given an exception based solely on their sex. In addition, Williams argues that this will lead to less sexual harassment; women will be freed from that culture which allows such depredations to occur. Ehrhart would argue otherwise, celebrating roles for women that are not tied to the same militaristic culture. In one of his finest poems, "Song for Leela, Bobby and Me," Ehrhart recalls a friend, Robert Ross, who was killed in Vietnam. He brings that memory forward, balancing it against more recent military actions in the Persian Gulf, Panama, and other places. The past interpenetrates the present; Ehrhart, still thinking of Ross, records this beautiful connection:

>   In the middle
>   of this poem, my daughter woke up crying.
>   I lay down beside her, softly singing;
>   soon she drifted back to sleep.
>   But I kept singing anyway.
>   I wanted you to hear.[25]

So Ehrhart's work is contentious and yet its values are admirable, his arguments compelling, and one engages the world at great peril if one is not conversant with the moral and ethical discourse his work presents. Ehrhart wants us all to hear.

Notes

1. Written in 1918 it was published in the anthologies *Minds at War* and *Out in the Dark*.
2. Jarrell, Randall. *Kipling, Auden & Co.* (New York: Farrar, Straus & Giroux, 1980). "Death of the Ball Turret Gunner" was published in 1945. Partly as it is short, this poem has been widely anthologized.
3. "Ode to My Socks" ("Oda a los calcetines") was written in 1956. It was published in the second tome of a series of four volumes of odes written between 1954 and 1959. It was translated into English by Robert Bly.
4. "Explico Algunas Cosas" was translated in English by Nathaniel Tarn in *Selected Poems: A Bilingual Edition,* by Pablo Neruda (London: Cape, 1970).
5. An American citizen Alan Seeger joined the French Foreign Legion to fight in World War I. He wrote poetry before and while he was at the front. His poems were not published until 1917, a year after his death on July 4, 1916.
6. Moore, Marianne. *The Complete Poems of Marianne Moore* (New York: Macmillan, 1981).
7. Balaban, John, "To P.T., a Poet, Who Holds That Good Poets Are Always Nice People (Even Robert Frost)," *After Our War* (Pittsburgh, PA: University of Pittsburgh Press, 1974), 41.
8. Frost, Robert, "Mending Wall," *North of Boston* (New York: Henry Holt, 1915).
9. Ehrhart, W.D., *The Distance We Travel* (Easthampton, MA: Adastra Press, 1993), 39–41.
10. Sassoon, Siegfried, *The Old Huntsman and Other Poems* (New York: Henry Holt, 1918).
11. "That Was Then, This Is Now: Reflections on the Late American War in Vietnam," Joe Patterson Smith Lecture, Illinois College, October 12, 2009. This lecture is an amalgamation of "'They Want Enough Rice': Reflections on the Late American war in Vietnam" and "One, Two, Many Vietnams?" published by W.D. Ehrhart in *Dead on a High Hill* (Jefferson, NC: McFarland, 2012), 112–125 & 131–133.
12. Ehrhart, W.D., "On Common Sense and Conscience" was first published in *Los Angeles & San Francisco Daily Journal*, January 15, 1993. It was then reprinted in *The Madness of It All: Essays on War, Literature, and American Life* (Jefferson, NC: McFarland, 2002), 40–42.
13. Larkin, Philip. *Collected Poems* (London: Faber and Faber, 2003).
14. Fall, Bernard. B., *Street Without Joy* (Mechanicsburg, PA: The Stackpole Company, 1961).
15. Ehrhart, W.D., *Beautiful Wreckage: New & Selected Poems* (Easthampton, MA: Adastra Press, 1999), 87–88.
16. Ehrhart, W.D., *Ordinary Lives: Platoon 1005 and the Vietnam War* (Philadelphia, PA: Temple University Press, 1999).
17. Ehrhart, *Ordinary Lives*, 72.
18. Ibid., 89.
19. Ibid., 39.
20. Ibid., 50.
21. Ehrhart, *Beautiful Wreckage*, 159.
22. Balaban, *Locusts*, 103–105.
23. Ehrhart, *Beautiful Wreckage*, 131.
24. Ibid., 114–116.
25. Ibid., 153–154.

W.D. Ehrhart and Chimei Hamada: War Memories of a Poet and of a Print Artist

Yoko Shirai

When a piece of poetry touches a reader's heartstrings, the poetry may lead the reader to a pictorial scene of its imaginary world. W.D. Ehrhart's "Making the Children Behave" evoked such a scene for me when I read it for the first time. It fully awoke my imagination of a rural community and its people, in Vietnam during the war: American soldiers are passing through a throng of villagers; wide-eyed children are gazing at stern strangers as if they are devils from hell; and the elderly people behind the children whisper in their ears, "Look at those monsters carefully. If you don't behave yourselves, they will take you away from home." Here, Ehrhart, himself a former soldier who once acted in a capacity similar to that of the strangers he depicts, identifies with the feelings of the villagers, particularly as seen by the eye of the Vietnamese children. The poem shows that the soldier-poet, nervously but with strong conviction, is speaking his mind and warning that something is wrong with his side in the war.

In the summer of 2010, I was unexpectedly reminded of Ehrhart's poem "Making the Children Behave" by an exhibition entitled "The World of HAMADA Chimei: Elegy and Humor in Prints and Sculptures" at the Museum of Modern Art Hayama in Kanagawa, Japan. Chimei Hamada is a world-renowned artist for his masterpiece series "Elegy for a New Conscript," which was based on his experience of war in China in the first half of the 1940s. The exhibition contained well over 300 prints and sculptures, and as I passed through the very last section of the display, I found myself transfixed by two sketches of a child's face; these drawings were entitled "Unforgettable Face A and B." Hamada's two "Faces," simply drawn in pencil and ball-point pen, acutely expressed the horror of war and the truth of

Chimei Hamada, "Unforgettable Face A 2008" (The Museum of Modern Arts, Hayama; photo by Kempachi Fujimoto).

war. At the same time those two sketches instantaneously reminded me of W. D. Ehrhart's "Making the Children Behave." Both the sketches and the poem are based on their creators' harsh experiences of war at different times and different places, but these works tell the truth of war through the eyes of the children who reside near battlefields. As I stood in the museum, Hamada's "Faces" became unforgettably entwined with Ehrhart's "Making the Children Behave."

> Do they think of me now
> in those strange Asian villages
> where nothing ever seemed
> quite human
> but myself
> and my few grim friends
> moving through them
> hunched
> in lines?
>
> When they tell stories to their children
> of the evil
> that awaits misbehavior,
> is it me they conjure?[1]

Chimei Hamada, "Unforgettable Face B 2008" (The Museum of Modern Arts, Hayama; photo by Kempachi Fujimoto).

Hamada's "Unforgettable Faces" were drawn in 2008, and are his most recent works, together with two other sketches entitled "Marching in the Night: Rain" and "Marching in the Night: Artillery Soldiers Marching through Mountains." He did these latter sketches based on his war memories of early 1940s China. People who are familiar with Hamada's work might have been amazed to see these sketches of scenes from the Sino-Japanese War at the exhibition in 2010 since his series of prints "Elegy for a New Conscript" (along with some other related prints) have been considered his definitive depiction of war, and it was understood that he had moved away from the war to different themes.[2]

The artist is ninety-six years old now but he still keeps trying to convey what the war did to Chinese people. It is amazing that a maestro of print and sculpture, more than half a century after publishing his masterpiece series of war landscapes in China, and almost seventy years after his experience in the battlefield, has shown us his memory of war through the eyes of a Chinese girl in small pieces of simply drawn sketches.

Hamada explains the background for the "Unforgettable Faces" as follows: It was May and June of 1941 at the Battle of Chugen in Northern China between the Japanese Army and the Chinese. One day after an important victory the Japanese regiment took a rest near a local village. Hamada and a fellow soldier walked around and went up the terraced ricefields. He recalled, "There was a house and a young girl with her mother who watched us through the window. The girl, although her face was sooty, looked very young. When they found us, they were seized with fear...." His fellow soldier broke into the house despite Hamada's plea that he should not do that. After a while he came out of the house grinning and pulling up his trousers. Hamada instantly understood what had happened in the house. "I wanted to kill the fellow who had acted so brutally," he writes. The Unforgettable Face A is her "expression of terror" when she found the Japanese soldiers coming into her village, says Hamada.³

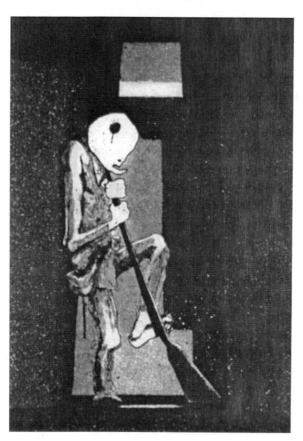

Chimei Hamada, "Elegy for a New Conscript: Sentinel 1954" (Property of Museum of Modern Art, Hayama).

Chimei Hamada was born in December of 1917 in Kumamoto, Japan. Upon his graduation from Tokyo Art School (present-day Tokyo National University of Fine Arts and Music) in 1939, he was drafted into the Army, into the Kumamoto 13th Infantry Regiment. In early 1940 he was sent to the front in the northern part of China and there he went through the training regime for new conscripts. He recalls feeling as if he were enclosed by invisible iron bars without a ray of sunshine, and he survived the daily military training only by thinking about committing suicide. Hamada actually produced two prints depicting a new conscript committing suicide: "Legend of a Latrine 1951" and "Sentinel 1954." Hamada said:

> I was hit hard everyday [by soldiers who had served longer than me.] It was only in the latrine and at night on sentry duty that I could feel at ease. I knew that the Japanese Army committed a tremendous number of atrocities in China such as burglary, rape, setting fire to the houses in villages, and massacres.... In the loess zone there were corpses of men and women stripped off of their clothes and revealing even their private parts against the sky. There were throngs of Chinese soldiers made prisoners and forced to march in the lines of Japanese soldiers....
>
> I kept thinking that I would draw those scenes and the tears of the miserable new conscripts when I was discharged from the military service. As an artist I pursued beauty and formative arts, but first of all I thought I should draw the unjustness and outrageousness of war and of the inhuman military. Human beings, once enrolled in the military, could behave as brutally as demons.[4]

He had spent a total of five years in the army by the end of World War II.

After the war Hamada tried to find an artistic technique to represent what he had seen and encountered in China, and he finally and firmly became convinced that etching was the best medium. In the first half of the 1950s Hamada devoted himself to producing etching prints of various war landscapes one after another. His prints in "Elegy for a New Conscript" express the sorrow of a young soldier and his sympathy with the Chinese people. He recalled later: "My starting point, as an artist, is in my experience of war. Since I belonged to an army that was full of brutality and I indescribably hated its barbarity, I was able to acquire a critical mindset towards the military. So maybe I should be thankful to the war for opening my eyes fully as an artist."[5]

In contrast to Hamada's experience of being conscripted into the army and sent to China against his will, W. D. Ehrhart voluntarily joined the U.S. Marine Corps upon finishing high school and went to Vietnam out of a feeling of great patriotism in early 1967. He had no doubts about what he was doing, but rather believed that he would fight against communism on behalf of the Vietnamese people and his own country. However, his poem "Making the Children Behave" shows the contrast between the insights of the poet and the mindset of a gung-ho U.S. Marine. Here, in a sketch-like poem of only forty-eight words, Ehrhart conveys the scene of American soldiers moving among the villagers. The soldiers are "hunched in lines" with grim faces, but they look somehow uncomfortable among the native Vietnamese people. The soldier Ehrhart, as depicted in the poem, seems to be calm and humble enough to observe himself as one of the invading soldiers from an outside perspective, and to be lucid enough to imagine what he and his fellow soldiers look like to Vietnamese villagers, and, especially, to the villagers' children.

Ehrhart wrote "Making the Children Behave" in the year the war ended, seven years after his return from Vietnam in 1968. His experience of war in Vietnam is vividly conveyed in the first volume of his autobiographic memoirs *Vietnam–Perkasie: A Combat Marine Memoir* (1983). Although he didn't have enough knowledge about Vietnam and its people when he arrived there, Ehrhart's inherent sensitivity was directed immediately and fully towards the country and the Vietnamese. One of his earliest poems "Viet Nam-February 1967" compiled in *Winning Hearts and Minds: War Poems by Vietnam Veterans* (1972), not only describes the rural landscape of a rice-producing country in Southeastern Asia, but also observes the people and their life amidst the roaring sounds of battle.

> ...
> Thundering roar of aircraft on the prowl,
> Roads clogged with troops and trucks,
> Distant growl of artillery,
> Crackling whine of small arms.
> Ramshackle buses crammed with people,
> Bamboo huts with straw-thatched roofs,
> Women bearing baskets from the markets;
> A ragged child stares at passing soldiers.[6]

The last line tells us that the poet's eyes keenly discern a poor child in the street gazing at passing American soldiers. The description of the child makes readers imagine what the war brought to children in Vietnam in a variety of ways.

When he returns to his role in the battlefield, however, the poet's warm view of the native child naturally turns to that of a combatant. He does not regard the Vietnamese enemy as enemies, or even as human beings. He writes in "Full Moon":

> We were on patrol last night;
> And as we moved along,
> We came upon one of the enemy.
>
> Strange, in the bright moon
> He did not seem an enemy at all.
> He had arms and legs, a head...
>
> ... and a rifle.
> I shot him.[7]

In "Hunting," Ehrhart depicts shooting a Vietnamese enemy as a form of hunting, as if he chased and aimed at wild game.

>   ...
>   The thought occurs
>   That I have never hunted anything in my whole life
>   Except other men.
>   ....[8]

Having described Vietnamese enemies without showing any of his feelings in the poems above, Ehrhart felt uneasy when he saw Vietnamese detainees for the first time at the battalion compound northwest of Hoi An. He was only a newcomer in Vietnam but he was deeply disturbed at finding civilians, who were not even prisoners, treated brutally by the U.S. Marines. Most of them were old men and women, and some were younger women with small children. Their hands and feet were all bound with wire. The Americans called this the County Fair to pick up Vietcong suspects and their sympathizers in the bunch of detainees.[9]

Children always caught Ehrhart's attention in Vietnam. One day on the way to Dien Ban his jeep was stalled after ramming into a rice paddy. While Ehrhart and his senior soldier were waiting for help, he noticed a boy in the rice-field. Ehrhart felt something strange, as if the boy was watching the two Americans carefully:

> I felt like a naked man as we stood on the open road, bare fields on either side laced with paddy dikes, treelines within sniping range beyond them, and a kid on a water buffalo in the middle of one of the fields suspiciously pretending to ignore us.[10]

And when he was patrolling with scouts, he often noted the expressions on the faces of the farmers or women carrying big basket of produce on their heads. He writes, "They ignored us for the most part, the deep untouchable silence of their almond eyes causing my stomach to tighten."[11] It had not been long since Ehrhart had arrived in Vietnam. Since he had no doubt that he had come to Vietnam to fight for the Vietnamese against the aggression of communism, he could not understand why he was being ignored by them. But their pretense of ignorance sometimes and suddenly revealed violent hostility against American soldiers. One time in Hoi An a boy less than ten years old tried to flip a grenade into the jeep Ehrhart and his fellow Marine were driving. The grenade missed but killed some civilians instead.[12] He knew later that the war in Vietnam was a guerrilla war and that old men and women and even children could possibly be enemies of the U.S. soldiers. He writes in "Guerrilla War":

>   It's practically impossible
>   to tell civilians
>   from the Viet Cong.

> Nobody wears uniforms.
> They all talk
> the same language
> (and you couldn't understand them
> even if they didn't).
>
> They tape grenades
> inside their clothes,
> and carry satchel charges
> in their market baskets.
> Even their women fight.
> And young boys.
> And girls.
>
> It's practically impossible
> to tell civilians
> from the Viet Cong.
>
> After awhile
> you quit trying.[13]

Here, the poem is written in a dry and cynical tone that reflects the poet's honest amazement at the Vietnamese people's strong will to fight against their enemies. Ehrhart realizes that guerrilla war is a total war, a people's war in Vietnam. He writes in "Christ":

> I saw the Crucified Christ three days ago.
> He did not hang upon The Cross;
> But lay instead on a shambled terrace
> Of what had been a house.
> There were no nails in His limbs;
> No crown of thorns, no spear wounds.
> The soldiers had left nothing
> But a small black hole upon His cheek.
> And He did not cry: "Forgive them, Lord";
> But only lay there, gazing at an ashen sky.
>
> Today on the Resurrection,
> Angelic hosts of flies caress His brow;
> And from His swollen body comes
> The sweet-sick stench of rotting flesh—
> Three days old.[14]

"Christ" here seems to be a Vietcong guerrilla. The cool eyes of the poet on the weather-beaten corpse, however, never seem to be virulent nor indifferent, but rather hint at some sympathy with their "Lord."

It was Staff Sergeant Trinh, the interpreter of the Army of the Republic of Vietnam attached to the battalion Ehrhart belonged to, who gave him a hard time and caused him to think about the war and himself. From the moment that Ehrhart noticed Trinh's "deep burning eyes set in an expressionless face" focused on him during the brutal interrogation of an old man by a merciless U.S. Sergeant, he felt uneasy, as if Trinh's eyes had penetrated deep inside his vague skepticism about the meaning of the war: "You Americans come here with tanks and your jets and your helicopters, and everywhere you go, the vc grow like new rice in the fields. You do not understand Vietnam. You have never bothered to understand us, and you never will bother because you have all the answers."[15]

When Ehrhart tried to explain to him that he came to Vietnam not as a draftee, but as a volunteer who wanted to help the Vietnamese, Trinh answered back sharply:

> I did not ask you for anything! ... you take the people from the land where their ancestors are buried and put them in tin cages where they cannot fish or grow rice or do anything but hate and die—and if they do not want to leave the bones of their ancestors, you call them communists and beat them and put them in prison and kill them. You Americans are worse than the vc.[16]

Because of Ehrhart's sensitivity and humility, he ultimately faced Trinh's words, and repeatedly asked himself what the war was for.

Considering that Ehrhart's early poems were written after his return to America, which he thought of as no longer his home, writing his poems meant struggling with the nightmares of traumatic war memories, and with his country which had sent its sons and daughters to fight against the Vietnamese. His "A Relative Thing," also written at this time, was the voice of young soldiers' grief and agony over the war:

> We are the ones you sent to fight a war
> you didn't know a thing about.
>
> It didn't take us long to realize
> the only land that we controlled
> was covered by the bottoms of our boots.
>
> When the newsmen said that naval ships
> had shelled a VC staging point,
> we saw a breastless woman
> and her stillborn child.
>
> We laughed at old men stumbling
> in the dust in frenzied terror
> to avoid our three-ton trucks.
>
> ...
>
> We have been Democracy on Zippo raids,
> burning houses to the ground,
> driving eager amtracs through new-sown fields.

> We are the ones who have to live
> with the memory that we were the instruments
> of your pigeon-breasted fantasies.
> We are inextricable accomplices
> in this travesty of dreams:
> but we are not alone.
> ....[17]

The poem suggests that young soldiers' grievances and agony were deeply rooted in American arrogance and ignorance toward Vietnam and its people. It might be that turning his eyes toward others made the poet overcome his traumatic memories of war, and face what the war did to the Vietnamese. His imagination regarding the Vietnamese, at the same time, made it possible for him to see the war through the eyes of children. "Making the Children Behave" was what resulted from Ehrhart's view of the war in Vietnam after all the painful struggling with his "Vietnam."

Both Hamada's "Unforgettable Faces" and Ehrhart's "Making the Children Behave" clearly show their views of the wars their creators had fought. Both the print artist and the poet struggled to express the images of the wars that they maintained in their minds. Hamada pursued "poetic expression"[18] by creating a simple world in black and white; Ehrhart visualized his new perspective of the war in his pictorial world of poetry. Both artists exclusively followed their sensitivity and inner voices. Hamada's art reminded me of Ehrhart's poem, and this was no coincidence. What seemed coincidental at first actually confirmed that their art, based on their own harsh experiences of war, captured the universal truth of war by depicting war through the eyes of children. The poetic drawings and the sketch-like poem simply convey their creators' experience of war at different times and in different places.

Notes

1. Ehrhart, W.D., *Beautiful Wreckage: New & Selected Poems* (Easthampton; MA., Adastra Press, 1999, 3rd printing, 2005), 15.
2. Kikuhata, Mokuma, "Ippeisotsu no Sengo" (A Soldier after World War II) *Mizue* no. 904 (July 1980), 43–51; Hidefumi Hashi, "Hamada Chimei" *The World of HAMADA Chimei: Elegy and Humor in Prints and Sculptures* (The Museum of Modern Art, Kamakura & Hayama, 2010), 10–13.
3. *Mainichi Newspaper* August 16, 2011; Interview by Shirai 27 March 2012.
4. Yoshida, Hiroshi, *HAMADA Chimei: Oral History* (Nishinihon Shimbun, Co., 1996), 13.
5. Ibid., 21.
6. Rottmann, Larry, Jan Barry, and Basil T. Paquet, eds., *Winning Hearts and Minds: War Poems by Vietnam Veterans* (Brooklyn, NY: 1st Casualty Press, 1972), 5.
7. Ibid., 14.
8. Ibid., 33.

9. Ehrhart, W.D., *Vietnam-Perkasie: A Combat Marine Memoir* (Jefferson, NC: McFarland, 1995), 25.
10. Ibid., 29.
11. Ibid., 47.
12. Ibid., 56.
13. Ehrhart, *Beautiful Wreckage*, 5.
14. Rottmann, *Winning Hearts and Minds*, 38.
15. Ehrhart, *Vietnam-Perkasie*, 148.
16. Ibid.
17. Ehrhart, *Beautiful Wreckage*, 9–10.
18. Takahama, Sugako, and Masafumi Sakamoto, eds., *Chimei Hamada: Prints and Sculptures "What Is Human Being?"* (Kumamoto: Kumamoto Prefectural Museum of Art, 2001), 31, 39.

The Poetry of W. D. Ehrhart: A Bibliographic Essay

N. Bradley Christie

> "I show my poems to friends now and then..."
> —*To Maynard on the Long Road Home* (1977)
>
> "I write poems you admire."
> —*A Confirmation* (1978)

Among the most admired, if not the most lauded or renowned, W. D. Ehrhart may be the most prolific American Vietnam veteran author. Since first emerging as the "dean" of Vietnam veteran soldier-poets, Ehrhart has published extensively in nearly every genre but long-form fiction or drama. This range of material and its import have been addressed in hundreds of conference papers, scholarly articles, and doctoral dissertation or monograph chapters; yet no comprehensive descriptive bibliography of Ehrhart's output has been compiled. Indeed, as he continues to produce, such a task looms large and must necessarily remain unfinished, hopefully for some time to come. Meanwhile, scholars and general readers may benefit from a glimpse of such a comprehensive project and its potential, which the following pages aim to provide by focusing on the poetry—more specifically, self-contained volumes and anthologized groupings of W. D. Ehrhart's poems from the early 1970s to the present. Each volume is described in general, with key representative poems described critically and contextually.[1]

The Emerging Voice

- **Rottmann, Larry, Jan Barry, and Basil T. Paquet, eds. *Winning Hearts and Minds: War Poems by Vietnam Veterans*. Brooklyn: 1st Casualty, 1972.**

In a 1996 interview W. D. Ehrhart admitted that when he first began figuring out how to write about his Vietnam experience, he lacked his own poetic voice.[2] But over two years at Swarthmore College that voice emerged and began to sound clearly for the first time in the eight poems included in *Winning Hearts and Minds: War Poems by Vietnam Veterans* (*WHAM*).

Several of the poems Ehrhart contributed to this first anthology of its kind—including "One Night on Guard Duty," "Hunting," and "Christ"—reappear often in later volumes. Three of these first poems, however, never resurface in later collections. Typical of these three, "Viet Nam—February 1967" is plodding and almost imagistic in its starkness, standing in marked contrast with later, increasingly narrative poems. Similarly, the second poem to appear only in *WHAM*, "Full Moon," depicts the reality of killing in war rather like a verbal snapshot of one such event. "[I]n the bright moon" of the title, "one of the enemy" is frozen in space and time. "He had arms and legs, a head... / ...and a rifle." "I shot him," the speaker tells us, as if merely clicking the shutter to render this image permanent (ll. 6–8). Finally, "Fragment: 5 September 1967" employs longer lines and imagery reminiscent of First World War influences and thus less reflective of any vivid, authentic war experience of Ehrhart's own. Nonetheless, "Fragment: The Generals' War," "Hunting," and "Christ" contain internal commentary that prefigures Ehrhart's later, more multi-layered poems. Even "Full Moon" steers inward for one line: "He did not seem an enemy at all" (l. 5).

- *A Generation of Peace*. New York: New Voices, 1975.
- *A Generation of Peace*. SAMISDAT, 1977. *Samisdat* 14.3 (chapbook).

Between *Winning Hearts and Minds* and his first self-contained volume of poetry in 1975, the also ironically titled *A Generation of Peace*, Ehrhart seems to have fully developed his poetic voice. Only two years after the 1975 publication of *Generation*, *Samisdat* editor Merritt Clifton published a chapbook edition of the same volume, containing the twenty-eight selections from the 1975 hardback and four additional Vietnam-related poems.

Both volumes include "Farmer Nguyen" and "Guerrilla War," which comment on the ambiguous, painfully blurred lines of a war fought largely by Vietnamese civilians. Other poems, such as "The One Who Died" (editorially corrected from "The One *That* Died" in the 1975 text[3]) and "Night Patrol," also paint the harsh realities of war in jarring shades of grey. The speaker of the former, for instance, observes in first person plural that the one who died "could too easily take our place / for us to think about him / any longer than it takes / to sort his personal effects": (ll. 3–6). The list that follows—"a pack of letters, / some cigarettes, / photos and a wallet"—recall the stark imagism of Ehrhart's earliest verses. But the edgy closing lines are more nuanced:

> We'll keep the cigarettes,
> divide them up among us.
> His parents have no use for them,
> and cigarettes are hard to get [ll. 10–13].

The whole poem happens in real time; that is, about the same time as the action it describes, rifling through a dead comrade's effects while trying not to think about him as a person, or trying not to think about him as a stand-in for oneself. In two other poems, "Time on Target" and "Hunting" (one of Ehrhart's most frequently anthologized texts), the poet powerfully foregrounds the dehumanizing effects of war on all its participants. He also underscores a characteristic distinction between the perspective of those whose jobs distanced them from the war's worst brutality, and the foot soldiers in the jungles and rice paddies who daily came into contact with the vivid, awful consequences of their actions.

Following the first section of twenty-eight Vietnam War poems in the 1975 *Generation of Peace* is a section of twelve Other Poems. Main themes among these jejune verses are the bonds of friendship, the mutability of the world, and the pangs of disillusionment. For the most part, these Other Poems read like they were written by the college student Ehrhart was when he first composed them. Few appear in later volumes, even in the 1977 *Samisdat* chapbook.

The Emerging Editor

- **Barry, Jan, and W. D. Ehrhart, eds.** *Demilitarized Zones: Veterans after Vietnam.* Perkasie, PA: East River Anthology, 1976.

Barely a year after the 1975 publication of *A Generation of Peace*, Ehrhart contributed some of the same poems to a second landmark anthology of Vietnam War poetry, this time as a co-editor, with a fellow veteran and friend, Jan Barry. *Demilitarized Zones: Veterans after Vietnam* (*DMZ*) contains ten Ehrhart poems which, although interspersed throughout the volume, flow in a loose chronology from the trope of the veteran's return home and the slow penetration of aching disillusionment to a public indictment of the American people and a trenchant plea for change. *DMZ* is interesting in part because it discloses Ehrhart's evaluation of his early output: he selected none of the poems from *Winning Hearts and Minds* and only four from *Generation* (1975)—and two of those he revised.

The revised poems, "Coming Home" (eventually titled "Coming Home, March 1968" in the 1977 *Generation* chapbook) and "Imagine," appeared first in *DMZ*. The speaker of the latter poem, presumably the poet himself, proceeds to imagine the frightening tales that Vietnamese villagers might tell of him and his "few green friends" (l. 6) as a means of disciplining naughty children in "Making the Children Behave," a poem of which Ehrhart has remarked: "If I'm lucky enough to have one poem outlive me, I won't mind if it's this one."[4] Many pages later, Ehrhart voices a chilling indictment of the American people in "A Relative Thing," unchanged from its appearance in *A Generation of Peace* (1975), except for a single word ("Local" in the phrase "the wives of Local 104"), which was likely a simple omission in the original. This pointed poem introduces what would become a recurring theme: the culpability of all involved in the war, whether directly as soldiers or indirectly as the ones sending them.

This set of poems ends with one of Ehrhart's finest, "To Those Who Have Gone Home Tired." Chosen to close the *DMZ* anthology, "Tired" employs that most traditional of poetic devices, the catalogue, in this case a litany of injustices perpetrated by mankind, not all of them in war. The final lines pose this mini-catalogue of troubling questions: "What answers will you find / What armor will protect you / When your children ask you / Why?" Thus, by putting a summary question about injustice, violence, and poverty in the mouths of children, Ehrhart lays universal ills at the reader's feet and issues a direct, personal challenge not only to answer but to act.

The *Samisdat* Chapbooks

- *Rootless*. SAMISDAT, 1977. *Samisdat* 14.2 (chapbook).
- *Empire*. SAMISDAT, 1978. *Samisdat* 17.3 (chapbook).

In addition to *A Generation of Peace* (1977), Ehrhart published two other early chapbooks with Merritt Clifton's support at Samisdat: *Rootless*, also in 1977, and *Empire* in 1978. Of the twenty-four poems in *Rootless*, only two—"The Obsession" and "To Those Who Have Gone Home Tired"—were not new.[5] Ehrhart changed only the capitalization of words at the beginning of lines for these poems' second appearance. In any event, none of the other twenty-two poems in *Rootless* are explicitly Vietnam poems. The dominant themes of this collection are lost love, concern for the preservation of nature, and the haunted life. Several poems (such as "At Last" and "Wanting") deal with seeking fulfillment in romantic relationships and are poignant accounts of lost loves, while the final poem, "Granddad," evinces a young boy's pride in knowing that he is like his grandfather. Appreciation of and concern for nature are expressed in "Colorado, June 1976" and "The Death of Kings." In yet another direction, "Money in the Bank," muses on the plight of the artist in an increasingly mechanized and utilitarian age.

In several ways the 1978 chapbook *Empire* is Ehrhart's most varied early collection. All twenty-four poems in the volume were new, though their topics by now are familiar: family; revels in (disappearing) nature; love, lost and found; aging; loneliness; spiritual renewal; and war. *Empire* contains formal variety, too, including two poems based on original texts by Hungarian poet Gyorgy Faludy. Several others are considerably longer than most Ehrhart poems, including the title poem, which appears in five numbered sections, and the closing poem, "A Confirmation," one of four new Vietnam poems. Another longer poem, "Twodot, Montana," employs longer free verse lines than Ehrhart's usual, reading almost like a lineated prose paragraph and looking more like a poem by Whitman or Ginsburg.

The best of the new Vietnam poems in *Empire* is "A Confirmation." Here the speaker goes camping with Gerry Gaffney, "a good friend in a bad time [Vietnam, 1967]" (subtitle). Through most of the poem, like Hemingway's Nick Adams returning to the Big Two-Heart, these two veterans pitch a tent "in the perfect stillness of the shadows / of the Klamath Indians" (ll. 7–8, 41–42, 81–82); they cook from cans over a campfire, and "test [their] / bonds and find them, after all / these years, still sound..." (ll. 82–84). Best of all, they fish "the wild waters of the Upper Umqua" (l. 3). With guidance the narrator catches a fourteen-inch rainbow trout, which he releases back into the life-renewing waters. "[I]n the awkward silence ... you / slip your arm around my shoulders / gently for a moment, knowing why" (ll. 65–67). That awkward silence is the crucible of the veterans' brotherhood. In the end that "perfect stillness" pervades this poem, also health and cleansing worship.

In "Letter" Ehrhart extends this sense of kinship to his former enemy, a North Vietnamese soldier "whose life crossed paths with mine in Hue, February 5th, 1968" (subtitle). It is fascinating to see a former foe here associated with a lifelong "good friend" like Gaffney. Neither man will the poet likely see again, but "once is enough" ("Confirmation" l. 102) in both cases. Both of these comrades are figured as lively, active participants in life after war; both are portrayed as fathers; and both are urged to celebrate "communion," particularly in nature. For the poet himself, the other party in both of these abiding relationships, "Letter" makes a concluding plea and a final association that in 1978 would still have shocked many: "Remember Ho Chi Minh / was a poet: please / do not let it all / come down to nothing" (ll. 36–39).

The First Reprints

- *The Samisdat Poems of W. D. Ehrhart.* **SAMISDAT, 1980.** *Samisdat* **24.1 (chapbook).**
- *The Awkward Silence.* **Stafford, VA: Northwoods, 1980.**

By 1980 W. D. Ehrhart had published some one hundred poems, many debuting singly or in small groupings in diverse literary papers and magazines with titles like *Halcyon*, *Wind*, and *Front'n Center*. These first appearances need to be compiled and catalogued, but many more poems initially appeared in the edited volumes and chapbooks described above. After a decade of serious writing and plenty of experience with various publishers, Ehrhart sought to expand the reach of his work and secure his reputation as a didactic poet by releasing reprints of his output to date. Merritt Clifton again accommodated by reprinting the contents of *A Generation of Peace*, *Rootless*, and *Empire* complete, with thirteen additional new poems, as *The Samisdat Poems of W.D. Ehrhart* (1980). For the most part the new poems are "civilian" verses, though, as in the other *Samisdat* volumes, such works often reverberate with echoes from the Indochina war. In the poem most overtly related to Vietnam, "The Teacher," Ehrhart explains to his high school students why he has sworn to teach them "all I know— / and I know things / worth knowing" (ll. 27–29). It all goes back to things he learned when he was "Hardly older then / than you are now" (ll. 8–9). Though the speaker's job is new to the poetry, the driving idea is already vintage Ehrhart: the veteran possesses a sacred trust, a fixed purpose of teaching the next generation what they need to know to avoid the mistakes of earlier ones. The theme is frequent in Ehrhart's work, as is the pattern of vacillating between stages of passionate drive to impart truth and jaded frustration over the seeming futility of such a task.

A second 1980 reprint volume, *The Awkward Silence*, compiles poems from early volumes divided into the sections "Winning Hearts and Minds" and "Demilitarized Zones." Despite what the headings might imply, only five poems in the first section appeared in the 1972 anthology *Winning Hearts and Minds*; the majority come from "The Vietnam War" section (I) of the 1975 *A Generation of Peace*. Similarly, The *DMZ* section of *The Awkward Silence* includes only four poems that originally appeared in the 1976 anthology that Ehrhart co-edited. Other selections here include four more poems from *Generation* and several from *Rootless* and *Empire*. Clearly, Ehrhart's choices for these first reprint volumes suggest which poems he viewed early as most effective and enduring.[6]

The 1980s and 1990s: New Materials

- *Matters of the Heart*. Easthampton, MA: Adastra, 1981. (chapbook)
- *Channel Fever*. With *In the Restaurant* by Jeptha Evans, and *Skunk Missal* by Kraft Rompf. New York: Backstreet Editions, 1982.
- *To Those Who Have Gone Home Tired: New & Selected Poems*. New York & Chicago: Thunder's Mouth Press, 1984.
- *The Outer Banks & Other Poems*. Easthampton, MA: Adastra, 1984.
- *Winter Bells*. Easthampton, MA: Adastra, 1988. (chapbook)

- *Just for Laughs: Poems by W.D. Ehrhart*. Silver Spring, MD: Vietnam Generation Inc. & Burning Cities Press, 1990.
- *The Distance We Travel*. Easthampton, MA: Adastra, 1993.
- "Mostly Nothing Happens." Easthampton, MA: Adastra, 1996. (chapbook)
- *Beautiful Wreckage: New & Selected Poems*. Easthampton, MA: Adastra, 1999.

In 1979 Gary Metras, a teacher and poet from Easthampton, Massachusetts, founded an old-school letterpress with the singular purpose of publishing "short collections of quality contemporary poetry using the methods and equipment of the antique book arts."[7] By 1981 Metras and Bill Ehrhart had found each other, and a mutually beneficial, long-term relationship began with the publication of *Matters of the Heart*. This would prove to be only the first of many volumes of Ehrhart's poems produced by Adastra Press. *Matters of the Heart* is an elegant chapbook of ten poems, all of them new, and all exemplifying the poet's growing preference for more narrative verses. As a group these poems give new voice to a favorite Ehrhart theme: a call to stand against the tide and to speak the truth regardless of the personal hardship and difficulty that may result.

In the title poem, Ehrhart dialogues with Tom and Jim, products of the World War II generation; he explains to them with bitter frustration that faith in man's essential goodness simply cannot hold up "In the age of the MX missile and the Trident / nuclear submarine and the 20-megaton bomb / multiplied by a couple of thousand or so..." (ll. 22–24).[8] Other poems, such as "The Eruption of Mount St. Helens" and "Near-sighted," expound other familiar themes of concern for the preservation of nature and fear that the swifter erosion of life by means of war will allow nothing to survive but "a dark cold lump / whirling through the silence / between the stars..." (ll. 19–21). Despite the soberness of tone and much of the content of this book, human lives and words, like those of Tom and Jim—and the steady resolve of Nature, as witnessed at Rehoboth Bay or Mount St. Helen's—strike a note of encouragement in many poems. "'Don't give in. Go on. Keep on,'" the title poem concludes, "'Resist. Keep on. Go on'" (ll. 49–50).

In 1982 another small letterpress publisher, Backstreet Editions, released Ehrhart's *Channel Fever* with two other slender collections by other poets in a single-volume edition limited to 526 copies. "The Obsession" reappears here revised from *DMZ* and *Rootless*; also from the latter chapbook "Rootless" itself, "Geese," and "Death Wish" significantly revised for *Channel Fever* as the opening poem, "The Hunter." One poem, "Growing Older Alone," is considerably revised from its first appearance in *Empire*.[9] Several new poems—including "Meeting," "Shadows," and "After the Fire"—render verbal snapshots of sensations or freeze-frame moments in the imagist style of Ehrhart's earliest work.

Each of these new poems also figures a couple—the speaker (Ehrhart) and a woman each time associated with his dreams, a woman he comes to love deeply. The titular poem, for example, depicts a solitary man adrift at sea, fighting for survival and a safe passage. He is sometimes accompanied by dolphins, whose laughing song for a time he imagined he was following (ll. 18–21). In the end, though, he reaches the shore guided by

> ...your
> invisible hand on the tiller, your
> breath drawing my small boat steadily on:
> your lips open to greet me, your thighs
> open to anchor me, your heart waits
> to secure me in the harbor
> shaped like a heart. It was you.
> It is your song I heard [ll. 32–39].

In sum, most of these poems are tributes to Ehrhart's wife, Anne, whom he married in 1981. *Channel Fever* closes with "Why I Am Certain," a touching poem that describes a love deeper and fuller than the "sudden surge of tangible joy" (l. 5) "or the absence of fear" (l. 6) he once associated with meaningful relationship. Rather, he finds healing and lasting contentment in sharing the simple things of daily life with someone he loves.

At least one reviewer, writing for the *Small Press Review*, noted that "Ehrhart is a lover.... Each of his poems is informed by landscape and by dreams, and by a passion for authentic relationship, a healing of a wound that we call 'Vietnam'...." That excerpt is quoted on the back cover of Ehrhart's second book published by Adastra, the 1984 volume *The Outer Banks and Other Poems*. Another blurb on the same cover remarks that "Nearly all of Ehrhart's poems are narrative," which certainly applies to most of the eighteen poems in *Outer Banks*, all of them new. Even after the passage of almost twenty years, Ehrhart is still hounded by shame and guilt over what happened in Vietnam. Thus, poems such as "Sound Advice" and "The Blizzard of Sixty-Six" convey a sense of disillusionment, sometimes even despair, over the rampant injustice and violence that plague humankind. In another poem, Ehrhart figures himself as a "farmer of dreams" working "soil / guaranteed by poverty to fail" ("The Farmer" ll. 11–12), laboring on in defense of what he sees as right even when no one else listens and the labor seems futile. Reminiscent of "Sound Advice" and the earlier *Samisdat* poem "The Teacher," in "A Warning to My Students," Ehrhart admonishes his charges at the George School not to make the mistake he did of going overseas to "kill / somebody else's enemies / for somebody else's reasons" (ll. 22–24).

Written in November 1981, "Warning" opens by lamenting U.S. Congressional approval for the B-1 bomber (ll. 1–4ff.). A few other poems in *The Outer Banks* pointedly reference events in Central America in the early 1980s. "Pagan" is *"for the people of El Salvador"*; "Warning" describes "another / petty upper-class junta" there that "needs American aid / to fight the communists" (ll. 10–13); and in "Responsibility" the happy life of the American dream is juxtaposed with the atrocities abetted by soldiers "in another country to the south" (l. 9).[10] The handful of remaining poems in *The Outer Banks* address familiar themes of love for family, as in "Continuity" and "Everett Dirksen, His Wife, You & Me," and wistful reminiscences of friends who have passed away in "the light that cannot fade…" and "Climbing to Heaven."

1984 also saw Ehrhart's first book-length reprint edition, *To Those Who Have Gone Home Tired: New & Selected Poems*, from Thunder's Mouth Press out of New York. This significant volume includes almost five dozen poems from earlier works—25 poems from *A Generation of Peace* (all but five of the Vietnam poems in the 1975 original); 10 from *Rootless*; 9 from *Empire*; all 8 new pieces from *The Samisdat Poems*; 5 from *Matters of the Heart*; 2 from *Channel Fever* (of only eight new poems in the volume); plus seven New Poems. Most of the reprinted poems appear unchanged or only lightly edited from their earlier versions. The powerful titular poem, for instance, appears exactly as it first did in *Demilitarized Zones*, except for a few lower case letters at the beginnings of some lines and a couple of (missing?) spaces between lines. Here, though—notably, for example, "The One That Died," "Geese," and "After the Fire"—Ehrhart restored early poems to their first, unedited or unrevised forms.

The seven new poems in *Tired* voice some of Ehrhart's preferred themes—a satirical explanation for the proliferation of missiles; a boyhood memory of death; tender experiences with his wife; appreciation for nature; and the relentless cycle of war. The strongest poems here relate indirectly to Vietnam, and most are overtly political. The best of the lot, "The Invasion of Grenada," reflects Ehrhart's ingrained bitterness, born of both service to country and subsequent remonstration. "I didn't want a monument," he still protests (l. 1ff.).

> What I wanted was a simple recognition
> of the limits of our power as a nation
> to inflict our will on others.
> What I wanted was an understanding
> that the world is neither black-and-white
> nor ours.
> What I wanted
> was an end to monuments [ll. 8–15].

Ehrhart's next chapbook, *Winter Bells*, was released by Adastra in 1988. In these twelve new poems, each a story-like vignette, the plain but still trenchant style of the maturing craftsman persists, as do familiar subjects and themes. For example, the titular poem, which opens the collection, recounts the redemptive power of a wife's love for the haunted veteran, much like the woman guiding the sailor home in "Channel Fever." The volume closes with a similar poem, "What Keeps Me Going," that celebrates the healing Ehrhart derives from the sheer innocence of his infant daughter, Leela, born in 1986, who spends "the long night dreaming / darkness into light" (ll. 23–24).[11] Other poems, such as "The Ducks on Wissahickon Creek" and "Water," recall the appreciation of and concern for the natural environment expressed in earlier poems like "Colorado," "A Confirmation," and "The Eruption of Mount St. Helens." Others, namely "*Adoquinas*" and "*Nicaragua Libre*," extend Ehrhart's commentary on U.S. involvement in Central America, where he visited in 1986.

The remaining handful of poems in *Winter Bells* concern more fallout from the Indochina war, all occasioned by a return visit to Vietnam with a pair of fellow veteran writers in 1985, a trip Ehrhart had recounted in his prose memoir *Going Back: An Ex-Marine Returns to Vietnam*.[12] In Vietnam Ehrhart met a Mrs. Nguyen Thi Na in the Cu Chi District and an Amerasian girl, Nguyen Thi My Huong, in Ho Chi Minh City. Each of these acquaintances would show up in poems addressed to them, and these would become among the most anthologized of Ehrhart's works. "We have lost so much, you and I; / it is better to keep things simple." Ehrhart directs these lines to one of his traveling companions in "Last Flight Out from the War Zone" (ll. 11–12), but they apply to all of the survivors he met, American and Vietnamese alike. Mrs. Na will live the rest of her life without any of the five sons she lost in the war, and Nguyen Thi My Huong remains "Twice Betrayed" in "the city that was once called Saigon" (l. 6). But they live on, with their respective losses not only acknowledged but shared, in these simple, lovely poems.

By 1990 the scholarly field of Vietnam studies was burgeoning, one sign of which was the emergence of another kitchen press, Burning Cities, which would publish Ehrhart's next volume that year. *Just for Laughs* appeared as a special issue (Vol. 2, No. 4) of *Vietnam Generation*, a fledgling journal founded in 1988 "to promote and encourage interdisciplinary study of the Vietnam War and the Vietnam War generation" (*Laughs* iv).[13] For a decade or so, Ehrhart was, in effect, the poet laureate of Vietnam Generation, Inc., and *Just for Laughs* is a fitting tribute. The largest self-contained volume of original poetry Ehrhart has published to date, *Laughs* includes all twelve poems from *Winter Bells*, plus thirty-four new poems.

The content is divided into five sections which collectively address a characteristically broad range of subjects, beginning with a Vietnam section. As in *Winter Bells*, the title poem opens the volume. Here the poet recalls himself as a ten-year-old, lighting firecrackers in frogs and once, with three other boys, beating a pregnant water snake to a particularly messy death. "Years later, I volunteered for war, / still oblivious to what I'd done, / or what I was about to do, or why" (ll. 42–44). The next two poems recount episodes in the boonies during the war. The five Vietnam poems from *Winter Bells* follow, all concerning events in 1985; namely, a March flare-up of the POW/MIA controversy, and Ehrhart's return trip to Vietnam that December. The section closes with two new poems from the 1985 trip. In "Second Thoughts" Ehrhart shares a smoke with Nguyen Van Hung, a North Vietnamese veteran who lost one of his arms during the war. Ehrhart rolls a cigarette for each of them; then, "Together we discover what we share: / Hué City. Tet. 1968...." Remarkably, whereas Ehrhart still carries "second thoughts" about the war and his part in it, "like an empty sleeve" (ll. 26–27), the maimed "partner" seems "happy just to share / a cigarette and *lua moi*, the simple joy / of being with an old friend" (ll. 28–30).

Section II includes two new poems for Anne and four about Leela. "A Small Romance" and "Small Song for Daddy" are also notable exercises in form. Not since *Empire* (1978) had Ehrhart published a poem like "A Small Romance," which approximates a kyrielle in form: four quatrains of rhyming couplets in iambic tetrameter, with a refrain. This last element is the most approximate in this poem—Ehrhart is clearly playful with the "two sapphires" plucked first from the sleepy child's eyes, then later from the sleepy father's—but it is good to see him honing his craft and technical skill.

Sections III–V of *Just for Laughs* are less tightly focused. The third section begins with a memory poem recounting a time when the poet nearly lost his life at sea. Two poems recall former lovers; three poems reflect on nature; three others reflect on the nature of poetry: "What You Gave Me," "The Poet as Athlete," and "The Heart of the Poem." More overtly political poems comprise section IV, many of them again responding to events in Central America. "*Adoquinas*" and "*Nicaragua Libre*" reappear from *Winter Bells*; and the new poems "What We're Buying" and "Not Your Problem" extend Ehrhart's scathing critique of U.S. involvement in El Salvador and, by corollary, of the capitalist system that facilitates such involvement. Meanwhile, at home, Ehrhart's Leela is growing up, shown learning to walk in "Chasing Locomotives."

This poem segues nicely into the closing section, where a number of poems expound upon the endless cycle of violence in the world, the soon-to-be-shattered innocence of childhood, and the depth of the bond among veterans. Again there is considerable variety here, in both content and form. In "The Way Light Bends" Ehrhart shows his hand at perfect blank verse in five tercets and a closing quatrain that refrains the opening line, "A kind of blindness, that's what's needed now." The remaining poems include three more about Leela, one for "The Children of Hanoi," and two strong narrative poems for fellow veterans—one who didn't survive ("Song for Leela, Bobby and Me") and one who did ("Unaccustomed Mercies").

Ehrhart returned to Gary Metras's Adastra Press for his next self-contained book, *The Distance We Travel*, published in 1993. An especially lovely letterpress volume, the first edition of only 400 copies nonetheless contains some dozen errata to be corrected in subsequent reprints. Nearly half of these twenty-one new poems and one short prose piece relate to Vietnam—a few as flashbacks ("How It All Comes Back," "Governor Rhodes Keeps His Word"); several as more "snapshots" of another return trip to Vietnam (e.g., "The Lotus Cutters of Hô Tây," "Finding My Old Battalion Command Post"); and several more relating past events in Southeast Asia to current ones in Central America or the Middle East ("More Than You Ever Imagined," "Why the Kurds Die in the Mountains"). And some of these combine with updated pictures of his love for wife and child. The opening poem, "How It All Comes Back," and the closing one, the title poem, both work this way.

In between, several other good poems employ dream references reminiscent of Ehrhart's earliest chapbook pieces. The simple summative poem "For a Coming Extinction" in some ways encapsulates Ehrhart's entire output, at least through the 1980s and '90s.[14] "Vietnam," it begins, "Not a day goes by / without that word on my lips" (ll. 1–2). Leela is here, being tucked in to the punny "rattle of small-arms fire" (l. 3–4). Anne is here, inspiring those same "stillborn dreams of other men" like Bobby Ross, who didn't make it back alive (ll. 5–6). Then, right at the heart of the verse, is Ehrhart's enduring point: "Already / it's become what it never was..." (ll. 11–12). Ironically—or maybe not—this is one of the lines Metras inadvertently misprinted in the limited first edition of *Distance*: he left out the second "it," which renders the line perhaps closer to the poet's true sensibility. Already Vietnam has become what never was—anywhere, at any time—

> heroic, a noble cause. Opportunity
> squandered, chance to learn turned
> inside out by cheap politicians
> and *China Beach*. So many so eager
> so soon for others to die ... [ll. 13–17].

Here are the same callous politicos now turning things inside-out in more recent trouble spots, addressed in so many poems from "*Nicaragua Libre*" to "Guatemala" or "Why the Kurds Die...." Here is the same made-for-television packaging that Ehrhart has excoriated since *WHAM*. Most of all, here is the poet himself. Here is that lone sailor seeking harbor, that solitary resistor refusing to get on the train, who in plain, uncluttered verse insists that these things be remembered. Here is W. D. Ehrhart the teacher of both history and literature, continuing to postpone extinction—his own, and "what was or is, / what might have been and was lost" (ll. 22–23)—with every line he writes.

Ehrhart published two other self-contained works, both with Adastra, before the new millennium. The first, another handsome letterpress chapbook, contains a single poem, his longest to date, "Mostly Nothing Happens" (1996). The 156-line text begins with Ehrhart's internal dialogue as, passing a group of young black men on his way home in the East Mt. Airy section of Philadelphia, he is ashamed that their very presence makes him uneasy. He proceeds to recall the friendship formed on Parris Island between himself and a fellow trainee, a young black man named John Harris. The poet fondly describes how Harris surprised him in many ways, not least by being as scared as he was and by having "a heart so big / I thought that mine would burst" (ll. 59–60).

Now, as he walks down Upsal Street, Ehrhart recalls the reason he moved to an integrated neighborhood in the first place: "because I didn't want a child of mine / to reach the age of seventeen / with no one in her life / who isn't white" (ll. 67–70). But several violent incidents, including a recent break-in attempt at Leela's bedroom window, make him acutely aware of the potential danger in which he places his family by choosing to live where he does. Struggling with the tension, so familiar in Ehrhart's poems, between the reality he knows around him and the reality he knows is possible, the poet decides to seek the advice of his old friend, Harris, only to find his name on the Vietnam Veterans Memorial Wall. The poem ends with characteristic poignancy. Ever idealistic at heart, yet ever frustrated by the brokenness of the world, Ehrhart concludes:

> I don't want to leave this neighborhood.
> I want to think we'll be okay
> if only we can touch the best
> in others and ourselves.
> I still don't keep a gun around
> because I'm through with guns,
> but every day is like a day at war:
> mostly nothing happens,
> but you never know what's waiting
> when or where or how.
> The first black friend I ever had
> died one day when something happened.
> Every day I'm always on patrol [ll. 144–56].

As the 20th century closed out, Adastra published a large compendium of Ehrhart's work under the title *Beautiful Wreckage: New & Selected Poems*

(1999), his first selected works volume since *To Those Who Have Gone Home Tired* fifteen years earlier. In contrast to the 1984 volume, *Wreckage* includes fewer works from the earliest chapbooks: only 8 poems from the original *Generation of Peace* and 2 from the 1977 chapbook; only 4 from *Rootless* (with one, "To Those Who Have Gone Home Tired," misattributed); 8 from *Empire*; 5 from *The Samisdat Poems*; and, most notably, only 2 from *Tired*—the revised "Channel Fever" and "The Invasion of Grenada." But later volumes are much more extensively represented: 14 poems from *The Outer Banks*, including excerpts from the long title poem; 8 from *Winter Bells*; 22 from *Just for Laughs*; 15 from *The Distance We Travel*; and "Mostly Nothing Happens" complete.

Eight poems written between 1988 and 1992 first appeared in various journals and literary reviews but had not been included in one of the earlier self-contained works. Two of these poems express the poet's rekindled love for his dying mother; two others recount dark nights at home long after the war; and "America in the Late 20th Century" echoes the drift of "Mostly Nothing Happens," as Ehrhart concludes that today's world is quite different from the one he grew up in. The three remaining poems in this section present various conclusions about the Vietnam War. "A Vietnamese Bidding Farewell to the Remains of an American," adapted from a Vietnamese poem, makes a gentle companion to "POW/MIA." In "What I know About Myself" Ehrhart addresses another writer friend from the war period, Gloria Emerson, who also spent time in Vietnam and shares Ehrhart's sense of guilt and complicity—"Our hands will never be clean," / she said, "but we must try" (ll. 30–31).

The twenty-four New Poems in the final section of *Beautiful Wreckage* comprise a miscellany of Ehrhart's repeated subjects and themes, if not their finest expressions. Less than a handful of these poems concern Vietnam; the best of these are "Purple Heart," addressed to Ehrhart's good friend and fellow veteran poet, Dave Connolly, recovering from a heart attack; and the volume's title poem, which plays on the perennial question, "What if...?" "What if none of it happened the way I said? / Would it all be a lie? / Would the wreckage be suddenly beautiful? / Would the dead rise up and walk?" (ll. 21–24).

A new Leela poem also exemplifies another feature of many of these last few poems of the 20th century. Until the closing lines, "Dropping Leela Off at School" is written in perfect iambic trimeter; then those final two lines step down, one syllable at a time, to "me"—which is where the poem begins, with another first-person pronoun, "My," referring to Ehrhart himself. Other poems like "Cycling the Rosental," "Nothing Profound," and "Variations on Squam Lake," employ his favorite meter, iambic tetrameter, and his preferred sound device, slant rhyme. These three poems even display various formal rhyme schemes, which Ehrhart seldom practices. In fact, several of these poems feel like practice works, like the poet doing his linguistic exercises while new ideas, or new versions of old ones, percolate.

One striking exception is "Red-tailed Hawks," a poem about a field-trip with Leela and her classmates. They're being kids, "chattering children" full of such "raw exuberance" (ll. 1, 2) that the wonders of a historic site like Mill Grove seem inevitably lost on them, when precisely in the middle of the poem one of them shouts, "'There's a hawk!' And points. / 'There's another!' 'There!' 'Another!' / other children cry: four red-tailed hawks lazily circling, gliding, whirling, wheeling..." (ll. 13–15). The children, of course, are entranced, "so intent, so silent one can almost hear / wings they want to lift them / where the hawks have gone" (ll. 22–24). Poetry like this also lifts readers' spirits. Fortunately for us, this powerful poet has more to say for the 21st century.

The 1980s & 1990s—Edited Anthologies

- *Carrying the Darkness: American Indochina—The Poetry of the Vietnam War.* **New York: Avon, 1985.**
- *Carrying the Darkness: The Poetry of the Vietnam War.* **Lubbock: Texas Tech University Press, 1989. (reprint)**
- *Unaccustomed Mercy: Soldier-Poets of the Vietnam War.* **Lubbock: Texas Tech University Press, 1989.**

During this period Ehrhart also edited two more book-length anthologies of poetry by Vietnam veteran poets, providing for several of them exposure like only Ehrhart and a handful of other peers enjoyed. The publication history of these volumes is complicated, but the essence is that for his memoir *Passing Time*[15] Ehrhart had worked with a senior editor at Avon Books, John Douglas, who also assisted with *Carrying the Darkness*, published by Avon in 1985. The book was poorly proofed and weakly marketed; Ehrhart objected and almost immediately sought to have the rights returned to him for subsequent publication. Before that happened, though, Texas Tech University Press enlisted him to produce another anthology, which became *Unaccustomed Mercy*. As it was being prepared, Avon released the rights to *Carrying the Darkness*, and Texas Tech agreed to publish a corrected reprint edition of *Darkness* and the new second volume, both in 1989.

Among others, Douglas at Avon had urged Ehrhart to include some of his own poems in *Carrying the Darkness*. Thus, fourteen poems appear there: including "Hunting" from *WHAM*, "Farmer Nguyen" and seven others from *A Generation of Peace*; "To Those Who Have Gone Home Tired" (first from *DMZ*) and "The Invasion of Grenada" from *Tired*; "Letter" and "A Confirmation" from *Empire*; and "The Blizzard of Sixty-Six" and "the light that cannot fade..." from *The Outer Banks*. Eight of these same poems appear among the dozen included in *Unaccustomed Mercy*. New to the latter volume are "The Next Step" (replacing "The One That Died" and "Time on Target" in *Darkness*); and "Twice Betrayed," replacing "the light that cannot fade...."

In his Introduction to *Unaccustomed Mercy*, Ehrhart referenced "the vast body of poetry" that this slim volume only narrowly represents (1ff.).[16] He mentions several other veteran poets not included here, as well as other volumes by non-veteran activists and Vietnamese poets. In the late 1990s Ehrhart advised another editor, Phillip Mahony, in compiling an anthology aimed at finally representing all—or at least many more—perspectives on the war. *From Both Sides Now: The Poetry of the Vietnam War and Its Aftermath*[17] includes six Ehrhart poems: 3 early works—"The Next Step," "Guerrilla War," and "Coming Home"; and three more recent—"POW/MIA," "For Mrs. Na" (from *Just for Laughs*), and "Midnight at the Vietnam Veterans Memorial" (*The Distance We Travel*).

Poems for a New Age: 2000–present

- *Greatest Hits: 1970–2000*. Johnstown, OH: Pudding House Publications, 2001. (chapbook, Greatest Hits Series #122)
- *Sleeping with the Dead*. Easthampton, MA: Adastra, 2006. (chapbook)
- *The Bodies Beneath the Table*. Easthampton, MA: Adastra, 2010.

In 2001, Ehrhart was asked to contribute to a series of *Greatest Hits* chapbooks produced by Pudding House Publications. Although considering inclusion in the series "a singular honor, not a punishment,"[18] selecting just twelve poems to represent his extensive body of work proved quite a challenge. In the end, he selected a handful of Vietnam poems, including "Making the Children Behave," "Song for Leela, Bobby, and Me," and "Sleeping with General Chi"; a couple of texts about preserving and appreciating nature ("New Jersey Pine Barrens" and "Red-tailed Hawks"); and several poems about and favored by his family. In this final category, "Last of the Hard-hearted Ladies," "Small Song for Leela," and "A Scientific Treatise for My Wife" reappear. The volume closes with his longest poem, "Mostly Nothing Happens," complete. Ehrhart chose to exclude many of his most anthologized poems because, he remarks, "relatively few scholars, editors, and publishers are familiar with the full range of [his] work," and he hoped to help counterbalance what he sees as an excessive emphasis on his war poems.[19]

After several experiences with other publishers—some of the operations large and a few of the relationships unhappy—Ehrhart returned to Gary Metras at Adastra for his 2006 chapbook, *Sleeping with the Dead*. Another lovely handpress work initially printed in only 390 copies, *Dead* contains eleven new poems clustered by various subjects but all of them, as the title suggests, focused on death. For instance, "All About Death," which personifies Death in some striking ways, is paired with "All About Love," which excoriates "sentimental / Hollywood romance" (ll. 27–28). The next two poems describe visits to very different gravesites. These are followed by two poems—"Home Before Morning" and "Seminar on the Nature of Reality"—addressed to dear friends, Lynda Van Devanter and Tom Deahl, who passed away in 2002. These remembrances, both in strong lines of iambic pentameter, are followed by a third, in which the poet waits all night (with his grumpy cat, Emily Dickinson) for the arrival of another friend who is contemplating suicide.

Here also are Ehrhart's responses to the most signal events marking the first decade of the 21st century: the turn of the new millennium ("What Better Way to Begin"), 9/11 ("Manning the Walls"), and Columbine ("Kosovo," clearly a poem that cuts in more than one direction). The volume closes with the title poem, addressed to a former lover whose welcoming arms temporarily rescued the poet from "all those dead [he] slept with every night" some two decades ago (ll. 12–13).

Ehrhart's most recent book of poetry, *The Bodies Beneath the Table* (2010), contains forty-one poems—thirty new works, plus the eleven selections from *Sleeping with the Dead*. These verses articulate some of Ehrhart's most mature, most elegantly styled musings on life, death, love, and purpose. They also include some of his most autobiographical works since the early chapbooks. "The Secret Lives of Boys" and "The Damage We Do," for example, recall boyhood experiences in a home that appeared idyllic from the outside but was, as the grown speaker explains, in many ways broken, always "crackling with rage" ("Damage," l. 22). Some texts, such as "Burning Leaves," are pervaded by a rather uncharacteristic nostalgia for the past, while several others, such as "Music Lessons" and "Epiphany," express joy over the healing presence of his wife and daughter.

A number of poems express Ehrhart's latest take on other familiar concerns: the abuse of natural resources, U.S. intervention in other countries, and the blindness of the next generation to the lessons of the past. Like many earlier poems, "The Bodies Beneath the Table" conflates such current affairs with a pointedly grotesque and tragic scene Ehrhart witnessed in Vietnam. The volume closes with "Temple Poem," a translation from Japanese, adapted by Ehrhart into six couplets of near-perfect blank verse.

But it is this volume's penultimate poem that, in a way, brings W.D. Ehrhart's journey as a poet full circle. The text, "Turning Sixty," is a slight revision of "Turning Thirty" from the 1980 *Samisdat Poems*; only two words have changed—obviously, "thirty" has (somehow/quickly, "just like that") become "sixty," and the "man" of 1980 has become the "gray-haired man" of 2010 (ll.

27, 30). Against the backdrop of his lingering frustration over the world's indifference to injustice and its unwillingness to listen to the truths he has uncovered, Ehrhart closes this latest volume with winsome lines that reclaim a sort of innocence. In spite of all he has suffered and lost so far, he repackages and republishes a poem that both acknowledges his inability to fully understand the world and exhibits a brand of child-like wonder and appreciation for the beauty in life. As in 1980, he continues to wonder "what causes laughter, why / nations go to war, who paints the startling / colors of the rainbow on a gray vaulted sky / and when I will be old enough / to know" (ll. 34–38). As life continues to settle and he sees himself and others aging, as he fears that he has wasted his life or failed in various ways—poetry abides. It continues to ease and to heal. It continues to teach. It continues to provide a vehicle for the poet's unflagging convictions. It continues to postpone extinction in the face of all the world's ills.

Notes

1. Much supporting research was conducted and an early version of this essay was drafted by Erskine College student Victoria Christine Unthank. For a similar assessment of Ehrhart as the "most important" Vietnam veteran poet, see Don Ringnalda, *Fighting and Writing the Vietnam War* (Jackson: University of Mississippi Press, 1994), 144ff. See also Lorrie Smith's excellent overview, "Resistance and Revision in Poetry by Vietnam War Veterans," in *Fourteen Landing Zones: Approaches to Vietnam War Literature*, ed. Philip K. Jason (Iowa City: University of Iowa Press, 1991), 49–66.

2. Anderson, Donald and Thomas G. Bowie, Jr., interviewers, "A Conversation with W. D. Ehrhart," *War, Literature & the Arts: an International Journal of the Humanities*, 8:2 (Fall/Winter 1996), 154–55.

3. The poem's title was always "The One That Died." Although not grammatically correct, the impersonal pronoun conveys a distance and coldness that Ehrhart wanted. Merritt Clifton at *Samisdat* insisted on "correcting" it, but Ehrhart restored the original title at the first opportunity.

4. Ehrhart, W. D., *Greatest Hits: 1970–2000*. Greatest Hits Series #122 (Johnstown, OH: Pudding House Publications, 2001), 7.

5. In John Newman's seminal bibliography *Vietnam War Literature: An Annotated Bibliography of Imaginative Works about Americans Fighting in Vietnam* (3rd edition, Lanham, MD & London: Scarecrow, 1996) poetry editor Stephen P. Hidalgo describes "To Those Who Have Gone Home Tired" as "one of Ehrhart's most important war poems," appearing in *Rootless* "for the first time," 512. But we have seen that this poem (and "The Obsession") debuted in *Demilitarized Zones*. Hidalgo also miscounts the number of poems in these early chapbooks.

6. Ehrhart utterly dismisses this volume. He twice had to sue the publisher–once in state court, once in federal court–over copyright infringement.

7. "Adastra Press," *Poets & Writers*. *Poets & Writers Magazine*, 9 July 2012. Web, accessed 8 November 2012.

8. "Tom and Jim" are the great American poet Thomas McGrath and the innovative publisher James Cooney. Ehrhart dedicated the poem to them and addresses himself to

them because their lives inspired him in his own struggles against complacency and compromise.

9. As with "The One That Died," the significant revisions in *Channel Fever* were largely editorial and ones that Ehrhart subsequently rejected.

10. "Responsibility" and "The Dream," the first piece in *The Outer Banks*, resemble "And what would you do, ma..." by Steve Hassett, which Ehrhart and Barry selected for inclusion in *Demilitarized Zones*:

> And what would you do, ma,
> if eight of your sons step out
> of the TV and begin
> killing chickens and burning
> hooches in the living room,
> stepping on booby traps
> and dying in the kitchen,
> beating your husband and
> taking him and shooting
> skag and forgetting in
> the bathroom?
> would you lock up your daughter?
> would you stash the apple pie?
> would you change channels? [*DMZ*, 121]

11. In many poems about Anne and Leela, music or song serves as an implicit metaphor for healing.

12. Ehrhart, W.D., *Going Back: An Ex-Marine Returns to Vietnam* (Jefferson, NC: McFarland, 1987).

13. Ehrhart, W.D., *Just for Laughs* (Silver Spring, MD: Viet Nam Generation & Burning Cities Press, 1990), iv.

14. See Lorrie Smith's excellent analysis of this and other Ehrhart poems in "Against a Coming Extinction: W.D. Ehrhart and the Evolving Canon of Vietnam Veterans' Poetry," *War, Literature & the Arts* 8:2 (Fall/Winter 1996), 1–30.

15. Ehrhart, W.D., *Passing Time: Memoir of a Vietnam Veteran Against the War* (Jefferson, NC: McFarland, 1989).

16. Ehrhart, *Unaccustomed Mercy*, 1ff.

17. Mahony, Phillip, ed., *From Both Sides Now: The Poetry of the Vietnam War and Its Aftermath* (New York: Scribner, 1998).

18. Ehrhart, *Greatest Hits*, 5.

19. Ibid., 6.

The Art of Writing Poetry: An Interview with W. D. Ehrhart

Jean-Jacques Malo

I first met W. D. Ehrhart at the Popular Culture Association/American Culture Association Conference in Toronto in March 1990 where he was a guest presenter in the evening of March 8th. This is also when I got my first Ehrhart book, *To Those Who Have Gone Home Tired*.[1] For a Frenchman living in the U.S.A., he was some kind of an oddity in his desire to educate people the way he did, being direct, trying to make sure people understand his point of view. Consequently I became interested in the man, in his writings, in his poetry, of course, but as well in his prose and in his essays. Over a period of more than twenty years, I have had the chance of meeting Ehrhart on the American continent and in Europe. We have had a number of exciting discussions on a wide variety of subjects.

W. D. Ehrhart has been a talking head in television documentaries,[2] and has been featured on local, regional and national radio shows.[3] However, there are only three published interviews of Ehrhart, two of which are in English (1991 and 1996) and one is in Italian (2000, with John S. Baky).[4] Unpublished interviews do exist, when Ehrhart was recorded by scholars (e.g. Subarno Chattarji, Stephen McVeigh, or Adam Gilbert) or students, but they have not been made available to the general public or readership. Therefore, it was time to have W. D. Ehrhart in his own words and in print. In the summer of 2012, by email I conducted a very long interview of Ehrhart. Hopefully, it will be published in full one day as Ehrhart the writer-educator has a lot to share with readers. I have selected questions and answers relating to poetry which I proffer in this chapter.

General aspects

JJM. You enlisted in the U.S. Marine Corps at seventeen in 1966, you served three years of active duty, including a 13-month tour of duty in Vietnam in

1967–68. Upon your return home you held quite a variety of jobs for many years before eventually becoming a fulltime high school teacher in 2001. You started writing at 15 whilst still in high school. As a teenager, a soldier, a young veteran, did you foresee that you would become a poet and a writer of nonfiction? In those early years, how much did you yearn to write?

WDE. Goodness, where do I begin? I was 15 years old the first time I wrote a poem that a teacher didn't make me write. (I still have a poem I wrote in 9th grade when I was 14 as an assignment for Miss Hershberger.) I no longer have the poem I wrote when I was 15, which is probably a blessing—it was about running away to a desert island where no one would ever hassle me again and I could live like a contented cow (a reference to Elsie the Borden's Cow). Talk about mixing metaphors.

Anyway, I have been writing poetry pretty much ever since. All through my last two years of high school, certainly. I was not going to be the star of the football team or anything like that, so poetry was a way of getting attention from the girls. Which actually worked pretty well. Also, I was dimly aware that all those dead white poets we used to read in English class had cheated the Reaper. (The only female poets I remember reading in those days were Dickinson, Bishop, and Barrett Browning, but this was the early '60s, and anyway those dead white guys were pretty good writers.) And they were dead, but they weren't. Here they were on the printed page right before my very eyes. That was cool.

Ultimately, of course, who can say why I took up writing? I don't really know. Something in my DNA? I certainly wasn't going to be a painter (my artistic skills don't go beyond stick figures) or a musician (can't get the hang of playing guitar), but I do seem to have a facility with words. As for the nonfiction, I didn't start writing that until the very late 1970s, but that's a different story.

As for all those jobs, I never have been very good at doing what other people want me to do. Before I began teaching at The Haverford School in 2001, the longest job I ever had lasted three years. That was the time I spent in the Marine Corps working for Uncle Sam, and I'd have quit that one sooner except that they put you in Portsmouth Naval Prison if you try to quit. The longest fulltime job I ever had that I could quit lasted 21 months. And that was back in the mid–70s. I realized by the age of 25 that I didn't really care about a career or financial security or much of anything except poetry. This posed a problem because poets don't generally make a living being poets. I did an assortment of jobs over the years to pay the bills—reporter, construction worker, merchant seaman, whatever I could pick up—but all that mattered was being able to write. And to write what I wanted to write. What I discovered, of course, is that people will only pay you to write what they want you to write. I worked as a reporter for awhile, but I just didn't care about the New Hope Water and Sewer Authority. I worked as a health writer for awhile, but I didn't care about vitamin C and back pain. Eventually, I stumbled into teaching while I was getting a Master's degree from the University of Illinois at Chicago Circle (that decision itself was a way of avoiding having to get another job), and I have taught sporadically ever since. Indeed, I enjoyed teaching very much, and proved to be pretty good at it in my early 30s, but when I was younger I didn't play well with adults, especially the kinds of adults who rise to the top of the bureaucratic food chain. When I got married and my wife turned out to be a very good computer programmer, I went back to mostly writing and picking up short-term jobs and part-time jobs for years while she graciously went to work every day and paid the household's major bills. (I became a feminist when I realized Professor Judith Gardiner at UICC wasn't talking about liberating women; she was talking about liberating me. My father could never have lived the life I've lived. He would have been the laughing stock of Perkasie. Can't support your own family. What kind of a man are you?) That worked fine for about two decades, although now the roles have been reversed in the last ten years or so, which seems only fair, with me working fulltime and Anne able to do more artistic endeavors like the vocal group she and my daughter helped found and still sing with, Svitanya.

JJM. You wrote eight books as well as ten chapbooks of poetry published between 1975 and 2010. You edited or co-edited three anthologies of Vietnam poetry between 1976 and 1989. In 1999 with Philip K. Jason you also co-edited an anthology of poems and short stories of the Korean War. You also published eight books of non-fiction between 1983 and 2012. You published twenty books as well as ten chapbooks of verse. Out of all these publications, twenty-two are devoted to poetry which is very much your focus. Your verse deals a lot with the Vietnam War, but not only. From your early poems you have also been dealing with nature, love, friendship, family, politics—an actual variety of themes.

My question is two-fold: first, did you want to become a poet (and decided some day to be one), and second, did you want to become a Vietnam War poet, or even *the* Vietnam War poet as many consider you the dean of Vietnam War poetry?

WDE. As I said, I began writing poetry when I was 15. By the time I was 25, I realized that this was the only thing I really cared about in terms of what to do with my life. This was not entirely a happy realization because I was smart enough to know that I would have a problem keeping a roof over my head and food in my belly.

As for the war poet thing, yes, I actually went off to Vietnam imagining that I might become the Wilfred Owen of the Vietnam War. I knew Owen's poetry well by then, although I obviously didn't get what he was trying to tell me or I wouldn't have enlisted in the Marines at 17 (too young even to register for the draft). I also conveniently neglected to fully absorb the fact that Owen didn't survive his war. Within a week after I got to Vietnam, I started writing. What I was writing, however, was bad high school imitation Wilfred Owen. Sadly, one of those poems survived to be published in *Winning Hearts and Minds*, a poem called "Viet Nam—February 1967."[5] (A measure of how little the editors had to pick from.) Years later, Philip Beidler used it as the paradymatic example of the worst poetry ever written about the Vietnam War, which it was (although Beidler might at least have added a footnote explaining that I had since written some better poems than that one). Within a few months, however, the war became so troubling and confusing, the questions arising in my own mind became so frightening, that I didn't want to think anymore. And if you don't think, you can't write. So I stopped writing not by conscious choice, but because I willfully stopped thinking. I didn't begin to write again until about two years later, just before I got released from active duty. Then I had to teach myself how to write, which I did through much of my college years, during which I was reading a lot of good poetry, which is a good way to learn how to write. In my first year of college, I wrote another lousy poem that, much to my chagrin, managed to survive into *WHAM*, the central image of which is a bayonet. A bayonet? Well, I had one, and when my John Wayne can opener broke, I could use the bayonet to bash open a can of C-rations. But I never put my bayonet on the end of my rifle and I certainly never killed anyone with it. That's an image straight out of Owen's war. It took me some years to realize that I needed to tap into my own war, not his war, for my imagery. Eventually I figured that out.

As for this "dean of Vietnam War poetry," what the heck does that mean, anyway? I think John Pratt was the first one to call me that, and it has been picked up by others and often repeated. Isn't a dean the person who is responsible for discipline and other bureaucratic details in institutional settings? At the school where I teach, The Haverford School, we have a dean of students who checks on student attendance and gives out detentions and suspensions. We had a dean of men at Swarthmore College who called me on the carpet for dumping water in another student's dorm room. So what does it mean that I'm the dean of Vietnam War poetry? I don't get it.

JJM. Some themes and ideas in poems from *A Generation of Peace* have subsequently found their way in longer prose versions in *Vietnam–Perkasie*. When you wrote these short poems, did you plan to expand then into prose?

WDE. I never thought about writing prose until 1978 or 1979, so when

I was writing those poems I had no thought of expanding the poems into prose. It is the events themselves that recur simply because those events left indelible impressions on me.

I only decided to try to write the prose nonfiction after I got a phone call late one night from a friend of mine who had just seen *The Deer Hunter*. He had known me for several years, and knew I was a Vietnam War veteran, but never gave much thought to what that meant. Now, having seen the movie, he was very upset, in tears, and wanting to apologize because he hadn't realized how terrible my experience must have been. I was touched by his emotions, but it was all I could do not to laugh or scold him for being tricked by Hollywood. The movie is bullshit. It turns the Vietnam War on its head. In the movie, the sweet innocent American boys go off to Vietnam where they are brutalized and tortured by the evil Asian communists. We're the victims in that movie, but that isn't really what happened. The Vietnamese were the victims, not us. Indeed, the central "metaphor" of the movie, the Russian roulette stuff—no American POW ever claimed that the Vietnamese made any Americans do that, not even once. I held my tongue because Daniel was clearly sincere and upset, but by the time I hung up the phone that night, I had determined to tell America the real story of the Vietnam War. (Talk about hubris!) That's how what became my accidental Vietnam War Trilogy (*Vietnam-Perkasie, Passing Time, Busted*) got started.[6]

Writing technique and poetry

JJM. How do you write? Do you sit down every morning like the Moroccan poet Abellatif Laâbi, and work until lunchtime and then quit whether you've written one line or ten pages? Or do you go to crowded and noisy cafés like some French 19th century writers used to do?

WDE. My "technique" for writing poetry isn't really a technique at all. I have always been at the mercy of the creative muse. When I am inspired to write a poem, I write. When I'm not, I don't. As I've gotten older, I have written less and less poetry. I'm not sure why. I do know that having a child created some wrinkles because ideas often come to me late at night in that twilight zone between wakefulness and sleep, and once Leela was born, I knew that she would wake up at 6AM and want my attention whether I'd had seven hours of sleep or two hours of sleep. This made it harder to force myself to work ideas that came to me in the night. Then when Leela was five, I quit smoking, and this changed my sleep pattern enormously. Nicotine is STP for the brain. It's a stimulant. It keeps you awake. I used to roll my own cigarettes, and most of the time when I'd be writing, I wouldn't be writing at all; I'd be staring at the page wondering what to write next, all the while rolling and smoking, rolling and smoking. When I quit smoking, I lost both the stimulant to keep me awake into the night and something to do while I'm trying to figure out what to write next. Though I've obviously continued to write poetry, I've never fully adjusted to writing without smoking. (By the way, I started smoking the same summer I started writing poetry, and though the two activities were not connected initially, they quickly became so.) It took me ten years to accumulate the 41 poems in 2010's *The Bodies Beneath the Table*.[7] I used to write that many poems in a year or two, though in my defense, these days a much higher percentage of what I write is worth keeping than was true thirty and forty years ago.

Prose is a different matter. I am much more workmanlike with prose, but that's because my prose is not creative. I have something to say, and I just have to figure out how best and most effectively to say it.

JJM. What are your writing tools? Do you use a No. 2 pencil (like Norman Mailer did) or do you compose your texts directly on a typewriter in older times or nowadays on a computer?

WDE. I still compose poetry longhand. Speed is not an issue, and I can make changes on changes on changes in longhand, even as I'm writing the next line, and thus see multiple versions all at once in a way I can't do on a computer. Only when the poem has more or less taken shape and I'm working on polishing it will I type it into the computer (or in the old days, on a typewriter). I also wrote all of the memoirs longhand initially, not beginning to end, but in sections. Write a section, type it up with editing and revising, then write the next section, then type that one up the next day. I've gotten lazy, however, and out of practice with longhand. When I'm writing prose now, I tend to do a lot of the composition directly on the keyboard, as I'm doing right now in answering your questions. I think my writing actually suffers from not using longhand much anymore, but my handwriting has never been very good, and as I've gotten older, it has gotten sloppier and sloppier and more difficult for me to do; my hand actually gets tired much more quickly than it once did. Alas, I think the computer has not helped my writing, but I have allowed myself to fall victim to convenience.

As I said, however, this does not apply to the poetry. That I still compose initially by hand.

JJM. Do you walk around with a notebook, and jot down ideas, words, phrases, images, visions?

WDE. The short answer to your question is no. On a few occasions, something has so struck me that I will write it down on whatever is handy, but I don't do that on any kind of a regular basis. In my 20s, I did finally discipline myself to keep a notebook by my bedside because, as I said, that's when ideas most often came to me. After many a morning when I'd wake up remembering that I'd had a good idea the night before, but unable to remember what it was, I trained myself to turn on the light and write down what I was thinking: an idea, a phrase, a line. Sometimes I would work it on the spot, though as I said, the more life intruded, especially after Leela's arrival, the harder it became to sacrifice sleep. But at least I had the idea down and I could come back to it. Nowadays, I'm usually in bed by 9 and asleep by 10. Spending day after day in the company of the teenaged boys I teach, I need to be rested and ready!

JJM. Do you go through several drafts? Do you complete your poems in a short time or over a period of several weeks or even months? Do you let your texts sit and then do you get back to them before you send them off to journals for publication?

WDE. Sometimes poems come to me fairly readily and don't require a lot of revision, but more often than not I do many drafts. However, these don't take the form of a complete poem, then a new draft, then another draft. I am constantly revising as I write. Lines, phrases, words. Arranging. Rearranging. Deleting. Adding. Often, what triggers a poem gets written out of the poem as it develops. I seldom know where a poem is going until it is well along. Some poems, as I said, come quickly. Others take much longer, although I no longer fuss with a poem as long as I used to. I've gotten to where I can pretty much tell if a poem is going to go somewhere or not, and if it's not, I won't worry over it; I'll just let it go. I used to try to save every poem I started, even the ones that were not salvageable.

JJM. Do you write, somehow with an audience in mind?

WDE. I write for thoughtful people who can read and understand the English language. Beyond that, I don't think much about audience.

JJM. You almost never write in rhymes. For example, in 1990 in *Just for Laughs*[8] you have only four rhymed poems out of 46; the rest is free verse. Your 2010 *The Bodies Beneath the Table* has only two rhymed texts out of 41. I take it you prefer the straightforwardness of free verse, this apparent simplicity to a more classic poetry writing with rhymes and metered verse? How and why do you decide to rhyme or not?

WDE. I learned when I was still very young that if I tried to work in rhyme, I mostly spent my time trying to figure out a word that rhymed with "alligator" (How about "refrigerator?") instead of figuring out how best to say what I needed to say. I suspect at least part of the problem is that I'm not all that good a poet. After all, Frost managed to do it poem after poem. So did a lot of other poets. On the other hand, for many centuries, poets writing rhyme could get away with stuff I can't. In the good old days, if a poet needed a single syllable, he or she could simply turn "never" into "ne'er." Try that these days, and you'll find your poem in some editor's wastebasket.

In any case, I abandoned rhyme almost from the start of my career as a poet, although as you point out, now and then I'll end up using rhyme. Not sure why. Sometimes it just works. Two of my favorite poems, "A Small Romance" and "A Scientific Treatise for My Wife,"[9] are written in rhyme. They just seemed to want to do that, and it worked (at least *I* think it worked).

JJM. You sometimes use a classic structure with a fixed form in your poems. I compared two books published twenty years apart, *Just for Laughs* and *The Bodies Beneath the Table*. In the former, nearly half of your texts (precisely 21 out of 46) are written in fixed forms. They range from couplets to tercets, to quatrains, to five-line, six-line or even seven-line or eight-line regular stanzas. However in *The Bodies* only two poems have a fixed form—tercets and/or couplets. What compels you to choose a complete free form or a more classic one?

WDE. Generally, the poem chooses its own form as it is getting written. I don't decide in advance to use tercets or octets or whatever. If the logic of what I have to say matches some stanzaic structure, I'll use it, but that invariably happens only after the poem is well along. And if no form presents itself, that's just the way it is. Why there are more fixed forms in the former book than the latter, I have no idea.

By the way, it was Vince Gotera at *North American Review* who suggested that alternation of tercets and couplets in "Home Before Morning," the poem for Lynda Van Devanter. I don't remember how I had set it up when I sent it to him, but he showed me that it would work very well as 3, 2, 3, 2. I didn't see it myself.[10]

JJM. Do you like to play on language, on words, on phrases in your writing?

WDE. Why do you ask me this? What do you see in my poetry? You can answer this question as well as I can, and probably better.

JJM. When you revise your own work, do you cut words, superfluous language, or do you add words, change phrases?

WDE. I do all these things pretty much simultaneously.

JJM. Do you get your wife, your daughter, or other people to read your poems when you think they are ready, and then make changes if you get a negative, or even a positive response?

WDE. For years, I sent drafts of poems to my college roommate, Don Cassidy, who is a very good critic. And over the past 32 years (I'm writing this in 2012), my wife has become my first reader, and is very good at it. When we first were a couple, she felt she didn't know anything about poetry, but I convinced her that you don't have to be a carpenter to recognize a good piece of furniture or an artist to recognize a good painting, and once she got over her lack of confidence, she got very good very quickly at critiquing my writing. She is almost invariably the first person to see anything I've written, poetry or prose.

Inspiration and writing

JJM. What are your sources of inspiration? Vietnam certainly was for a while. In your last books of poetry over the past twenty years, the themes are quite diverse. You talk about your wife Anne, your daughter Leela, and the value of friendship; all these are themes related to love. Is love and/or friendship nowadays, or the lack of it one of your main sources of inspiration?

WDE. Actually, the Vietnam War has never been more than one of many sources of inspiration. Of course, my extended prose works—the memoirs, *Going Back*,[11] and *Ordinary Lives*,[12] all deal in one way or another with my encounter with the Vietnam War. But my poetry and my essays have always been more reflective of the multiplicity of interests that have occupied my life. What are my main sources of inspiration? You can see them in the poems. Certainly love, my wife and daughter in particular, friendship, the natural world, the conflict between humans and that natural world, the desire to understand myself and others, geez, I don't know. Again, look at the poems. What's in the poems is what inspired them.

JJM. You also deal with politics, for instance mainly Latin America in *Just for Laughs*, and later other parts of the world. Do you believe poetry can influence politics in the same way politics influences poetry, especially yours?

WDE. When I was much younger, I thought poetry could influence politics. In some countries, it does. In some countries, poets are jailed and tortured or shot for what they write because they are so influential. But I have slowly over the course of my lifetime had to accept the fact that in this country no one pays any attention to the poets. I no longer write with any expectation that it will change anything. I write because I have to. Because it is who and what I am. But I am a very small man in a very big world. There isn't much I can do, in poetry or otherwise, to make much of a dent in the stupidity and greed and venality and narrowmindedness and intolerance and boneheadedness that seems to be the human condition.

JJM. Have you considered publishing a whole book of political poems, ranging from Vietnam to Latin America to the Middle East, and encompassing your political thinking about the state of the U.S. and the world?

WDE. Short answer: no. People have from time to time noted my "personal poetry" and my "political poetry," but it's all the same to me. I write about my life and the world I live in. It is others—you, for instance—who make the distinction, not me.

JJM. After you came back from Vietnam, was writing therapeutic? And is it still? Do you need to write as part of your life, as some people need regular physical exercise.

WDE. I dislike the notion of poetry as therapy. Got PTSD? Write poetry. Got AIDS? Write poetry. Disabled? Write poetry. No matter what ails you, if you write poetry, you'll feel better. That seems to be the prevailing belief these days. And I suppose it's true that anybody can write poetry. But not everybody can write good poetry. I've spent a lifetime trying to perfect and improve my art, and I resent the idea that anyone can do it.

That said, however, in retrospect I have to recognize that writing about the war was indeed very therapeutic for me, especially in the early years of my 20s when I was struggling to understand what had happened to me in Vietnam. I came home an emotional wreck, confused, broken, lost, damaged. Writing was a way of making sense of what had happened. I learned what I thought through what I wrote. We imagine that writing is a mechanical process, but it's not. It's really a process of thinking (go back to what I said at the beginning of this interview about thinking and writing). What's up in our brains is a kind of alphabet soup. It's all up there, but it's just a jumble. You have to take your spoon and dip it into the soup and form the letters of your name on the spoon. "Bill" emerges only when you find a B, an I, and two L's, and arrange them in the right order on your spoon. That's what you're doing when you write.

I remember trying to write a poem during my first few weeks in college in the fall of 1969. It was a rant about how these privileged kids at Swarthmore College could go around protesting the war only because guys like me had put our lives on the line for their freedom of speech. But as I worked on the poem, I had to recognize that what I had done in Vietnam had had nothing whatever to do with freedom of speech in the United States of America. I was merely parroting the same stupid shit I'd been fed by the assholes who sent me to Vietnam. I balled up the paper and threw it away.

JJM. Could you stop writing tomorrow and lock your pens away?

WDE. I don't know. I hope I never have to face that situation.

JJM. You were born and raised in Pennsylvania, and you have been living in Philadelphia since 1985. Do you find that Pennsylvania—the place itself, or the people you've met here, has influenced your work?

WDE. Probably, but I'd be hard-pressed to explain how.

JJM. Do music, paintings, landscapes, dance, etc.—the arts in general—influence your writing?

WDE. Again probably, but again, I'd be hard-pressed to explain how. Everything influences my writing in the end; it's all part of the world I live in, part of my life.

JJM. When do you decide that a poem is finished?

WDE. When it feels right. Beyond that, it's hard to say. So much of what happens in writing is intuitive, taking place at a level well below the conscious, deliberate level. Then someone—like you—asks for an explanation, and it is very unsatisfying to get the response, "I don't know." So the poet tries to come up with some coherent explanation, but that explanation may or may not have anything to do with what is really going on because the poet doesn't really know. It just feels right.

And sometimes I'm wrong. There's a poem in the first 1984 printing of *To Those Who Have Gone Home Tired*, "The Invasion of Grenada,"[13] that has a closing couplet you won't find in any other printing of that poem. The moment I saw it in print, I realized, "Oh, crap. Why did I put that in?" Conversely, the last line of "What Makes a Man"[14] in my most recent book is missing something, and I didn't realize it until the book was published and I read the poem in public a few times. That line reads, "and nothing I could do to change a thing." But it should read, "and nothing either one of us could do / to change a thing." I thought the poem was finished, but it wasn't. I hope I get a chance to correct the error in print.

JJM. You often break up the lines of your poems. Is it because when they are spoken they sound different from the lines on the page, and consequently the rhythm works better that way? Is this an influence of your many public readings in various venues and on very different occasions?

WDE. I try to create line breaks that reflect how I want the poem to read. Sometimes it's the integrity of a phrase or idea, sometimes I am working in a rough iambic pentameter or some other syllabic measure, sometimes I want to put emphasis on certain words or phrases (words at the ends or beginnings of lines get more attention from readers than words in mid-line).

Every now and then, I'll discover that I read a poem differently than it appears on the printed page, and when that happens, I've tended to leave the printed page alone anyway. Most of the time, the format on the page reflects how I want it read aloud.

JJM. Do you occasionally face a white page and cannot fill it with words, either in the case of poetry or prose?
   WDE. Of course. Often, especially with poetry.

JJM. What do you do in that case? Do you think there are any generic and efficient ways to answer writer's block?
   WDE. I get up and walk away. But more often than not, what happens is that I simply feel no inspiration to write. The spark is not there. I don't even try. Many years ago, when I was in my 20s still, I was complaining to Merritt Clifton, then editor and publisher of a small magazine called *Samisdat* who gave me a lot of encouragement in those years, about a dry spell I was in. He said something to me that I've never forgotten and have often fallen back on: "You can't rape the Muse, Bill. If you do, it'll be sex, but it won't be love." When you're not writing, he was saying, don't worry about it, don't try to force it. I took that to heart, and still do. Let the blank page be blank. Go have a beer, or watch TV, or read a book, or go jogging. Sooner or later, you'll write again. Or you'll die. One or the other will happen when it happens.
   One of the nice things about teaching high school at this stage of my life is that I get enormous emotional satisfaction out of what I'm doing. Teaching a good class is like writing a good poem. It's a work of art. So if I'm not writing so much these days, that's okay. Teaching and writing, for me, are two sides of the same coin. If I never write another poem, but continue to teach effectively, I'll die a happy man. Of course, I hope I do write another poem, but if I don't, that will not be a tragedy.

JJM. When you start a poem with an idea in mind, does it always become what you meant it to be? For example, I am thinking of "Responsibility" which appears in *The Outer Banks & Other Poems*.[15] It seems to start as a love poem, and then shifts to politics. This one obviously did not follow the primary direction—or did it?
   WDE. "Responsibility" is a perfect example of a poem that wants to be something other than what I want it to be. It did indeed start out as a love poem. I had done something stupid, and my wife went off to work upset with me, and I figured it would be good if I greeted her that night with a poem (it had worked before). So I started writing, and you can see the love poem in the first stanza. This was 1984, in the midst of the Reagan Wars against the peasants of Central America. And as I wrote, these hideous, ugly images kept popping out of my pen onto the paper, and I'd go, "No, no, go away, I don't want

you here." And this went on for several hours before I finally got my head out of my ass and realized that if I were smart, I'd let the poem go where it wanted to go. Which I finally did.

JJM. Does self-censorship play an important part in your writing? Are there taboos or inviolable topics that prevent you from tackling certain subjects?
WDE. Not that I'm consciously aware of. I've written about my wife's underwear, dressing up in my mother's lingerie, torturing animals, killing civilians. I can't think of anything I've been afraid to tackle.

JJM. Some of your poetry has been translated in a number of languages, including French by myself, Italian, German, Japanese, Chinese, Arabic, even Vietnamese. How important is it for you personally—and for a poet more generally—to be published in other idioms?
WDE. Poetry is the art form least easily translatable into another language. I have no idea how well any of those translations of my work convey the feel, the emotion, the message of my English language poems. Like so many Americans, I am limited only to English (which, in the case of reading my poems in other languages, may be a blessing). All I can say is that it is very gratifying for me personally when someone thinks enough of a poem of mine to want to take the time and trouble to translate it into another language. It pleases me very much.

JJM. What does the birth of a poem represent for you?
WDE. If it's a good poem, I am happy. If it's a bad poem, I hope I have sense enough to recognize that and put it out of its misery.

JJM. Is it writing which compels the writer, or is it the writer who compels writing?
WDE. Which came first, the chicken or the egg?

JJM. You regularly dedicate some of your poems to people (Lynda Van Devanter, Jim Beloungy, Lisa Coffman, Nguyen Thi My Huong, Diana Bedell, Nguyen Van Hung, your wife Anne amongst others). I would say you do it much more than any other poets. Why is it so?
WDE. Credit where credit is due, basically. In almost every case like this, I am either speaking directly to that person or that person inspired the poem. Sometimes both.

JJM. So, really, why do you write? And why do you write so much?
WDE. Because I can't play the guitar and I can't paint. Which is true.

Beyond that, I have no idea. It's just something I've done virtually all my life, or at least since I was 15. It gives me satisfaction. I like to see my name in print. I seem to have things to say that I want others to read. At least some people apparently enjoy what I write. I enjoy writing. I'm no good at architecture or engineering. This is one of those questions I referred to earlier: the real answer is, I don't know. I just write.

JJM. Some people might describe your writings—particularly your poetry—as "pacifist." Is this a characterization you agree with?

WDE. Well, no, I wouldn't agree with that characterization because it isn't accurate. I'm not a pacifist. Actually, for a while in the early/mid–1970s, I kind of thought I was a pacifist. But especially as I watched the struggle to end apartheid in South Africa, I gradually realized that pacifism is a luxury of white middle-class westerners. Can you imagine what the white racist regime in Pretoria would have done with a street full of Blacks singing "We shall overcome?" It would have given new meaning to the notion of blacktopping a highway. What good would pacifism have done the Jews against Nazi Germany? Indeed, most Jews didn't resist, and look what it got them. Gandhi and India were operating in very unusual historical circumstances, and look what happened to non-violence as soon as the British left. Indeed, what good would pacifism have done the Vietnamese in the face of French and later American violence? I am certainly anti-war. I'm anti-greed, anti-jingoist, anti-chauvinist. I'm eternally opposed to wars started by the old and fought by the young, to wars fought by the poor for the benefit of the rich. But that doesn't make me a pacifist. If the Russians invade Ocean City, New Jersey, I'll be the first one out on the beach to try to stop them. If you mess with my wife or my daughter, watch what I do to you. If I had been a 17-year-old Vietnamese instead of a 17-year-old American, I hope I'd have had the courage and patriotism to join the Viet Cong. I've never believed that the Vietnam War should not have been fought, at least by the Vietnamese, because the Vietnamese had every reason to fight. I was simply on the wrong side.

Notes

1. Ehrhart, W.D., *To Those Who Have Gone Home Tired* (New York: Thunder's Mouth Press, 1984).
2. *Vietnam, A Television History* (13 episodes, 1983; series director: Bruce Palling) and *Making Sense of the Sixties* (6 episodes, 1991; director: David Hoffman).
3. For example, on "Radio Times," host Marty Moss-Coane, NPR affiliate WHYY-FM (in the Philadelphia area), August 6, 2012. Ehrhart has also been featured on national radio, e.g. on NPR's "All Things Considered" and "Morning Edition."
4. See Anderson, Donald and Thomas G. Bowie, Jr., interviewers, "A Conversation with W.D. Ehrhart," *War, Literature & the Arts: an International Journal of the Human-*

ities, 8:2 (Fall/Winter 1996), 149–157. Ronald Boughman, ed., *The Dictionary of Literary Biography Documentary Series*, vol. 9 (Farmington Hills, MI: Cengage Gale, 1991), 63–82. Stefano Rosso, "Conversazione con William D. Ehrhart e John S. Baky, Philadelphia, ottobre 1997," *Ácoma* (no. 19, Primavera-Estate, 2000, anno VII), 40–47. Republished in Stefano Rosso, *Musi gialli e Berretti Verdi. Narrazioni Usa sulla Guerra del Vietnam* (Bergamo: Bergamo University Press, 2003), 233–249.

    5. Rottmann, Larry, Jan Barry, and Basil T. Paquet, eds., "Introduction," *Winning Hearts and Minds: War Poems by Vietnam Veterans* (New York: McGraw-Hill Book Company, 1972).

    6. Ehrhart, W.D., *Vietnam-Perkasie: A Combat Marine Memoir* (Jefferson, NC: McFarland, 1983). *Passing Time: Memoir of a Vietnam Veteran Against the War* (Jefferson, NC: McFarland, 1989). *Busted: A Vietnam Veteran in Nixon's America* (Amherst, MA: University of Massachusetts Press, 1995).

    7. Ehrhart, W.D., *The Bodies Beneath the Table* (Easthampton, MA: Adastra Press, 2010).

    8. Ehrhart, W.D., *Just for Laughs* (Silver Spring, MD: Viet Nam Generation & Burning Cities Press, 1990).

    9. Both poems appear in *Just for laughs* and subsequently in *Beautiful Wreckage*.

    10. Ehrhart, W.D., "Home Before Morning," *Sleeping with the Dead* (Easthampton, MA: Adastra Press, 2006), 17.

    11. Ehrhart, W.D., *Going Back: An Ex-Marine Returns to Vietnam* (Jefferson, NC: McFarland, 1987).

    12. Ehrhart, W.D., *Ordinary Lives: Platoon 1005 and the Vietnam War* (Philadelphia, PA: Temple University Press, 1999).

    13. Ehrhart, *To Those Who Have Gone Home Tired*, 71.

    14. Ehrhart, *The Bodies Beneath the Table*, 32–33.

    15. Ehrhart, W.D., *The Outer Banks & Other Poems* (Easthampton, MA: Adastra Press, 1984), 34–35.

PART THREE.
The Influential Writer

The Heart of the Poem

Split the ribcage open
with a heavy-bladed knife,
a hatchet or an axe.
Be careful with an axe;
it can do more damage than you need.

Grasp the ribs and pry them back.
They won't want to give at first:
pull hard and steadily;
keep pulling till they snap.

Forget about the skin;
it'll tear when the ribs give way.

After that, it's easy:
push the other guts aside,
let your fingers dig until the heart
seats firmly in your palm
like a baseball or a grapefruit,
then jerk it out.

Get rid of it.
Sentiment's for suckers.
Give us poetry.

—W. D. Ehrhart

Just for Laughs, 58; *Beautiful Wreckage: New & Selected Poems*, 143.

Ehrhart Effect

Jan Barry

Bill Ehrhart's impact on my work as a writer and on my life has been, over the course of more than 40 years, profoundly rewarding and challenging.

One of my fondest memories is of Bill and me in old military field jackets vigorously pushing a swing to put my very young son flying high in a playground full of chattering moms and tots, as we plotted a poetry anthology focused on war's grim aftermath.

Beginning with the creation of *Winning Hearts & Minds: War Poems by Vietnam Veterans,*[1] where we met in the winter of 1971–72 as novice writers seeking collaborators in confronting war with poetry, we fostered a friendship that survived working together to compile a sequel, *Demilitarized Zones: Veterans after Vietnam,*[2] published in 1976. *DMZ,* as we called it, was conceived in a partnership forged in maintaining that soaring pendulum of a playground swing, while brainstorming ways to publish what we saw as a new kind of poetry.

Bill's relentless push to publish a veritable library of literary works probing every aspect of the war in Indochina challenged me to write more than I otherwise might have done. His brash way of writing about seemingly every facet of life delighted me so much that I shed some of my Scots/Anglo-Saxon reserve to reveal more about myself in my writings. And his fearless, unflagging tweaking of the conventions of journalism, book publishing and other aspects of American society encouraged me in my work as a journalist, as well as in writing poetry.

Our literary ties survived despite going our own ways after bringing out *DMZ*. We've managed, for decades, to maintain a long-distance affiliation punctuated by periodically getting together for poetry readings in various places, to discuss new book projects (usually Bill's, who seemed to always have one or two in the works) and compare notes on forays into the daunting thickets of publishers and editors, and for family gatherings to catch up on our lives.

Yet I still am often startled to read a new poem or prose piece that reveals another facet of Bill's life that I had not known. Bill Ehrhart has an uncanny knack for publicly plumbing emotional depths that make most American males of our generation squirm.

"My kiss surprised you, but you didn't / Turn away," he wrote in "Unaccustomed Mercies," a 1980s poem dedicated to a fellow Vietnam veteran writer that first appeared in the *American Poetry Review*.

> After your reading about the war,
> it was only a way of saying thanks
> for surviving, for writing, your
> murderous humor slicing the sinew
>
> of what men do to be men
> to the white bleeding bone.
>
> ...Think of it: all that steel,
> the hatred, the generations consumed
> for want of unaccustomed mercies men
> might receive, if only they knew how.
>
> What shall we give our children?
> Paco's company blown to jungle junk
> by our own obsessions—or a graceless kiss,
> my weaponless hands, your smile.

Bill also has a knack for stating his opinions so bluntly that, by his own reckoning, he's infuriated family members, at least one judge, journalists and assorted other writers. Called to jury duty, for instance, he challenged the judge's instructions to the prospective jurors.

> I raised my hand.
> "You can't do that?" the judge asked.
> "I can't swear to it, your honor," I said.
> "You can't allow me to interpret the law?" he asked, his voice rising a little.
> "I can't swear to it, your honor," I said....

And so he went, back and forth with an increasingly ticked off judge, as Bill wrote in "On Common Sense and Conscience," a jaw-dropping treatise on the independent duties of juries that is just one of numerous prickly newspaper op-ed essays reprinted in *The Madness of It All: Essays on War, Literature and American Life*, published in 2002.[3]

I mostly saw a much more cooperative, less abrasive side of Bill. The worst blow-up we had was a harsh disagreement over which should be the final poem in *Demilitarized Zones*. Bill insisted it had to be his poem "To Those Who Have Gone Home Tired," which ends with the word "why?" I argued for something else. After a dark night of the soul and some more anguished reflection, I realized that Bill's instincts as a poetry editor were better than mine.

With that realization, I felt compelled to do another poetry anthology, *Peace Is Our Profession: Poems and Passages of War Protest*,[4] on my own. That feat, I magnanimously felt, was a great accomplishment to pull off by myself, and I took a long breather. Bill, meanwhile, churned out chapbook after chapbook and then book-length collections of his own poetry. He compiled and edited an acclaimed series of anthologies of poems on the Vietnam war and the Korean war. He wrote an acclaimed series of memoirs, and acclaimed collections of selected essays. His literary pace and output—20 books as well as 10 chapbooks, at last count according to Ehrhart's website—left me feeling exhausted.

The expanding bookshelf of works by W. D. Ehrhart, however, further challenged me to do more with my writing, to carve out time in a hectic schedule as a newspaper reporter to occasionally turn out a chapbook of poetry, then eventually a collection of selected poems—each of which Bill insightfully reviewed in one publication or another.

What drew us together was a shared background of growing up in flag-waving small towns and enthusiastically joining the military at a young age—and getting rudely disillusioned by U.S. military actions in Vietnam. We each set out to convey what we learned in the war to the patriotic, conservative, Bible-thumping America that raised us to be decent, hard-working, honest, straight-shooting citizens. The weapon we chose, after participating in shooting up a lot of other places on behest of our war-boostering, peace-loving hometowns, was the pen.

We both delighted in trying out various ways, in poetry and prose, of skewering the militaristic mumbo-jumbo that enthralled us as kids.

"I saw the Crucified Christ three days ago," Bill wrote in "Christ," one of the set of poems he submitted for publication in *Winning Hearts & Minds* that instantly caught my attention as one of the editors.

> He did not hang upon The Cross;
> But lay instead on a shambled terrace
> Of what had been a house.
> There were no nails in His limbs;
> No crown of thorns, no spear wounds.
> The soldiers had left nothing
> But a small black hole upon His cheek....

We who grew up joyfully singing "Onward, Christian Soldiers" were the executioners of a cruel U.S. military mission that was killing holy men and other innocents in distant lands—Buddhists among others, targeted as troublemakers by a far-flung, self-righteous American empire. That was the breathtakingly blunt theme of this poem by a United Church of Christ minister's son, which Bill expanded upon in subsequent writings, including *Empire*, a poetry chapbook published in 1978.

Such brashly dissident poems by Bill and other vets excited me so much I composed several poems for inclusion in *WHAM*—our sardonic acronym for *Winning Hearts & Minds*. Before working on that project with fellow editors Larry Rottmann and Basil Paquet, I'd published just one brief poem on the war.

For reasons that likely had to do with post-traumatic stress disorder (which had no name at the time), the ad hoc collective that compiled, edited and published *WHAM* under our own imprint, First Casualty Press, fell apart. In what in hindsight was surely irrational, I began feeling I couldn't trust other vets or anyone angling for a commercial piece of *Winning Hearts & Minds*—which was briefly staged as an off–Broadway play created by my wife Paula Pierce, until we had a bitter falling out with New York Public Theater producer Joseph Papp. As I'd previously done in resigning from a leadership role in Vietnam Veterans Against the War when I felt burnt out, I severed my relationship with First Casualty Press and the other editors, who brought out a stunning collection of short stories, *Free Fire Zones*,[5] and folded up the vets' publishing project.

In the sour aftermath, Bill convinced me to work with him on a sequel, *Demilitarized Zones*. On more than one occasion, when one damn thing or another riled me up, I was ready to drop the whole thing. But Bill persistently kept us on track. In the absence of finding another publisher, we created our own small press called East River Anthology. The literary reference point of that name was the salty waterway between Manhattan and Brooklyn, NY, where I was living at the time.

Several of Bill's poems that laced *DMZ* like whiplash marks inspired or otherwise challenged me to write more poetry. In "The Obsession," for instance, he wrote of arguing with a girlfriend who found him obsessive that he needed to stay the night, every night, with her:

> Dark shapeless things
> Moving
> Through the twilight pools
> Beneath the surface:
>
> Swift bullets flying
> Without warning...
>
> How much like death
> To sleep alone.

I responded with a poem titled "Sleeping with a Light On," which described a recurring nightmare of being jolted out of bed by explosions at a base camp in Vietnam, which reawakened me for years, until I took to sleeping with a light on, wearing all my clothes.

In "To the Asian Victors," Bill reexamined again how it was that he ended up in Vietnam in the role of the British Redcoats fighting a losing campaign against an historic anti-colonial revolution, and concluded:

> But I cannot ever quite remember
> What I went looking for,
> Or what it was I lost
> In that alien land
> That became
> More I
> Than my own can ever be again.[6]

That poem propelled me to write "Viet Nam," a tribute to "a strange, alien ... hostile land" that became "my foster, second home" where I learned "to be not just a man / but a human being." In my sometimes crisis-punctuated life after the war, I repeatedly learned similar lessons from Bill Ehrhart.

When I insisted, wanting to make my own literary mark, on doing the next poetry anthology myself, Bill cordially submitted several new poems for *Peace Is Our Profession* and offered to help with anything else I needed, such as pasting copy onto the thick stack of page boards. The publisher was our cobbled together East River Anthology. Bill transferred the press' files and boxes of unsold copies of *DMZ* from his parents' home in Perkasie, PA, to my new digs in Montclair, NJ. For years after, Bill would periodically retrieve a box of *DMZ* for another audience or class of students he had cultivated. It was another spur to me that we had to reach out and build a readership, rather than wait for readers to discover us.

Among the poems in *Peace Is Our Profession* that further inspired me were a wry, kind-hearted "Letter" to a North Vietnamese soldier whose rocket blast nearly killed Bill during the 1968 battle of Hue; a fishing story ("A Confirmation") about a camping reunion with a fellow wounded Marine, where a hard-fighting rainbow trout is unhooked and released back into the river, as Bill's old battle buddy slips an arm around his shoulders; and a raw revelation of his thoughts on undertaking a new career ("The Teacher"), where he holds out a torch "to keep my heart from freezing / and a strange new thing called / love / to keep me sane...."

Around the same time that *Peace Is Our Profession* came out in 1981, a very different set of poems by Bill Ehrhart were published by Adastra Press in a hand-typeset volume titled *Matters of the Heart and Other Poems*.[7] His approach to writing about life after war further challenged me, down to this day.

"I cherish my friends," he wrote in "Again, Rehoboth." Among his cherished friends at the time was Thomas McGrath, an aging prairie populist and social action poet, and James Cooney, publisher of *The Phoenix*, a radical journal that had nurtured Henry Miller and other literary outcasts of the 1930s and was revived after a long hiatus to protest the war in Vietnam. Bill paid tribute, in the title poem "Matters of the Heart," to these two "old tired fighters' unbowed hearts" encouraging him to keep writing about tough social issues.

In 1985, Avon Books published a mass market paperback titled *Carrying the Darkness: American Indochina—The Poetry of the Vietnam War*, edited by W. D. Ehrhart.[8] It was an astounding confirmation of my previous observation that Bill had discovered (and nurtured) an extraordinary talent as a poetry editor. I was delighted that he included several of my poems, including two newer ones from a chapbook titled *War Baby*, published by Samisdat, thanks to another of Bill's networking connections.

We had totally reversed roles, from when I was an editor of *WHAM* and considering poems by a hyperactive Marine vet from Pennsylvania who burst into my apartment in Brooklyn with an infectious enthusiasm that we could pin down the elusive truth of the war in Vietnam in poetry. Bill had now forged far ahead and was opening publishing doors for me and for many other veterans.

Four years later, Texas Tech University Press published another literary bombshell edited by W. D. Ehrhart, titled *Unaccustomed Mercy: Soldier-Poets of the Vietnam War*.[9] It was a tremendous morale booster for me to be included among this select group, hailed by famed Vietnam war novelist Tim O'Brien as among "many of the finest poets and finest poems to emerge from America's trial in Vietnam." It was clearly Bill's talents and persistence that made this wondrous tribute happen.

However, it was also damn discouraging. By then, Bill had published a dozen collections of poetry, two memoirs, a book about returning to Vietnam, and scads of poems in major literary journals. Besides that, he had gone back to college and gotten a master's degree in poetry. I felt exceedingly challenged.

Along with the economic precariousness of the news business, Bill's literary successes provided another kick in the seat of my pants to return to college and finish a B.A. degree and get better focused in advancing my writing career. Most of that renewed energy, for years that stretched into decades, went into my work as a journalist.

This is one area where Bill and I had a great divergence of views. Bill loathed war correspondents, from his time as a Marine under heavy fire in Vietnam. He didn't like working as a journalist, from a chafing experience as a reporter for a local newspaper in Pennsylvania. And he hated newspaper editing, from wincing at the chopping block results in feature stories and op-ed essays that he provided to Philadelphia newspapers and to other papers across the country.

I thrived on the frenzied pace of daily newspaper reporting, the hardball gamesmanship with editors, the opportunities to be on the leading edge of educating the public to harsh realities, from fatal fires and car crashes to health effects of Agent Orange and other chemicals used in the war impacting Vietnam veterans and their families at home. And I applied to my reporting what I liked about Bill's blunt, but well-considered writing style.

In 1995, the University of Massachusetts Press published yet another Ehrhart literary explosion, titled *Busted: A Vietnam Veteran in Nixon's America*.[10] This one topped his previous memoirs in exposing the madness at home of the authoritarian mentality that fueled the war in Vietnam. "Here is the haunting and turbulent and heartbreaking history of many in a generation of American men used up in an insane war," stated Gloria Emerson, the noted author and *New York Times* war correspondent.

Gloria Emerson, not incidentally, was tremendously supportive of *Winning Hearts & Minds*, helping generate wide attention in the news media when it was published. She mentored, in a tough love sort of way, a number of veteran poets and writers for years. When she died in 1994, Bill and I and others were asked for comments on her influence on our writing careers. I liked Bill's recollection better than my own. Here's why:

"Everyone who ever met her has a 'Gloria Story' to tell," Bill wrote in an appreciation that appeared in *The VVA Veteran*. "She was one of a kind, and I was often thankful I only had one of her to cope with. But it was impossible not to love someone who could write, 'I don't know even now, twenty years after I left [Vietnam], how to harden my heart so it won't be punctured yet again by the war.' Someone who could say to a discouraged writer, 'Don't keep track of where the other writers are, either behind or ahead. We are all doing what we can, no more no less. It isn't a race, is it?'"

That was a comforting thing to read by a guy whose literary pace left me reeling, now generously sharing with a generation of war veterans and writers trained to be fiercely competitive such a memorable quote by a mutual friend.

Busted rattled me to the bone. For one thing, it featured me as a character in Ehrhart's story. Among his litany of abusive encounters with the forces of law and order during the Nixon administration's widening of the war in Southeast Asia to include home front political "enemies" was a bizarre entanglement Bill and I had with New York City police in the wake of a poetry reading. It felt further bizarre to see my name changed in the book, in the interest of protecting "the privacy of living persons and the families and relatives of the dead."

Far more troublesome than being anonymous in a story I was part of is that I couldn't imagine revealing the turmoil of my thoughts or my life so starkly as Bill did.

My response to this unsettling exposure as a poet ensnarled in a police dragnet in *Busted* was to begin formulating a very different sort of public affairs book. Given Bill's disciplined publishing schedule, I created a deadline for writing a book that I'd been thinking about doing for years. In 2000, Rutgers University Press published *A Citizen's Guide to Grassroots Campaigns*, my community workshop approach to organizing for social change. It featured an array of personal anecdotes that illustrated how various people tackled a variety of social issues. That was a technique I learned in newspaper reporting and honed in emulating Bill's well-crafted weaving of personal and political aspects of life.

Bill Ehrhart's apparent style of letting it all hang out is deceptive. He doesn't in fact reveal all, but is highly selective in the details he uses to tell a story. The account of his disagreement with a judge over the duties of jurors doesn't reveal he'd studied law for a job as a paralegal aide. The blow by blow rendering of the run-in with New York City police after a poetry reading doesn't mention that fact, either; he didn't want the cops to know that, in his day job, he worked with a federal task force investigating police corruption.

Under the surface of Bill's seemingly dashed off venting lies a lot of scholarship. He marshals his material to create teachable moments.

"I began to write about the war. I didn't know it then, but the writing was a way to get at what had happened to me and why and how I felt about it," he noted in "Why Didn't You Tell Me?," an essay in *The Madness of It All* that first appeared in *Studies in Education* in 1994. "My writing has been for me a continuing education, as I hope it is for those who read it. Somewhere along the way, I came to understand that I have been an educator all my adult life."

And then there's the strategy he developed as a poet, pieced together from prodigious study of classical and contemporary poetry.

"As a poet, that's what I want a poem to do. Shake things up. Get under people's skin. Get into their heads and stay there," he wrote in "Batter My Heart with the Liquor Store: or, Teaching Poetry to Teenagers," a speech he gave at a teachers' conference, reprinted in *Dead on a High Hill: Essays on War, Literature and Living, 2002–2012*.[11] "I want to make my readers laugh and cry and ache and gasp and see the world in ways they never thought of made suddenly familiar by my words. And when they put down a poem of mine, I want them to say to themselves, 'Wow.'"

That's how I've felt on reading—and rereading—many of Bill's poems.

A couple of winters ago, I was in my usual cold weather funk, exacerbated that season by my wife dying during the Christmas holidays ten years before. When I get blue beyond the soothing realms of jazz, I reach for poetry. The rhythmic kick of well-placed words works better for me than pills or booze. So it was that I grabbed from a pile of books near my desk a copy of Ehrhart's latest poetry collection, *The Bodies Beneath the Table*. Through that dark night, I read each poem aloud, awash in thunderstorms of emotions set in motion by Bill's poems and my life, and got up refreshed.

One of the poems that made me feel Bill was right there in the room talking with me is "All About Death." The concluding kicker is:

> My mother-in-law
> died twenty-five years ago, but my wife
> still cries out in her sleep for her mommy.
> Sometimes my wife isn't even asleep.[12]

Much of this collection of poems is about death or dying, in Vietnam and other wars and at home. "Letting Go" is about Bill's mother, yet it describes in chillingly detail my wife's last moments as well—from laying in a coma "willing herself to live / in spite of the cancer that wanted her dead," to the son whispering to her

> It's okay, Mom.
> You've done your best. Your work is done.
> It's time to rest. Let go.[13]

Bill's interweaving of "wow"-level poetry, provocative essays and classroom teaching often resonated with me. After decades of guest appearances reading my poetry in college and high school classes, sometimes alongside Bill or more often in his wake, I began to focus on teaching college courses, which I've been doing since retiring from newspaper work.

I'm still working on how to be as challenging a teacher as Bill is. Consider this address he gave to seniors at The Haverford School, where over the past decade he's created a crucible of life lessons by way of teaching American and British literature and history:

> Are you going to continue to make the same mistakes humanity has been making since time out of mind? Are you going to continue to think in terms of me and mine, us and them, my good fortune and your tough luck, my country versus your country, my way or no way, this is mine and I deserve it? Are you going to continue to live as the generations before you have lived, as if the future will always be there?
>
> Or are you going to do what has never been done before: learn to think truly and genuinely, creatively, imaginatively, globally, selflessly, beyond borders and boundaries and horizons, beyond old fears and comfortable truisms that are leading us inevitably toward irreversible disaster?[14]

Bill's teachable moments don't just occur in classrooms, conferences and auditoriums. On June 14, 2012, I was at a Warrior Writers workshop for veterans of the wars in Afghanistan and Iraq that was held at the Wounded Warriors offices in New York City. As a writing prompt for the dozen or so military veterans looking to learn how to write about haunting experiences, workshop director Lovella Calica handed out copies of an Ehrhart essay titled "If This Be War."[15] The Warrior Writers project has been using many of Bill's poems and essays to help spur participants to tackle war demons in workshops in various locales around the country for several years.

It is another of his literary legacies that I've run into, and gotten another boost from, in working with the Warrior Writers program and other projects with veterans.

Perhaps as a consequence of his academic studies, certainly from his enthusiastic explorations of the range of poetry, Bill developed a fine eye for the telling details in other poets' work. Over the years, he's written numerous essays that assessed an astounding variety of poets, from the well-known to, by his lights, the unjustly overlooked. So it was with some trepidation that I read his review of *Earth Songs: New & Selected Poems*, my book-length collection that appeared in 2003.[16] The review was titled "What's the Point of Poetry," reprinted in *Dead on a High Hill*.[17]

After duly noting the historic nature of my involvement in putting together *Winning Hearts & Minds*, a set of my war poems that were widely anthologized and several lesser known and newer poems he felt were worthy of mention, he made this observation: "Most moving of all, I think, are Barry's poems to his wife, Paula Kay Pierce, from the early love poem 'Paula Kay' ... to 'Death in America,' where he writes of Paula's losing battle with cancer ... to her return to him in dreams...."

Yet again, I'd been greatly influenced, or perhaps coaxed to expand my poetry beyond war themes by Bill Ehrhart's attentively focused poetry about his family. "For Anne, Approaching Thirty-five" is one of Bill's signature poems to his wife. "What Keeps Me Going," was the title of an early poem about his infant daughter, Leela, who kept him afloat when he felt "pressed down by the weight / of despair...."[18]

A poem of mine on the same theme in *Earth Songs* was titled "Saved":

> Despair
> tears black holes
> sucking in dreams,
> hopes, plans—
> shredding my soul—
> until a call to dinner,
> round up the kids;
> "Hey, help me out!"
> pulls me out

Memories get hazy at my age. But I'm certain that it was my long and intense interaction with Bill Ehrhart, probing the width and depth of poetry, pondering the meaning of it all, that sparked the poem I wrote in 1981 for *Peace Is Our Profession* that he quoted in reviewing *Earth Songs*.

> What's the point of poetry?
> Might as well ask what's the point of spring.
> What's the point of a flower opening....

Bill Ehrhart—as a poet, author, editor, teacher and cherished friend of many folks—provokes such elemental and challenging thoughts.

Notes

1. Rottmann, Larry, Jan Barry, and Basil T. Paquet, eds., *Winning Hearts & Minds: War Poems by Vietnam Veterans* (Brooklyn, NY: First Casualty Press/McGraw-Hill, 1972).

2. Barry, Jan and W.D., Ehrhart, eds., *Demilitarized Zones: Veterans after Vietnam* (Perkasie, PA: East River Anthology, 1976).

3. Ehrhart, W.D., *The Madness of It All: Essays on War, Literature and American Life* (Jefferson, NC: McFarland, 2002).

4. Barry, Jan, ed., *Peace Is Our Profession: Poems and Passages of War Protest* (Perkasie, PA: East River Anthology, 1981).

5. Rottmann, Larry, Wayne Karlin, and Basil T. Paquet, eds., *Free Fire Zones: Short Stories by Vietnam Veterans* (Brooklyn, NY: First Casualty Press/McGraw-Hill, 1973).

6. First published in *Demilitarized Zones*, 157; and subsequently in several other books.

7. Ehrhart, W.D., *Matters of the Heart* (Easthampton, MA: Adastra Press, 1981).

8. Ehrhart, W.D., ed., *Carrying the Darkness: Poetry of the Vietnam War* (Lubbock: Texas Tech University Press, 1989).

9. Ehrhart, W.D., ed., *Unaccustomed Mercy: Soldier-Poets of the Vietnam War* (Lubbock: Texas Tech University Press, 1989).

10. Ehrhart, W.D., *Busted: A Vietnam Veteran in Nixon's America* (Amherst, MA: University of Massachusetts Press, 1995).

11. Ehrhart, W.D., *Dead on a High Hill: Essays on War, Literature and Living, 2002–2012* (Jefferson, NC: McFarland, 2012).

12. Ehrhart, W.D., *The Bodies Beneath the Table* (Easthampton, MA: Adastra Press, 2010), 23.

13. Ehrhart, *The Bodies Beneath the Table*, 34–35.

14. Ehrhart, W.D., "What the Fuss Is All About," *Dead on a High Hill*, 80–83.

15. Ehrhart, "If This Be war," *The Madness of It All*, 10–12.

16. Barry, Jan, *Earth Songs: New & Selected Poems* (Bloomington, IN: iUniverse, Inc., 2003).

17. Ehrhart, "What's the Point of Poetry," *Dead on a High Hill*, 67–69.

18. Ehrhart, W.D., *Just for Laughs* (Silver Spring, MD: Vietnam Generation Inc. & Burning Cities Press, 1990), 79.

The Importance of Being Earnest: A Veteran's Eye View of W. D. Ehrhart's Vietnam War Poetry and Prose

EDWARD F. PALM

In November 1994, at the Sixties Generation Conference, Adi Wimmer[1] and H. Bruce Franklin[2] advanced essentially the same theory about why W. D. Ehrhart is not for the masses, or at least not for a commercial publisher. Wimmer likened the Vietnam War to the Holocaust and Ehrhart to a Holocaust survivor. He suggested that Ehrhart's unpopularity stems from his insistence on "bearing moral witness" to events the country is trying to forget or even deny. Franklin agreed with Wimmer but suggested that the problem also lies with officialdom. He credited Ehrhart with "piercing the mantle of plausible deniability"—with running afoul of the "ours was a noble cause" wave of revisionism our national leadership was then promoting. To Franklin, Ehrhart was "a modern-day Jeremiah who had made himself unwelcome in polite literary circles."

The common ground between the two was the implication that our so-called "liberal media establishment" had closed ranks against someone who challenges the conservative agenda. Wimmer and Franklin, I think, were overreaching. Ehrhart's unflinching honesty indeed may have accounted for his unpopularity among a public sentimentally inclined to kick, or even deny, the "Vietnam syndrome." But I have to believe that the reason he remained largely on the margins, while Vietnam writers like Tim O'Brien and Michael Herr achieved both commercial and critical success, may finally have more to do with his poetics than his politics.

Back when people first started taking Vietnam War literature seriously, Philip Beidler published a seminal essay that still applies today. In this essay, entitled "Truth-Telling and Literary Values in the Vietnam Novel," Beidler argues that two elements account for the peculiar character of that first generation of Vietnam literature: first, Vietnam writers began writing in close proximity to the historical events, often while the war was still being fought; and, second, they were usually writing with polemical purpose, to bear moral witness to "the horror" of the war. These elements led to a generally intractable demand for "truth-telling" in the sense of verisimilitude.[3]

That first generation of Vietnam writers felt they had to conform realistically to the audience's media-created vision of what the Vietnam War was "like"—greatly limiting the writer's prerogative to reorder and shape the raw materials of life, arriving at some more imaginative or innovative vision of the underlying Truth (with a capital "T") of the experience than straight realism would allow. In short, in stressing polemical purpose, these writers limited literary value. The prevailing mood at the time was that the message was too important to leave to "literature" lest the reader miss the point. Hence, the message became the medium. The essential character of Vietnam literature, according to Beidler, is a compromise between telling it "like it was" and asserting the writer's traditional artistic license to generalize in innovative ways.

Beidler goes a long way toward explaining Ehrhart's limited success. Ehrhart hails from that first generation of truth-tellers and, insofar as his Vietnam War poetry and prose go, is essentially still *of* it. This, I believe, is why he got a modicum of recognition for his Vietnam War writing but not publishing contracts from the commercial literary establishment. It is also why someone like Tim O'Brien is still the darling of that establishment. There is an expectation that literature take the long view and that it be fresh and innovative. O'Brien became a commercial and critical success because he met this expectation. While O'Brien soft-pedals, and even obscures, his polemical purpose in favor of literary value, Ehrhart is first and foremost committed to truth-telling—to telling it like it was.

Recalling the deep divisions of the war in fact, by the 1990s, imaginative recreations of the American war in Vietnam were polarizing people along critical lines. The older "sense making" cultural critiques that first won serious attention for this literature were losing ground to a "literature of trauma," as Sixties Generation founder Kalí Tal had termed it. While Vietnam writers and critics alike once found their "usable past" in the myths associated with America's founding and its frontier,[4] the proponents of this new school drew on the existential, mysteries of the human heart, suggesting that the Holocaust is finally a more meaningful parallel to the Vietnam experience than anything endemic to the American cultural narrative. And they adopted Ehrhart as the writer who best exemplified their politically correct view of the holocaust America had visited upon Vietnam.

The first, and still the best, comprehensive statement of this new critical school was Kalí Tal's *Worlds of Hurt: Reading the Literature of Trauma*. Tal essentially outlined a new set of literary rules of engagement with this literature. The literature of trauma, she maintains, is defined by the following elements, all of which she locates in Ehrhart's work: First, the experience of trauma; second, the urge to bear witness to that trauma; third, a sense of community with [his] fellow survivors; and, fourth, "the struggle to prevent his own traumatic experience from being appropriated and incorporated into an American national myth that does not reflect his experience."[5]

Superficially at least, Ehrhart's life and work do fit within Tal's paradigm. While his war-related poems and memoirs are not without literary merit, they are unabashedly polemical. Ehrhart remained in O'Brien's shadow, it still seems to me, because he wrote primarily for the "never again" crowd.

I shared this assessment with Ehrhart not long after sharing it with the Sixties Generation online discussion forum. He wrote back to me, disputing my assessment with the self-deprecating honesty characteristic of so much of his writing:

> I don't write, and never have written, for the "never again" crowd." I write what is in my heart.... If I were more clever, more subtle, more talented, more astute, perhaps I too could take the long view, be fresh and innovative, and thereby become a darling of the commercial literary establishment. But I am, alas, a plodding dullard who cannot seem to imagine issues larger or more important than the myriad issues raised by the American destruction of Indochina.[6]

In a subsequent letter, he expressed his gratitude for Tal's thoughtful and sympathetic exploration of his writing, but also admitted his discomfort at "being pegged as the paradigm of a 'survivor poet.'"[7]

Whatever else Ehrhart may be, he is certainly not a "plodding dullard." But the rest of his last sentence, in my view, belies his premise. There is an earnestness about his Vietnam writings—an insistence on "bearing moral witness," as Wimmer put it—that makes his work more polemical than poetic in the larger aesthetic sense of the term.

This earnestness is certainly in keeping with the poststructuralist push toward relevance and away from "empty aestheticism." But the literary establishment of the eighties and nineties remained committed to traditional "literary values" (albeit in a postmodern sense), and that is why they merely blessed Ehrhart but canonized O'Brien. In short, they saw Ehrhart as more of a Vietnam writer than a writer exploring larger issues within a Vietnam setting. As a Vietnam veteran turned academic, I have always been plagued by a peculiar double-vision in viewing Ehrhart's life and work. I appreciate the literary values of writers like Michael Herr and Tim O'Brien—who draw on analogy, metaphor, myth, literary parallels, and metafiction—in interpreting and making sense of our Vietnam experience. But, as a veteran, I initially found myself drawn toward those writers who dwell on the individual disillusionment and pain of the war. These are the writers who bear witness to the "horror" of the war in an effort, as Tal notes, to make it "real" to the victim, his own community of sufferers, and to sympathetic readers.[8]

The writer who first made the Vietnam War "real" to me, validating my trauma and cementing my fellowship with a community of veterans, was W. D. Ehrhart.[9] A meaningful popular culture parallel, it seems to me, can be drawn between Ehrhart and the musical voice of my generation, Bob Dylan. Dylan was widely credited with re-creating the authentic, rustic voice of American folk music—in "a voice that came from you and me," as Don Mclean characterized it in his ballad "American Pie." Ehrhart, likewise, can be credited with re-creating the authentic voice of a subset of our generation—those of us who served in Vietnam.

To fall back on one of Tal's key terms, I first recognized in Ehrhart's work the "basic wound,"[10] the common trauma suffered by all of us who went to Vietnam. The single-greatest obstacle to understanding why America could not prevail in Vietnam, ironically, is to persist in viewing that sad experience as just a war. Vietnam was finally a metaphor for a world that simply was not the way it was supposed to be—at least not from the standpoint of those who saw action in either of the war's theaters, "in country" or back "in the World." To expand upon Jonathan Shay's focus in his masterful *Achilles in Vietnam*,[11] our Achilles' heel in Vietnam was neither the liberal media nor our irresolute political leadership, but rather the naïve idealism of the 1960s generation.

Raised in relative prosperity and nurtured by the great American myths that had seemingly been validated by the outcome of the Second World War, most of us who came of age during the 1960s held "these truths to be self-evident": "Truth, justice, and the American way" was a redundant phrase, and America always had been, and always would be, on the side of right. Of course, the civil rights movement, coming as it did on the eve of our Vietnam involvement, marked the beginning of my generation's painful trek from innocence to experience. But the journey's end proved to be Vietnam, where our American dream vanished and we all awoke to an American nightmare.

In my opinion, Ehrhart remains the best, and certainly the most accessible, chronicler of this process of individual and collective disillusionment. Unlike so many of us who were enlisted Marines in those years, Ehrhart had been a promising student with the means to go to college when he graduated from high school in 1966. He could easily have gotten a deferment, but he chose to enlist instead, intent upon demonstrating his faith in the old verities at a time when so many others were beginning to doubt. The erosion of that faith is the subject of much of Ehrhart's early poetry as well as his three artfully written and moving memoirs—all of which are written in a voice that rings true to those of us who were there.

In *Vietnam–Perkasie*, for instance, Ehrhart describes his arrival in Vietnam and how while being driven to his unit he was chided for waving to the people. "Who do you think you are? Douglas MacArthur?" his driver asked. The driver went on to enlighten him about the people he was waving to: "We get sniped at along this road all the time. Half the people you're waving to are probably VC. Couple of weeks ago, some gook tossed a grenade into a truck right here in this marketplace. Messed up a few guys real good."[12]

In the preface to *Vietnam–Perkasie*, Ehrhart describes how the realities of the war soon dashed that naïve self-image of himself as a liberator:

> In Vietnam, there were few things worse than having time on your hands—time to think about what you'd been doing and what was going on around you; time to compare the America you'd enlisted for with the one you saw blowing up villages, and tearing up rice fields with tanks and amphibious tractors, and bullying old men and women, and generally running around with your rifle and your name shooting anything that moved.[13]

This process of disillusionment is exacerbated by the character of the conflict. As Ehrhart complains in his poem "Guerrilla War," "it's practically impossible / to tell the civilians / from the Vietcong. / After a while / you quit trying."[14]

What rings true to me here is the existential ethos that prevailed among the troops in Vietnam. Plunked down in an alien culture we didn't understand and unable to distinguish friend from foe, we viewed Vietnam as an absurd, naturalistic universe unto itself where everything and everyone was a potential threat and where the ordinary rules of civilized society did not apply. Not for nothing did we refer to the States as "the World." The absurdity, moreover, was compounded by the individual rotation policy. We had no stake in the outcome of the war; we only had to survive our 12- or 13-month tours of duty.[15] Hence, survival become the only moral touchstone, and a primal ethic of mutual dependency became the norm. As the narrator of Vietnam veteran Larry Heinemann's novel *Close Quarters* puts it, "You cover me and I'll cover you and we'll all go home."[16] Hence, for too many of us in Vietnam, whatever seemed to enhance our chances of survival, including unprovoked preemptive action against civilians, could seem justified.

A good example of this existential attitude can be found in Ehrhart's poem "Time on Target," an account of the effects of the harassment and interdiction (H & I) artillery fire we engaged in as a terror tactic in Vietnam. Essentially, we chose trail junctions and other possible places where the enemy might gather and fired artillery, often at random, at those targets. The idea was to keep the enemy off balance and apprehensive, making him feel that there were no safe havens for him. Some of the targets were chosen on the basis of intelligence reports, but as Ehrhart explains in *Vietnam–Perkasie*, those reports were rarely reliable.[17] In any event, it did not seem to concern us that the enemy lived and moved among the people and that these likely assembly points were often in or adjacent to villages.

As a mere corporal, moreover, Ehrhart found himself responsible for choosing the targets. His poem "Time on Target" concludes with an account of how on patrol one day he finally gets to see the results of his work: "a woman / with her left hand torn away; / beside her lay a child, dead."[18] Ehrhart's reaction is characteristic of that existential mindset most of us succumbed to in Vietnam: "It gave us all a lift to know / all those shells we fired every night / were hitting something."[19] Ehrhart's intention is not simply to shock but rather to illustrate how the conditions we endured and the things we witnessed in Vietnam could warp the sensibility of even a good middle-class American boy.

In her study, Tal suggests that the survivors of trauma inhabit a world in which the dead are more real to them than the living.[20] This insight is somewhat borne out by Ehrhart's third memoir *Busted*[21] (which I will examine later). But it really does not apply to the existential in-country mindset that Ehrhart recreates in much of his poetry. A case in point is "The One That Died":

> You bet we'll soon forget the one that died;
> he isn't welcome any more.
> He could too easily take our place
> for us to think about him
> any longer than it takes
> to sort his personal effects....

The third line inverts our expectation, speaking to the process of dissociation that typically took place among survivors in Vietnam. There is a subtext here that only a veteran is likely to recognize and fully appreciate. The only way to maintain that youthful illusion of immortality is to hold the man who died responsible for his own death and to practice a kind of shunning. He is dead to the rest of the men in an existential sense. He is never to be thought of or mentioned again. His only residual value lies in what the men can use—his cigarettes.[22]

Tal—again, in my view and in my experience—overstates the case in viewing Ehrhart as reacting to an unfathomable Evil comparable to that of the Holocaust. What Ehrhart's Vietnam poems illustrate is a perfectly understandable existential reaction to a naturalistic setting we didn't understand and where everything seemed to present a threat.

Where Tal is completely correct, however, is in noting how trauma survivors resist and resent any appropriation of their experience. Ehrhart's poem "The Invasion of Grenada" is a case in point:

> I didn't want a monument,
> not even one as sober as that
> vast black wall of broken lives.
> I didn't want a postage stamp.
> I didn't want a road beside the Delaware
> River with a sign proclaiming:
> "Vietnam Veterans Memorial Highway."

Aside from an end to the sort of arrogance and ethnocentricity that took us to Vietnam in the first place, the narrator wants no less than "an end to monuments."[23]

Ehrhart especially resents the distortion of his Vietnam experience in order to reinscribe the cherished myth of America as the redeemer nation. This is the theme of Ehrhart's most bitter Vietnam War poem, "A Relative Thing." After vividly describing the ugly realities behind the official euphemisms and the inadequacies of the misplaced and uninformed gestures of support, the narrator describes the crux of the problem. The World War II generation was trying to force-fit their sons "into the uniforms of photographs / of [them] at twenty-one."[24] The selling of the Vietnam War, as Ehrhart realized, involved the pretense that the aims were as noble and clear-cut as those of World War II. Ehrhart here puts his finger on the source of the generational tension that was so much a part of the Sixties.

The thought that nothing was learned from the American experience in Vietnam is a particularly painful realization among veterans. Ehrhart has given eloquent voice to this sense of disillusionment and disappointment in his poem "Letter," addressed to the North Vietnamese soldier who had tried to kill him in the battle for Hue during the Tet Offensive of 1968:

> Remember Ho Chi Minh
> was a poet: please,
> do not let it all come down
> to nothing.[25]

This sense of retrospective longing for some ameliorative result runs throughout the prose trilogy in which Ehrhart recounts his Vietnam experience and his painful, prolonged period of readjustment: *Vietnam–Perkasie, Passing Time,* and *Busted*. To return to Beidler's distinction, Ehrhart's memoirs, like his Vietnam War poetry, are concerned first and foremost with truth-telling, but they are hardly devoid of literary value or artistic merit.

The first in the series, *Vietnam–Perkasie,* is not simply a linear, chronological account of Ehrhart's in-country experience and its immediate aftermath. Ehrhart employs an *in medias res* opening, and in the preface to the first edition, while he does not actually use the term "nonfiction novel," he makes it clear that he has reordered events, created composite characters, and even appropriated the experiences of others as his own.[26]

At this stage of his life, Ehrhart felt that the underlying Truth—with a capital "T"—of the Vietnam experience was larger than that of any individual veteran's experience and that testifying to that Truth was too important to be left to fiction lest the reader fail to appreciate how the war traumatized those of us raised to trust in the old American verities. Many of the experiences Ehrhart recounts in *Vietnam–Perkasie* recall the war stories we used to hear and pass on in Vietnam, most of which were exaggerated and some of which probably never happened.

As Tim O'Brien points out in *The Things They Carried*, war stories are not about the factual truth. They are a means of illustrating and testifying to the existential truths of how the war affected the teller.[27] The experience of trauma is essentially ineffable,[28] but some sense of how it affected the survivor can be conveyed through metaphor and analogy, even if the effect is only to shock the listener or reader into the realization that he or she cannot imagine how it really felt.

Ehrhart's trilogy is especially notable for recreating the sense of anomie that, to some extent, we all suffered from upon returning from Vietnam. There is an almost embarrassing degree of candor regarding his rowdy behavior and his difficulties in establishing meaningful relationships with women. To those of us in his "community of survivors," Ehrhart's confessions are not merely self-indulgent attempts at unburdening himself. The fact is that many of my own post–Vietnam missteps parallel the ones Ehrhart relates.

In 1996, I reviewed Ehrhart's trilogy for a tough audience, the readership of *Marine Corps Gazette*, the professional journal of Marine officers.[29] I reassured the *Gazette*'s readers that *Vietnam–Perkasie* is not simply another angry screed whose author pretends to a smug moral superiority. At every step along the way, Ehrhart recreates, and remains faithful to, his point of view at the time, leaving readers to draw their own conclusions.

Vietnam has been called our first rock-and-roll war.[30] As O'Brien's narrator in *Going After Cacciato* remind the reader, "Everyone was so incredibly goddamned young."[31] It was not just a matter of chronological age or even of youthful inexperience and naïveté. The post–World-War-II baby boom generation brought its manners and mores to Vietnam, accounting for the war's peculiar tone and the moments of levity found in both O'Brien and Ehrhart's works.

O'Brien, it must be admitted, creates moments of piercing and insightful irony that challenge the reader. An apt analogy would be the kind of clever repartee and quips found in situation comedies on television. We admire that sort of wit, mainly because it is seldom found or sustained in real life. Hence, in terms of Beidler's distinction, O'Brien's work wins out in terms of purely literary value. Ehrhart, on the other hand, leavens his account of his Vietnam experiences with liberal doses of self-ironic humor and playful exaggeration that ring true to me in terms of my own Vietnam experience. His hilarious hyperbolic account of how well-meaning people deluged his unit with chocolate chip cookies is a case in point.[32] Ehrhart instinctively knows what so many of our Vietnam writers either forgot or never knew: literature does not have to strike a tone of unrelenting high seriousness in order to be serious.

In the same vein, the worst thing a writer can do is take him- or herself too seriously, a fault Ehrhart certainly avoids in his middle memoir, *Passing Time*.[33] Ehrhart looks back on his days at Swarthmore College from the perspective of the temporary repose he later found as a merchant marine seaman.

While *Passing Time* may fall short of O'Brien's metafictional heights, it is artfully written and self-contained. The narrative frame consists of Ehrhart's attempts to explain himself to an older shipmate. He finds he must confront the war and what it made him. Interwoven throughout his poignant and often humorous account of his attempts to fit in as a college student and dormitory adviser, therefore, are many of the same experiences recounted in *Vietnam-Perkasie*, this time rendered as short, sharp dramatic vignettes or flashbacks. The effect is one of ironic contrast. How does a Marine accustomed to facing real life-and-death issues adjust to a liberal college campus, where term papers, tests, and protests take on an absurd life-and-death urgency? Ehrhart never really did, and the missteps he recounts in *Passing Time* are sometimes funny, sometimes sad, but never self-indulgent or self-pitying. He remains self-ironic throughout, displaying the candor and wisdom to laugh at himself and his own foibles.

The final volume in the trilogy, *Busted*, recounts how Ehrhart lost his pleasant sanctuary at sea when he was "busted" for bringing marijuana aboard his ship and how he fought to keep his merchant marine credential. Ironically, at the same time Ehrhart was contesting the loss of his credential the country was struggling with the Watergate scandal.

Busted essentially poses the rhetorical question, who among us in 1966 could have envisioned the America of 1974? It also supports Tal's contention that "the Vietnam veteran inhabits a land peopled with the dead."[34] Throughout the novel, Ehrhart manages to keep the innocent past alive in a cynical present. He is visited periodically by the ghosts of three friends who had been killed in Vietnam. They become his Greek chorus, guiding him through his interrogation of the past and the present. All of us who were in Vietnam, to some degree, carry our ghosts from that war with us. But more importantly, in terms of Ehrhart's artistry, the ghosts in *Busted* function as a kind of objective correlative, evoking the bitter sense of disillusionment and alienation Vietnam veterans in general were feeling by the 1970s.

There was a time when my graduate-trained sensibility preferred the metafictional tour-de-force of Tim O'Brien and the brilliant analogies and cultural allusions of Michael Herr. But along the way I realized that not many veterans, much less the general reading public, have read or can fully appreciate *Going After Cacciato* or *Dispatches*. Both are intensely literary books that demand much of the reader. They recall how James Joyce expected his readers to devote their lives to studying his works.

There is, of course, a place in the literary pantheon for James Joyce and, at less exalted rungs, for Tim O'Brien and Michael Herr. But there also needs to be a middle-brow rung for the writers who can reach the reasonably educated general reading public. It is an important place because the writers who fit there have the greatest chance of shaping opinion and influencing public policy. This, to my mind, is where Ehrhart fits. To return to Beidler's distinction, Ehrhart may be essentially a "truth-teller," but he is an artful one. And some truths are just too important to be left to the literati.

Notes

1. Wimmer, Adi, "The Violence We've Inherited: W.D. Ehrhart's Post-Vietnam Poetry and the Labor of Mourning," Sixties Generations Conference, Danbury, CT, 5 Nov. 1994, lecture.

2. Franklin, H. Bruce, "Busted, or, the Strange Case of W.D. Ehrhart," Sixties Generations Conference, Danbury, CT, 5 Nov. 1994, lecture.

3. Beidler, Philip D., "Truth-Telling and Literary Values in the Vietnam Novel," *South Atlantic Quarterly*, 87:2 (1979), 141–156.

4. Palm, Edward F., "The Search for a Usable Past: Vietnam Literature and the Separate Peace Syndrome," *South Atlantic Quarterly*, 82:2 (1983), 115–128.

5. Tal, Kalí, *Worlds of Hurt: Reading the Literatures of Trauma* (Cambridge: Cambridge University Press, 1996), 78.

6. Ehrhart, W.D., Letter to the author, 17 Jan. 1995.

7. Ehrhart, W.D., Letter to the author, 25 Jan. 1996.

8. Tal, 21.

9. I first met Ehrhart in 1991 at the U.S. Naval Academy. I was a Marine major assigned to the English Department at the time, and Professor Philip Jason had invited him to visit classes we were both teaching in Vietnam War literature. Having both been enlisted Marines in Vietnam, we struck up a conversation, and I shared with him a copy of my own two-part Vietnam memoir, "Tiger Papa Three," first published in *Marine Corps Gazette*. Ehrhart read my memoir and was kind enough to write, praising my writing. In 1996, he visited my class "Vietnam in Fact, Fiction, and Film" at Glenville State College, in West Virginia. We have remained friends and have stayed in touch ever since first meeting at the Naval Academy.

10. Tal, 78.

11. Shay, Jonathan, *Achilles in Vietnam: Combat Trauma and the Undoing of Character* (New York: Macmillan, 1994).

12. Ehrhart, W.D., *Vietnam–Perkasie: A Combat Marine Memoir* (Jefferson, NC: McFarland, 1983), 21.

13. Ibid.
14. Ehrhart, W.D., *Carrying the Darkness: The Poetry of the Vietnam War* (Lubbock: Texas Tech University Press, 1985), 93–94.
15. Soldiers had to stay for 12 months, Marines for 13.
16. Heinemann, Larry, *Close Quarters* (New York: Farrar, Straus, Giroux, 1977), 329.
17. Ehrhart, *Vietnam–Perkasie*, 103.
18. Ehrhart, *Carrying the Darkness*, 94–95.
19. Ehrhart, *Carrying the Darkness*, 95.
20. Tal, 87.
21. Ehrhart, W.D., *Busted: A Vietnam Veteran in Nixon's America* (Amherst, MA: University of Massachusetts Press, 1995).
22. Ehrhart, *Carrying the Darkness*, 92–93.
23. Ehrhart, *Carrying the Darkness*, 103.
24. Ehrhart, *Carrying the Darkness*, 95–97.
25. Ehrhart, *Carrying the Darkness*, 98–99.
26. Ehrhart, *Vietnam–Perkasie*, xi.
27. O'Brien, Tim, *The Things They Carried* (Boston: Houghton Mifflin, 1990), 73–91.
28. Tal, 78,
29. Palm, Edward F., "Perkasie Lost: W.D. Ehrhart's Vietnam Saga," *Marine Corps Gazette*, Apr. 1996, 65–67.
30. Michael Herr, in *Dispatches*, first popularized the connection in one of his most provocative and insightful passages: "The Sixties had made so many casualties, its war and its music had run power off the same circuit for so long they didn't even have to fuse." *Dispatches* (New York: Knopf, 1978), 223.
31. O'Brien, Tim, *Going After Cacciato* (New York: Dell, 1989), 179.
32. Ehrhart, *Vietnam–Perkasie*, 76.
33. Ehrhart, W.D., *Passing Time: Memoir of a Vietnam Veteran Against the War* (Jefferson, NC: McFarland, 1989).
34. Tal, 87.

Authentic Voices:
Echoes of Bill Ehrhart and Me

Robert C. Doyle

Vietnam–Perkasie seemed to be an innocuous title by W. D. Ehrhart, an author I had heard of but not yet read. I had just finished my doctorate in American Culture Studies in 1987 and landed an instructor job in the American Studies Program at Penn State. Little did I know at that moment when my chair, Dr. Dan Walden, suggested that I needed an "authentic voice" to stimulate the class I lovingly called "The American Dream and the Vietnam War" that my relationship with this writer, Vietnam veteran, and former Marine would change my life and touch the lives of so many of my students in three countries for so long.

In a real sense, Bill Ehrhart and I are true birds of a feather. Both of us are Baby Boomers, born and raised in very traditional families in the Philadelphia area. Bill recalled those years, "In elementary school, I read books about John Paul Jones and Pecos Bill, and at Halloween I collected money for UNICEF to help the children in countries less fortunate than my own."[1] We grew up around World War II veterans who above everything else showed a true pride in their military service. Deep inside of us, we wanted to be just like them, maybe even a little better. Bill noted: "Once Jeff Alison and I sneaked into his father's bedroom and found the Silver Star cradled in velvet in a black box with gilt trim."[2] We were Kennedy-era kids who took our hero John F. Kennedy at his word when he called us to action in his 1961 inaugural speech. We wanted to see the world, be part of what was going on at the time, be part of something larger than ourselves, and maybe walk away heroes, stamped with the "Well Done" brand on our foreheads just like the generation that gave us life. We feared very little except failure. We were bulletproof with pimples on our faces. They were heady days.

John F. Kennedy was assassinated in November 1963, the year I became a Navy ROTC midshipman at Penn State University. In August of 1964, while blissfully life guarding my summer away in a small community swimming pool in West Germany, I learned about the Tonkin Gulf Incident from some German friends. At eighteen years old, I shrugged it off; my frowning friends said it meant war for the United States, maybe a war we could not win this time. What did Germans know about war anyway? More than I did, for sure.

By 1965, my junior year in college, my German friends seemed more correct: President Lyndon B. Johnson ordered the U.S.M.C. to go on offensive operations in the northern part of South Vietnam. Casualties mounted rapidly. One year later, Bill Ehrhart enlisted in the United States Marine Corps. Asking the fundamental question, his friend said, "You've really joined the Marines?" They'll send you to Vietnam. You could get killed." "I know," Bill replied. "You're crazy," she said, "but I really admire you."[3] Soon, the 1966 civilian high school graduate and patriot Bill Ehrhart found himself facing drill sergeants screaming at him in boot camp at Parris Island, South Carolina.

Marine Corps boot camp at Parris Island is nothing short of a rite of passage that every enlisted Marine endures. It takes young men and now women from civilian life and forms them into what the U.S.M.C. calls "the roughest, toughest, most destructive fighting force the world has ever known." Everything changes, including the common language: yes becomes aye aye sir; food becomes chow; floors become decks; ceilings become the overhead; walls become bulkheads; clothes become fatigues; hair simply disappears; toilets become heads; sergeants become gods, and recruits become the scum of the earth. For a while, that is, until they shed the veneer of their civilian world and become United States Marines. Bill recalled his arrival at Parris Island:

> The DI who got into the bus was eight and a half feet tall. And he was ugly. He blocked the huge windshield of the bus completely. His chest strained at the buttons of his shirt, so that they seemed about to fly off at any moment like buckshot from a scattergun. Standing there with his hand on his hips, he looked like a cross between Paul Bunyan, Babe the Blue Ox, and Godzilla.... "Get in the building." Three of four more identical copies of Godzilla, the Blue Bunyan materialized out of nowhere, all of them shouting, "Get in the building. Line up in front of the tables. Double Time. Get in the building." We began to surge forward frantically in one lump, bodies in back climbing over the ones in front of them like stampeded cattle, stumbling and falling and crawling on hands and knees and getting up and falling again.[4]

Without this thoroughly shocking transition, no one can become a Marine. Maybe that is why I joined the Navy.

My encounter with the U.S.M.C. was very different. My father served in World War II as a Navy Chief Shipfitter, and he never screamed at anybody. At Penn State, I encountered the Assistant Marine Instructor, Gunnery Sergeant John C. Smith, a Korean War veteran. "Gunny" Smith, a kind man who loved his midshipmen, never raised his voice to us. Yet Gunny Smith had his moments. I once asked him what it was like to "fight those people." I am certain he misunderstood my question. In 1966, I meant the Vietnamese communists; he thought I meant the North Koreans or Chinese. "Well, RC, it ain't all that bad if you have plenty of ammo and some extra barrels." I did not reply, but my inner self screamed "Oh my God, what have I gotten myself into?"

Bill endured and finished boot camp at the same time. He wrote:

> One million push-ups, eleven hundred and eighty-six obstacle courses, and twelve thousand "Aye, aye sirs" later, the good Lord did in fact deliver me, creating a lifetime convert in the process. As I stood in graduation formation on the parade deck, facing a replica of the statue of the Marines raising the flag at Iwo Jima, I thought back to the first night in June when I couldn't begin to conceive of this day. I burst into a broad grin, barely able to contain the pride struggling to get out of me in a mighty shout. In a few moments, I would be meritoriously promoted to Private First Class W.D. Ehrhart, United States Marine.[5]

At home on leave, his Quaker friend Sadie Thompson, knowing that Bill was going to Vietnam, asked him, "try not to kill anybody."[6]

In 1968, I received orders to the USS *Steinaker* DD 863, home-ported in Norfolk, Virginia. Trouble was that in August 1968, the ship was on a Western Pacific cruise, meaning it was sailing and fighting off the Vietnam coast. Seven months before I arrived in the western Pacific, Bill was fighting for his life with the 1st Battalion, 1st Marine Regiment at Con Thien and Hue City against the Viet Cong and the North Vietnamese Army.[7]

Up to January 1968, Bill served nearly twelve months with a Marine infantry battalion, amazingly without a scratch. The Marine Corps served thirteen month tours; everyone else—U.S. Army, Navy, Air Force, and Coast Guard—served twelve months to the day unless one got lucky and received the "million dollar wound" or went home in a box. When we got close to the date of departure—DEROS to us—we called ourselves "short" or "shortimers." Bill was "short" when the Vietcong and North Vietnamese attacked all forty-four provinces of South Vietnam at the end of January 1968, "Tet," the Vietnamese New Year of the Monkey.

The Marines had to rescue the Army in Hue City, and for the first time in the war, house to house fighting replaced jungle fighting, and it was just a mess. Bill wrote: "I mean everybody was getting hit.... That first day, we lost almost half our fighting strength." And in typical U.S.M.C. style, he blamed the Army: "It took us nearly fourteen hours to fight our way six blocks north from the edge of the city to the MACV (Military Assistance Command, Vietnam) compound one block south of the river—and when we got there, we had a few choice words for the goddamned Army and their goddammed light sniper fire."[8]

Bill took the opportunity to explain to his audience why most of Vietnam's Marine casualties took place early in a Marine's tour of duty. He explained quite correctly that they just "hadn't yet learned enough to avoid getting it. But guys got it in their last few months because they got stupid in a way that the new guys never could."[9] I saw that too when I finally got incountry in 1970, but as Bill and I agree, we fought different wars. His was a blood-drenched, angry, personal, infantryman's war. He never knew a Vietnamese who was not an enemy or a potential enemy. His Vietnamese were rarely allies or friends; rather, they were usually just targets when he could find them. Power to him came through the barrel of his rifle. He was in the middle of it all at the worst combat period of the war. As he wrote, "I was terrified."[10] Then, boom, a sudden explosion to his rear while he tried to boil water for coffee. The sound deafened him, and later corpsmen (Navy medics who served with the U.S.M.C.) removed lots of jagged shrapnel and rubble from his flak jacket, nothing permanent, but the utter chaos of combat was all around him. He had a month left in Vietnam, his thirteenth.

My war started in 1968 too, in August, a few months after Bill went home. I met the USS *Steinaker* DD-863 in Japan at the tail end of a Vietnam tour. From offshore, we conducted lots of gunfire support operations mostly for Marines and Navy Coastal Groups, and real naval war off the coast of North Vietnam shooting at North Vietnamese trawlers heading south loaded with war supplies.

I landed in Vietnam for the next tour of duty in 1970, and was flown south to Ben Tre City in Kien Hoa Province, a really beautiful province town along the Mekong River about sixty miles south of Saigon. I did not know yet that Ben Tre had been made famous in 1968 as the town that had to be destroyed to save it. I became the Naval Intelligence Liaison Officer, the NILO. In April 1970, the Navy decided to remove almost all its river patrol boats from the Mekong for rehabilitation and transfer to the Vietnamese Navy. Except for the Cambodian invasion to our west, there was very little war, and my hopes to be useful ground nearly to a halt. Instead of working with aggressive U.S. Navy riverine forces, I had to find other things to do. In a short time, I convinced Navy Special Warfare in Saigon that we might have work for a SEAL team or two. By May, I now had a team of Navy SEALs to work with. This work became central to my job for the remainder of 1970 up to March of 1971 when I left Vietnam.[11]

There were occasions when the Central Intelligence Agency, known as OSA (Office of the Special Ambassador, that is, Ambassador William Colby) would call upon SEAL services. For OSA operations, a guide was always available, but their guides were quite different from the low level guides we often used, often actual agents whom OSA decided it would take the risk of exposing in order to accomplish a mission. OSA missions were always secret, well thought out, political, dangerous, and ultimately those missions which really meant something to the war effort at the time. We called these operations, "snatch ops" because the objective was to capture, not kill, the target. Dead VC have no intelligence value.

The most interesting operation took place in 1971. CIA asked the SEALs to meet a Vietcong political cadre on the Mekong about 0200. The team escorted him to the Ben Tre pier/helipad, and he was flown to Saigon for a conference. By 0500 the cadre was returned by Air America helicopter to Ben Tre, and the SEALs escorted him back to his sampan on the river. Once the SEALs came home, and I was informed about the nature of the mission, I was puzzled why I had not been informed before the mission. OSA told me it was just an oversight, but that if anything significant came of the mission I would be informed. I asked several times what happened and learned informally that the target was a COSVN (Central Office of South Vietnam) cadre who was acting as an emissary. The nature of the OSA-COSVN conversation was a discussion of life in the region once they took over, basically the terms of agreement for dismantling and withdrawal of the American apparatus. The OSA people enjoyed irony, and unlike us, were convinced from that time that the Vietcong would eventually take over the region. To the OSA field operatives it was a matter of time. In my naïveté I was aghast over this kind of defeatism from men I trusted, and from that time on I began to reconsider my own position and that of the SEALs. If OSA was considering throwing in the towel, why should we fight? If OSA had already thrown in the towel, why bother? Like Bill Ehrhart earlier and unknown to me then, I was beginning to ask: why don't we just pack up the guns, say that we did the best we could, and leave? Ultimately, that is exactly what we did, but that event waited until 1973. In 1971, I resigned from the Navy, returned to Philadelphia, and started to look around for a future. It was elusive, but I began seeing some writing on the walls.

A friend was teaching at a local high school and told me that I could begin substituting. Well, that was simply not satisfying enough. I earned an MA in Comparative Literature in 1976, and in 1983, a friend suggested an interdisciplinary doctoral program at Bowling Green State University in Ohio. I finished the degree in 1987 and returned to Penn State to a job teaching American Studies part time. In 1989, I became a full time Instructor of American Studies and began to develop more new classes, one of them called The American Dream and the Vietnam War, which became the reason why Bill Ehrhart's experience and writing skills first entered my solar system.

My chair, Dr. Dan Walden, suggested that a former Marine who wrote a fabulous memoir about his experiences in Vietnam from 1967 to 1968 might come to speak to the class and read some of his war poetry. He arranged it, and I orchestrated it. I asked the class to read Bill's memoir, *Vietnam-Perkasie*, but I neglected intentionally to tell them he was coming. He came into the room with me, and I introduced him to my fifty students whom he mesmerized for the next hour. Ms. Alisa Giardinelli of Philadelphia attended that class and commented:

> I do remember Bill's visit to our class. He was pretty engaging—with big glasses, big hair, big mustache. I think I was (and still am) just impressed that someone could go through an experience like his and deal (even in part) so effectively with it through poetry and verse. So when I think of Bill, I think of how he represented this broader perspective and approach, and how without him, our understanding of the war would not have been nearly as multidimensional as it was.[12]

In a subsequent communication, she reflected on what seemed to be a glaring inconsistency. "I remember," she writes, "something else about Bill's visit, more emblematic of my lack of age and experience at the time. I remember thinking, 'he's a poet, how could he have been a soldier?' It didn't seem possible, and I may have even not believed it at first."[13]

While serving as a Fulbright scholar in Germany at the Wilhems Universität Münster, I conducted a seminar about the Vietnam War and used *Vietnam–Perkasie* yet again. It moved the German students the same as it did my American students at Penn State. I believe it is safe to conclude that Bill's prose has a kind of universality to it that really crosses cultural boundaries. Although Germany does not have a Marine Corps, Germans certainly understand soldiering.

In 1995, I accepted a position as a visiting professor of American Civilization at the University of Strasbourg II in France. While in France I asked Bill Ehrhart to send me a tape so that I could share his Vietnam experience with my French students who were studying his *Vietnam–Perkasie* in class with me. The students were very grateful, and so was I. In 1998, I left France because my three-year visa expired.

I started teaching American history at the Franciscan University of Steubenville, Ohio, in 1999 and yet again developed another class on the Vietnam War, and again Bill Ehrhart entered my life, this time with Mr. Ryan Rousseau, a student majoring in English in my class. Because of Ryan's interest in war poets and narrators in general and a good grounding in authors like Ambrose Bierce, Wilfred Owen, Sigfried Sassoon, James Dickey, and many others from many past wars, I pointed this young student to the work of W. D. Ehrhart, and soon they were corresponding. To be sure I count Bill Ehrhart as a most trusted friend, colleague, and fellow Vietnam veteran who cares for and about students as I do.

In the foreword to the original McFarland edition of *Vietnam–Perkasie*, John Clark Pratt tells us that the memoir is a kind of *Bildungsroman*, a coming-of-age story of the evolution of a boy becoming a man in the late 1960s. In *Ordinary Lives: Platoon 1005 and the Vietnam War* (1999),[14] Bill tells us about the men he trained with, what their lives were like both in combat and after it. We were both volunteers in our respective military services. His decorations and mine are nearly identical, and he left the Marine Corps a few months after I left the Navy. In a way though, the U.S.M.C. never left him as the Navy has never left me. Although it is clear that he hated the Vietnam War and all war by now, he still loves his Marine Corps. He wrote:

> Though I came to hate the American War in Vietnam, I have never hated the Marine Corps, and I will always be grateful to Staff Sergeant J. J. Oliver, Sergeant T. W. Evans, and Sergeant D. S. Bosch, and to the training program for which they served as point men, for preparing me as well as anyone could have prepared me to bear up under the awful obscenity of war.[15]

Although in later life Bill has commented in prose and poetry about a myriad of topics, what touches me is his extensive writing that concerns our war, the Vietnam War, our warriors, and the pain it leaves with us all. In *Beautiful Wreckage: New & Selected Poems* (1999), Bill gives life to his thoughts about fighting the Viet Cong in his poem "Guerrilla War."

> It's practically impossible
> to tell civilians
> from the Viet Cong.
>
> Nobody wears uniforms.
> They all talk
> the same language
> (and you couldn't understand them
> even if they didn't)
>
> They tape grenades
> inside their clothes,
> and carry satchel charges
> in their market baskets.
>
> Even their women fight.
> And young boys
> And girls.
>
> It's practically impossible
> to tell civilians
> from the Viet Cong
>
> After a while,
> you quit trying.[16]

He is absolutely right. In one of the districts in Kien Hoa Province in November 1970, two Vietcong posed as women, came into the Huong My district marketplace, and began shooting at everyone. Like most terrorist attacks, it stopped only when they were shot and killed by the police on the scene. Politically and tactically, the Vietnam War changed from 1968 to 1970; in other ways it remained the same.

Another poem that struck home for me is "Souvenirs."

> "Bring me back a souvenir," the captain called.
> "Sure thing," I shouted back over the amtrac's roar.
>
> Later that day,
> the column halted,
> we found a Buddhist temple by the trail.
> Combing through a nearby wood,
> we found a heavy log as well.
>
> It must have taken more than half an hour,
> but at last we battered in
> the concrete walls so badly
> that the roof collapsed
>
> Before it did
> I took two painted vases
> Buddhists use for burning incense.
>
> One vase I kept,
> and one I offered proudly to the captain.[17]

Again, the poem connected with my experience in Vietnam. In my inventory of souvenirs, I have a cone hat, a pair of black pajamas, chop sticks, gold medallions, some crude Vietnamese pottery, and a pastoral oil painting with bullet holes in it. Other veterans have more interesting souvenirs, like AK-47s and Chinese pistols. The prize, however, was a Viet Cong flag. Americans over there would do some really bizarre, often stupid and very dangerous things to get one. Why flags are so important, perhaps can be traced to the Civil War, when taking the enemy's flag or "colors" could earn the Medal of Honor for a common soldier. Japanese and German flags are in basements and attics throughout America from wars past. How many Viet Cong flags are out there, no one really knows, but a few of them come from me. I paid an old lady in Ben Tre to sew a few I could use in Saigon to swap for some items I really needed. No one was disappointed, and in terms of my flags, no one got killed trying to capture them.

Bill, I, and over two million other Vietnam veterans share more than we know. Each veteran's war was his and her own. We can never share a foxhole anymore, but we do know what a foxhole is. We share diseases that come in older age, but do not share the way we deal with them. We never really grow old when we think of Vietnam—and we think of it every day—because we always remember the faces of both the living and the dead. We always look up when we see and hear helicopters flying by. We all have our heroes and villains, our Robert McNamaras, Lyndon Johnsons, and Richard Nixons, but we remember each other much better. As Bill wrote in *Ordinary Lives*, "no life is ordinary." He goes on to say, "Every life is fascinating if you take the time to notice. Everyone has a story to tell if you take the trouble to listen. Every life is its own little drama."[18] How true!

Bill was and is correct: we fought two different wars and have very different feelings about them. His was on the battle line, in the mud, and bloody; mine was bloody but less so than Bill's, two years later, and more about "Spookin' the Cong" than conducting combat against them.[19] My combat forces were SEALs, SEABEES, Swiftboats, Riverine and naval air forces all of whom I provided intelligence that I hoped would save their lives and complete their missions. Yet, in Vietnam there were no front lines. There never are in guerrilla wars.

We like to remember the good days and forget the bad ones. Remarkably, Bill Ehrhart remembers the bad days much better than many other authors do. Of course, we all have both. Some Vietnam veterans lost their sense of patriotism; some say nothing; others, like Bill and me, are teachers and cannot live our personal and professional lives in silence. We soldier on, knowing that we are the authentic voices.

Notes

1. Ehrhart, W.D., *Vietnam–Perkasie: A Combat Marine Memoir* (Jefferson, NC: McFarland, 1983), 7.
2. Ibid., 7.
3. Ibid., 10.
4. Ibid., 12–13.
5. Ibid., 19.
6. Ibid., 19.
7. See W.D. Ehrhart, *Ordinary Lives: Platoon 1005 and the Vietnam War* (Philadelphia, PA: Temple University Press, 1999), for an explanation of how the U.S.M.C. creates its unit designations.
8. Ehrhart, *Vietnam–Perkasie*, 3.
9. Ibid., 5.
10. Ibid., 247.
11. My complete debrief of my NILO tour of duty was taken by the Naval Historical Center, Washington Navy Yard, Washington, DC in 1978 and the Vietnam Oral History Center at Texas Tech University, Lubbock, Texas, in 2012.
12. Personal correspondence, 20 June 2012.
13. Personal correspondence, 6 July 2012.
14. 15. Ehrhart, *Ordinary Lives*, 19.
16. Ehrhart, W.D., *Beautiful Wreckage: New & Selected Poems* (Easthampton, MA: Adastra, 1999), 5.
17. Ibid., 6.
18. Ehrhart, *Ordinary Lives*, 318.
19. "Spookin' the Cong" was the term used by Naval Intelligence Force Vietnam to describe its mission.

W. D. Ehrhart and Adastra Press: A Publisher's Perspective

Gary Metras

When Bill mentioned to me in 1998 that he was beginning to assemble a selected poems volume and suggested he send the manuscript on to me, I was immediately flattered. At that point in our relationship, I had published six titles of Bill's: a broadsheet, three chapbooks, and two full-length books. Each was handset, handsewn letterpress editions, though the two full-lengths later went into offset, perfect bound reprint editions. Each sold well (for small press poetry). Each was a well-deserved notch in both poet and publisher's reputations. Each was a deepening in our relationship of mutual respect and admiration. Bill told writer Joshua Bodwell for an article on Adastra Press, "This guy could print your grocery list and it would bring tears to your eyes."[1] I replied to Bill that a selected volume deserved a publisher bigger and better than Adastra Press.

My motives for turning it down were twofold: First, I sincerely felt that Bill's poetry deserved a wider audience than my limited distribution could provide. He needed a good university-based or larger independent publisher that could promote the title more widely, get more reviews, and could get it into a wider range of book stores than I, a one-man publisher, could. Second, I knew this book would be expensive to produce, that, indeed, it might bust the Adastra budget for a couple years, thus delaying the printing/publication of at least a few chapbook titles and one anthology already in the works.

Paraphrasing Bill's answer to me is telling: Gary, you have been the truest friend to both my poetry and to me that there is no better publisher for my selected poems than Adastra Press.

With that, what else could I do but accept the book sight unseen, which left just the editing process itself, and since I had worked closely with Bill in editing earlier manuscripts, I knew we'd arrive at a mutually agreeable selection of poems fairly quickly. After all, I already had handfuls of my personal favorites of Bill's poems and I knew he did also. The only difficulty during the editorial process was based exactly on the fact that there were so many poems that I personally liked, really liked, that were not in the original manuscript Bill sent me, such as his very early poem, "Making the Children Behave," that haunts me still today for its marching-in-step rhythm and its stark, brutal truth. Bill had struggled to keep the manuscript under 150 pages and therefore cut out many good poems that I felt should be in the collection. I gave him a list of these poems. As it happens, Bill had two other close poetry friends read the manuscript and each reacted in the same way I did: why isn't this poem or that poem included? They also gave Bill lists of additional poems, which they loved. So the typescript grew to 200 pages. After doing desktop design and layout, the book was 239 plus pages long. Quite large. Quite expensive.

I was also concerned with what might be perceived as egotism on the part of both poet and publisher in having such a large selection. Here are some points of reference: William Carlos Williams's *Selected Poems* clocks in at 140 pages; the *Selected Poems of Thomas Merton* is 135; *Kenneth Patchen Selected Poems* is 145; Joseph Langland's *Selected Poems* is 118; *The Granite Pail: The Selected Poems of Lorine Niedecker* is 111; George Oppen's *Collected Poems* is 256; *The Collected Poems of Theodore Roethke* is 266. And here's small press poet Bill Ehrhart with 239 pages of poems that he and I felt were essential for his career to be fairly assessed. Who reads Merton or Patchen these days? Niedecker may be more widely read today than when she was alive. Langland has been dead almost a decade and it seems as if he's disappeared from the literary map. Oppen's fans are probably as small as they were when he was writing, but they are dedicated. Roethke's reputation has, unfortunately, dwindled. These are each great poets who are now dead. If we examine the trend with living poets and their selected volumes, we find *The Blessing: New and Selected Poems* by Adastra chapbook poet Richard Jones at 384 pages; two other Adastra poets I share with other publishers: Thomas Lux's *New and Selected Poems 1975–1995* at 174, while his Adastra volume, *The Blind Swimmer: Selected Early Poems 1970–1975* is 64; Ed Ochester's *Unreconstructed: Poems Selected and New* is 171; Galway Kinnell's first *Selected Poems* is 148; Rita Dove's *Selected Poems* is 202; *Sailing Around the Room: New and Selected Poems* by Billy Collins is 172; Lawrence Raab's *Visible Signs: New and Selected Poems* is 188; and then there is James Tate, whose 1991 Pulitzer winner *Selected Poems* wasn't long enough so that in 2012 he published *The Eternal Ones of the Dream: Selected Poems 1990–2010* at 252 pages.

Each is a substantial volume. Does this mean that the current generation of poets is "better" than the previous? That they have more individual poems that should be canonized? Of course because each is still alive and writing, their selected books also include a sizable group of new poems. Or does it merely indicate the state of publishing in America today where such big books are the norm regardless of the quality of each and every poem included? Or did the editors and their readers keep adding personal favorites as happened with Bill's *Beautiful Wreckage*? In any case, I, as long time publisher of Bill, felt he and his poetry, his vision, his experience, his message deserved such a large book of selected poems.

Beautiful Wreckage: New & Selected Poems by W.D. Ehrhart was published on November 30, 1999, all of 239 pages, as Adastra's 54th title, and has gone into four printings through 2009. At a June 2012 reading by Bill at University of Massachusetts-Boston, I had a table displaying and offering for sale three titles of Bill's, his newest full-length poetry book, *The Bodies Beneath the Table* (2010), the few remaining copies of his limited edition chapbook, *Sleeping with the Dead* (2006) and *Beautiful Wreckage* (1999). People bought all of the selected and I could have sold more if I had more copies. Only a couple copies of the others sold. So it seems that poetry readers want a large selected edition; they want a full view of the poet and not just the latest work.

As part of the process of editing Bill's selected, I went through his previous Adastra titles and some of our correspondence about them. Here's some background: Bill and I met in the pages of *Samisdat Magazine*, published in San Jose, California, then Sherbrooke, Quebec, in the late 1970s. We were both publishing our poems there. We were young, energetic, idealistic, and because of that idealism, we were angry at what reality had offered us. I was married with two small children, and trying to establish a high school teaching career. Bill was unattached and searching for the meaning of his having volunteered for the Vietnam War and of the war itself. His poems were mostly about that. Mine were mostly about my working class roots and experience working construction. We each admired the other's poems. We met face-to-face at a book fair in Northampton, Massachusetts, the next town over from where I live. *Samisdat* editor Merritt Clifton had procured a table at the fair and invited me to join him as I had just begun Adastra Press with two titles in print. Merritt also invited Bill to drive up from Philadelphia for the weekend book fair and the camaraderie. Here's how Bill described the event: "Well, it was one of those raw, cold, wet New England early spring days—just miserable weather—and the book fair turned out to be craft fair. We were the only booksellers there, and people had come to buy macramé plant holders and handmade earrings and glass elephants, not books. So we froze our asses off for two days, but ended up having a great time drinking Yukon Jack and engaging in increasingly silly banter with disinterested passers-by."[2] Very accurate, except that I sold all the Adastra books, two titles, both hand printed and sewn, on my side of the table, whereas Merritt's chapbooks and magazines, all stapled and cheaply printed on his own small duplicator press, barely got glanced at by people. Since I was the one flush with cash, so to speak, I bought the booze we all enjoyed. It was great to meet our mutual publisher, talk up literature, radical politics, and bitch about the weather.

Soon after that meeting, Bill began to lobby me in letters about publishing his next chapbook. He was so certain about their quality and in the audience he was slowly building, that he boldly said, "You won't lose money on me. I guarantee it. I'll buy whatever copies you need to sell in order to break even."[3] I wasn't that worried about sales and money. I was busy with two other chapbooks at the time and the letterpress craft is so labor intense that I couldn't really focus on another title, but I did know I was interested in having a book by Bill on my small list. I suppose I just kept stringing him along to see how far he'd go in wanting an Adastra chapbook. So after he guaranteed the success of it, I accepted the manuscript: *Matters of the Heart* (1981) 23 pages in an edition of 325 handset, handsewn copies. It was the fourth title from the press and sold for $2.50. Some rare book dealers now have it priced over $150. Nice. Of course, neither Bill nor I get any of that. But the point is, Bill was absolutely correct. His audience became fans who are pretty loyal to his poetry, his politics, his person, and they buy his books, often in multiple copies.

My standard royalty with all my authors is 10 percent of the print run in copies upon publication and a 50 percent discount off cover price. Over the next year, Bill bought ten to twenty copies at a time for a total close to a hundred copies, which he sold at his readings. He made money and I made money. Bill has consistently bought copies of his books at discount and sold along the way. Not all Adastra poets have bought their own books, and never as many as has Bill. In a closet at his house, Bill keeps copies of his current books inventoried and neatly lined up on a shelf in his office. When he has an upcoming reading or workshop, he checks his stock and if short, orders more copies from the publisher. Bill is that certain of his audience, especially at public readings. I can remember when he read at Amherst College in Amherst, Massachusetts, with Bruce Weigl and John Balaban after the three returned from a trip to Vietnam in 1985. Each is a veteran of the Vietnam War, though Balaban, who is a recognized and published translator of Vietnamese poetry, served in a non-military capacity. This night, Bill read last, then the three poets chatted with audience members and signed copies of their books. Soon, Weigl, Balaban, and myself were outside waiting for Bill to finish and join us for a drink; we waited longer, then longer, to finally give up and head to the bar. The three had been giving readings around the country and John and Bruce told me this wasn't the first time they had to wait for Bill. Afterward, Bill told us he sold every one of the books he had, including the ones in his hands that he read from. Just amazing. But Bill as reader and public persona, if a poet can be said to have such, is so believable that people want to keep sharing in his life's story and his poems long after the reading, so they buy his books.

But we're not talking salaries here, nor the kind of royalties that allows the writer to pay off the mortgage, let alone buy a second house along the ocean. Fifty dollars here, a hundred there, maybe a thousand or two in a year or longer. This is small press publishing where selling a hundred or two hundred copies of one title in a year is an achievement. Poetry in America is a hobby for both the poet and the poetry publisher. There was a period of time in the mid 1980s to '90s when Adastra Press was publishing more poetry per year than Random House, then the largest publisher in America. Poetry in America is a hobby and we write it and publish it because we love it without concern for money. As simple as that.

Four years after *Matters of the Heart* and eleven titles from other poets later, I released Bill's *The Outer Banks & Other Poems*, 52 pages of handset Garamond types, double handsewn signature, in both paper (275 copies) and cloth (25 copies signed & numbered). It took less than a year to sell out and I had it reprinted commercially: offset, perfect bound, but with a letterpress cover that I printed. I kept that book in print for twenty years. It's that good. A review in *Small Press Review* (10/85) opened with "This is the only book of poems that I am aware of that has the possibility of attaining the wide readership and celebrity status, of Carolyn Forché's *The Country Between Us*." The 1984 edition of *The Dictionary of Literary Biography Yearbook* ends its review of *The Outer Banks* with "It is a great pity that a poet this strong has to struggle in the small presses. He deserves a great audience." And why? Because for the first time in Bill's poetry, there were poems of hope and love, poems that grew out of his Vietnam War experiences without directly mentioning them while that sense of loss and increased sensitivity informs poems about U.S. foreign intervention, his students, his friends, his wife. He had fallen in love, gotten married, and honeymooned on North Carolina's Outer Banks, and returned with a renewed sense of life, and a handful of new poems that grew into a bookful. Bill didn't have to lobby me or make outlandish promises, but there was the understanding that I wouldn't lose any money publishing him, which is still the way it is today, and it is still true that I haven't lost a dime on Bill. In fact, he's my largest selling poet in terms of copies sold over forty years and he's my most popular poet with ten titles published (two being broadsides) since 1980.

As for the poet/editor relationship between Bill and myself, the following are instructive. There were two poems I wanted cut from *The Outer Banks* manuscript, "Gifts" and "On the Plain of Marathon." Of my objection to the latter, Bill wrote, "No need to worry about hurting my feelings with your criticism…. Praise is nice, but doesn't help me grow. I like people who wield a sharp knife. Your thoughtful comments are much appreciated and very helpful."[4] Because of such straightforwardness from Bill and because I knew how strongly he felt about it, I decided to let "Gifts" stay in the collection. Yes, it's a sentimental poem to his wife on their wedding, but it vividly shows the love and promise of a future life together unlike anything else he had written to this point. As a side note: Bill asked me in summer 2003 how much it would cost him to have me print "Gifts" as a broadsheet for Christmas gifts. It's obviously a poem he loves dearly. And he also knew I wasn't that enamored with it. When I told him I'd print and publish it and pay him royalties, he was genuinely surprised and asked what the deal was. I replied that while "Gifts" was certainly honest though sentimental, those were exactly the qualities that would make for an effective broadsheet poem. I printed it in an edition of 100 signed & numbered copies, as is my custom with broadsheets, and "paid" Bill with half the print run. At bookfairs, I usually display a few broadsheet poems and "Gifts" invariably sells a copy or two or three at the reasonable price of $10 And so our own working together was always a give-and-take negotiation with author and publisher having the goal of birthing the best book possible from the manuscript at hand. Bill's acceptance of my thoughtful criticisms were balanced with what I learned over years of this kind of working together toward the limits of Bill's sense of any given poem's worth and its place in any one of the collections to be published. We both had and have strong beliefs in our own works and abilities to produce a poetic art and could each be stubborn with the other when needed. Our mutual respect always won out. Our common goal of the best book possible always won over any minor disagreements.

Such exchanges did not always orbit around a submitted manuscript. Sometimes Bill would send or e-mail me a new poem, wanting comment, and I sent Bill some of my own new poems to get his keen perspective on them. Here's one such poem with commentary, beginning with my e-mail reply to Bill (with apology to Anne, who may not have seen the original version):

Bill,
   I'm attaching "Where Beauty Is Found" with comment and suggestion (and a somewhat similar poem of my own—with comment on that, too!
Gary

> I don't care how old you get.
> I don't care about thickening thighs
> and heftier hips and breasts
> that have lost the struggle with gravity.
> I don't care that your hair's going gray
> and your belly's gone slack and the wrinkles
> around your eyes aren't going away.

> I remember you at twenty-five
> in the shower naked beside me,
> soap cascading the length of that
> heavenly body, me like a kid
> in a candy shop and no one around:
> most beautiful woman in all the world
> and mine. All mine. All I see to this day.

Bill, I like this poem very much. But I'd cut the entire first stanza and use just the second. If you title the poem something like: Growing Old Together, or Long Married, etc. then the first stanza is not needed. It's implied and leaves you free to celebrate the memory of beauty without having to mention any of the aging negatives, which we all know about anyway, and which our wives simply love to be reminded about (not!).

—Gary

Here's a recent memory of taking a shower together poem of my own:

> *When I saw the Wild Rabbit*
>
> When I saw the wild rabbit licking
> seeds off the February ground beneath
> the bird feeder, dark tongue impervious
> to all but its need, I didn't think of
> the struggle life can be. Instead, I saw us
> years ago in the shower of a Salzburg hotel
> as you turned off the spray and we stood
> in that small enclosure, dripping and gleaming,
> your tongue licking the wet from my shoulder,
> impervious to all but our love.

P. S.: So what does this say about folks (or at least guys) our age both writing about showers with our babes when younger? Are we yearning just a little too much for that lost youth? that physical love? Or are these memories simply sustaining our machismo as we begin to lose it? And when's the last time we did shower with our wives? (...By the way, our 40th is this October and we're going to Greece, the Islands, and Istanbul on a tour in Oct.)

I think, too, the simple fact that you and I both obviously still actively remember our younger selves and our love, even honor the memories (hence we put them in a poem), keeps us still loving that same woman, keeps and prevents our marriages from becoming stale, preventing our eyes and minds from wandering, as the saying goes. Yes, it is good we write these things down.

June 17, 2008.
Dear Gary,

An interesting suggestion to drop the entire first stanza. Let me ponder that. I have revised the poem somewhat since I sent you the version you saw, but most of the revision is in the second stanza anyway.

Your poem, I think, is better. And your commentary on both poems is cogent. I'm not sure if I am having to remind myself of the physical beauty of the woman

I married—or if it is more a matter of reassuring her that I don't care what age and time have done to her appearance. Maybe a little of both. Certainly, I am not the slim athletic-looking guy she fell in love with.

Anne hasn't seen the poem yet. I've made a little card with the poem incorporated into it; I'll give it to her on June 27th, which will be our 27th. But 40 ... geez, that's an achievement. One of the nice things about my having gotten married relatively late, however (I was 32), is that I know the value of a one-night stand. I've never been seriously tempted to risk what I have for one more tumble in the hay....

    Bill

June 18, 2008
Dear Bill,

I know Anne is not the typical vain woman-wife-mother, but I do believe that any reminders of an individual woman's aging (especially in such a formal way as in a poem), does more harm than good (at least in my experience). So my recommendation to drop the first stanza is not based on ignoring the truth, but more on emphasizing the memory of youthful bodies. Tactful? Perhaps. Diplomatic? Maybe. But neither of those are really concerns. Of course you don't care what time has done to her shape. But she may, and even if she does even only a tiny bit, then the first stanza becomes a reminder of what she now is not. And that negative could be hard to overcome even with the beautiful ending to the poem. The most important is the love, active and current. And based on the history (or memories) of that love.

Christ, I first met Natalie when she was 16! Tell me she hasn't changed a lot! Or me! I was a stud back then—worked construction on weekends, boxed at the Boy's Club, knew all the lyrics of Dion and the Belmonts and the then new Beatles. This was winter of 1965. When we were introduced, I said in response to her name, "Oh, just like Natalie Wood" (who at the time was extremely popular—*West Side Story* was 1 or 2 years old). She answered me with, "Only this Natalie wouldn't." That's what got me right away, that wit, that presence. I was smitten. (Are we still allowed to use that word?!) I'll compound it: I relentlessly though discretely wooed her until she let me put a ring on her finger, 2 and a half years later.

...

Anyway, I hope your 27th went well and that Anne did indeed like the poem.
    All best,
    Gary

July 1, 2008
Dear Gary,
  Having had several weeks to contemplate your suggestion, I had decided to follow your advice even before this e-mail arrived. Thanks very much....
    Bill
    July 2, 2008

And here's the poem as it appears in *The Bodies Beneath the Table* (2010):

> *Epiphany*
>> *for Anne*
>> *28 years later*
>
> What I remember is you at twenty-six
> in the shower naked beside me,
> soap cascading the length of that
> heart-stopping, eye-popping sight,
> me like a kid in a candy shop:
> most beautiful woman in all the world
> and mine. All mine. All I see to this day.[5]

Because the initial suggested revision was mine, my attempts to persuade Bill go to some lengths in terms of both literary argument and personal appeal; the latter could only work in the professional/personal relationship Bill and I have built up over the years. And in Bill's terse replies, you can hear his wheels turning, weighing his inspiration against the truth of my explanations so that his sensitivity of and affection for his wife came to overrule the initial impulse of the poem.

Further along in Bill's July 2 e-mail, he says, "I am getting itchy to put together something new of my own—either a new chap[book] or a slightly longer work of about 25 poems including those 11 poems in *Sleeping with the Dead* [chapbook 2006]—but not until all of *Sleeping with the Dead* are gone. Don't know how long that will take, but this new one would certainly not be imminent. 2009? 2010?" Bill's concern with having *Sleeping* sold out before the new book was released is evidence of his concern and respect for the publisher and his readers; he didn't want me to be stuck with boxes of unsold copies of a moot chapbook; he didn't want his readers to feel they had to buy both titles when the new one would contain most of the chapbook. In late summer and during the fall, Bill sent me several individual poems he was working on. Here's my comment on "The Secret Lives of Boys": "Your new poem 'Secret Life...' is excellent. One of the best you've done in a while. Quite moving.... You get more such as this and the next book we do is gonna be better than good."[6] So without any formality, the next book became a given right there. All it needed was the time and patience for the poems to arrive.

That's the kind of working relationship Bill and I have enjoyed over the years. As Bill told interviewer Joshua Bodwell, though this part was cut from the published article, "In 28 years of working with Gary Metras, through nine different publications, we have never signed a contract of any kind; we have worked together with nothing but integrity and a handshake, and we have never had any kind of dispute or disagreement." I'd say it's pretty close to the ideal author/publisher affiliation, and I am blessed having Bill as an Adastra poet and a friend.

Notes

1. Bodwell, Joshua, "A Letter at a Time," *Poets & Writers Magazine*, Sept./Oct. 2008.
2. Unpublished interview 2008.
3. Letter 15 Sept. 1980.
4. Letter 15 March 1984.
5. Ehrhart, W.D., *The Bodies Beneath the Table* (Easthampton, MA: Adastra Press, 2010), 62.
6. Email 6 September 2008.

PART FOUR.
The Educator Who Knows Things Worth Knowing

The Teacher
    for my students at Sandy Springs
    Friends School, September 1978

A cold moon hangs
cold fire among the clouds,
and I remember colder nights
in hell when men died
in such pale light as this
of fire swift
and deadly as heart of ice.

Hardly older then
than you are now,
I hunched down shaking
like an old man
alone in an empty cave
among the rocks of ignorance
and malice honorable men
call truth.

Out of that cave I carried
anger like a torch
to keep my heart from freezing,
and a strange new thing called
love
to keep me sane.

A dozen years ago,
before I ever knew you,
beneath a moon not unlike
this moon tonight,
I swore an oath to teach you
all I know—
and I know things
worth knowing.

It is a desperate future
I cling to,
and it is yours.
All that I have lived for
since that cold moon long ago
hangs in the balance—
and I keep fumbling for words,
but this clip-clapper tongue
won't do.

I am afraid;
I do not want to fail:

I need your hands to steady me;
I need your hearts to give me courage;
I need you to walk with me
until I find a voice
that speaks the language
that you speak.

—W. D. Ehrhart

The Samisdat Poems, 65; *To Those Who Have Gone Home Tired*, 48–49; *Beautiful Wreckage: New & Selected Poems*, 49–50.

Bill Ehrhart as Educator

Martin Novelli

It should be a given, if we stop to think about it, that artists by the very nature of what they do in whatever art is in question, are also educators. They lead us into new realms of esthetic experience but they also, through those esthetic experiences, lead us to old and new truths about life and the burden of being human.

Bill Ehrhart is justly celebrated as poet, memoirist, essayist of the Vietnam War and beyond. *Vietnam–Perkasie*, *Passing Time*, and *Busted*[1] are key documents to help us understand the magnitude of the folly, waste, and outright criminality that encompass the American invasion of Vietnam. The poetry, and not just the Vietnam poems, reminds us of the power of language to open worlds never imagined by the reader. The essays take us into the hearts of many kinds of darkness from the Vietnam years to the present day catalog of folly, waste and criminality that encompass the American invasion of everyone and everywhere, foreign and domestic.

Bill Ehrhart's huge contributions to his countrymen which, for the most part as he ironically observes, go unnoticed and unwelcomed, include his tireless willingness to speak to and with students about the folly he lived through and the folly he has been observing for the last four decades. For students, a visit by Bill Ehrhart is an enlightening and electrifying experience.

In my particular case Bill Ehrhart has been visiting classes that I have taught and continue to teach in a variety of college settings. He has been a guest lecturer in classes at a New Jersey community college—Ocean County College; at Rutgers, the State University of New Jersey; and at the University of the Arts in Philadelphia. These visits have occurred on a regular basis since 1986 when I first met Bill at a conference on the Vietnam War at Manchester Polytechnic in the UK. Discovering we both lived in Philadelphia, we began to communicate and thus began the multiple visits over the next two and a half decades.

At Rutgers University until 1992 and at Ocean County College since

1993, the course has been "America in the 1960s" and the text used was and is *Vietnam–Perkasie*; at the University of the Arts since 1987, the course has been "Images of Vietnam" and the texts used have been both *Vietnam–Perkasie* and *Passing Time*. The length of the visit ranges from 75 minutes at OCC to 150 minutes at UARTS.

Bill and I usually arrive at the classroom between five and ten minutes before the start time. As students begin to arrive they notice a graying, middle aged man standing with me at the front of the room. Bill watches as they take their places and begin to remove *Vietnam–Perkasie* from their bags. He jokingly praises the students who have "new" books rather than ones with a "used" sticker on the front, saying that those who have purchased the "new" books have put a couple of dollars in royalties in his pocket whereas he receives nothing for the "used" copies.

As we begin I distribute a copy of Bill's bibliography to each student; on the flip side are the lyrics of "Round Eyed Blues" a song by a rock group named Marah. The song was written after one of the brothers (David and Serge Bielanko—who constitute the band) read *Vietnam–Perkasie* back in the early '90s; it appears on the Marah album *Kids in Philly*.

I mention that over the years, after Bill became acquainted with the brothers, he has appeared on stage with them in various venues, not, obviously, to sing with them but to recite some of his poems as a complement to the song. I jokingly designate Bill as a "rock-n-roll" star as a consequence. I follow this up by indicating that Bill is *also* a "comic book hero" holding up a fading copy of *Real War Stories*, a one-issue publication from 1987 featuring seven pages—done by Alan Moore—illustrating material from both *Vietnam–Perkasie* and *Passing Time*. Many of the students are fans of the "graphic novels" of Alan Moore, especially *Watchmen*, *From Hell*, and *V for Vendetta*, and are stunned to learn that he illustrated Bill's words. Bill jokes that Moore was able to do in seven pages what took him a couple of hundred pages in the two books.

I then introduce Bill describing his various academic degrees and his current teaching position and then turn the session over to him.

Bill usually begins by saying that if they read his book (or books in the UARTS class) they know he is not a particularly private person so they should not hesitate to ask him anything; no question they ask will embarrass or annoy him. He adds, again jokingly, that if they have a question they better ask it during the session because if they come up to him after class ends and say they have a question to ask him, he will reply sorry you missed your chance; I'm going to lunch. In reality Bill always stays after each class and will patiently autograph copies of *Vietnam–Perkasie* no matter how long it takes and certainly *will* answer any question anyone asks at that point.

After some hesitation, the questions begin. Over the years, the first question—and not always from the women in the class—is about "Jenny." Did he ever see her again? Does he know what happened to her? The "no" to the first question gives way to a longer response to the second question where he describes what he knows about her through first hand and second hand accounts. He indicates he long ago gave up the bitterness he once felt and has only sympathy for a young woman who faced a difficult situation and probably felt guilty for years about the "Dear John" letter. If he had gone to college, rather than Vietnam, he believes they would have broken up relatively soon, especially if he had gone to UCLA which had been his goal.

The second question, over the years, usually is some variation of if you had it to do all over again, would you still go to Vietnam? The answer to that question is always a resounding "No!" and from there Bill outlines how his naïve belief that he was fighting for freedom in Vietnam and the disillusionment that followed after his thirteen months there compounded by all he learned about the origins and the truths of American involvement there have "fucked up my life" for 40 years. Bill usually takes a long time to discuss his response in detail going from his actual experiences in Vietnam to his attempt to put the war behind him to his discovery, prompted by the Kent State killings in 1970, that he had to take some action to try and stop the war to everything that has been his life since then. He makes it clear that he is not anti-military or even anti-war. He credits the military, especially the Marines, in teaching him how to survive, joking that if he had been in the Army instead of the Marines, he would never have survived Vietnam. He declares he would fight, even now, if there was a "just" war and America was actually under attack but there have been neither in his lifetime.

Bill makes it absolutely clear that the "enemy" was (and is) those in power who sent young men like him to Vietnam (or South America or Lebanon or Iraq in 1991 or the Balkans or Iraq again in 2004 or Afghanistan; the list of course is nearly endless). Naturally, his greatest rage is still centered on the Kennedy, Johnson, and Nixon "experts"—those "best and brightest"—who created and sustained the American invasion of Vietnam and then lied to a generation of young men into participating in that invasion. These moments are the epitome of "Bill Ehrhart as Educator" as he informs these young men and women about aspects of American politics and history that they have never been taught. Interestingly, despite his ironic assertion that he is a writer who no one listens to, Bill describes emails that he has received and still receives from soldiers in Iraq (1991 and 2004) and Afghanistan and elsewhere who have come upon his books and have communicated to him how much they have learned from them. Thus, Bill has an impact far beyond an average American college class on the 1960s in general or Vietnam in particular. Especially in the class sessions at UARTS that can go beyond 75 minutes, Bill can outline in *savage* detail the crippling effect of Vietnam both during and after the war finally ended. The hope that Vietnam would teach Americans some kind of lesson about invading other countries soon faded as the Reagan years inaugurated thirty plus years of imperial adventuring all over the globe with the attendant loss of life by individuals and groups who either refuse to accept American interference in their country or, worse, are innocent civilians who happen to be in the wrong place at the wrong time (as the current drone war is proving every day to everyone in the world except an American public who are never informed by the mainstream media the carnage that is being carried on in their name). All these things and more Bill tells students and watching their faces as he speaks I can see the tops of their heads metaphorically exploding as they listen.

The discussion of Bill's experiences in Vietnam and their impact on him inevitably leads to questions about the writing of the books. Bill always indicates that, to him, *Passing Time* not *Vietnam–Perkasie* is the more important book; the book he set out to write initially but which had to wait until he had gotten *Vietnam–Perkasie* out of his system. He is asked about some of the Marines he knew in Vietnam and how much or how little contact he has had with them. He describes contacts made and broken, friendships renewed and then lapsed. He describes the years of research and writing *Ordinary Lives: Platoon 1005 and the Vietnam War*[2] as he tried to locate and speak to as many men as possible who went through Marine boot camp with him. He describes locating some of the officers he served under and even the fact that he has attended Marine Corps reunions over the years. Sometimes I interrupt to tell the students that despite Bill's reputation as an *anti-war* writer, he has visited (and been relatively [sic!] well-received) at all three military academies and that the United States Air Force Academy devoted an entire issue of its journal—*War, Literature & the Arts*—to Bill's poetry and prose.

The highlight of the stories is how he and Ken Takanaga—"Kenny Amagasu" in *Vietnam–Perkasie*, the Japanese, not Japanese-American, Marine who showed up in Vietnam in the summer of 1967 and astounded everyone into constantly asking what in the world was he doing in both the Marines and in Vietnam—found each other three decades later after both were wounded (Takanaga much more seriously) in Hue City during the Tet Offensive. As Bill is being treated for his own wounds, he asks "Where's Kenny?" Because Bill can't hear at this point, the medic scribbles on a piece of paper: "Medevac out. Left arm gone below the elbow." Thirty-two years later in 2000, by a karmic coincidence, Bill locates Ken Takanaga in Japan and they resume their friendship. Bill is delighted to learn that doctors saved Takanaga's arm (for the full story, including their trip back to Vietnam in summer, 2011, go to "Ken and Bill's Excellent Adventure" at Bill's website wdehrhart.com).[3]

For my Ocean County College '60s class in fall, 2006, there, along with Bill, was Ken Takanaga in the flesh. He happened to be visiting Bill at the time and eagerly participated that day much to the amazement of the class.

Once the subject of Vietnam and Bill's experiences there and his writing about his experiences there starts to be discussed then the questions come quickly and without hesitation. Obviously the 150 minute sessions at UARTS allow for much more detailed discussion but even the 75 minute sessions at OCC allow for an enormous amount of give and take. From Vietnam the discussion usually leads to questions about Bill's views on current American politics and politicians, views that are generally unflattering to all concerned, both Republicans and Democrats alike. Bill also blisters the mainstream media for its cowardice and its eagerly accepted role as mouthpiece for the government rather than watchdog that it sometimes claims to be (universal laughter anyone!!).

There are two issues that I always make sure I ask Bill to comment on. The first is the POW-MIA myth which, fortunately, has pretty much faded away although the POW-MIA flag still flies over public buildings in New Jersey and elsewhere and barely legible bumper stickers of that flag can occasionally be seen on cars and motorcycles. The students in the '60s class generally only have the vaguest (or no) idea of what the POW-MIA myth was/is all about but I ask Bill to discuss it as a poisonous after-effect of the war that lingered for years. Bill talks about the myth and sometimes reads his moving anti-myth poem "POW/MIA" from *Winter Bells*.[4] For the Vietnam class at UARTS, one of the assigned books is H. Bruce Franklin's *M.I.A. or Mythmaking in America* (1993) which details and dissects the whole fraudulent creation of the myth. Bill has nothing but sympathy for the families of men whose bodies could not be recovered and who spent years living with the false hopes that this myth tricked them into believing. He writes in "POW/MIA": "God forgive me, but I've seen / that triple-canopied green / nightmare of a jungle / where a man in a plane could go down / unseen, and never be found / by anyone. / Not ever."[5]

The second issue I ask Bill to comment on is the myth of the returning soldiers being "spit on" by anti-war activists, often at an airport when the men return from Vietnam. Of course, Bill reports on his return to America near the end of *Vietnam–Perkasie* and there is not a spitter in sight! In both the '60s class and the Vietnam class, students watch the explosive documentary *Sir! No Sir!*[6] about the anti-war movement within the military. They also read several essays on the size and power of that anti-war movement and, especially, the close and friendly ties between the civilian and military movements. The documentary includes an interview with Jerry Lembcke, Vietnam veteran, professor of sociology, and author of the absolutely essential study *The Spitting*

Image: Myth, Memory and the Legacy of Vietnam.[7] Lembcke spent several years researching the myth and concludes that there is not a single scrap of evidence that any returning vet was ever spit on by an anti-war activist, despite the occasional claim by a vet or vets that it actually happened to him. (I might add that "myth-busting" is a Lembcke specialty. His 2010 book, *Hanoi Jane: Sex, and Fantasies of Betrayal*,[8] shreds the bizarre stories that grew out of Jane Fonda's 1972 visit to North Vietnam, a visit that Lembcke points out had no impact whatsoever on the outcome of the war which ended [*sic*!] with the Paris Peace Accords in early 1973 and the release of American POWs.

Bill, of course, has no time for this particular lie, emphasizing, as Lembcke does, that the myth has been used by Nixon, Reagan, Bush I and Bush II to demonize opponents of their various wars as unpatriotic and hateful toward the "brave men and women who are serving their country and preserving American freedom" in—take your pick—whatever country (countries) Nixon, Reagan, Bush I and Bush II decided to invade. He is scathing about this myth.

By now students are usually reeling. No one has ever told them these things; things that they must know, as Bill insists, if they are to be enlightened citizens.

Bill usually concludes with some words about his wife and daughter and his teaching at an exclusive boys school outside of Philadelphia where he, ironically, teaches the children of American ruling class and does his damndest to counter the poison their parents have poured into them since birth.

I always make sure some time is saved so Bill can read a few of his poems—both Vietnam and non–Vietnam poems—to the class. This becomes a powerful educational moment for the class. Students, for the most part today, read poetry only under what can be called "duress," i.e., in "Introduction to Literature" classes, and poetry plays no real role in their world view. The direct, plain-spoken force of Bill's poems slams into them and "educates" them on the poetic possibilities of direct, plain-spoken language to open their eyes to every possible human moment. The Vietnam poems, to just name a few, such as "A Relative Thing"; "Making the Children Behave"; "For Mrs. Na"; "Second Thoughts" (Bill tells the story behind this poem—a night spent drinking in Hanoi in 1985 with a one-armed NVA veteran who lost his arm in Laos in 1971; at the end of the night as they stagger out of the bar together, the man puts his arm around Bill and says "Mr. Bill, I'm glad I didn't kill you!"); the heart-breaking "Song for Leela, Bobby and Me" and the equally heart-breaking long poem "Mostly Nothing Happens." One poem—"Guns"—from *The Distance We Travel*[9] is particularly moving since it translates the lengthy prose of *Vietnam–Perkasie* into the compressed images of poetry. Bill understands that someday he will have to tell his now (in the poem) four-year-old daughter Leela about his time in Vietnam. He writes: "Just eighteen, I killed / a ten-year-old. I didn't know. / He spins across the marketplace / all shattered chest, all eyes and arms. / Do I tell her that? Not yet, / though one day I will have / no choice except to tell her / or send her into the world / wide-eyed and ignorant. / The boy spins across the years / till he lands in a heap / in another war in another place / where yet another generation / is rudely about to discover / what their fathers never told them."

And the post–Vietnam poems such as "A Warning to My Students" and "Responsibility" remind them that they are now the vulnerable ones, the ones who will be propagandized into going to war(s) against people(s) who offer no threat to them.

Finally there are the personal poems; I always try to end with a few of these. Bill writes with great tenderness about his wife Anne and their daughter Leela. He has no hesitation in describing what a difficult, forbidding presence he was after he left the Marines: angry, drinking too much, raging against civilian and military alike. It took him a year to convince his wife to risk a date with him. One poem "A Scientific Treatise for My Wife" ranges over the history of science, from the ancients to Galileo to Newton to Einstein to Stephen Hawking. And what does cosmology have to do with his love for his wife? The poem ends: "Okay, I'm not a physicist. / But even geniuses can miss the obvious, / and I don't need a Ph.D. to know / the universe begins and ends with you." As he finishes, he usually breaks out into a big grin and says to the students: "Now how can you not love a man who writes poems like that about you."

At the end of class, several of the students stay around, getting their books autographed, and telling Bill how much they enjoyed his visit. I have had students who were so moved that they began an email correspondence with him.

As a follow-up, at the next class I distribute a copy of Bill's great speech, delivered in October 2009 as the "Joe Patterson Smith Lecture" at Illinois College. The title: "That Was Then, This Is Now: Reflections on the Late American War in Vietnam"[10] brilliantly summarizes the forty years that Bill has been thinking about and writing about Vietnam and its continuous presence in our lives. I also give them a writing assignment to describe their reactions to Bill's visit. The papers, without exception, for the past couple of decades indicate the enormous impact that Bill's visit has on them. Occasionally, at Ocean County College, there has been a Vietnam veteran (or even a veteran from a more recent war) in the class. They too react to Bill's visit as if blinders had been removed from their eyes and they can now understand the pointless and grotesque folly(ies) that robbed them of their youth and their dreams.

As long as I teach about Vietnam and/or the 1960s, I will ask Bill Ehrhart to come help "educate" my students.

Notes

1. Ehrhart, W.D., *Vietnam–Perkasie: A Combat Marine Memoir* (Jefferson, NC: McFarland, 1983). *Passing Time: Memoir of a Vietnam Veteran Against the War* (Jefferson, NC: McFarland, 1989). *Busted: A Vietnam Veteran in Nixon's America* (Amherst, MA: University of Massachusetts Press, 1995).

2. Ehrhart, W.D., *Ordinary Lives: Platoon 1005 and the Vietnam War* (Philadelphia, PA: Temple University Press, 1999).

3. See also W.D. Ehrhart, "Ken and Bill's Excellent Adventure," in *Dead on a High Hill* (Jefferson, NC: McFarland, 2012), 163–185.

4. Ehrhart, W.D., *Winter Bells* (Easthampton, MA, Adastra Press, 1988). It was reprinted in *Beautiful Wreckage: New and Selected Poems* (Easthampton, MA: Adastra Press, 1999).

5. Ehrhart, W.D., *Winter Bells* (Easthampton, MA, Adastra Press, 1988); *Just for Laughs* (Silver Spring, MD: Vietnam Generation Inc. & Burning Cities Press, 1990), 19–21; *Beautiful Wreckage: New & Selected Poems* (Easthampton, MA: Adastra, 1999), 106–7.

6. Director David Zeiger, 2005, 85 minutes.

7. Lembcke, Jerry, *The Spitting Image: Myth, Memory and the Legacy of Vietnam* (New York: New York University Press, 2000).

8. Lembcke, Jerry, *Hanoi Jane: Sex, and Fantasies of Betrayal* (Amherst, MA: University of Massachusetts Press, 2010).

9. Ehrhart, W.D., "Guns," *The Distance We Travel* (Easthampton, MA: Adastra Press, 1993), 42.

10. This lecture is actually an amalgamation of "'They Want Enough Rice': Reflections on the Late American war in Vietnam" and "One, Two, Many Vietnams?" Both of these were published in *Dead on a High Hill* (Jefferson, NC: McFarland, 2012). Information courtesy of W.D. Ehrhart.

W. D. Ehrhart: Teacher-Poet

Charles L. Yates

I met Bill Ehrhart for the first time in 2001, just a few weeks after the Twin Towers collapsed in clouds and America's simple, unexamined sense of innocence and nobility went down with them. However, I had known him already for a long time before that. I encountered him first in the PBS documentary, *Vietnam, A Television History*. Then we crossed paths again in another retrospective television documentary, *Making Sense of the Sixties*.[1] In both places, he was one of many talking heads the producers had brought in as witnesses and participants, to tell viewers about the lives they lived in those times, who they were when they began, how they changed, and who they have become since then.

But from the first sight, Bill was more than just another talking head. He kept saying things I would have said, and he kept saying them in ways I would have said them. Repeatedly, the guy was channeling me, and I realized that for years I had been channeling him whenever someone asked me about my experiences in Vietnam and my thoughts about them since. It was fairly spooky. I found myself thinking, "I know this guy. What a conversation we could have. We could sit down together and talk for days and never run out of more to talk about."

Of course, it never occurred to me that I'd ever actually meet him, and prove by doing it how right I was about that conversation. But then, many years later, I began team-teaching a course on narratives about the U.S. war in Vietnam at Earlham, the little college where I worked.

Me, the token Vietnam veteran in the history department at a Quaker college, and my colleague, a Quaker himself and a veteran of the war at home, the massive protests people staged in the United States while I was in Vietnam doing the work of war. In the course, we read novels, poems, histories, and documents. We watched movies and TV shows and documentaries and propaganda films. We watched most of *Vietnam, A Television History* (13 episodes), and I told my colleague about the sense of kindred I felt with that one talking head guy. We wanted our students to grapple with the question of what happens when an event becomes a story. We wanted them to try to come to grips with the distinction between what one author has called "happening-truth" and "story-truth."[2] We wanted them to grapple with the ambiguity of truth—better yet, with the multiple truths—that arise and compete for our loyalty when a narrator takes an event and makes a story of it, and then when all who remember the event are gone and all that's left is the story.

One year, we used one of Bill's anthologies of Vietnam war poetry, *Carrying the Darkness*.[3] Not long after that, the editor of the college alumni magazine asked us to write a piece about the course and what we were trying to do in it. And in the piece, one of the names we mentioned was Bill Ehrhart.

A few weeks after the magazine came out, the editor received a letter from Bill. It turned out that Bill's wife is an alumna of the same college, and when he saw his name in the magazine, he wrote to the editor to introduce himself and let him know that he could be available to come to campus and give a poetry reading. I wrote to Bill immediately and invited him to visit campus, speak to our class, and read some of his poems for a larger audience, and though we had no idea at the time of what was to come, we scheduled his visit for just a few weeks after that September day in 2001. So naturally, when Bill came, he had plenty to talk about.

He spoke to our class, and that was a golden moment. None of those students was quite ready for what Bill had to give them, and none of them was quite the same after their encounter with him. And he also gave that public reading of his poetry we'd asked him for, but there, because of a fluke coincidence of timing, his audience consisted almost entirely of Vietnam veterans from the community.

Only a few people from the college attended. They had already spent what energy they had for the day in a massive protest on campus against the appearance of Ann Coulter, who had signed a contract to speak at our campus on the same day Bill was scheduled to read his poems. It was a tragic missed opportunity. Those of us who went to Bill's reading came away not only moved and stimulated but with a renewed sense of moral clarity. I doubt that those who staged the protest against Ann Coulter could have said that, because in the end, the only effect the protest had on her was to give her the opportunity for headlines saying something like "Ann Coulter Speaks to Standing Room Only Audience at Quaker College," not at all the kind of publicity we would have wanted.

The friendship with Bill that began on that occasion continued to grow, and a couple of years later I brought him back to campus for another appearance, in connection with another class I was teaching. This time, one of the students who came to hear Bill was the daughter of one his lifelong friends, a young woman who had grown up playing with his daughter Leela, and who consequently had known Bill most of her life. When he was done speaking, he greeted her with a huge hug, and then she asked Bill and me how long we had known each other. I said, "Bill and I met just a few years ago, but we've known each other all our lives." Her jaw dropped open in astonishment and she said, "That's exactly what Bill said when I asked him about you."

Ten years later, Bill and I rarely see each other, but we stay in touch, we trade stories, and occasionally we find an opportunity to get together and continue that conversation. And there are things I've learned about Bill in those conversations that exemplify the kinds of insights we can have when we bond with kindred spirits—and of course, there are things I've learned about myself too.

Like me, Bill Ehrhart doesn't always win friends and influence people, sometimes not even when he's dealing with people he thinks of as friends, and particularly not with people he hopes to influence. One of the gentlest and most loving men I've ever known, Bill can be pretty hard-edged when he's talking about the convictions he holds most passionately, and those he addresses don't always know how to understand the force of that passion, especially not when he directs it at them because they've refused in some way to be morally affected by what he tells them.

Actually, it's pretty simple. He wants people to know what he thinks about war and those who make it, about the military and organized state-sponsored violence, about pacifists and pacifism, about government and the way it throws away the young people in its care in pursuit of goals it cannot define or defend, about the culture of the United States and the high status it grants to the military and to military values. He wants people to know what he thinks, and he doesn't always go out of his way to protect their sensibilities or spare their feelings when he tells them.

Make no mistake: Bill knows why he chose to become a Marine. He knows about the kinds of motives that lead young men to join the military. He knows that some of those motives are noble, and he recognizes and honors that kind of motivation in others who've served. But he also distinguishes carefully between the reasons people serve and the kinds of things they actually end up doing in the name of service. And he wants the rest of us to make that same careful distinction.

He refers to himself as an "ex-Marine." Of course, as any "former Marine" will tell you, there's no such thing as an "ex-Marine." For Bill, though, that "once a Marine always a Marine" mentality is one of the main reasons why young people keep joining the Corps and going off to kill and be killed in wars whose purposes they don't understand. And he makes no effort to conceal the truth he discovered for himself as soon as he arrived in Vietnam. As he likes to put it, "I didn't serve my country; I served my government." He might add that nobody either in Vietnam or in the United States derived any benefit of any kind from what he did while he was a Marine, either while he was in Vietnam or after he came home. Not even the United States government or the Marine Corps, *semper fi*, gained anything from the personal sacrifices Bill made, the property he destroyed, the lives he took, or the permanent scars he carries on his body and his soul as a result of the things he did, all in the name of honor, duty, and country.

He passionately wants to educate people, to make them know that the elaborate apparatus of military culture serves to conceal the truth about the military and its special reality. He wants them to understand how the monuments, memorials, and cemeteries, the parades, ceremonies, and vast geometric rows of identical tombstones, all function as the magician's other hand, the one he flourishes flamboyantly to keep us from seeing what he's doing with the hand that matters, the one actually holding the cards. He wants us to realize that powerful and moving phrases like "this great country of ours" and "all gave some, some gave all" and "freedom isn't free," by appealing directly to our affect rather than to our intellect, function primarily to keep us from thinking clearly about military policy and military action, about the human consequences of the latter, and the moral, ethical, cultural, and economic consequences of the former.

Of the many moves Bill makes in a typical performance, one of my favorites comes when he asks members of the audience to tell him how many people died in whatever the most recent popular war movie happens to be. He waits patiently while they try to work it out and add up how many distinct deaths they can remember seeing on the screen. And after a few of them have tried to get it right, Bill tells them what they already knew: "Nobody died. It was a movie and they were all actors. When they were done filming they dusted themselves off, got into their limousines, and rode off to whatever the next Hollywood event was."

The movie audience member's casual willingness to conflate death on the screen with death on the battlefield, and thus fail to come to grips with the messy, undignified, and embarrassing reality of death in combat, is one of the main reasons why so many people find it so easy to feel so good about whatever may be the most recent war their government has asked them to pay for—with taxes always, with the integrity of their national economy, more often than not, but, all too often, with the lives of their own children as well. Deep down, they know that already, but all the official and unofficial bloviating about war in the culture makes it easy for them to keep from knowing what they know.

They'd rather get all warm and fuzzy listening to Lee Greenwood holler about how he's "proud to be an American" and how he won't forget the men who died to keep America free.[4] They'd rather get all red-eyed and righteous listening to Toby Keith promise "a boot in the ass" to whole countries full of people he's never met, who never did anything to harm him, just because "it's the American way."[5] Maybe, Bill wants to say to Keith and his loving fans, maybe if we did a better job of understanding why they kicked us, we wouldn't be quite so eager to kick back, or quite so sure that it's obviously the right thing to do.

And Bill also wants us to pause and ask ourselves—ask Greenwood—what about the men who lived, Lee, the ones who get to spend the rest of their lives trying to figure out how to live with themselves and the knowledge of what they did in war, how to believe once again that they deserve to be among their families and their neighbors, in whose name they did those things, but who always manage to get on with their lives as if none of it has anything to do with them—the ones who keep saying to Bill and the others, get over it and get on with your life.

Bill wants to push against that, to keep us from falling for it. As the consummate teacher, doing one of those things that teachers do best, Bill wants to remind us of what we know but would prefer not to know. After all, to know is to be responsible—for the knowledge, for its implications and consequences, for the changes it calls us to make in ourselves, in the way we see the world, and in the way we behave.

Bill is angry. He's been angry most of his life, and like most of us Vietnam vets, he was already pretty well steamed up before he went to Vietnam.[6] But when he came home, again like the rest of us, he brought with him a very special new kind of anger—a new dimension of anger, the kind we produce when we realize that those in whom we placed our trust have taken advantage of us and our motives; the kind of anger we feel when we come to know that people we trusted have sent us to do dishonorable, despicable things in the name of honor, in the name of that proverbial Truth, Justice, and the American Way in whose defense we initially decided to join up and do our part. It's the kind of anger we feel when some unexpected agency forces us to acknowledge that we already knew it, we knew it all along, but we sheltered ourselves from it, and we allowed terrible things to happen because it was easier to pretend we didn't know. Bill wants to remind us, and he does it in ways we can't dodge.

Pick up any one of his poems. He'll tell you a story, familiar or strange or some combination of both, and you'll follow along, unsuspecting, until right at the end, when he drops that punch line that you can't avoid. "I didn't want a monument," he'll say. "What I wanted was an end to monuments."[7]

Gotcha.

"We are the ones you sent to fight a war you didn't know a thing about," he'll start off. And after a catalog of revelations that stop you in your tracks, he'll wind up, "We are your sons, America, / and you cannot change that. / When you awake, / we will still be here."[8]

He'll string out a series of reminders of things going on all around you that you know about but so far have avoided doing anything about, and then he'll get right in your face and ask you, "What answers will you find / What armor will protect you / when your children ask you / Why?"[9]

He'll take you to unfamiliar, unsettling places, places you're really glad you have never been, with an opening like, "It's practically impossible / to tell civilians / from Viet Cong." Details will follow, until you're already there with him when he gets to the end and hits you with, "After awhile, / you quit trying."[10] Back home, we safe ones wonder what goes wrong in wars to cause the children we raised with such care to turn into cold, steely-eyed, indiscriminate dispensers of death and destruction. How do we get massacres of civilians? How do we get a My Lai, a No Gun Ri, a Wounded Knee? Bill has the answer, he knows we're not going to like it, and he shoves it at us anyway, because he knows that we know it already ourselves and it's his mission to make sure we let ourselves know that we know, know what we know.

After that, you're not terribly surprised when, in another setting, he starts you off in the car, riding along with him and his daughter in the everyday peace and normalcy of their home town: "Again we pass that field / green artillery piece squatting / by the Legion Post on Chelten Avenue, / its ugly little pointed snout / ranged against my daughter's school."[11] She asks him if he ever used a gun like that, and then there's a conversation where, before long, she dismisses the whole idea of guns and war with "That's dumb." Bill picks it up there: "How do you tell a four-year-old / what steel can do to flesh?"

"Just eighteen," Bill says, "I killed / a ten-year-old. I didn't know. / He spins across the marketplace / all shattered chest, all eyes and arms. / Do I tell her that? Not yet," he decides, "though one day I will have / no choice except to tell her / or to send her into the world / wide-eyed and ignorant. / The boy spins across the years / till he lands in a heap / in another war in another place / where yet another generation / is rudely about to discover / what their fathers never told them."[12]

And then we send our children to places like Grenada, Panama, Beirut, Baghdad, Fallujah, Kabul—it seems we never grow tired of finding new places to send our children—and then they meet that boy, all shattered chest, eyes and arms, spinning across the years and collapsing, lifeless, into their lives, there to remain, haunting them for the rest of their days—as in "Patrick."[13]

Do you see what we do? Bill asks. Do you see these lessons we seem always to avoid learning? How many more times must we do this to our beloved children, to the beloved children of others, to ourselves? Are we insatiable? And will we always blame the children when they come home from our wars dark, sullen changelings? Will we always refuse to see? For decades, Bill has never stopped asking.

Instead, he keeps reminding us, as he says to his students, who haven't taken things as seriously as Bill wants them to: "And now I see it all / coming / one more time; one / by one, all the old flags / resurrected / and ready / for the rocket's red glare / still another time—."[14] He wakes terrified in the night, reaches for his wife, and she reassures him, tells him it's just a dream. "And she's right, too," he says, "these days, for me / it's just a dream / because the next time they come looking / for soldiers, they won't come looking / for me. I'm too old; / I know too much. / The next time they come looking / for soldiers, they'll come looking / for you."[15]

Gotcha.

After enough of those—after Bill has backed you into enough corners and pinned you there, summoning your conscience in ways you can't ignore—you have to admit to yourself that you knew that already, you already knew the answer, and what Bill has just done is not to teach you something you didn't know, but to make you acknowledge something you did know. You already know the answer—and you know you can't escape the moral implications of the answer—when he asks you, "When they tell stories to their children / of the evil / that awaits misbehavior, / is it me they conjure?"[16]

Gotcha.

Unfortunately, Bill's anger, like that of most of us Vietnam vets, is impotent, and all the more dangerous for that reason, because the people against whom we feel it are beyond our reach, beyond our control, and beyond caring about us, or what we think, or how we feel. They don't read Bill's poetry. They don't listen when he reads it out loud to audiences full of skeptics in the hope that maybe one or two of them will have a few fleeting second thoughts. Nothing illustrates this more graphically than the offhand remark attributed to Donald Rumsfeld, that "you go to war with the army you have, not the army you might want or wish to have at a later time."[17]

Rumsfeld didn't say this just anywhere. He said it in Iraq, to troops he had sent there, troops who had asked him to explain why the American government had not provided them with the equipment they needed to do even a marginally adequate job of the fighting it had sent them to do, and at the same time manage somehow to stay alive themselves. They wanted Rumsfeld to explain why he and his president had thrown them away. And as he made clear in his reply, he didn't care, and he didn't care that they could see he didn't care, because he also knew that there was nothing they could do about it. And he knew that, because of the motives that led them to become soldiers in the first place, they'd go on doing what he had sent them to do, go on killing and being killed, wasting lives and dreams in service to a cause he knew perfectly well he didn't even understand himself.

It's an impotent anger. Over the course of time, those of us who are lucky—those who manage to be in the right place, at the right time, so we can get the right kind of help: loving friends, counseling, mood altering drugs—we find ways to live with that anger, but it never goes away, and it's always there, just beneath the surface. As Bill puts it in the title of that anthology of war poetry I mentioned a while back, we carry our darkness with us wherever we go, though it's important to add that there's more to it than just that. As the title of another of Bill's anthologies makes clear, eventually we also learn a kind of "unaccustomed mercy" that makes it just marginally easier for some of us to keep getting out of bed one day at a time and trying to do the best we can in spite of the weight of that darkness.[18] Knowing that Bill is out there, watching with his unsparing moral vision, speaking of what he sees in always new poems, makes it just a bit easier for me to keep going, returning to the fray time after time. I think Bill would say the same thing about me, and about his other friends whom he sees only rarely but with whom he's always in contact, and with whom, when he can, he likes to sit for hours, sipping a good single malt whiskey and following that conversation wherever it leads.

And of course it's not just Vietnam vets any more. Many of the kids coming home from the wars in Iraq and Afghanistan are angry too, for the same reasons, and with the same slender prospect of meaningful relief. Vietnam Veterans against the War (VVAW) was founded in 1967, and Bill became involved in 1971 and has been a long-time member ever since.[19] Now we have IVAW and AVAW as well, and we talk to each other, at meetings, over the internet. Remember: "We are your sons, America, [and your daughters too, now] / and you cannot change that. / When you awake, / we will still be here."[20] As one of America's best known Vietnam vet authors puts it, "send guys to war, they come home talking dirty."[21] And now the girls are talking dirty too. Such is the legacy of the American errand into the wilderness. Such are the citizens of that shining city on a hill.[22]

It's an impotent anger, and consequently it's one of the main reasons why Bill doesn't always win friends and influence people. Even when he doesn't let them see it, they sense it, and rather than acknowledge that it scares them, they turn their backs on Bill, and blame him for their discomfort. I think Bill is more or less content even if this is all he achieves. If he can leave an audience feeling uncomfortable—even if he also leaves them blaming him for their discomfort—he has achieved his most fundamental goal. He has undermined complacency just a little bit; as teachers like to put it, he has created a teachable moment, and within it he has taught. He has subjected yet another audience to his Gotcha.

In many ways, Bill is the Smedley Butler of our time.[23] Everywhere he goes, he tells people that war is a racket, and he tells them why, and he requires them—politely when he can, but rudely when he must—to acknowledge that it's a racket in which they're all complicit, a racket that works in significant degree because they support it, they approve of it, they believe it speaks of the best there is in themselves and their country. Or, worse, they simply remain disengaged and complacent—examples of good men and women who do nothing and thus allow evil to triumph, as the old wisdom has it[24]—good men and women who prefer to go on pretending that Bill's not talking to them when he wonders how they will answer when their children ask them why.

Here is what this means: unlike many veterans, who return home and quickly bury all of the truths they discovered on the battlefield, Bill has figured out that deliberate wrongdoing is not the main culprit in the ongoing global spree of organized violence visited on harmless peoples that has defined the American imperial enterprise from the beginning. There is no clean line separating the guilty from the innocent, and the innocent are just as guilty. The main culprit is the complacency of the bystanders, who continue to watch, to applaud, as the destruction goes on. And he wants to tell people that when their sons and daughters come home in plastic bags, or worse, come home physically intact but emotionally, psychologically, and morally damaged and deformed for the rest of their lives, they have not suffered these wounds to anyone's benefit. As I've already said, even the government that uses them and then tosses them aside has gained nothing worthwhile from the maiming and the death—not that which they've inflicted on others, and not that which they've suffered themselves.

Bill wants people to know this. He wants them to know that they have fallen for what Wilfred Owen and others have called the old and terrible lie: "dulce et decorum est, pro patria mori."[25] In fact, Bill says over and over, there is nothing sweet or noble about dying for one's country. It's messy, vulgar, disgusting, degrading, dehumanizing, and permanent.[26] And he adds, dying for the country is not the hard thing. The hard thing is killing for the country and then trying to learn to live with it. The lucky ones die. The less lucky come home—to families and neighbors who realize they don't much want them any more, don't like who they've become. The less lucky get to spend the rest of their lives listening to the Lee Greenwoods of the world forget about them and care only for the ones who are beyond caring. The less lucky get to struggle as they try to explain why they lose their tempers so easily over such small things, why they don't just instantly overflow with gratitude when someone thanks them for their service.[27]

And so, for much of his life, since long before he went to war, but especially since he came home from it, Bill has written poetry. It's not all about war, as even a casual glance through any of his chapbooks, collections, or anthologies quickly shows. In fact, some of his most beautiful and arresting poems are those he has written to his wife Anne over the years, as the passage of time has brought them to a better knowledge of themselves, of each other, and of the astonishing gamble they took when they decided to become a couple, the breath-taking discoveries they've made along that road, and the beauty they've bequeathed to the world, both in the person of their daughter Leela and in the commitment to each other that they've managed to sustain in spite of the many challenges they've faced in doing so. But, that said, a lot of Bill's poetry is about war, and many of the images, themes, and motifs of the war poems also inform poems about other subjects.

Bill has also written a great deal of prose—a three-volume memoir, an account of a return journey to Vietnam, a record of his effort to locate and reestablish contact with all the members of his Marine unit, and several collections of essays, among others. He is a very prolific writer, and what is striking about all of his output is its coherence, its integrity as a body of work. In poetry or in prose, regardless of the details of any given piece, Bill is always writing about the same things. And what I've found most consistently distinctive and reliable about his work, most compelling, most unforgettable, is his genius for that Ehrhart Gotcha I've been referring to.

As I've already suggested, Bill's Gotcha reminds us of what we knew already, but it does more than that: it calls us to remember fundamental moral and ethical truths that we knew but had perhaps set aside or looked away from, case by case, so that we could remain complicit in things of which we would disapprove otherwise, things for which we would prefer fastidiously not to share responsibility.

In one of my favorite poems, "The Simple Lives of Cats," one immaculate stanza at a time, Bill leads us into a scene in a dark and empty house in the middle of a rainy night, a house from which wife and daughter have just fled in terror after he has "lost it, temper flaring, / patience at a too-quick end, my daughter crying, / my wife's heart sinking / at the sadness of another good day gone bad. / If sorry has a name, it must be mine." But the cats are fine with it, and "don't suspect a thing. / One turns her head to lick my hand. / The other ... settles in my lap."[28] Some of us remember. We've been there. We know exactly what's going on. The war we brought home with us has roared into life once again, and we've aimed its full force at those we care about most, even if only because they happened to be nearby. Reading this, some of us let ourselves wonder fleetingly what may have become of loved ones who never came back after escaping that one last time.

Bill winds it up, pulling no punches: "Tonight my wife and child are sleeping / somewhere else. I've done this to myself / often enough to wonder just how many / chances I've got left. I stroke the cats, / who purr like engines; happy to be near, / they see no need for my improvement."[29]

Gotcha.

Notes

1. *Vietnam, A Television History* (13 episodes, 1983; series director: Bruce Palling) and *Making Sense of the Sixties* (6 episodes, 1991; director: David Hoffman).
2. O'Brien, Tim, *The Things They Carried* (New York: Penguin Books, 1990), 203.
3. Ehrhart, W.D., ed., *Carrying the Darkness: The Poetry of the Vietnam War* (Lubbock: Texas Tech University Press), 1985.
4. Greenwood, Lee, "God Bless the USA," 1984.
5. Keith, Toby, "Courtesy of the Red White and Blue (The Angry American)," 2002.
6. For example see Ehrhart, "The Damage We Do," *The Bodies Beneath the Table* (Easthampton, MA: Adastra Press, 2010), 16–17.
7. Ehrhart, W.D., "The Invasion of Grenada," *Beautiful Wreckage: New and Selected Poems* (Easthampton, Massachusetts: Adastra Press, 1999), 75. (hereafter *BW*)
8. Ehrhart, "A Relative Things," *BW*, 9–10.
9. Ehrhart, "To Those Who Have Gone Home Tired," *BW*, 25.
10. Ehrhart, "Guerrilla War," *BW*, 5.
11. Ehrhart, "Guns," *BW*, 173–74.
12. Ibid.
13. For explicit commentary on this point, cf. W.D. Ehrhart's new poem, "Patrick," *The Veteran*, 42:2 (Fall 2012), 18, where he ends with: "The army said he was fine and sent him home / with so much blood his hands will never be clean. / The VA gives him pills. Frozen in time, / he can't get out of his head the carnage he's seen."
14. "A Warning to My Students," *BW*, 85–86. This one is subtitled "George School November 1981." It dates from when Bill was a member of the faculty at what is probably the best known Quaker high school in the country.
15. Ibid.
16. Ehrhart, "Making the Children Behave," *BW*, 15.
17. http://crooksandliars.com/2006/12/15/remebering-rumsfeld-you-go-to-war-with-the-army-you-have-not-the-army-you-might-want-or-wish-to-have-at-a-later-time/
18. Ehrhart, W.D., ed., *Unaccustomed Mercy: Soldier-Poets of the Vietnam War* (Lubbock: Texas Tech University Press), 1989.
19. VVAW was founded by Jan Barry, Mark Donnelly, David Braum, and three other Vietnam war veterans, in New York City in June, 1967 after they marched together in the April 15, 1967 Spring Mobilization to End the War anti-war demonstration with over 400,000 other protesters. After talking to members of the Veterans for Peace group at that march, Barry discovered there was no organization representing Vietnam veterans. James S. Olson, *Dictionary of the Vietnam War* (Westport, CT: Greenwood Press, 1988), 475.
20. Ehrhart, "A Relative Thing," *BW*, 9–10.
21. O'Brien, *The Things They Carried*, 77.
22. Winthrop, John, aboard the *Arbella*, bound for North America, 1630, https://www.mtholyoke.edu/acad/intrel/winthrop.htm
23. Butler, Smedley, *War Is a Racket* (Los Angeles: Feral House, 2003).

24. Burke, Edmund, http://www.quotationspage.com/quotes/Edmund_Burke/

25. Owen, Wilfred, "Dulce et Decorum Est," *The Collected Poems of Wilfred Owen* (New York: New Directions, 1963), 55. Invoked in O'Brien, *The Things They Carried*, 76.

26. Bill also likes to point out the obvious: no matter how graphically realistic those movie special effects may be, the one thing they can't convey is the smell. Or, as another of Bill's favorite poets, Siegfried Sassoon, likes to put it, "the rank stench of those bodies haunts me still." Jon Silkin, ed., *The Penguin Book of First World War Poetry* (New York & London: Penguin Books, 1996), 124–127.

27. Bill explains this issue elegantly in his own terms. Cf. W.D. Ehrhart, "Thank You For Your Service," *The Veteran*, 42:2 (Fall 2012), 16.

28. Ehrhart, "The Simple Lives of Cats," *BW*, 192.

29. Ibid.

W. D. Ehrhart:
Transformational Teacher

Joseph Cox

In the final pages of *Passing Time,* W. D. Ehrhart is passionately discussing American history with his friend and shipmate Roger, third engineer on the SS *Atlantic Endeavor,* the oil tanker out of Long Beach, California, where Bill has finally found some respite from his Vietnam past. Roger asks Bill for a list of books to read, and suggests to Bill, "You could be a teacher. Christ I wish *my* kid could have a teacher like you. I wish I could have a teacher like you— I mighta learned something."[1] Fortunately, since 2001, boys at The Haverford School in Pennsylvania have had W. D. Ehrhart as their English and history teacher, track coach, and mentor. Those who know his passion and compassion know that he is an engaging and transformational teacher/coach/mentor who makes those fortunate enough to be in his class think, and he changes lives for the better.

In his poem, "Unaccustomed Mercies," W. D. Ehrhart, Bill to his friends, asks the question, "What shall we give our children?"[2] In his many poems about his daughter, Leela, his recurrent answer is love. The passage in "Song for Leela, Bobby and Me" where Bill tells us that he has "friends who wonder why I can't / just let the past lie where it lies, / why I'm still so angry. / As if there's something wrong with me"[3] resonates with those who know his work and him personally. Those who have followed his narrative from Perkasie to Vietnam and beyond know that Bill is driven by love for those for whom he cares and for what he hoped his country could and should have been. His most consistent love in his writing, public speaking, and in his classroom is his passionate efforts to tell the truth, especially to the next generation. If there ever were something "wrong" with Bill, and God knows there are so many justifiable reasons for someone to suffer given what he has experienced, it is not present in his classroom where he becomes the bedrock of compassion and honesty we hope for in all our teachers. Love and truth are what he gives our children.

In his post–Vietnam memoir *Passing Time,* Bill describes his relationship with Jamie McAdams (actually James J. McAdoo, Jr.), the men's swimming coach at Swarthmore College, "I just wanted to be around Jamie (Jimmy). He made me feel good. He was one of the gentlest, most sensitive men I'd ever known."[4] During a time when Bill, like many other Vietnam veterans, was wrestling with the demons of unacknowledged Post Traumatic Stress Disorder (PTSD), Coach McAdams (McAdoo) could see his angst and encouraged him to "do something to unwind." In his 2007 *Swarthmore College Bulletin* article Bill says, "Jimmy was the kind of coach who changed lives for the better, who taught young men how to be men in the finest and most inclusive sense of the word."[5] The coaching emphasis was less on the body than the soul, less on the results of a race than the preparation for life. Bill's teaching duties at Haverford extend to the winter track season where he, like his college swimming coach, empathetically coaches his young men for life and teaches his "young men how to be men in the finest and most inclusive sense of the word." The "teacher-coach" model in American independent schools is an archaic but effective way to involve educators in all phases of a student's development and one well suited to Bill's personality. In the classroom and on the track, Bill finds ways to encourage best performance, and his intervention in a boy's life at a time of stress has been just as reaffirming and supportive as Coach Jimmy McAdoo's (Jamie McAdam's) role in Bill's education.

Nationally ranked middle distance runner Lucas Elek bears witness:

> The whole school recognizes his famous "Winter Track Rocks" graffiti tag, which can be seen on various white boards throughout the school year. Dr. Ehrhart is constantly on the lookout for fresh track recruits and his famous catch phrase, "This Sport Ain't for Pansies" echoes throughout the halls. He coaches from the heart, motivating with boisterous praise. Always cheeky, his rowdiness cranks up a notch at meets. His cheers are always positive and encouraging to team. It doesn't matter if a boy is a beginner or a superstar, Dr. Ehrhart hollers at the top of his lungs and waves his arms frantically all the way to the finish line. Off the track, he is always a loyal patron at other school sporting events and major after school events. While his school spirit soars higher than any other teacher I can think of, his true talents shine with individuals. A one-on-one can leave you deeply pondering or laughing so hard you cannot stand upright. I have been blessed to witness these natural talents on more than one occasion. At one of the lower points of my life, Dr. Ehrhart took me in his room one afternoon and cured my blues with a marathon of Monty Python until I was laughing right along with him. The experience was honest, insightful and came with the rare gift of genuine human kindness. I know I am not unique in receiving such a wonderful gift.[6]

Bill's rare "gift of human kindness," his empathy is ever present in his poetry and classroom. In an anti-bullying poem, "Sins of the Fathers," that resonates with his students, Bill shares his memories of his daughter being taunted and coming home from school in tears, "it makes me think—O Christ, it makes / me think of things I haven't thought about / in years. How we nicknamed Barbara Hoffman / 'Barn,' walked behind her through the halls and mooed / like cows. We kept this up for years, and not / for any reason I could tell you now / or even then except that it was fun. / Or seemed like fun. The nights that Barbara must have cried herself to sleep, the days / she must have dreaded getting up for school."[7] In the poem, "Just for Laughs," Bill also describes the world through the perspective of a child, this time when he was a ten-year-old boy who "thought that I / would live forever, I could kill / whatever I pleased."[8] The plump pregnant snake being stoned by small boys becomes the metaphor for a war being perpetrated by equally vicious and dangerous young men who are "oblivious" to the carnage being done on innocents. The power Bill's poems achieve from the empathetic persona who speaks to us as man reflecting on childhood informs our best teachers. Our very best teachers sympathize with the difficulties at every stage of life and are there to offer support. Bill Ehrhart is the kind of teacher who dispenses kindness along with knowledge and has a lasting affect on his students.

As Headmaster of The Haverford School, I am in a unique position to know both W. D. Ehrhart's poems and his work in the classroom as a teacher of literature and history. In his December, 1997, *Swarthmore College Bulletin* article, "Military Intelligence," Bill outlines our fortunate (for me) friendship. I first met Bill at the 1993 University of Notre Dame Vietnam Reconciliation Conference where he read his poetry. At that influential conference, Bill's session was the only one to draw a deserving standing ovation. I presented a paper on "American War Myths and Vietnam Veteran Narratives," which Bill attended and actually remembered in later conversations. Because of their craft and their honesty, the poetry and narratives of W. D. Ehrhart were well known among military professionals and those of us who taught at our military academies. Bill was surprised to learn that *Passing Time* was part of the Air Force Academy curriculum. Several years later, I was fortunate to be able to teach an elective at West Point entitled "The Art of War," a nondescript title that allowed its teacher to select any topic related to war and shape a course that would help prepare future officers make sense out of military careers before them. I decided to explore with my students the best of each artistic medium to come out of the Vietnam War.

I thought Tim O'Brien was the best fiction writer, and we read his works and he visited West Point to discuss his Vietnam War and fiction with my students. Phil Caputo wrote what I thought was the best personal memoir (although I find Bill's a close second), and he, too, visited my class. Oliver Stone made the best movies, and, yes, even Mr. Stone was generous enough to share his experiences with cadets without any financial remuneration. I thought an artist named John Wolf was the best painter to have experienced and to have represented the Vietnam War, and I believed W. D. Ehrhart was the best Vietnam veteran poet. During his visit to West Point, I also could see that the poet W. D. Ehrhart was also an incredible teacher who connected authentically with the cadets. He had an enormous capacity for empathy and never talked down to students. His basic decency and unflinching honesty made the students understand the emotional reality of his wartime experiences, and they respected his perspectives on war even if Bill's opinions were not politically compatible with the majority of service academy students. Bill says that his encounters with us military types were a "kind of epiphany" for him, and for us it was also the beginning of a remarkable friendship.

When, after I retired from my thirty-year Army career and became Headmaster of a boys' school outside of Philadelphia, and was suddenly in need of an English teacher to take the place of a much beloved man taken ill, I asked Bill to take the job. Bill's first year was not easy for him. Teaching is hard work, lots of preparation, and, especially in a school full of very bright young men, a credibility challenge. Boys sniff out insecurity, and Bill was not sure during his first few months that he was comfortable with the challenges of teaching Haverford boys who were making it clear that he was trying to take the place of a beloved icon. I remember talking to several boys who missed the teacher he replaced very much and were perhaps holding their loyalty to him against Bill. I told them that they would see that Bill's heart was as big as that of the man he replaced. I knew that he would love his students as much if not more than the man he replaced, and students would respond, but it took a little time. In a matter of months "Dr. Ehrhart" was well on his way to iconic teacher status that is a staple of American independent schools. Bill told me he knew he had arrived when the boys nicknamed him "Big Dawg" for reasons I cannot fathom, but having a nickname in a boys' school is about as honorific as it gets. Poems by boys dedicated to "Big Dawg" now adorn his classroom bulletin board, and his selection by graduating class after graduating class to be their senior banquet speaker attest to their respect for a life-changing educator. Once when giving Bill his yearly contract, a fair but, for what teachers do to benefit our society, paltry sum, Bill confessed he would do the job for nothing. "I love these boys" he said with a hitch in his voice. I knew he meant it, and his students return that love.

One recent graduate shared the following with me when he heard I was writing this chapter:

> Taking Dr. Ehrhart's class, whether it is English or History, is a privilege as a Haverford student. His enthusiasm for teaching is unmatched, as it is so clear after spending time in his classroom how much he loves teaching. He demands

respect in the classroom, and his students adapt early to his unique style of teaching. A major highlight of his class is the multitude of personal anecdotes he shares always intriguing his students. His ideology on politics often clashes with that of his students, but it always leads to good conversation of relevant current events and broadens the horizons of the boys. His opinions, although seen as unpopular, are based on first hand experiences and therefore are completely justified. Students learn not only from the material he teaches in class, but also from the life lessons he has learned and passes on. Haverford is lucky to have a teacher like Dr. Ehrhart.[9]

Bill has become a pied piper of sorts as another student explains:

As the second semester drew near, and "senioritis" started to get into full swing, it was time to pick classes for my last semester of high school. Generally the rule for picking classes, especially for those who have already been admitted to the college of their choice months in advance, is which class is the easiest and has the least work. I'd be lying if I said I didn't keep this in mind in some of my class choices; however, there was one exception. Dr. E! In my ten years at Haverford, my interaction with Dr. Ehrhart had been limited to his amusing announcements at assemblies and the outspoken appreciation that my friends had for his style of teaching and honest approach. So I signed up for his poetry elective, even though poetry has always been one of my least favorite subjects. Once I got acclimated to the daily quizzes and write-ups, I was truly grateful to have forty minutes of my day with Dr. Ehrhart. He brought an honest, raw, and well-thought-out approach and explanation to the material. His class was a true joy and learning experience. Dr. E. finds a way to transcend the prototypical teacher-student relationship in an unparalleled and graceful way. I can truly say that my ten years at Haverford are complete now that I have had Dr. Ehrhart.[10]

In a *New York Times* article, a public middle school teacher, Clair Needell Hollander, makes the point that summer reading should be purposeful on two levels. Students should read for "word knowledge" as well as "world knowledge,"[11] and the best books provide both. I would add that the best teachers balance their teaching with "word knowledge" and "world knowledge." In my opinion and in the opinion of his students, Bill Ehrhart's classes are heavily laden with "world knowledge." No one will experience a literature or history class taught by Bill without his sharing with them the nominally unseen horrors visited on other human beings during the course of history. In his poem "Coaching Winter Track in Time of War," he asks. "How do you tell them it's not that simple? / How do you tell them: question it all. / Question everything. Even a coach. / Even a President."[12] You can be sure that if his students stop short, Bill will "question everything." His "world knowledge" and positive relations with his students forged out of their respect for his sincerity make Bill a very effective educator. Australian education researcher John Hattie[13] reports that teacher subject-matter expertise matters far less than positive student relations to their teacher in producing positive student learning results.

Bill's rich teaching formula for success is a fusion of very positive student-teacher, teacher-student respect mixed with a rich sauce of "world" and "word" knowledge. His lessons will stick with his students throughout their lives.

Bill shared with me the story of his first teaching experience. When he was 28 and enrolled in a master's program in English/creative writing at the University of Illinois Chicago Circle (UICC), he asked for outright tuition assistance but instead was given the opportunity to be a teaching assistant to help make ends meet. The other teaching assistants (TA's) spent their first quarter at UICC taking a class on how to teach composition, but Bill didn't begin until the second quarter and did not take the class. Instead, he was paired with an experienced teacher to watch for a quarter, and then he would be given his own class in the spring. After two weeks, his mentor got called for jury duty and ended up on a murder trial that lasted for three weeks. Bill took over the class. Bill was terrified, but followed the first day's lesson plan. When he called the experienced teacher the next day to ask for the next lesson plan, his mentor told him, "You're not stupid. Figure something out. Stop calling me." Bill says he somehow managed to fumble his way through the next two and a half weeks. He didn't bother the experienced teacher because he had the power to tell the English Department Bill shouldn't be a TA the following year. When the trial ended, the experienced teacher returned and finished the quarter, though he had Bill continue to teach one of the three weekly sessions the class met.

Bill and the experienced teacher became pretty good friends, which was good because his mentor was head of the education certification program at UICC. Sitting in his office one day just before he graduated, Bill was scolding him for hanging him out to dry. His mentor told Bill that he believed you can't really teach people how to teach; his job was to give a lot of people who had no business being teachers at least a fair chance of surviving a few years in a classroom. He claimed some people are natural teachers, and he claimed he sensed very quickly that Bill was one of them. He was confident that he could leave his class in Bill's hands, even though Bill had no experience. It would work out okay. "And," he said, "I was right." Bill still has the recommendation he wrote for him when at age 30 Bill applied for his first high-school teaching job at Sandy Spring Friends School, where Bill began his intermittent teaching career.

He wrote,

> [Bill] and I worked very closely together on the teaching of a section of freshman composition in the winter quarter of last year. He came to the task without the usual preparation we give to our teaching assistants, and he was intelligently hesitant at first to make suggestions or to take over the class. But when I had to go for jury service he was compelled to take over, and he did an admirable job.

He was thoroughly prepared and professional in every way. Though he was still inclined to be a little over-conscientious, I stress that this stemmed from the best of all possible motives: he simply wanted to be sure of what he was doing, and I also think he was a little put off by the difference between his teaching experience and mine. He learned a great deal.

He has since, of course, had classes of his own to teach. His confidence has increased, and he has been continually concerned about how to do things even better. I've seldom known anyone who comes to teaching with such caring. I'm glad to say, too, that he still stops by to chat about teaching, and he now has a marvelous combination of confidence *and* a sense of the need to continue to grow. His poetry, too, reflects this fine combination of unassuming diction and real technical control. In sum, I'm delighted to recommend Bill as a teacher, and I'm proud to have him as a friend.[14]

In the Haverford classroom Bill is still "over-conscientious" and "caring." He strives to make learning history a living, breathing, life-changing experience. Rather than concern himself primarily with conveying facts and content, he captures and immerses his students in the exploration of human interactions, and connections between events while investigating their causes, ramifications, and the choices people made along the way. His students emerge with a respect and enthusiasm for history along with a confidence to look below the surface narratives. Bill wears his emotions on his sleeve and has no patience with false piety and conventional hypocrisy. Some parents love to see conventions challenged. Some do not. Those who complain to me usually get a response along the lines of, "Wow, Bill is really holding back what he really thinks. I am surprised he has provided such a balanced critique." I encourage them to read his works to truly appreciate how hard he works to maintain a balanced approach in the classroom.

Bill subordinates himself to the greater good in ways those familiar with his iconoclastic narratives might be surprised. Bill has the absolute professional respect of his peers. The Dean of our Faculty describes him as "A professed rebel of the status quo and a man of honor: his word is his word." Although he despises the Haverford coat and tie dress code, he adheres to it from the first day of school to the last, demanding the same correctness from his students. There is a sign on his classroom door that reads, "Shirt-tail out? Think before you enter."[15] The Dean of the Faculty goes on to say that, "His word is also his work. Bill's poetry tells of his interior life as a young soldier, a friend, a husband, a father. His teaching encourages his students, all young men, to know and express their own inner selves as they grow into manhood."[16]

Another colleague wrote:

> Over the course of the last two school years, Bill Ehrhart and I have become friends. Enjoying some good meals together and partaking in some excellent conversations. I have not read a lot of Bill's poetry, but I am very confident I

understand why it is so highly regarded and has the impact that it does. When I listen to Bill talk about his life experiences, which include protests, wars, passionate loves, bitter disappointments, profound successes and devastating failures, I can only conclude that Bill has lived his life to the fullest and traveled a path forged by his beliefs, convictions, and passions. Given a reservoir of experiences and feelings like that to draw upon it is no wonder that what he chooses to write about is both compelling and moving.[17]

That the line is blurred between Bill's life and what he teaches, and that he successfully straddles the academic demands of literature and history should surprise no one familiar with his published opus. Bill is a living reflection of the fascinating period of American culture he inhabited. He wears that culture, literally, in his dress and hair style and his emotional and moral framing of the world around him. Paul Fussell's admonition that "once a pissed off infantryman, always a pissed off infantryman" applies to SGT and Purple Heart recipient W. D. Ehrhart in ways that would make the late Professor Fussell proud. What they have in common is the striving for truth and living an authentic life in the face of a world that constantly sugar-coats the truth.

American Transcendentalists saw miracles in the everyday. Ralph Waldo Emerson "crossing a bare common, in snow puddles, at twilight, under a cloudy sky" enjoys "a perfect exhilaration" and is "glad to the brink of tears."[18] I have seen Bill Ehrhart's students, even the most common of them, bring him to the brink of tears. Having known Bill's poetry before I knew the man, now knowing "Dr. Ehrhart, Big Dawg" the teacher enhances my appreciation of his poetic gifts of finding the divine in the everyday and in every boy. Bill models in his classroom and in his life Emerson's adage, "to be yourself in a world that is constantly trying to make you something else is the greatest accomplishment," and he has the moral courage to expect his students to live equally authentic lives. Most learn the lesson well, sometimes to their parents' dismay.

Notes

1. Ehrhart, W.D., *Passing Time* (Jefferson, NC: McFarland, 1989), 276.
2. Ehrhart, W.D., *Just for Laughs* (Silver Spring, MD: Vietnam Generation, Inc. & Burning Cities Press, 1990), 84.
3. Ibid., 81.
4. Ehrhart, *Passing Time,* 148.
5. Ehrhart, W.D. "Knock Their Jocks Off, Boys!" *Dead on a High Hill* (Jefferson, NC: McFarland, 2012), 89.
6. Elek, Lucas, Haverford School Class of 2013, 31 July 2012.
7. Ehrhart, W.D. "Sins of the Fathers," *The Bucks County Writer*, 5:3 (Spring 2004), Doylestown, PA, 109; *The Bodies Beneath the Table* (Easthampton, MA: Adastra Press, 2010), 19.
8. Ehrhart, "Just for Laughs," *Just for Laughs,* 12.
9. Selverian, Mac, Haverford School Class of 2012, 27 July 2012.

10. Koven, Eli, Haverford School Class of 2012, 30 July 2012.

11. Hollander, Claire Needell, "Some Books Are More Equal than Others," *The New York Times*, 24 June 2012, 5.

12. Ehrhart, W.D., "Coaching Winter Track in Time of War," *Pegasus*, Fall, 2005, 33; *The Bodies Beneath the Table* (Easthampton, MA: Adastra Press, 2010), 74.

13. Internationally acclaimed education researcher John Hattie is the director of research at the Melbourne Graduate School of Education. Author of 14 books, Hattie's 2008 *Visible Learning* synthesized the results of more than fifteen years of research involving millions of students and represented the biggest ever collection of evidence-based research into what actually works in schools to improve learning.

14. Lindley, Daniel A. Jr., associate professor and chairman, English education, UICC, 5 December 1977.

15. Among the many other warnings on Bill's classroom door is "Change Takes Courage," a Eugene Debs quotation, "The class which has the power to rob upon a large scale has also the power to control the government and legalize their robbery," and an Andy Rooney warning that, "Computers make it easier to do a lot of things, but many of the things they make it easier to do don't need to be done." Bill does not get high marks in use of classroom technology in his formal evaluations.

16. Davis, Rebecca, dean of the faculty, the Haverford School, 28 June 2012.

17. Trocano, Thomas, chair of the Science Department, the Haverford School, July 10, 2012.

18. Emerson, Ralph Waldo, "Nature," *Selected Writings of Emerson* (New York: Random House, 1950), 6.

"I have learned by now where such thoughts lead": W. D. Ehrhart's Poetry and Rethinking How We Study and Teach History

MATTHEW K. IRWIN

Many of us who study and teach in the American academy habitually rely on traditional means and methodologies. In doing so, however, we often satiate ourselves (and sedate our students) with tedious, uninspired essays and lectures more inert with facts and figures than alive with dynamic substance colored and textured by our humanity's complexity. For instance, in my field, we historians seek to analyze, explicate, and if we're particularly inventive, animate the past. And while we may succeed to some degree, more often it seems we only manage to quiet or even silence history's humanity. How do we rethink and retool in order to amplify history's human voice, especially when evidentiary conservatism and exclusive methodologies have inhabited our field for so long? Upon encountering W. D. Ehrhart's poetry many years ago, I immediately discerned a less-traveled road that scholars and educators could take if we wish to encounter primary sources positively teeming with the "beautiful wreckage" of real life experiences.

Historians have studied the Vietnam War from countless angles. However, none have seriously explored the historical impact, importance, or relevance of poetry like Ehrhart's to help posterity understand Vietnam. Yet if we would permit ourselves to pause and look carefully, we'd discover that much of the verse that combatants and witnesses produced concerning the war touches on the very same subjects as our traditional histories: how and why it started; what happened during the war; and the social, cultural, political, physical, emotional, psychological, and spiritual ramifications of U.S. involvement in Vietnam. Unfortunately, though, few of us outside English departments and creative writing programs have deigned to consider Ehrhart's poems or their merit for historical inquiry, let alone allowed ourselves to harvest and partake in the rich bounty his pen yields.

Worse than merely overlooking verse, some traditionalists inexplicably dismiss it nearly altogether, arguing that poetry contributes little worthwhile to our knowledge of the past. Noted historian Arthur Marwick contends that

> the use of literature and art raises problems.... A novel or poem or painting, if it is a source at all, is a source for the period in which it was written or painted, not for the period *about* which it is written or what it is *purporting to represent*.... For the concrete facts of everyday existence ... spurn the novelist, and turn instead to the government papers, statistical series, company records, ... trade union archives....[1]

Marwick believes that our knowledge of the past must be derived from sources like the latter, and unfortunately, his works campaign to diminish the artistic voice's significance and value. He suggests that if historians want to know "concrete facts of everyday existence," we'd be better served adhering to the methodology and pedagogy he outlines in his historiographical "catechism."[2]

Distinguished military historian John Keegan discounts such ideas. Keegan allows that Marwick's traditional archival sources do indeed function to answer certain questions, but he finds the "featureless prose" in such technical histories inherently insufficient to understand the humanity behind the history. Further, Keegan criticizes historians who cling stubbornly and solely to "highly traditional forms," who unbendingly accept only those conventions in which they work:

> The "rhetoric of history"—that inventory of assumptions and usages through which the historian makes his professional approach to the past—is not only, as it pertains to the writing of battle history, much more strong and inflexible than the rhetoric of almost all other sorts of history, but is so strong, so inflexible and all so time-hallowed that it exerts virtual powers of dictatorship over the military historian's mind.[3]

And yet Marwick perseveres, resounding and reiterating that historians must "never forget [artistic and literary sources] are *fiction*," that we should spurn the artistic for the technical, the governmental, for the traditional.[4]

Few methodological philosophies seem more misguided. In seeking to understand the Vietnam War combat experience, no responsible historian should ever discount any primary source media, especially poetry, without careful scrutiny and protracted reflection. As Ehrhart so eloquently phrases it, "If one wants to know the essence of the Vietnam War, how it felt and smelled and tasted, what it did to those who fought it and why it will not go away ... one is likely to find more truth in these poems than any history ever written."[5]

In case one deems it suspect to cite the soldier-poet Ehrhart himself to bear witness for poetry's historical value (despite his indisputable experience both in Vietnam War poetry and the combat realities that inhabit and inspired it), consider eminent folklorist and oral historian, Lydia Fish. She has written numerous works treating artistic primary sources, advocating tirelessly for the place in the historical canon they so richly deserve. Fish notes, "Some historians argue that the real scope of history has no place for the artistic voice. I contend that the scope of history could never be trusted as real without it."[6]

Piecing together our past from scant sources is challenging, largely because most human experiences remain unspoken. Considering our paucity of sources, one can only wonder at Marwick's selectivity and exclusivity. He must certainly have overlooked a serious evidentiary problem: government papers and ledger-laden statistical series remain predictably silent as to what our troops felt in their somersaulting guts upon witnessing, for example, a decomposing, sun-bloated, bullet-perforated corpse at that gruesome moment when

> Angelic hosts of flies caress His brow
> And from His swollen body comes
> The sweet-sick stench of rotting flesh—
> Three days old.[7]

In fact, when pressed, traditionalists will have to acknowledge that most of their traditional archival records offer little to help our imaginations inhabit those moments, say, when troops recognized that the Vietnam War had altered them irreparably, had stolen whatever purity remained of their youth. Even Pentagon-endorsed, combat-centric after-action reports, renowned for all their mind-numbingly inclusive data, omit many of the war's most pivotal, human battlefield events, such as the violent death of a young Marine's idealistic optimism and the hemorrhagic, premature birth of a tragically disfigured, sarcastic cynicism:

> We used to get intelligence reports
> from the Vietnamese district offices.
> Every night, I'd make a list
> of targets for artillery to hit.
>
> It used to give me quite a kick
> to know that I, a corporal,
> could command an entire battery
> to fire anywhere I said.

> One day, while on patrol,
> we passed the ruins of a house;
> beside it sat a woman
> with her left hand torn away;
> beside her lay a child, dead.
>
> When I got back to base,
> I told the fellows in the COC;
> it gave us all a lift to know
> all those shells we fired every night
> were hitting something.[8]

Horrific scenes and disillusioning epiphanies seared into Ehrhart's memory through combat experience. And their graphic nature survives time's ravages intact because of the artistic voice. As Ehrhart reasons, "when a poem is written, it becomes a singular entity with an inextinguishable and unalterable life of its own. It is a true reflection of the feelings and perceptions it records, and as such, it is as valuable a document as any history ever written."[9]

Poetry strikes chords in its audiences because it resonates with all the sensory detail and personal emotion that combat summons but that traditional sources rarely contain and even more rarely articulate. Indeed, how fully will we ever really come to know or understand our past, ever hope to capture our colleagues' and students' imaginations and spur genuinely enthusiastic discussion if we deliberately marginalize or dismiss potential primary sources simply due to their artistry? Arguably, we cannot.

That poetry endures as one of the most compelling means to voice human emotion seems a literary truism almost beyond dispute. But the notion that verse also serves as one of the most reliable time capsules for preserving actual human experiences may yet surprise most historians. We needn't fear poetic sources as literary curiosities too fraught with historical abstraction because Ehrhart's verse, as our case in point, is anything but. On the contrary, his poems abound with real human events. They chronicle not only some of the most resonant moments of one Vietnam-era Marine's life, they arguably also voice the hearts and minds of countless Americans and Vietnamese, meeting them in those very moments and contexts of their own Vietnam War history. As primary sources go, Ehrhart's poems live, breathe, and speak history more authentically and more personally—and thus, more *compellingly*—than most records to emerge from the war.

Three ever-present characteristics of Ehrhart's poems exemplify how verse can foster greater understanding and appreciation of Vietnam War history: their narrative qualities; their descriptive power; and their unmistakably human voice. Examining several poems will more fully illustrate their historical merit. Consider first "Fragment: The Generals' War." Comprised of a grisly montage of images from Ehrhart's tour, it documents the bitterness he felt toward commanders who could somehow separate themselves and their orders from the undeniable human toll their orders exacted:

> Paper orders passed down and executed;
> straggling back in plum-colored rags,
> one-legged, in slings, on stretchers,
> in green plastic bags,
> with stubbled faces
> and gaunt eyes hung in sockets;
>
> returned to paper
> for some general to read about
> and pin a medal to.[10]

How generals could ever perceive people as paper seems baffling to anyone with an ounce of human decency, and Ehrhart jarringly registers his disgust with the disgraceful practice. Nothing dehumanizes quite like death, but by personalizing and personifying commanders' orders, Ehrhart rehumanizes those orders' consequences and forces his audiences to see the obscene human cost war incurs. As a historian's resource, the poem preserves a grunt's wartime images and sentiments while simultaneously animating his disdain. It succeeds pedagogically, too, teaching historical irony as no statistical series ever could. Students regularly comment that the ragamuffin characters, haggard images, and solemn circumstances Ehrhart highlights hardly seem worth commemorating with the self-absorbed pomp and ritual of generals' medal ceremonies.

But Ehrhart's poems do more than animate imagery or teach irony. They also document specific events and catalogue concrete facts about his in-country tour, providing narrative testimony, evidential slivers, and microhistorical glimpses that speak *his* history as clear as any source can. Both the literal and the figurative weight of a grunt's tour come alive in works like "Another Life":

> The long day's march is over.
> Ten thousand meters through the bush
> with flak jacket, rifle, helmet,
> three hundred rounds of ammunition,
> three days' rations, two canteens,
> hand grenades, a cartridge belt;
> pack straps grinding at the shoulders,
> feet stuffed in boots that stumble forward
> mile after hill after hour;
> the sun a crushing hundred-and-two,
> sweat in the eyes and salt on the lips;
> and always aware that Charlie only waits.

> The march is over for today.
> Now, heaped against a paddy dike
> and fighting back the sweetness of exhaustion,
> I close my eyes
> and struggle to recall
> another life.[11]

After witnessing such an inventory of burdens, one might say that in fact, poetry far outstrips most archival sources' descriptive power, as when it forcefully recounts the horrifying moments that frequently imprinted on the consciousness of those who witnessed combat death. For example, during the 1968 Tet Offensive battles over the old Vietnamese imperial capital, Hue, Ehrhart witnessed several comrades killed by sniper fire. He recalls, "Sometimes, they would simply die. Sometimes they would thrash and struggle as if they were drowning. It was not pretty."[12] Such eyewitness testimony should silence any objection to acknowledging "The Sniper's Mark" as a disturbingly accurate account of a soldier suffering a fatal head shot:

> He seemed in a curious hurry
> To burn up what was left
> Of the energy inside—
>
> A brainless savage flurry
> Of arms and legs and eyes.[13]

Another perfect case in point, "Hunting" recounts precisely what Ehrhart thought in those moments in which he engaged many of his enemy targets:

> Sighting down the long black barrel,
> I wait till the front and rear sights
> form a perfect line on his body,
> then slowly squeeze the trigger.
>
> The thought occurs
> that I have never hunted anything in my whole life
> except other men.
>
> But I have learned by now
> where such thoughts lead,
> and soon pass on
> to chow, and sleep,
> and how much longer till I change my socks.[14]

Even still today Ehrhart describes his primary in-country duty as "hunting." He admits, "Christ, it's what I did every day. I hunted human beings. It's what we were sent there to do. Hunt them and kill them."[15] Historians love finding the proverbial evidential "smoking gun," and "Hunting" chronicles for the very first time a heretofore undocumented event: that grimly surreal, grotesque epiphany wherein Ehrhart consciously realized he was hunting people.

As shocking as that may sound, the last stanza's seemingly aloof nonchalance is what usually fuels the most heated classroom debate. Some students argue that Ehrhart's ability to coolly contemplate his next meal or the mundane task of changing socks—all after killing someone—proves the war turned our troops psychopathic. I affirm that in some cases, sadly, it did, but encourage the students to think harder, to look deeper and consider his motivations at that moment. Some wonder whether "Ehrhart's in denial." I say, "Maybe, but if so, why? In the middle of the war, what possible realities might he have felt the need to deny?" Ehrhart provides his own personal insights, responding that "Hunting" and other poems articulate his growing suspicions, sobering realizations, and worsening ambivalence about the war:

> I remember sending a tape to my then girlfriend in the spring of 1967 in which I went on at some length about how we were winning the war, however slowly and painfully progress was being made. What the fuck did I know about who was winning the war? In fact, I had already begun to realize that, as far as I and my battalion were concerned, we were getting nowhere fast. But how on earth could I admit that to myself? I'm 18 years old. I've got another ten or eleven months to serve before I can go home. And I'm supposed to admit to myself that I've made the biggest mistake of my life and might well die for it? That my country is at best terribly wrongheaded, at worst playing me for a sucker? So at first I kept trying to tell myself that we were the good guys, and when that would no longer wash, I just stopped telling myself anything but "March 5th, 1968" (my rotation date).[16]

Ultimately, students arguing over "Hunting" get the message: that Ehrhart and other infantry *had* to disengage their unsettling internal tensions over killing people and focus instead on much more innocuous and routine tasks. Otherwise, they'd lose their minds, their military effectiveness, maybe even their lives.

Ehrhart's verse doesn't just preserve his personal epiphanies and self-preservation strategies at specific points in time. It also documents specific states of mind amid the events and circumstances in which he fought, detailing those emotions that haunted him throughout his tour. On Ehrhart's very first in-country maneuvers, Operation Stone [February 1967], Bravo Company commander Captain Bob Lain stepped on a mine that blew both his legs off. On another occasion ten months later, Ehrhart's unit was sweeping an area to the northwest of Con Thien when they came under enemy mortar fire. As the Marines sought cover in a tree line, several tripped booby traps with disastrous results.[17] After these and many similar incidents, in "The Next Step," Ehrhart put to paper his virtually inescapable inner-monologue, chronicling the dread that plagued him relentlessly on every hump, throughout every operation:

> The next step you take
> may lead you into an ambush.
>
> The next step you take
> may trigger a tripwire.
>
> The next step you take
> may detonate a mine.
>
> The next step you take
> may tear your leg off at the hip.
>
> The next step you take
> may split your belly open.
>
> The next step you take
> may send a sniper's bullet through your brain.
>
> The next step you take.
> The next step you take.
>
> The next step.
> The next step.
>
> The next step.[18]

Vietnam veteran and master of combat narrative history, Tim O'Brien, corroborates the paralyzing fear to which Ehrhart testifies, noting a sense of the absurd combination of perpetual certainty and uncertainty—certainty that indeed death lurked everywhere, the uncertainty of how to avoid it:

> You look ahead a few paces and wonder what your legs will resemble if there is more to the earth than silicates and nitrogen.... You try to second-guess the mine. Should you put your foot to that flat rock or the clump of weed to its rear? Paddy dike or water? You wish you were Tarzan, able to swing with the vines. You try to trace the footprints of the man to your front. You give it up when he curses you for following too closely; better one man dead than two.... The moment-to-moment, step-by-step decision-making preys on your mind.[19]

O'Brien's narrative prose lacks Ehrhart's degree of poetic artistry: his deliberate, trudging structure that itself conjures a weighty, plodding, nerve-wracking mission of trespassing through Charlie's turf. Nonetheless, the uncanny similarity of his supporting testimony unquestionably acquits "The Next Step" of any accusations of historical worthlessness.

In fact, Vietnam War history lives everywhere in Ehrhart's poetry. He records truths that virtually no one who served in an actual infantry unit would dispute. For example, Ehrhart penned "Guerrilla War" after a ten year-old boy tried to throw a grenade into his and his buddy's jeep as they drove through the small coastal village of Hoi An one day in the spring of 1967. It perfectly encapsulates his and countless other troops' frustrations with operating among and trying to fight a maddeningly elusive, essentially anonymous enemy:

> It's practically impossible
> to tell civilians
> from the Vietcong.
>
> Nobody wears uniforms.
> They all talk
> the same language,
> (and you couldn't understand them
> even if they didn't).
>
> They tape grenades
> inside their clothes,
> and carry satchel charges
> in their market baskets.
>
> Even their women fight;
> and young boys,
> and girls.
>
> It's practically impossible
> to tell civilians
> from the Vietcong.
>
> After a while,
> you quit trying.[20]

The surprise ending openly confesses an all-too-common in-country metamorphosis. Ehrhart elaborates, "While I was shocked when I first got to Vietnam at the way Marines would toss civilians off the tops of amphibious tractors with their hands and feet bound, by the summer of 1967 during Operation Pike [after the adolescent grenadier and other disillusioning incidents], I was the one tossing the civilians off the tractor."[21] Chasing anonymous, chameleon enemies—VC hiding in plain sight as farmers by day, roving as guerrillas by night—frustrated American troops endlessly, eventually darkening many hearts and justifying unconscionable actions, if not in posterity's eyes, then at least in troops' own minds at the time. And while Ehrhart and most others never devolved into atrocity anywhere approaching My Lai scope and scale, "Guerrilla War" discloses some of the reasons why troops commonly surrendered to the dark indifference and fatalism that the war's frustrating combat realities engendered.

In light of these dark revelations, perhaps the most compelling (and refreshing) asset of Ehrhart's poetry is its bare, blunt truthfulness. Dr. Laurie

Smith of St. Michael's College contends that poets like Ehrhart muster more personal and historical truth because their marginal position in the literature canon frees them from the cultural hegemony of the academy and marketplace. Or as Ehrhart simplifies it, poets write for themselves, not to woo, please, and placate audiences or win arguments. He posits that other writers, artists, and commentators constantly "hedge their vision of the truth against what they think their potential audiences will buy, both figuratively and literally."[22] If not, then why, Ehrhart asks, did Ron Kovic in his memoir *Born on the Fourth of July* omit

> that at the time he was wounded he had already served one full 13-month tour in Vietnam, come home to America, and then volunteered to go back for a second full 13-month tour? Does Kovic obscure this fact in order to present himself in a more sympathetic light, to make himself appear to be the naïve kid suddenly struck down in his innocence instead of an experienced veteran who knew what he and his country were doing, thus to make his book more appealing? If that is not the reason, how else does one explain Kovic's disingenuousness? Did he just forget to mention it?[23]

Poetry simply exhibits fewer agendas, biases, and truth gaps because, unlike Westmoreland's inflated body counts and McNamara's chronically dishonest "We are winning" refrain, poetry makes no pretense, requires no subterfuge to slant or sell its ugly truths. In fact, Ehrhart questions whether *any* historical primary sources prove more viable and honest than poetry. Certainly, given Westmoreland's widely known tendency to lie, it's reasonable for Ehrhart to ask:

> [How can historians possibly] give more credence to a press release from MACV HQ in 1967 than to a poem written about the same event by an honorably discharged combat-wounded Marine sergeant? Are they really going to give ANY credibility to ANYTHING Secretary of Defense Robert Strange McNamara said between 1962 and 1967 when in 1995 he turned around and finally admitted, "We were wrong. Terribly wrong"? What about Henry Kissinger when he looked straight at the camera in 1972 and pronounced, "Ve believe peace is at hand." As usual, he was lying. So which sources do historians want us to trust, exactly?[24]

Of course, poetic accounts aren't the most complete or comprehensive, but to equate poetry's historical incompleteness with historical inaccuracy is both unfair and unwise, and we should think twice before discarding sources simply because they don't contain all the facts or look and sound like the primary sources we hold dear. As Ehrhart puts it,

> If [historians] won't accept what I've written in a poem like "A Relative Thing" unless I tell them the exact time, date, and location I saw an amphibious tractor driving through a newly sown rice field or Vietnamese refugees in a squalid refugee camp, then my task and yours [of understanding and animating the Vietnam War] is hopeless."[25]

Certainly more encouraging, however, is the fact that during classroom activities in which we learn to evaluate sources' reliability, even young college students [skeptics, most all], recognize poetry's historical honesty. While it startles students, Ehrhart's transparency impresses them, especially when he confesses:

> We laughed at old men stumbling
> in the dust in frenzied terror
> to avoid our three-ton trucks.

And:

> We have been Democracy on Zippo raids,
> burning houses to the ground,
> driving eager amtracs through new-sown fields.[26]

Ehrhart admits that he and other grunts "routinely brutalized Vietnamese civilians," explaining some of the historical context and events that inspired and find voice in "A Relative Thing":

> We often made a game of running Vietnamese civilians off the road, trying to get as close to them as we could without hitting them, scare the hell out of them. We were kids and scared and didn't give a fuck; it passed the time. One time, we were going up a road in trucks and we saw a bunch of kids up ahead begging, holding out their hands, shouting, "G.I., G.I.!" The guys in my truck all hunkered down and when we got up to the knot of kids, we all rose up and tossed cans of C-rations at these kids as hard as we could. From point-blank range. This was in November 1967 on our way to jump off on Operation Lancaster up near the DMZ.[27]

And even though the students understand that Ehrhart's "we" in "Farmer Nguyen" can refer also to U.S. troops in general, his unmistakably self-incriminatory, first-person pronoun use bears witness:

> When we swept through farmer Nguyen's hamlet,
> some people said that farmer Nguyen
> had given rice to the Vietcong.
>
> You picked the wrong side, farmer Nguyen.
> We took you in, and beat you,
> and put you in a barbed wire cage.

On one particularly memorable occasion when I asked whether we can trust this and other poems to relate Vietnam War history, a chronically flippant but nonetheless brilliant class clown surprised me by sobering up and echoing Ehrhart, speaking directly to authors' motivations:

> Yeah, we can trust them. They don't write these poems for money or legacy or to save the jobs they'll lose if they don't report something encouraging. Unlike

those lying to the American people and their bosses and birthing the Vietnam War's notorious credibility gap, Ehrhart vilifies himself. Why? What could he possibly hope to gain by describing how he and his buddies victimized Vietnamese villagers? Why subject himself to the storm of scrutiny and indignation that admitting his own violence is gonna unleash? I suppose because truth matters more to Ehrhart than reputation and royalties.[28]

Even having read only Ehrhart's poetry and none of his commentary, the students reach his conclusions: poetry is honest because poets gain nothing by being dishonest, and war poetry is where we find the truest relationship between war and memory.[29] These and other priceless moments where we witness students begin to understand and engage the Vietnam War's messy moral ambiguities, its painful paradoxes, its innumerable historical complexities only reinforce the value of utilizing poetry in our scholarship and classrooms. Students waking up intellectually and conversationally and enthusiastically contending with our course material I'd say constitutes an accurate barometer of classroom success, and that significant phenomenon alone should give us pause and cause us constantly to consider new and different methodological and pedagogical alternatives.

In the end, historians will research, write, and teach Vietnam War history however they choose. Still, millions of people's experiences comprise the totality of Vietnam War history, and we know little or nothing about almost all of them. Ehrhart illuminates the grunt's war with a narrative honesty, descriptive power, and human voice seldom united in nightly wartime newscasts, textbook histories of the war, or even soldiers' letters home. Thus, if we historians truly believe that it falls to us to advance our knowledge of the past, to knit more human accounts like his into the vibrant tapestry woven of our individual and collective histories, then we must learn to harvest those unorthodox resources as rich and enduring as W. D. Ehrhart's poetry. Neither we nor our colleague and student audiences will ever regret we did.

Notes

1. Marwick, Arthur, *The Nature of History* (London: Macmillan Press, 1989), 228–9 (emphasis, mine).

2. Ibid. [*Emphasis* mine]. See also, Marwick, *The New Nature of History: Knowledge, Evidence, Language* (Chicago: Lyceum Books, 2001), 179–185.

3. Keegan, John, *The Face of Battle* (New York: Military Heritage Press, 1986), 31, 36.

4. Marwick, *The New Nature of History*, 170.

5. Ehrhart, W. D., *Unaccustomed Mercy: The Soldier Poets of the Vietnam War* (Lubbock: Texas Tech University Press, 1989), 4–5.

6. Fish, Lydia M., interview with author, Salt Lake City, UT, Fall 1999.

7. Excerpt from Ehrhart, "Christ," in Larry Rottmann, Jan Barry, and Basil T. Paquet,

eds., *Winning Hearts & Minds: War Poems by Vietnam Veterans* (Brooklyn, NY: First Casualty Press/McGraw-Hill, 1972), 38 (hereafter cited as *WHAM*).

8. Ehrhart, "Time on Target," in *Carrying the Darkness* (Lubbock: Texas Tech University Press, 1985), 94–5.

9. Ehrhart, "The Poetry of Bullets, or: How Does a War Mean?" Keynote address to the *Conference on War in Memory, Popular Culture & Folklore*, sponsored by the Center for the Study of the Korean War and the National Archives and Records Administration, Central Plains Region, Kansas City, Missouri, 25 February 2000, 16. Published in *The Madness of It All* (Jefferson, NC: McFarland, 2002), 205–17.

10. Ehrhart, "Fragment: The Generals' War," in *WHAM*, 25.

11. Ehrhart, "Another Life," in *A Generation of Peace* (Flushing, NY: New Voices Publishing Co., 1975), 22.

12. Email correspondence with Ehrhart, 25 August 2012.

13. Ehrhart, "The Sniper's Mark," *To Those Who Have Gone Home Tired* (New York: Thunder's Mouth Press, 1984), 9.

14. Ehrhart, "Hunting," in *Beautiful Wreckage: New & Selected Poems* (Easthampton, MA: Adastra Press, 1999), 7.

15. Email correspondence with Ehrhart, 25 August 2012.

16. Email correspondence with Ehrhart, 16 July 2012.

17. Email correspondence with Ehrhart, 25 August 2012.

18. Ehrhart, "The Next Step," in *Unaccustomed Mercy*, 56–7.

19. O'Brien, Tim, *If I Die in a Combat Zone: Box Me Up and Ship Me Home* (New York: Delacorte Press, 1973), 120–21.

20. Ehrhart recounted the South Vietnamese boy's grenade-throwing and other incidents in email correspondence, 25 August 2012. Ehrhart, "Guerrilla War," in *Carrying the Darkness: The Poetry of the Vietnam War*, W.D. Ehrhart, ed., 93–4.

21. Email correspondence, 25 August 2012.

22. Ehrhart, "The Poetry of Bullets," 8.

23. Ibid., 9–10.

24. Email correspondence with Ehrhart, 25 August 2012.

25. Ibid.

26. Excerpted from Ehrhart, "A Relative Thing," in *Unaccustomed Mercy*, 59.

27. Email correspondence with Ehrhart, 25 August 2012.

28. Notes taken during a class discussion over an upper-division lecture, "American Wars at Home and Abroad, 1965–1974," in HIST 374, *U.S. History since 1945*, Texas A&M University at Galveston, 23 March 2011.

29. Ehrhart, "The Poetry of Bullets," 10.

Making the Wreckage Beautiful

Clint Van Winkle

In 1978, a year after my birth, W. D. Ehrhart wrote "The Teacher" for his students at Sandy Springs Friends School.[1] In the poem he says: "I swore to teach you / all I know— / and I know things / worth knowing." Nearly three decades later, Dr. Eric Wertheimer, a professor of mine at Arizona State University, would guide me to Ehrhart and to that knowledge "worth knowing."

Another series of wars brought yet another generation of veterans to Ehrhart's work, and the war-related baggage I brought to Ehrhart's writings influenced the reader-text relationship. Therefore, my interaction with Ehrhart's text must be viewed through the lens of transactive criticism, which is, simply, "a transaction between the reader and the text" where the "interpretation is a function of [the reader's] identity." With transactive criticism, "the true focus ... has to be the relation between oneself and the text."[2] My identity as a combat veteran, more specifically, a wayward combat veteran, made my Ehrhart readings very personal.

Only two years removed from combat in Iraq, where I took part in the invasion of that country, the stench of combat still lingered. My war had been a constant companion. I was wrestling with PTSD and didn't have many people who could relate to what I had experienced, nor did I feel that I could explain what had transpired in Iraq to anybody outside of the people who had been there with me. In my late twenties, I didn't fit what most Americans thought of as a veteran. I was too young, too reserved. People, especially my student peers, were not concerned with the war that consumed me—it was a war other people were fighting, and, without a draft, the students were safe at the university. The situation caused me to question my combat experience; my English professor mother and Dr. Wertheimer guided me to literature for answers.

However, reading about war didn't appeal to me. I'd gotten my fill of combat in Iraq. It was the homecoming experience I was interested in reading about, the ways others dealt with the trauma they'd incurred from fighting and seeing how other veterans processed their war adventures. Wertheimer suggested that I read W. D. Ehrhart.

I made short work of *Passing Time: Memoir of a Vietnam Veteran Against the War*[3] and *Busted: A Vietnam Veteran in Nixon's America*[4]; perused the combat poetry found in *Beautiful Wreckage: New & Selected Poems*. Bill's writings about war and the aftermath of war spoke to me more than anything else I'd read. Even though he'd waded through chest-high elephant grass in Vietnam and I'd kicked rocks on hell's prairie, his words were familiar. His ability to articulate the unspeakable gave lucidity to my chaos.

While many authors of war memoirs sugarcoat the psychological effects of combat, the forthrightness of Bill's collected war writings were especially helpful as I struggled to come to terms with my combat trauma. Much like Bill, I set out on my combat adventure blinded by patriotism; I was idealistic, believing the weapon I carried would make a positive impact. I came home unsure of everything. I felt like an outsider, a nomad who couldn't quite bring himself to terms with the fact that all I had so vehemently believed in (God, Country, and Democracy) might be a farce. And while I didn't take the same route as Bill to find my peace, seeing a fellow U.S. Marine ask questions I was afraid to ask (and afraid to have answered, in some cases) helped put my war experience in perspective.

With the help of alcohol, I mustered the courage to e-mail Ehrhart. It was Dr. Wertheimer's idea (the email, not the alcohol), and it was probably way too personal. I didn't think any author would care to talk to me and didn't have high expectations that an author of Bill's caliber would ever respond. I just wanted to let him know that his work had made an impact on me. I wanted him to know that I could relate to what he was saying. It was also an outlet, a way of communicating with the only person, outside of the Marines I'd served with in Iraq, who I felt truly understood. To my surprise, Ehrhart promptly responded with an 1,800-word email, a treatise on what a confused combat veteran could expect. Eight years later, I still have the e-mail.

The straightforward style he's known for was present in the response he sent to me. Ehrhart laid it all out in the open. It was exactly what I needed to hear:

> Yes, this is the hard part. The going on from day to day in a world that is forever alien, not the place you left behind, out of focus, ignorant, oblivious. No rotation date out of this place, no Freedom Bird to look forward to, you're here for the duration. It's taken me my entire adult life to come to terms with it, and still some days I can hardly stand it ... though it took about a gazillion years to get here, in my 50s I've finally achieved something resembling wisdom, peace, and happiness. Don't know what I'm trying to say except you got to keep plugging away.... If you find peace by the time you reach your 50s, you'll be a lucky man.

And

> All the years I sacrificed to try to change how we do business in the world—as a people, as a nation—and we end up with a draft-dodging empty-headed Christofascist for president and my own generation cheerfully sending their children off to die for God and country. When the First Gulf War happened, I almost went totally out of my mind. I could hardly believe how goddamned gullible Americans could be only 15 years after the end of the Vietnam War. I guess that's when I really had to take a long hard look at what I believe, at what I do, at what I CAN do, and why I do it. I do what I do because I can't NOT do it, not because I think it matters. That's the peace I've come to, and that only after many, many years. I hope you find your own peace eventually. I hope you eventually discover what you have to do, as opposed to what others think you should do or what you think you should do or whatever else gets in the way of seeing clearly.
>
> In the end, I had to make a choice: was I going to spend my life being at war with my country, my fellow citizens, and my government, or was I going to spend my life being at war with my own soul? Yes, it often seems easier just to stop thinking, put out your American flag and your yellow ribbon, tell yourself how evil those (insert whatever is appropriate: communists, Islamic militants, bleeding heart liberals) are, and how lucky you are to live in the freest, greatest nation on earth. But knowing what you know, take that path and see what it does to your insides. It isn't easy being an outsider in the land of my birth, but it's easier than betraying my own soul.[5]

The fact that Ehrhart took the time to e-mail a stranger is a testament to his character, and it shows the driving force behind his work: he wants to make a difference. Self identified as "an outsider in the land of [his] birth," he seems to be drawn to other outsiders, to those who have lived a life of hard knocks and have had the fortitude, or desire, to pull through it. This epitomized how he helped me, a combat veteran who, out of the blue, sent him a meandering email.

Like Bill, I found solace in writing and by the time Dr. Wertheimer introduced me to Ehrhart's writings, I'd already accumulated a pile of my own war writings in the form of essay and poetry. While the former were certainly amateurish at best, the latter, in my opinion, were just good enough to share with others. A month after first emailing Bill, I sent what I thought was my best piece of writing to him. Once again, Bill responded at length:

> After the murders at Kent State in May 1970, I let go of whatever reluctance I had to talk about what I saw and did in Vietnam. Nobody's been able to shut me up in all these 35 years since. It never occurred to me to worry about what my family or anyone else thought of me. I knew what I thought of me, and nobody else's opinion of me could have been any lower than my own. I don't know what kind of relationships you have with your family. But if they love you, they will learn to cope with what you did.
>
> As for why you can't just let it all go, here's my conclusion: somehow, I intu-

itively understood, way back there in the early 1970s when I was trying to sort this all out, that I could spend the rest of my life at war with my government, my country, and my fellow citizens, or I could spend the rest of my life at war with my own soul. The former, though not easy, seemed easier than the latter. I think that's what you're struggling with. You can't unlearn what you learned in your war. You can't make it go away. And you can ignore it or bury it inside only at great peril to your humanity, your soul, your psyche, whatever you want to call it. Why the gods chose to bestow this knowledge on you, neither of us can say. But you know what you know, and you can't unknow it. The only question is: what are you going to do with what you know?"[6]

What was I going to do with my knowledge? What had I gained by taking part in the worst aspect of humanity? Those were questions I hadn't thought about before. I'd started writing because it was the only thing I could do to keep sane, the only outlet I felt I had. I wrote because I had no other choice. I didn't think anybody would want to read, much less publish any of my writing. I was emboldened by Bill's writing and his advice. I had to attempt to share my knowledge. So, I submitted the essay I'd emailed to Bill, "Ghosts from Iraq" to several literary magazines, and it was eventually published in the literary journal *Cimarron Review*.[7] That essay led to a book contract.

I began working on the manuscript for *Soft Spots: A Marine's Memoir of Combat and Post-Traumatic Stress Disorder*.[8] Again, Bill was instrumental in the process, although in a different way this time and, unlike Oliver Stone, who seems to have borrowed from Ehrhart's *Passing Time* for scenes in his movie *Born on the Fourth of July*,[9] I'm okay with sharing what influenced my work.

In *Busted*, Ehrhart conveys being stuck in two worlds and the mind-fuck that occurs after returning from combat, by having his dead Marine buddies appear and reappear throughout the memoir. Non-veterans might view their appearance as magical realism, a literary technique he is using to show how veterans always carry the dead with them. However, for veterans, this is not a literary device, but reality. Since truth is relative, and I was attempting to bring to life my chaotic post-combat world, it also made sense for me to use a similar technique to tell my story. Instead of fallen Marines, my living Marine buddies—Paxson, Kipper, and Gunny—reappear and appear in my book as I hash out my war memories and struggle with PTSD. Additionally, as a nod to Bill's influence on my work, my book, and me, the epigraph is the last stanza from his poem "Beautiful Wreckage," which, not so coincidentally, is a poem that mentions Ames, Ski, and Gaffney—his dead Marine buddies that appear in *Busted*.

> What if none of it happened the way I said?
> Would it all be a lie?
> Would the wreckage be suddenly beautiful?
> Would the dead rise up and walk?[10]

In *The Guilt*, a short documentary film I made[11] as a sequel to *Soft Spots*, which is about two of the U.S. Marines from my memoir, Ehrhart is featured as the voice of reason—a Vietnam Veteran giving advice to three, struggling Iraq War veterans. He is the sage holding council, a role he has perfected from years of practice. Bill had more years as a veteran than we had of life, and his knowledge on the subject, and advice about dealing with the aftermath, left an indelible mark on us.

One anecdote he gave, about being asked how long it took him to readjust was especially helpful, as many have searched for the ways to "fix" combat veterans, without even considering that it may not be an option. Bill's reply to that question: "What makes you think I am readjusted? What, because I look kind of normal and I keep my shoes tied? What does it mean to be readjusted? You don't heal. You learn to live with it. You learn strategies to live with it, and that's what you guys will do."

Whether Bill believes it or not, his work has made an impact in a most profound way. He continues to affect all those who find his texts and come in contact with him. Instead of leaving his readers with something as authors have historically done, Bill magically relieves something horrific from those who have been through the fray and who, unfortunately, truly understand his words, which is a feat that validates the efforts of his life's work.

Bill's reply to that first email I sent to him started out like this: "Skip the 'Dr. Ehrhart' stuff. My school requires my students to call me that, but it's not my idea, and you're not my student. 'Bill' will do just fine." Now, I would like him to know that he was wrong. I've been his student since I first read a line of his work, since the day he replied to my email, and will continue to be his student. Many veterans from my generation, including my Marine buddies who met Bill as we filmed *The Guilt*, are pupils of his as well; many future generations of veterans will be his pupils, too. Bill is a teacher who knows things worth knowing. And, as long as society continues to wage wars, readers will look to him for guidance and understanding.

Notes

1. Ehrhart, W.D., *Beautiful Wreckage: New & Selected Poems* (Easthampton, MA: Adastra, 1999), 49.
2. Holland, Norman Norwood, *The Nature of Literary Response: Five Readers Reading* (New Brunswick: Transaction, 2011), 248.
3. Ehrhart, W.D., *Passing Time: Memoir of a Vietnam Veteran Against the War* (Jefferson, NC: McFarland, 1989).
4. Ehrhart, W.D., *Busted: A Vietnam Veteran in Nixon's America* (Amherst, MA: University of Massachusetts Press, 1995).
5. Ehrhart, W.D., email. to Clint Van Winkle, 13 Nov. 2005.
6. Ehrhart, W.D., email. to Clint Van Winkle, 21 Dec. 2005.

7. Van Winkle, Clint, "Ghosts from Iraq," *Cimarron Review* (Winter 2007), Issue 158, 76.
8. Van Winkle, Clint. *Soft Spots: A Marine's Memoir of Combat and Post-Traumatic Stress Disorder* (New York: St. Martin's Press, 2009).
9. Franklin, H. Bruce, Foreword in *Busted*, xi.
10. Ehrhart, *Beautiful Wreckage*, 49.
11. *The Guilt*, dir. Clint Van Winkle, perf. W. D. Ehrhart, Christopher Shawn Kipper, David Paxson. Brave New Foundation, 2010.

Appendix A:
Ehrhart's Military History

W.D. Ehrhart formally enlisted in the United States Marine Corps on 11 April 1966, while still in high school, beginning active duty on 17 June. He graduated from basic recruit training at the Marine Corps Recruit Depot, Parris Island, South Carolina, on 12 August, receiving a meritorious promotion to private first class, and completed basic infantry training at Camp Lejeune, North Carolina, on 12 September 1966. (While at Parris Island, he qualified as a rifle sharpshooter on 18 July 1966, subsequently qualifying as a rifle expert on 11 April 1968 and as pistol sharpshooter on 24 April 1969.)

Assigned to the field of combat intelligence, Ehrhart spent 10 October to 15 December 1966 with Marine Air Group 26, a helicopter unit based at New River Marine Corps Air Facility, North Carolina, meanwhile completing a clerk typist course at Camp Lejeune in November 1966 and graduating first in his class from the Enlisted Basic Amphibious Intelligence School at Little Creek Amphibious Base, Norfolk, Virginia, in December 1966. He also completed a Marine Corps Institute combat intelligence correspondence course in December while at New River.

Before leaving for Vietnam on 9 February 1967, Ehrhart received additional combat training with the 3rd Replacement Company, Staging Battalion, Camp Pendleton, California, in January and February. Upon arrival in Vietnam, he was assigned to the 1st Battalion, 1st Marine Regiment, first as an intelligent assistant, later as assistant intelligence chief. In March 1967, he was temporarily assigned to the Sukiran Army Education Center, Okinawa, where he graduated first in his class from a course in basic Vietnamese terminology before returning to permanent assignment.

While in Vietnam, Ehrhart participated in the following combat operations: Stone, Lafayette, Early, Canyon, Calhoun, Pike, Medina, Lancaster, Kentucky I, Kentucky II, Kentucky III, Con Thien, Newton, Osceola II, and Hue City. He was promoted to lance corporal on 1 April 1967 and meritoriously promoted to corporal on 1 July 1967.

Ehrhart was awarded the Purple Heart Medal for wounds received in action in Hue City during the Tet Offensive, a commendation from Major General Donn J. Robertson commanding the 1st Marine Division, two Presidential Unit Citations, the Navy Combat Action Ribbon, the Vietnamese Service Medal with three stars, the Vietnamese Campaign Medal, a Cross of Gallantry Meritorious Unit Citation, and a Civil Action Meritorious Unit Citation. He completed his Vietnam tour on 28 February 1968

Ehrhart was next assigned to the 2nd Marine Air Wing Headquarters Group at Cherry Point Marine Corps Air Station, North Carolina, from 30 March to 10 June 1968, where he was promoted to sergeant on 1 April. After a brief assignment with the Headquarters Squadron of Marine Air Group 15 based at Iwakuni Marine Corps Air Station, Japan, he was then reassigned to Marine Aerial Refueler Transport Squadron 152, Futema Marine Corps Air Facility, Okinawa, from 20 July to 30 October 1968, where he received a commanding officer's Meritorious Mast.

Ehrhart completed his active duty with Marine Fighter Attack Squadron 122, based alternately at Iwakuni and Cubi Point Naval Air Station, Philippines, from 31 October 1968 to 30 May 1969. While in the Philippines, he completed a field course on jungle environmental survival in February 1969.

On 10 June 1969, Ehrhart was separated from active duty, receiving the Good Conduct Medal. While on inactive reserve, he was promoted to staff sergeant on 1 July 1971. He received an honorable discharge on 10 April 1972.

Reprinted, slightly edited, from *Vietnam–Perkasie: A Combat Marine Memoir* (McFarland, 1983), pages 313–314

Appendix B: Ehrhart Poems Selected by Contributors

A Relative Thing

We are the ones you sent to fight a war
you didn't know a thing about.

It didn't take us long to realize
the only land that we controlled
was covered by the bottoms of our boots.

When the newsmen said that naval ships
had shelled a VC staging point,
we saw a breastless woman
and her stillborn child.
We laughed at old men stumbling
in the dust in frenzied terror
to avoid our three ton trucks.

We fought outnumbered in Hue City
while the ARVN soldiers looted bodies
in the safety of the rear.
The cookies from the wives of Local 104
did not soften our awareness.

We have seen the pacified supporters
of the Saigon government
sitting in their jampacked cardboard towns,
their wasted hands placed limply in their laps,
their empty bellies waiting for the rice
some district chief has sold
for profit to the Vietcong.

We have been Democracy on Zippo raids,
burning houses to the ground,
driving eager amtracs through new-sown fields.

We are the ones who have to live
with the memory that we were the instruments
of your pigeon-breasted fantasies.

We are inextricable accomplices
in this travesty of dreams:
but we are not alone.

We are the ones you sent to fight a war
you did not know a thing about—
those of us that lived
have tried to tell you what went wrong.
Now you think you do not have to listen.

Just because we will not fit
into the uniforms of photographs
of you at twenty-one
does not mean you can disown us.

We are your sons, America,
and you cannot change that.
When you awake,
we will still be here.

To Those Who Have Gone Home Tired, 17–18; *Beautiful Wreckage: New & Selected Poems*, 9–10.

Beautiful Wreckage

What if I didn't shoot the old lady
running away from our patrol,
or the old man in the back of the head,
or the boy in the marketplace?

Or what if the boy—but he didn't
have a grenade, and the woman in Hue
didn't lie in the rain in a mortar pit
with seven Marines just for food,

Gaffney didn't get hit in the knee,
Ames didn't die in the river, Ski
didn't die in a medevac chopper
between Con Thien and Da Nang.

In Vietnamese, Con Thien means
place of angels. What if it really was
instead of the place of rotting sandbags,
incoming heavy artillery, rats and mud.

What if the angels were Ames and Ski,
or the lady, the man, and the boy,
and they lifted Gaffney out of the mud
and healed his shattered knee?

What if none of it happened the way I said?
Would it all be a lie?

Would the wreckage be suddenly beautiful?
Would the dead rise up and walk?

Beautiful Wreckage: New & Selected Poems, 206.

Briana

for CJ, in memory of Jill

Death comes knocking and the silence descends
like a black bird alighting on the windowledge
on a black night with no candles.

Yet everything continues: bottle time,
nap time, play time, bath time, story time,
bed time—only a brief confusion:
for a few days you asked for mommy;
then you stopped asking.

You can't know the black bird will sit
for a lifetime in your father's heart.
I watch him with you now:
the tall slender frame
bending over your crib like a willow;
the large hands hesitantly poised—
wanting to touch,
not wanting to wake you;
the soft searching eyes permanently puzzling
an incomprehensible absence
he will never let you feel
if he can help it.

Years will pass before you understand
the secret tremble when your father holds you,
just how much such a small child weighs—
but that's okay;
            don't trouble your dreams
with wondering. Be what you are:
your mother's daughter. Be a candle.

Light the awful silence with your laughter.

Matters of the Heart, 22–23; *To Those Who Have Gone Home Tired*, 61; *Beautiful Wreckage: New & Selected Poems*, 68.

Coaching Winter Track in Time of War

The boys are running "suicides"
on the football field today:
ten-yard increments out to the fifty
and back again, push-ups in between.

It's thirty degrees, but they sweat
like it's summer in Baghdad,
curse like soldiers, swear to God
they'll see you burn in Hell.

You could fall in love with boys
like these: so earnest, so eager, so
ready to do whatever you ask, so
full of themselves and the world.

How do you tell them it's not that simple?
How do you tell them: question it all.
Question everything. Even a coach.
Even a president. How do you tell them:
ask the young dead soldiers coming home
each night in aluminum boxes
none of us is allowed to see,
an army of shades.

You tell the boys "good work" and call it a day,
stand alone in fading light while
memory's phantoms circle the track
like weary athletes running a race
without a finish line.

The Bodies Beneath the Table, 74.

Cowgirls, Teachers & Dreams

for Betsy in Montana

That day we fished Coyote Creek
from Pete's ranch to the upper barn,
dry pale prairie grass rippled
pastures mile on mile to mountains
shouldering sky. Cattle grazed the high
plateaus where men in winter still
go mad from loneliness and snow. Hard
land, its beauty self-composed; a long
way from anywhere. We shared one rod.
You showed me where the best spots were,
parted bushes—"Shhh," you said, "don't
scare the fish"—coached my clumsy casts.
It didn't help: you caught twenty; I
caught none. It didn't matter. Seven
hours working up the creek through
morning into afternoon toward evening.

Words passed softly back and forth
like dry prairie grass in wind. Magic
how that hot dry day in summer in Montana
passed so gently. At the upper barn,
we cleaned the fish: you deftly lopped
off heads and tails, taught me how
to slit their bellies, poke my finger
down the spines to clear the guts in one
swift stroke. How was I to tell you
I was squeamish? Biting flesh inside
my mouth, I did as I was shown. "It's late,"
you said, "we'd better take the horse."
How was I to tell you I was scared
of horses, hadn't ridden since that day
when I was ten and rode four wild miles
on a horse that wasn't stable-broken?
I climbed up behind you: no saddle,
nothing but your slender waist to hold—
a stalk of prairie grass in wind—and you
went straight for every ditch you saw,
jumping, laughing: "Hang on tight!"—stopping
only when you saw the mother antelope
and fauns, babies still with spots, all
three staring, undecided. Maybe next time
bobcats or wolves instead of riders.
The cook got fired while we fished.
Drinking on the job. A hard life in Big
Sky Country. I was only passing through;
I've never seen you since. Not that I
would have a reason: you were eight, and I
was twenty-two. The friends I stopped
to see were only summer help—married now,
a lawyer and a teacher in the East.
I'm a teacher, too. So were you.
And in my mind, you'll always catch
the fattest trout and ride the swiftest
horse, always stop to gaze at fauns,
and never lose your innocence or courage
in that lonely hard land you offered
to a stranger like a treasure,
like a blessing.

The Outer Banks & Other Poems, 29–30; *Beautiful Wreckage: New & Selected Poems*, 90–91.

Dancing

Having been where contrasts meet,
I perceive reality to be
whatever looms largest in the mind.

Thus, truths are never absolute;
nebulous, they never lose the shifting
beat of music changing time.

Books I read, and faces seen
in sunlight tell me where I am;
at night, this truth melts away;

an older truth looms within
and I submit, take my rifle,
rejoin comrades on patrol

until the sun returns the books,
and faces, and the other truth
I dance with to a kinder beat.

A Generation of Peace, 26; *A Generation of Peace (Revised)*, 23; *Beautiful Wreckage: New & Selected Poems*, 3.

Everett Dirksen, His Wife, You & Me

I read once that Everett Dirksen,
United States Senator, never slept
a night without his wife of fifty years.
One can almost see them, near the end:
two doddering old white-haired giggling
lovers climbing into bed, the undimmed
passion still glowing steadily from within—
enough to light the darkness one more night.

And yet I think that light was raised
against a darker darkness both, perhaps,
saw approaching years before the end.
I see it coming, too—saw it years
before I met you; it scared me then,
and still does, and you're the only one
who's ever made me feel the weight
a little less. We giggle, too, sometimes.

One might marvel at the long-enduring
passion of that husband and his wife:
fifty years without a night alone;
marvelous, indeed—
but it's other couples who amaze me:

their ignorance, their faith, their sheer
bravado. Whether we shall be together
or alone in death, I have no way of knowing;

but I know the weight, and how it feels
to pass the night without you.

The Outer Banks & Other Poems, 28; *Beautiful Wreckage: New & Selected Poems*, 89.

Farmer Nguyen

When we swept through farmer Nguyen's hamlet,
some people said that farmer Nguyen
had given rice to the Vietcong.

    You picked the wrong side, farmer Nguyen.
    We took you in, and beat you,
    and put you in a barbed wire cage.

When the Vietcong returned to farmer Nguyen's hamlet,
some people said that farmer Nguyen
had given information to the Round Eyes.

    Wrong again, farmer Nguyen.
    They took more rice, and beat you,
    and made you carry supplies.

A Generation of Peace, 5; *A Generation of Peace (Revised)*, 5; *To Those Who Have Gone Home Tired*, 8.

For Mrs. Na

Cu Chi District
December 1985

I always told myself,
if I ever got the chance to go back,
I'd never say "I'm sorry"
to anyone. Christ,

those guys I saw on television once:
sitting in Hanoi, the cameras rolling,
crying, blubbering
all over the place. Sure,

I'm sorry. I never meant
to do the things I did.
But that was nearly twenty years ago:
enough's enough.

If I ever go back,
I always told myself,
I'll hold my head steady
and look them in the eye.

But here I am at last—
and here you are.
And you lost five sons in the war.
And you haven't any left.

And I'm staring at my hands
and eating tears,
trying to think of something else to say
besides "I'm sorry."

Winter Bells, 13; *Just for Laughs*, 23–24; *Beautiful Wreckage: New & Selected Poems*, 110.

Guerrilla War

It's practically impossible
to tell civilians
from the Viet Cong.

Nobody wears uniforms.
They all talk
the same language
(and you couldn't understand them
even if they didn't).

They tape grenades
inside their clothes,
and carry satchel charges
in their market baskets.

Even their women fight.
And young boys.
And girls.

It's practically impossible
to tell civilians
from the Viet Cong.

After awhile
you quit trying.

A Generation of Peace, 15; *A Generation of Peace (Revised)*, 12; *To Those Who Have Gone Home Tired*, 12; *Beautiful Wreckage: New & Selected Poems*, p. 5.

Guns

Again we pass that field
green artillery piece squatting
by the Legion Post on Chelten Avenue,
its ugly little pointed snout
ranged against my daughter's school.

"Did You ever use a gun
like that?" my daughter asks,
and I say, "No, but others did.
I used a smaller gun. A rifle."
She knows I've been to war.

"That's dumb," she says,
and I say, "Yes," and nod
because it was, and nod again
because she doesn't know.
How do you tell a four-year-old

what steel can do to flesh?
How vivid do you dare to get?
How explain a world where men
kill other men deliberately
and call it love of country?

Just eighteen, I killed
a ten-year-old. I didn't know.
He spins across the marketplace
all shattered chest, all eyes and arms.
Do I tell her that? Not yet,

though one day I will have
no choice except to tell her
or to send her into the world
wide-eyed and ignorant.
The boy spins across the years

till he lands in a heap
in another war in another place
where yet another generation
is rudely about to discover
what their fathers never told them.

The Distance We Travel, 42–43; *Beautiful Wreckage: New & Selected Poems*, 173–174.

Appendix B

Hunting

Sighting down the long black barrel,
I wait till the front and rear sights
form a perfect line on his body,
then slowly squeeze the trigger.

The thought occurs
that I have never hunted anything in my whole life
except other men.

But I have learned by now
where such thoughts lead,
and soon pass on
to chow, and sleep,
and how much longer till I change my socks.

A Generation of Peace, 17; *A Generation of Peace (Revised)*, 14; *To Those Who Have Gone Home Tired*, 13; *Beautiful Wreckage: New & Selected Poems*, 7.

Letter

        to a north Vietnamese soldier
        whose life crossed paths with mine
        in Hue City, February 5th, 1968

Thought you killed me
with that rocket? Well, you nearly did:
splattered walls and splintered air,
knocked me cold and full of holes,
and brought the roof down on my head.

But I lived,
long enough to wonder often
how you missed; long enough
to wish too many times
you hadn't.

What's it like back there?
It's all behind us here;
and after all those years of possibility,
things are back to normal.
We just had a special birthday,
and we've found again our inspiration
by recalling where we came from
and forgetting where we've been.

Oh, we're still haggling over pieces
of the lives sticking out
beyond the margins of our latest
history books—but no one haggles
with the authors.

Do better than that
you cockeyed gunner with the brass
to send me back alive among a people
I can never feel
at ease with anymore:

remember where you've been, and why
And then build houses; build villages,
dikes and schools, songs
and children in that green land
I blackened with my shadow
and the shadow of my flag.

Remember Ho Chi Minh
was a poet: please,
do not let it all come down
to nothing.

Empire, 5; *To Those Who Have Gone Home Tired*, 34–35; *Beautiful Wreckage: New & Selected Poems*, 29–30.

Sleeping with the Dead

I dreamed about you again last night.
This time, you were living in Tennessee,
on a horse farm, married, children
I think, it wasn't clear—you know
how dreams can be—but I finally
got you to see that I don't love you,
not like that: as if my world would end
without you in it.
 O, to have been
so close, to have shared your bed, to have
felt like I'd been raised from the dead
after all those dead I slept with
every night. It almost drove me mad
to let you go.
 But that was years ago.
You were eighteen then, and here I am
married eighteen years and sorry only
that I've never had the chance to tell you
that it's okay, that I'm okay,
that no one could have saved me then,
not you nor God, that I don't love you
anymore, but hope that someone does.

Sleeping with the Dead, 28; *The Bodies Beneath the Table*, 56.

Souvenirs

"Bring me back a souvenir," the captain called.
"Sure thing," I shouted back above the amtrac's roar.

Later that day,
the column halted,
we found a Buddhist temple by the trail.
Combing through a nearby wood,
we found a heavy log as well.

It must have taken more than half an hour,
but at last we battered in
the concrete walls so badly
that the roof collapsed.

Before it did,
I took two painted vases
Buddhists use for burning incense.

One vase I kept,
and one I offered proudly to the captain.

A Generation of Peace, 4; *A Generation of Peace (Revised)*, 4; *To Those Who Have Gone Home Tired*, 8; *Beautiful Wreckage: New & Selected Poems*, 6.

Surviving the Bomb One More Day

For three days, iron cold gripped
the earth in a blue fist:
mucus froze in nostrils; lungs
ached with the weight of breathing;
cheeks turned red with pain.

Is this how we would finally end?
Not in fire; not consumed
in mushroom orange heat,
but laid out stiff and hard
like fish in a peddler's cart?

After all those nights of waking up
to thunder, sweating, thinking, "Christ,
we've finally done it," waiting
in the eerie fog of half-awake
for the final slap of the blast.

On the third day, it began to snow.
Into the night the snow fell,
and by morning the earth was white.
But by afternoon, the wind
was tailing off, and a warming sun

foretold another night
of waiting for the fire.

The Outer Banks & Other Poems, 27.

The Generals' War

Paper orders passed down and executed;

straggling back in plum-colored rags,
one-legged, in slings, on stretchers,
in green plastic bags,
with stubbled faces
and gaunt eyes hung in sockets;

returned to paper
for some general to read about
and pin a medal to

A Generation of Peace, 20; *A Generation of Peace (Revised)*, 17; *To Those Who Have Gone Home Tired*, 14.

The Lotus Cutters of Hô Tây

The lotus cutters gather morning
into their small reed boats.

Graceful as egrets, they weave
through mist so fine it curls

them into its gossamer arms
like a woman holding a child.

One turns to catch a ball
of sunshine balanced on a stalk.

Who would come ten thousand miles
to bomb them?

What have they ever done
but keep the sun from falling?

The Distance We Travel, 22; *Beautiful Wreckage: New & Selected Poems*, 162.

The Invasion of Grenada

I didn't want a monument,
not even one as sober as that
vast black wall of broken lives.
I didn't want a postage stamp.

I didn't want a road beside the Delaware
River with a sign proclaiming:
"Vietnam Veterans Memorial Highway."

What I wanted was a simple recognition
of the limits of our power as a nation
to inflict our will on others.
What I wanted was an understanding
that the world is neither black-and-white
nor ours.

What I wanted
was an end to monuments.

To Those Who Have Gone Home Tired, 71; *Beautiful Wreckage: New & Selected Poems*, 75.

To Maynard on the Long Road Home

Biking at night with no lights
and no helmet, you were struck
and hurled sixty feet,
dead on impact.
The newspapers noted the irony:
surviving the war
to die like that, alone,
on a hometown street.
I knew better.

Years before, on Christmas Day,
I met you on a road near Quang Tri,
a chance reunion of Perkasie boys
grown up together in a town
that feared God and raised sons
willing to die for their country.
"Who're you with?
Have you seen much action?
What the hell's going on here?"
All afternoon we remembered
our shared youth: the old boat
with Jeffy and the slow leak,
skipping Sunday School to read comics
and drink orange soda at Flexer's,
the covered bridge near Bryan's farm.
Though neither of us
spoke of it, we knew then
we had lost
more than our youth.

I show my poems to friends now and then,
hoping one or two might see
my idealistic bombast
in a new light:
the sharp turns of mood, anger
defying visible foundation,
inexplicable sadness.
How often they wonder aloud
how I managed to survive—
they always assume the war is over,
not daring to imagine our wounds,
or theirs, if it is not.
I think of you,
and wonder if either of us
will ever come home.

To Those Who Have Gone Home Tired, 21–22; *Beautiful Wreckage: New & Selected Poems*, 16–17.

To Those Who Have Gone Home Tired

After the streets fall silent
After the bruises and the tear-gassed eyes are healed
After the concensus has returned
After the memories of Kent and My Lai and Hiroshima
lose their power
and their connections with each other
and the sweaters labeled Made in Taiwan
After the last American dies in Canada
and the last Korean in prison
and the last Indian at Pine Ridge
After the last whale is emptied from the sea
and the last leopard emptied from its skin
and the last drop of blood refined by Exxon
After the last iron door clangs shut
behind the last conscience
and the last loaf of bread is hammered into bullets
and the bullets
scattered among the hungry

What answers will you find
What armor will protect you
when your children ask you
Why?

Rootless, 18; *To Those Who Have Gone Home Tired*, 28–29; *Beautiful Wreckage: New & Selected Poems*, 25.

Visiting My Parents' Grave

If you had told me thirty years ago
I'd miss this town, I'd have told you
—well, you know what I'd have said,
so smug it was, so self-content,
its point of view so narrow one could
get a better field of vision peering
through the barrel of a shotgun.
I, at seventeen, could see that much
and so much more I couldn't wait
to leave. It didn't help, of course,
that I was who I was:
the preacher's and the teacher's son,
blow my nose the whole town knew,
anonymous a word I used
to stare at in the dictionary,
wishing it were me. Yet here I am,
thirty years later, back again.

I've come at night because I know
in daylight I could walk these streets
from dawn to dusk, meeting no one
who would know my name, or even yours.
Peter Shelly's house lies buried under
Nockamixon Lake, the Bryan's dairy farm's
a shopping mall, tract housing's crowded
out the sledding run near Callowhill;
Jeff Apple's gone to Melbourne Beach,
Larry Rush went schizophrenic
paranoid, and just about the only
thing that hasn't changed is Larry's mom,
who's still convinced he'll come out right
if only he'll repent and turn to God.

Me, I'm pretty well convinced that she's
the reason Larry's nuts, but that's
the only thing I'm sure of anymore.
I've been to the other side of world,
said what I've thought, hedged no bets, had
no use for comfortable hypocrisies
or delicate interpretations
meant to keep the world the way it is.
I've quit every job I've ever had
for something else, for this or that, or else
because someone's always screwing someone
else, and silence to injustice
large or small is simply cowardice.

Which may be true, but what I've got
for all my years is unemployed
and unemployable, a dozen books
that no one reads, a wife who works
to earn what I cannot, a daughter
I have trouble looking in the eye
because I fear she'll recognize
her father for the failure he's become.
That's the worst of it: I don't trust
my own judgement anymore. What used
to seem so obvious has vanished
in the glare of consequences
prudent people manage to avoid.

So here I am: sitting on your gravestone
on a hill above this town I couldn't
wait to get as far away from
as the moon, and though I know it's only
an illusion, here's the moon just rising
over Skyline Drive so huge it looks
as if I'd only need to reach
my fingers out to touch it,
just like sitting here at night
makes the town appear like nothing's changed,
as if at any moment Jeff and Larry
might appear on bikes, wave to me, and shout,
"Let's chase the cows at Bryan's farm!"
As if the years might fall away
and let me start again.

Beautiful Wreckage: New & Selected Poems, 219–221.

The Last Time I Dreamed About the War

Ruth and I were sitting in the kitchen
ten years after Vietnam. She was six-feet-two
and carried every inch of it with style,
didn't care a fig that I was seven
inches shorter. "You've got seven inches
where it counts," she'd laugh, then lift her chin
and smile as if the sun had just come out.

But she didn't want to hear about the war.
I heard the sound of breaking glass
coming from my bedroom, went to look:
VC rats were jumping through the window.
They looked like rats, but they were Viet Cong.

Don't ask me how I knew. You don't forget
what tried to kill you.

I tried to tell her, but she wouldn't listen.
"Now look, Ruth!" I said so loud the woman
sleeping next to me woke up and did
what Ruthie in my dream refused to do:
she listened to me call the name
of someone she had never heard of,
anger in my voice, my body hard.

The woman I was sleeping with
would be my wife, but wasn't yet. I was
still a stranger with a stranger's secrets
and a tattoo on my arm. She'd never known a man
who'd fought in Vietnam, put naked women on
the wall, smoked marijuana, drank whiskey straight.
And here I was in bed with her,
calling someone else's name in anger.

She wanted to run, she told me later,
but she didn't. She married me instead.
Don't ask me why. I only know
you never know what's going to save you
and I've never dreamed again about the war.

Beautiful Wreckage: New & Selected Poems, p. 198.

An Ehrhart Bibliography

Books: Poetry

From the Bark of the Daphne Tree. Easthampton, MA: Adastra Press, 2013.
The Bodies Beneath the Table. Easthampton, MA: Adastra Press, 2010.
Beautiful Wreckage: New & Selected Poems. Easthampton, MA: Adastra Press, 1999.
The Distance We Travel. Easthampton, MA: Adastra Press, 1993.
Just for Laughs. Silver Spring, MD: Viet Nam Generation & Burning Cities Press, 1990.
The Outer Banks & Other Poems. Easthampton, MA: Adastra Press, 1984.
To Those Who Have Gone Home Tired. New York: Thunder's Mouth Press, 1984.
The Samisdat Poems. Richford, VT: Samisdat, 1980.
A Generation of Peace. New York: New Voices Publishing Company, 1975.

Books: Prose

Dead on a High Hill: Essays on War, Literature and Living, 2002–2012. Jefferson, NC, and London: McFarland, 2012.
The Madness of It All: Essays on War, Literature, and American Life. Jefferson, NC, and London: McFarland, 2002.
Ordinary Lives: Platoon 1005 and the Vietnam War. Philadelphia: Temple University Press, 1999.
Busted: A Vietnam Veteran in Nixon's America. Amherst: University of Massachusetts Press, 1995.
In the Shadow of Vietnam: Essays 1977–1991. Jefferson, NC, and London: McFarland, 1991.
Passing Time: Memoir of a Vietnam Veteran Against the War. Jefferson, NC, and London: McFarland, 1989 (reprint: University of Massachusetts Press, 1995).
Going Back: An Ex-Marine Returns to Vietnam. Jefferson, NC, and London: McFarland, 1987.
Vietnam–Perkasie: A Combat Marine Memoir. Jefferson, NC, and London: McFarland, 1983 (reprint: University of Massachusetts Press, 1995).

Editor

Unaccustomed Mercy: Soldier-Poets of the Vietnam War. Lubbock: Texas Tech University Press, 1989.

Carrying the Darkness: Poetry of the Vietnam War. Lubbock: Texas Tech University Press, 1989.

Co-editor

Retrieving Bones: Stories & Poems of the Korean War. New Brunswick, NJ, and London: Rutgers University Press, 1999, with Philip K. Jason.
Demilitarized Zones: Veterans After Vietnam. Perkasie, PA: East River Anthology, 1976, with Jan Barry.

Poetry Chapbooks

Sleeping with the Dead. Easthampton, MA: Adastra Press, 2006.
A Sort of Peace: Echoes and Images of the Vietnam War. Canandaigua, NY: Fox Photo Arts, 2005, with photographer Don Fox.
Greatest Hits: 1970–2000. Johnstown, OH: Puddinghouse Press, 2001.
Mostly Nothing Happens. Easthampton, MA: Adastra Press, 1996.
Winter Bells. Easthampton, MA: Adastra Press, 1988.
Channel Fever. Port Jefferson, NY: Backstreet Editions, 1982.
Matters of the Heart. Easthampton, MA: Adastra Press, 1981.
Empire. Richford: VT, Samisdat, 1978.
Rootless. Richford: VT, Samisdat, 1977.
A Generation of Peace. (Revised) Richford, VT: Samisdat, 1977.

Booklet

Going Back: A Poet Who Was Once a Marine Returns to Vietnam. Wallingford, PA: Pendle Hill Publications, 1987.

Selected Works About Ehrhart

Anderson, Donald, and Thomas G. Bowie, Jr., interviewers. "A Conversation with W. D. Ehrhart." *War, Literature & the Arts: An International Journal of the Humanities*, 8:2 (Fall/Winter 1996), 149–157.

Boughman, Ronald, ed. *The Dictionary of Literary Biography Documentary Series*, vol. 9. Farmington Hills, MI: Cengage Gale Research, 1991; 63–82.

Bova, Annalisa. *Every day I'm always on patrol: testimonianza a trauma di W.D. Ehrhart* [Witnessing trauma in W. D. Ehrhart]. Master's thesis, University of Bergamo, Italy, 2003.

Casale, Frank D. "W. D. Ehrhart and the Extremes of Foreign Policy, Ideology, and American Hegemony." *Entertext 6.2: War & Society*, 6:2 (Winter 2006–2007). http://people.brunel.ac.uk/~acsrrrm/entertext/issue_6_2.htm.

Chattarji, Subarno. *Memories of a Lost War: American Poetic Responses to the Vietnam War*. Oxford: Oxford University Press, 2001.

Goldensohn, Lorrie. *Dismantling Glory: 20th Century Soldier Poetry*. New York: Columbia University Press, 2004.

Gollner, Nicole. "Writing the War: The Works of William Daniel Ehrhart: From Patriot to Poet to Pacifist." Master's thesis, American Institute of American Studies, Karl Franzens-Universit Graz, Austria, 2005.

Gotera, Vince. *Radical Visions: Poetry by Vietnam Veterans*. Athens: University of Georgia Press, 1994.

Jason, Philip K., ed. *Critical Survey of Poetry*, 2d rev. ed. Ipswich, MA: Salem Press, 2002.

Jason, Philip K., and Mark A. Graves, eds. *Encyclopedia of American War Literature*. Westport, CT: Greenwood Press, 2001.

Rosso, Stefano. "Conversazione con William D. Ehrhart e John S. Baky, Philadelphia, ottobre 1997" [A conversation with William D. Ehrhart and John S. Baky, Philadelphia, October 1997], *Ácoma* (no. 19, spring 2000, vol. VII), 40–47. Republished in *Musi gialli e Berretti Verdi. Narrazioni Usa sulla Guerra del Vietnam* [Yellow faces and green berets: American stories on the Vietnam War]. Bergamo: Bergamo University Press, 2003, 233–249.

Slabey, Robert M., ed. *The United States and Viet Nam from War to Peace*. Jefferson, NC: McFarland, 1996.

Tal, Kalí. *Worlds of Hurt: Reading the Literature of Trauma.* Cambridge University Press, 1996. See esp. chap. 4, "The Farmer of Dreams: The Writings of W. D. Ehrhart," 77–114.

War, Literature & the Arts 8:2 (Fall/Winter 1996). Special issue on W. D. Ehrhart.

Waring, Brett. *The Individual in War Literature: A Case Study of W. D. Ehrhart and Modern War Narratives.* Master's thesis, California State University at Dominguez Hills, 2011.

About the Contributors

Ammiel **Alcalay**'s books include *Islanders, Neither Wit Nor Gold: From Then, Scrapmetal, Memories of Our Future, After Jews and Arabs*, and *The Cairo Notebooks*. He has translated widely from Bosnian and Hebrew and is the founder and general editor of *Lost & Found: The CUNY Poetics Document Initiative*.

Since 1989, Donald **Anderson** has been the editor of *War, Literature & the Arts: An International Journal of the Humanities*. He has edited or written several books, including *Aftermath: An Anthology of Post-Vietnam Fiction, When War Becomes Personal: Soldiers' Accounts from the Civil War to Iraq*, and *Gathering Noise from My Life: A Camouflaged Memoir*. A former Air Force officer, he directs creative writing at the United States Air Force Academy.

Jan **Barry** is a poet, author, editor, adjunct professor and award-winning journalist. He is the author of *A Citizen's Guide to Grassroots Campaigns, Earth Songs: New & Selected Poems* and *Life After War & Other Poems*. A Vietnam veteran, he is co-editor of *Winning Hearts & Minds: War Poems by Vietnam Veterans*, among other works. He was co-editor (with W.D. Ehrhart) of *Demilitarized Zones: Veterans after Vietnam*. His website is www.janbarry.net.

Subarno **Chattarji** is an associate professor in the Department of English, University of Delhi, India. He has a D.Phil from the University of Oxford. His publications include *Tracking the Media: Interpretations of Mass Media Discourses in India and Pakistan* and *Memories of a Lost War: American Poetic Responses to the Vietnam War*. He is co-editor of *Globalization in India: Contents and Discontents* and *An Anthology of Indian Prose Writings in English*.

N. Bradley **Christie** is a senior vice president for academic affairs at Erskine College in Due West, South Carolina. In 1988 he published one of the earliest doctoral dissertations on Vietnam War literature, "Another War and Postmodern Memory: Remembering Vietnam." He has since published articles, presented conference papers, and conducted workshops on teaching the war. He is at work on a comprehensive descriptive bibliography of the writings of W. D. Ehrhart.

Joseph **Cox** was the headmaster of the Haverford School, a boys' school outside of Philadelphia, until his recent retirement. He spent 30 years in the U.S. Army, a stint that included 14 years teaching literature at West Point. A Vietnam veteran, he commanded a battalion in the 101st Airborne Division. He holds a Ph.D. from the University of North Carolina at Chapel Hill, and has been the headmaster at Haverford for the past 15 years.

After serving as an officer in the U.S. Navy from 1967 to 1971, including two stints in South Vietnam, Robert C. **Doyle** earned a Ph.D. from Bowling Green State University. In 1994, he published the first study of the American captivity experience, *Voices from Captivity: Interpreting the American POW Narrative*, with a follow-up study, *A Prisoner's Duty: Great Escapes in U.S. Military History*. His recent book *The Enemy in Our Hands* covers the American treatment of POWs from the Revolution to the War on Terror. He is a professor of history at the Franciscan University of Steubenville.

Adam **Gilbert** is a Leverhulme Early Career Fellow in history at the University of Sussex in England. He recently completed a Ph.D. at Cambridge University, writing his dissertation on morality, soldier poetry and the American War in Vietnam.

Nicole **Gollner** earned a master's degree in English and American studies, media studies and Italian at the Faculty of Humanities, Karl-Franzens-University of Graz in Austria. Her thesis was on W. D. Ehrhart. She has worked as a freelance journalist, language teacher, translator, public relations officer, copywriter, editor and lector.

Matthew K. **Irwin** is a doctoral candidate at Texas A&M University. His dissertation explores what troops' cadences, graffiti, folksongs, pirate radio broadcasts, and poetry express about the Vietnam War that other histories omit. He contends that troops capture and confront the war more unflinchingly and honestly than any other records to emerge from Vietnam and argues for a more prominent place for them among the canon of Vietnam War history and literature.

Jean-Jacques **Malo** is the coeditor, with Tony Williams, of *Vietnam War Films* (McFarland, 1994, 2011). Once a professional technical translator, he taught French at the University College, Cardiff, in Wales, as well as at the University of Washington in Seattle. Since 2001 he has taught English at the IUT de Nantes, Université de Nantes in France. He has translated U.S. Vietnam War poetry into French and has published on the Vietnam War and cinema in France and the United States.

Gary **Metras** is the editor, publisher, and letterpress printer of Adastra Press. He has worked as a store clerk, tobacco picker, short-order cook, hod carrier, air traffic controller (U.S. Air Force), bookstore manager, high school English teacher, and college writing instructor. He holds degrees from the University of Massachusetts at Amherst and Goddard College. His poems, essays, and reviews have appeared in more than 200 journals and in 16 collections of poetry.

Martin **Novelli** is a professor of film, history, and humanities at Ocean County College in Toms River, New Jersey. He is also an adjunct professor of liberal arts at the University of the Arts in Philadelphia, Pennsylvania, and adjunct professor of history at Kean University at Ocean. He was formerly dean of humanities, fine arts and media studies at Ocean County College. With Frank Wetta, Novelli co-wrote *The Long Reconstruction: The Post–Civil War South in History, Film and Memory*.

Diederik **Oostdijk** is a professor of English and American literature at the VU University in Amsterdam and a board member of the Netherlands American Studies Association. He holds a Ph.D. from Radboud University Nijmegen, Netherlands. He is co-editor of *Tales of the Great American Victory: World War II in Politics and Poetics*, has published many articles on American literature and culture and is the author of *Among the Nightmare Fighters: American Poets of World War II* (2011).

Edward F. **Palm** is a Vietnam veteran and retired Marine officer. He earned a Ph.D. in English and American literature from the University of Pennsylvania and has published extensively on literature and military affairs. He has been a tenured full professor and department chair at Glenville State College and has held dean appointments at Maryville University of St. Louis and Olympic College. He writes an opinion column for his local newspaper, the *Kitsap Sun*.

Dale **Ritterbusch** is a Vietnam veteran and author of two books of poetry, including *Lessons Learned*, a collection of poems on the Vietnam War and its aftermath. He is a professor of English in the Department of Languages and Literatures at the University of Wisconsin–Whitewater but is working as, for the second time, the distinguished visiting professor in the Department of English and Fine Arts at the United States Air Force Academy.

Yoko **Shirai** teaches American history at Japan Women's University in Tokyo. She received a Ph.D. in American history from the University of Pennsylvania. She translated W. D. Ehrhart's poems "Making the Children Behave," "Invasion of Grenada," and "For Mrs. Na" into Japanese in her book on the Vietnam War in American history. Her research focuses on the Indian-white relations in Colonial Pennsylvania and on the poetry of Vietnam veterans.

Clint **Van Winkle**, an Iraq War veteran, is the author of *Soft Spots: A Marine's Memoir of Combat and Post-Traumatic Stress Disorder*. He is also the director of *The Guilt*, a documentary film about combat veterans, and an alumnus of Swansea University's master's program in creative and media writing. He is working on his second book and his website is Clintvanwinkle.com.

David A. **Willson** worked at Green River Community College in Auburn, Washington, as a reference librarian and instructor. He is a Vietnam War bibliographer and the author of four novels, *In the Army Now* and the trilogy *The REMF Diary*, about his tour of duty in Vietnam. Now retired, he reviews books for *The Veteran*.

In 1966 Charles L. **Yates** enlisted in the Navy and spent the next four years learning Vietnamese and putting it to use during 18 months at Da Nang, serving as an air crewman in reconnaissance aircraft. He completed his education with the help of G.I. Bill funds, including a Ph.D. in East Asian studies at Princeton. He teaches in the history department at Earlham College in Richmond, Indiana.

Index

Numbers in ***bold italics*** indicate pages with photographs.

Achilles in Vietnam 170
Adams, Nick 124
Adastra Press 8, 125–134, 160, 187–196, 272
"*Adoquinas*" 129–130
Afghanistan 65, 201, 214
After Jews and Arabs 271
After Our War 108*n*7
"After the Fire" 126, 128
Aftermath: An Anthology of Post-Vietnam Fiction 271
"Again, Rehoboth" 160
"Against a Coming Extinction: W.D. Ehrhart and the Evolving Canon of Vietnam Veterans' Poetry" 138*n*14
Against Forgetting: Twentieth-Century Poetry of Witness 75*n*65
Agent Orange 34, 43–45, 56, 162,
Agnew, Spiro T. 34
Alcalay, Ammiel 4, 50–58, 271
Alexievich, Svetlana 74*n*35
"All About Death" 70, 136, 164
"All About Love" 70, 136
"All Things Considered" 12*n*27
"America in the Late 20th Century" 133
American Civil War 54
American foreign policy 84, 92, 104
"American Pie" 170
American Poetry Review 33, 157
American politics and politicians 203
American Revolution 78
"American War Myths and Vietnam Veteran Narratives" 221
Amherst College 190
Among the Nightmare Fighters: American Poets of World War II 273
"And what would you do, ma..." 138*n*10
Anderson, Donald 3, 12*n*26, 14–21, 152*n*3, 271
Anderson, Doug 5, 77–87
"Another Life" 232–233

An Anthology of Indian Prose Writings in English 271
apartheid 152
Arizona State University 10, 241
"At Last" 123
"At the Vietnam Memorial" 80
Auden, W.H. 100
Austria 3
Autobiography of Frederick Douglass 55
Autobiography of Malcolm X 55
Avon Books 134–135, 161
The Awkward Silence 124–125
Axtell, James 26

Backstreet Editions 125, 126–127
Bacon, Francis 102
Baghdad 212
Baky, John S. v, 7, 12*n*23, 139
Balaban, John 33–34, 41, 90, 100, 102, 106–107, 190
Balkans 201
Barrett, Faith 53
Barry, Jan 6, 7–9, 56, 72, 120, 122, 156–166, 271
Bastide, Roger 23
"Batter My Heart with the Liquor Store: or, Teaching Poetry to Teenagers" 163
Battle of Chugen, Northern China 112
Beacon on the Hill 105
"Beautiful Wreckage" (poem) 133, 250–251
Beautiful Wreckage: New & Selected Poems (book) xx, 13, 49, 126–134, 184, 189, 198, 242, 244, 250–251, 253–263, 265–266
Bedell, Diana 151
Beidler, Philip 142, 167–168, 173–174, 176
Beirut 212
Beloungy, Jim 151
Ben Tre City 181–182, 185
Benjamin, Walter 23, 27
Bielanko, David 200
Bielanko, Serge 200

275

Bierce, Ambrose 183
Big Table 50
Bildungsroman 183
Bilgere, George 80–81
Billy the Kid 51
Binh Hoa 42
Bishop, Elizabeth 140
Bishop, Maurice 84
Black Mountain Review 50
Blackburn, Simon 60
The Blessing: New and Selected Poems 188
"Blighters" 102
The Blind Swimmer: Selected Early Poems 1970–1975 188
"The Blizzard of Sixty-Six" 127, 134
The Bodies Beneath the Table 135, 144–146, 164, 189, 194, 252, 259
Bodwell, Joshua 187, 195
Born on the Fourth of July (film) 244
Born on the Fourth of July (novel) 22, 237
Boughman, Ronald 152*n*3
Bowie, Thomas G., Jr. 12*n*26, 152*n*3
Bowling Green State University 182
"Briana" 251
Brodsky, Joseph 82
Browning, Elizabeth Barrett 140
Bryant, Charles 38
Bryant, William Cullen 53
Bundy, McGeorge 44, 46, 60
Bundy, William P. 34
Burke, Edmund 218*n*24
"Burning Leaves" 136
Bush, George Herbert Walker 46, 204
Bush, George Walker 204
Busted: A Vietnam Veteran in Nixon's America 3, 14–21, 143, 162, 172–173, 175, 199–206, 242, 244
Butler, Smedley 215

The Cairo Noteboooks 271
Calica, Lovella 165
Call Me Ishmael 51
Cambodian invasion 181
Caputo, Philip 24, 221
Carrying the Darkness: American Indochina—The Poetry of the Vietnam War 134–135, 161
Carrying the Darkness: The Poetry of the Vietnam War 9, 82, 134–135, 208
"Carrying the Ghost of Ray Catina" 37
Cassidy, Don 147
Catina, Ray 37
Catlin, Alan 37
Central America 1, 84, 128–130, 150
Central Office of South Vietnam 182
Channel Fever (book) 125–134
"Channel Fever" (poem) 129, 133

Chapman, Guy 24
"Chasing Locomotives" 130
Chattarji, Subarno 4, 7, 22–30, 84, 139, 271
"The Children of Hanoi" 131
Childress, William 38
Chimei Hamada: Prints and Sculptures "What Is Human Being?" 119*n*18
China 6
"Christ" 116, 121, 158
Christie, N. Bradley 7, 120–138, 271
Cimarron Review 244
A Citizen's Guide to Grassroots Campaigns 163, 271
City Lights (publisher) 271
Civil War 78, 82, 185
Clarion College 37
Clifton, Merritt 121, 123, 125, 150, 189
Close Quarters 171
"Coaching Winter Track in Time of War" 65, 223, 251–252
Cobley, Evelyn 24
Coffman, Lisa 151
Colby, William 181
Cold War 53–54, 84
Collected Poems (George Oppen) 188
The Collected Poems of Theodore Roethke 188
Collins, Billy 99, 188
"Colorado, June 1976" 123, 129
"Coming Home" 122, 135
"Coming Home, March 1968" 122
Con Thien 36, 180, 234
"Concord Hymn" 78
"A Confirmation" 124, 129, 134, 160
Connolly, David 34, 133
Conrad, Joseph 103
"Continuity" 128
Cooney, James 137*n*8, 160
COSVN *see* Central Office of South Vietnam
Coulter, Ann 208
The Country Between Us 191
"Cowgirls, Teachers & Dreams" 252–253
Cox, Joseph 10, 219–227, 272
Cu Chi District 129
Cuban Missile Crisis 15
"Cultural Effects of Vietnam (EVAC)" 40
"Cycling the Rosental" 133

Da Nang 274
"The Damage We Do" 136
"Dancing" 254
Davis, Rebecca 227*n*16
Dead on a High Hill: Essays on War, Literature and Living, 2002–2012 1, 31–48, 163, 165
"Dead on a High Hill: Poetry of the Korean War" 38
Deahl, Tom 136
dean of Vietnam War poetry 141–142

"Dear John" letter 201
"Death in America" 165
"The Death of Kings" 123
"Death of the Ball Turret Gunner" 99
"Death Wish" 126
The Deer Hunter 143
Delhi 4
Demilitarized Zones: Veterans After Vietnam 7, 56, 122–123, 126, 128, 134, 156–157, 159, 271
Dewey Canyon III 52
Dickey, James 183
Dickinson, Emily 53, 140
The Dictionary of Literary Biography Documentary Series 152*n*3
The Dictionary of Literary Biography Yearbook 191
Dien Ban 115
di Prima, Diane 57
Dispatches 176
The Distance We Travel 126–135, 204, 257, 261
DMZ see *Demilitarized Zones: Veterans After Vietnam*
Donne, John 100
Douglas, John 134
Dove, Rita 188
Doyle, Robert C. 8–9, 178–186, 272
"The Dream" 93–94
"Dropping Leela Off at School" 133
"The Ducks on Wissahickon Creek" 129
"Dulce et Decorum Est" 82, 99
Duncan, Robert 99
Dylan, Bob 34, 170

Earlham College 207
Earth Songs: New & Selected Poems 165–166, 271
East River Anthology 122, 159–160
Ehrhart, Anne Gulick (W.D. Ehrhart's wife) 33, 127, 130, 141, 147, 151, 192, 194, 205, 216
Ehrhart, Leela Gulick (W.D. Ehrhart's daughter) 33, 96, 129–134, 143, 145, 147, 165, 204–205, 209, 216, 219
Eisenhower, Dwight David 45
El Salvador 62, 130
"Elegy for a New Conscript" 109, 111
"Elegy for a New Conscript: Sentinel 1954" *112*
Elek, Lucas 220
Ellison, Ralph 79
Emerson, Gloria 68, 133, 162
Emerson, Ralph Waldo 53, 78, 226
Empire 123–125, 134, 158, 259
Emporia, Kansas 35
The Enemy in Our Hands 272
"Epiphany" 136, 195

Erskine College 137*n*1
"The Eruption of Mount St. Helens" 126, 129
The Eternal Ones of the Dream: Selected Poems 1990–2010 188
Evans, Jeptha 125–134
"Everett Dirksen, His Wife, You & Me" 128, 254–255
Evergreen 50
"Explico Algunas Cosas" 108*n*4

"Facing It" 77–87
Fall, Bernard 103
Fallujah 212
Faludy, Gyorgy 124
"The Farmer" 49, 127
"Farmer Nguyen" 121, 134, 238, 255
54th Massachusetts Volunteer Infantry 78
Fighting and Writing the Vietnam War 137*n*1
"Finding My Old Battalion Command Post" 131
First Casualty Press 120, 159
Fish, Lydia 230
The Floating Bear 50
Fonda, Jane 34, 38, 204
"For a Coming Extinction" 131
"For Anne, Approaching Thirty-five" 165
"For Mrs. Na" 135, 204, 255–256, 273
"For the Union Dead" 78
Forché, Carolyn 75*n*65, 191
Ford, Gerald 34
Fort Benning 100
Fourteen Landing Zones: Approaches to Vietnam War Literature 137*n*1
"Fragment: 5 September 1967" 121
"Fragment: The Generals' War" 121, 231
France 3
Franciscan University of Steubenville, Ohio 183
Frankl, Viktor 71
Franklin, H. Bruce 18, 55–56, 167, 203
Franks, Gen. Tommy 102
Free Fire Zones 159
Freud, Sigmund 79
Friday's Egg Calendar 45
From Both Sides Now: The Poetry of the Vietnam War and Its Aftermath 135, 138*n*17
From Hell 200
From the Warring Factions 271
Front'n Center 125
Frost, Robert 100–101, 145
"Full Moon" 114, 121
Fussell, Paul 226

Gaffney, Gerry 124
Gardiner, Judith 141
Gathering Noise from My Life: A Camouflaged Memoir 271

"Geese" 126, 128
"The Generals' War" 261
A Generation of Peace (1975) 1, 13, 121–122, 125, 133–134, 142, 254–256, 258, 260–261
A Generation of Peace (1977, *Samisdat*) 121–122, 128, 133, 254–256, 258, 260–261
"Ghosts from Iraq" 244
Giap, Gen. Vo Nguyen 33
Giardinelli, Alisa 183
"Gifts" 191–192
Gilbert, Adam 7, 59–76, 139, 272
Ginsberg, Allen 54
Girard, René 24
Globalization in India: Contents and Discontents 271
Glover, Jonathan 62
Goethe, Johann Wolfgang von 105
Going After Cacciato 174, 176
Going Back: An Ex-Marine Returns to Vietnam 91, 129, 147
Goldwater, Barry 34
Gollner, Nicole 6, 88–98, 272
Golubnichaya, A. 74n35
"Good Fences Make Good Neighbors" 37
Gotera, Vince 146
"Governor Rhodes Keeps His Word" 131
"Granddad" 123
The Granite Pail: The Selected Poems of Lorine Niedecker 188
"Great Balls of Fire" 43
Greatest Hits: 1970–2000 135
Greatest Hits series 135
Greek chorus 175
Green River Community College, Auburn, WA 43
Greenwood, Lee 210–211, 215
Grenada 212
"Growing Older Alone" 126
"Guatemala" 131
"Guerrilla War" 115, 135, 121, 171, 184, 235–236, 256
The Guilt 10, 245, 273
"Guns" 204, 257

Hagopian, Patrick 78, 84
Halcyon 125
Hamada, Chimei 6, 109–119
HAMADA Chimei: Oral History 118n4
Hanoi Jane: Sex, and Fantasies of Betrayal 204
Harris, John 132
Hart, Frederick 6
Harte, Bret 53
Hashi, Hidefumi 118n2
Hass, Kirsten Ann 78
Hassett, Steve 138n10
Haswell, Janis 69
Hattie, John 223

Haverford School 3, 10, 36, 140, 142, 164, 219–227
Hawkins, Tom 56
Heart of Darkness 103
"The Heart of the Poem" 130, 155
Hedrick, Wally 54
Heinemann, Larry 2, 34, 41, 54, 171
"Hell's Music: A Neglected Poem from a Neglected War" 38
Hemingway, Ernest 124
Henry V 100
Henry V 103
Herr, Michael 167, 169, 176
Hidalgo, Stephen P. 137n5
"High Country" 61
Hill, Matthew 68
Hinojosa, Rolando 38
Hiroshima 71
"History of Bop" 54
Hitler, Adolf 34
Ho Chi Minh 34
Ho Chi Minh City 129, 204
Hoffman, David 152n1
Hoi An 115
Holland, Norman Norwood 245n2
Hollander, Clair Needell 223
Hollenbach, Bob 33
Holocaust 24, 167–168
"Home Before Morning" (poem) 136, 146
Home Before Morning: The True Story of an Army Nurse in Vietnam (book) 44
"The Hooded Legion" 82–83
"How It All Comes Back" 131
Howe, Julia Ward 53
Howl 54
Hué City 5, 36, 180, 202, 233
Hughes, Langston 53–54, 56
"The Hunter" 126
"Hunting" 114, 121–122, 134, 233–234, 258
Huong My district 184
Hynes, Samuel 24

"I Have a Rendezvous with Death" 100
"I Want to Try It All Before I Go: The Life and Poetry of William Wantling" 39
"If This Be War" 165
The Iliad 100
Illinois College 102, 205
"I'm Explaining a Few Things" 99
Imaginative Representations of the Vietnam War Collection, La Salle University, Philadelphia 7, 12n23
"Imagine" 122
"In Distrust of Merits" 100
In the Restaurant 125–134
In the Shadow of Vietnam: Essays, 1977–1991 31–48, 92

Infantry School 100
"The Invasion of Grenada" 77–87, 128, 133–149, 172–173, 261–262, 273
Invisible Man 79
"Ippeisotsu no Sengo" (A Soldier After WWII) 118*n*2
Iraq 201, 213, 241
Iraq War 101
Irish, Jane 6, 12*n*23
Irwin, Matthew K. 10, 228–246, 272
Islanders 271
Iwo Jima 80

Jaffe, Maggie 98*n*14
James, William 78
"James Magner, Jr. William Meredith and Reg Saner: Reluctant Poets of the Korean War" 38
Jarrell, Randall 83, 99–100, 104
Jason, Philip K. 137*n*1, 141
Jaspers, Karl 63
Jay, Martin 27
Joe Patterson Smith Lecture 108*n*11, 205
Johnson, Lyndon B. 60, 179, 185, 201
Joll, James 62
Jones, John Paul 14, 178
Jones, Richard 188
jus ad bellum 66, 70
jus in bello 66, 70
Just and Unjust Warriors: The Moral and Legal Status of Soldiers 66
Just and Unjust Wars 66
"Just for Laughs" (poem) 221
Just for Laughs: Poems by W.D. Ehrhart (book) 126–135, 145–147, 256

Kabul 212
Kali (Hindu goddess) 79
Kanagawa, Japan 109
Kaplan, Steven 26
Keegan, John 229
Keith, Toby 211
"Ken and Bill's Excellent Adventure" 34, 38, 202
Kennedy, John F. 15, 89, 103, 178
Kenneth Patchen Selected Poems 188
Kent State killings 3, 63, 71, 201, 243
Kerouac, Jack 54
Khrushchev, Nikita 15
"Kids in Philly" 200
Kien Hoa Province 181, 184
Kikuhata, Mokuma 118*n*2
King, Nicola 24
Kinnell, Galway 188
Kirmayer, Laurence J. 29*n*22
Kissinger, Henry 46
Kitsap Sun 273

Komunyakaa Yusef 5, 35, 77–87
Korean War 54, 88, 141, 179; poetry 38; writers 38–39
"Kosovo" 136
Koven, Eli 227*n*10
Kovic, Ron 22, 237
Kurtz (novel) 103

Laâbi, Abellatif 143
Lambeck, Michael 28
Langland, Joseph 188
Larkin, Philip 102
La Salle University 7, 39, 81
"Last Flight Out from the War Zone" 129
"Last of the Hard-hearted Ladies" 135
"The Last Time I Dreamed About the War" 265–266
Latin America 147–148
Lebanon 201
"Legend of a Latrine 1951" 113
Lembcke, Jerry 203–204
"Lemonade 2 Cents?" 39
Lessons Learned 273
"Letter" 124, 160, 173, 258–259
"A Letter to McGeorge Bundy" 46
"Letting Go" 164
Levertov, Denise 9, 70
Lewis, Jerry Lee 43
Li Po 100
Life After War & Other Poems 271
The Life of Poetry 53
"...the light that cannot fade..." 134
Lin, Maya Ying 5–6, 77–87
A Little History 271
Loeb, Jeff 28*n*7
Logevall, Fredrik 60
Long Binh 41–42
The Long Reconstruction: The Post–Civil War South in History, Film and Memory 273
Longfellow, Henry Wadsworth 53
"Losses" 83
Lost & Found: The CUNY Poetics Document Initiative 271
"The Lotus Cutters of Hô Tây" 131, 261
Love My Rifle More Than You 107
Lowell, Robert 78
Luce, Don 41
Lux, Thomas 188

The Madness of It All: Essays on War, Literature and American Life 31–48, 102, 157, 163
Maguire, Barrie 32
Mahony, Phillip 135
Mailer, Norman 144
Making Sense of the Sixties 12*n*32, 152*n*1, 207
"Making the Children Behave" 6, 13, 57, 67, 109–119, 123, 135, 188, 204, 273

Malo, Jean-Jacques 7, 139–153, 272
Manchester, England 41
Manchester Polytechnical Institute 40, 199
Manning, Frederic 24
"Manning the Walls" 136
Maple Valley 38
Marah 200
"Marching in the Night: Artillery Soldiers Marching through Mountains" 111
"Marching in the Night: Rain" 111
marijuana 16
Marin, Pilar 41
Marine Corps Gazette 33, 174
Marwick, Arthur 229
Marx, Karl 34
Matters of the Heart and Other Poems 125–134, 160–161, 190–191, 251
The Maximus Poems 51
McAdams, Jamie 220
McAdoo, James J., Jr. 220
McCarthy, Gerald 82–83
McClure, Michael 54
McGrath, Thomas 137n8, 160
Mclean, Don 170
McLoughlin, Kate 80–81
McMahan, Jeff 67
McNamara, Robert 34, 60, 185, 237
McVeigh, Stephen 7, 139
Medal of Honor 185
"Meeting" 126
Mekong River 181
Melling, Phil 18
Melville, Herman 51, 53, 55
Memories of a Lost War: American Poetic Responses to the Vietnam War 271
Memories of Our Future 271
"Mending Wall" 100
Merritt, William 24
Metras, Gary 8, 126–135, 187–196, 272
M.I.A. or Mythmaking in America 203
Middle East 148
"Midnight at the Vietnam Veterans Memorial" 83, 77–87, 135
"Military Intelligence" 221
Miller, Cristanne 53
Miller, Henry 161
Mitchell, W.J.T. 80
Moby-Dick 55
"Money in the Bank" 123
Moore, Alan 200
Moore, Marianne 100
More, Thomas 104
"More Than You Ever Imagined" 131
"Morning Edition" 12n27
"Mostly Nothing Happens" 126–135, 204
multiple myeloma 41, 44–45
Münster, Germany 8

Museum of Modern Art, Hayama, Japan 109–112
"Music Lessons" 136
My Lai 71, 212

The Nature of Literary Response: Five Readers Reading 245n2
Naval Intelligence Liaison Officer 181
Navy SEALs 181–182, 186
Navy Special Warfare 181
"Near-sighted" 126
Neither Wit Nor Gold: From Then 271
Nelson, James Davis 12n22
Neruda, Pablo 99
The Netherlands 3
New and Selected Poems 1975–1995 (Thomas Lux) 188
New Hampshire Gazette 33
"New Jersey Pine Barrens" 135
New Jersey Waterways 42
New Voices 121
New York City police 162–163
New York Public Theater 159
New York Times 162, 223
Newman, John 137n5
"The Next Step" 135, 234–235
Nguyen Thi My Huong 129, 151
Nguyen Thi Na, Mrs. 92, 129
Nguyen Van Hung 130, 151
"*Nicaragua Libre*" 129–131
"Night Patrol" 121
NILO *see* Naval Intelligence Liaison Officer
9/11 99–100, 136
Nixon, Richard 63, 162, 185, 201, 204
No Gun Ri 212
"Los Norteamericanos y Centroamérica" 84
North American Review 146
Northwoods (publisher) 124
"Not Marble Nor the Guilded Monuments" 81
"Not Your Problem" 130
"Nothing Profound" xx, 51, 133
Novelli, Martin 9, 199–206, 273

Obama, Barack 27, 34
O'Brien, Tim 2, 14, 24, 26, 161, 167–169, 174–176, 221, 235
"The Obsession" 123, 126, 159
Ocean County College 199–206
Ochester, Ed 188
"Oda a los calcetines" 108n3
"Ode to My Socks" 99
Office of the Special Ambassador 181
The Old Huntsman and Other Poems 108n10
Olson, Charles 51, 54, 56
"On Common Sense and Conscience" 157, 108n12
"On Returning to the Front After Leave" 102

"On the Eve of Destruction" 71–72
"On the Plain of Marathon" 191
"One Night on Guard Duty" 121
"The One That Died" 121, 135, 172
"One, Two, Many Vietnams?" 206n8
"The One Who Died" 121
onomastics 80
Oostdijk, Diederik 5, 77–87, 273
Operation Stone 234
Oppen, George 188
Ordinary Lives: Platoon 1005 and the Vietnam War 104, 147, 183, 186, 202
Origin 50
"The Origins of Passion" 36
OSA *see* Office of the Special Ambassador
The Outer Banks & Other Poems 1–2, 49, 94, 125–135, 150, 191, 253, 255, 261
Owen, Wilfred 82, 99, 142, 183, 215

Pacek, Michael 44
pacifism 152
"Pagan" 128
Palling, Bruce 152n1
Palm, Edward F. 4, 8, 167–177, 273
Panama 107, 212
Papp, Joseph 159
Paquet, Basil T. 120, 159
Parker, Charlie 54
Parris Island 132, 179
Passing Time: Memoir of a Vietnam Veteran Against the War 3, 9, 14–21, 22–30, 134, 143, 175, 199–206, 219–220, 242, 244
Patchen, Kenneth 54
"Patrick" 6, 212
"Paula Kay" 165
Peace Is Our Profession: Poems and Passages of War Protest 158, 160, 166
Pecos Bill 14, 178
Pennsylvania State University 8
The Pentagon Papers 5, 23
"Perkasie Lost: W.D. Ehrhart's Vietnam Saga" 177n29
Persian Gulf 107
Philadelphia Inquirer 33
Philadelphia newspapers 161
The Phoenix 160
Pierce, Paula Kay 159, 165
Platoon 1005 105
"The Poet as Athlete" 130
"Poetry" (William Wantling) 39
Poetry Wales 33
Poets & Writers. Poets & Writers Magazine 137n7
Pol Pot 34
Popular Culture Association/American Culture Association Conference, Toronto, March 1990 139

Post-Traumatic Stress Disorder *see* PTSD
"POW/MIA" 133, 135
POW-MIA myth 203
Pratt, John Clark 40–41, 95, 183
Prints and Sculptures 118n2
A Prisoner's Duty: Great Escapes in U.S. Military History 272
PTSD 93, 148, 220, 241, 244
Pudding House Publications 135
Purple Heart 36
"Purple Heart" 133

Quaker college 207
Quang Tri 37

Raab, Lawrence 188
Rambo 43
Reagan, Ronald 34, 84, 150, 204
Real War Stories 200
"Red-tailed Hawks" 134–135
"A Relative Thing" 65, 117, 123, 173, 204, 238, 249–250
The REMF Diaries 274
REMF Diary 40
REMFs 37
"Resistance and Revision in Poetry by Vietnam War Veterans" 137n1
"Responsibility" 62, 128, 150, 205
Ringnalda, Donald 29n26, 137n1
Ritterbusch, Dale 6, 99–108, 273
Rivers, Mendal 45
"The Road Not Taken" 101
Rodin, David 66
Rompf, Kraft 125–134
Rootless 123, 125–126, 133, 263
Ross, Robert 107
Rosso, Stefano 7, 153n3
Rottmann, Larry 120, 159
"Round Eyed Blues" 200
Rousseau, Ryan 183
Rukeyser, Muriel 52–54, 57
Rumaker, Michael 271
A Rumor of War 25
Rumsfeld, Donald 213
Rusk, Dean 60
Russian roulette 143
Rutgers, the State University of New Jersey 199–206
Rutgers University Press 163

Sailing Around the Room: New and Selected Poems 188
Saint Gaudens, Augustus 78
Saint Michael's College 236
Sakamoto, Masafumi 119n18
Samisdat (magazine) 150, 189
Samisdat (publisher) 121, 123, 161

The Samisdat Poems of W. D. Ehrhart 124–125, 133, 136, 198
Sandy Spring Friends School 224, 241
Sassoon, Siegfried 24, 28n3, 100, 102, 183
"Saved" 165
Schlosser, Robert L. 44–45
"A Scientific Treatise for My Wife" 135, 146, 205
The Seattle Post-Intelligencer 33
"Second Thoughts" 130, 204
"The Secret Lives of Boys" 136, 195
Seeger, Alan 100, 102
Selected Poems (Galway Kinnell) 188
Selected Poems (James Tate) 188
Selected Poems (Joseph Langland) 188
Selected Poems (Rita Dove) 188
Selected Poems (William Carlos Williams) 188
Selected Poems: A Bilingual Edition 108n4
Selected Poems of Thomas Merton 188
Selverian, Mac 227n9
"Seminar on the Nature of Reality" 136
"Sermon on the Mount" 105
"Setting the Record Straight: An Addendum to the Life and Poetry of William Wantling" 39
"Sex, Death and Military Might" 40
"Shadows" 126
Shakespeare, William 81–82, 100
Shaw, Robert Gould 78
Shay, Jonathan 170
Shirai, Yoko 6, 109–119, 273
The Short-Timers 25
Shue, Henry 66
"The Simple Lives of Cats" 216
Sino-Japanese War 111
Sir! No Sir! 203
Six Gallery reading 54
Skunk Missal 125–134
Slabey, Robert 41
"Sleeping with a Light On" 159
"Sleeping with General Chi" 135
Sleeping with the Dead (book) 135, 189, 195, 259
"Sleeping with the Dead" (poem) 259
Small Press Review 127, 191
"A Small Romance" 130, 146
"Small Song for Daddy" 130, 135
Smith, John C. (gunnery sergeant) 179
Smith, Lorrie 64, 137n1, 138n14, 236–237
"The Sniper's Mark" 233
Soft Spots: A Marine's Memoir of Combat and Post-Traumatic Stress Disorder 10–11, 244–245, 273
soldier-poets 77, 91, 94, 230
"Some Books Are More Equal Than Others" 227n11
"Some Other World" 106

"Song for Leela, Bobby and Me" 107, 131, 135, 204, 219
Sonnet 55 (Shakespeare) 81
"Sound Advice" 104, 127
South Africa 1, 152
South America 201
"Souvenirs" 185, 260
The Spitting Image: Myth, Memory and the Legacy of Vietnam 203–204
Stallone, Sylvester 43
"Stealing Hubcaps" 25
USS *Steinaker DD 863* 180–181
Stone, Oliver 221, 244
Strasbourg, France 8
Street Without Joy 103
Studies in Education 163
"Surviving the Bomb One More Day" 260–261
Svitanya 141
Swarthmore College 11n13, 121, 148, 175, 220
Swarthmore College Bulletin 33, 220–221

Takahama, Sugako 119n18
Takenaga, Ken 7, 32, 37–38, 202
Tal, Kali 1, 71, 93–96, 168–170, 172, 175
Tales of the Great American Victory: World War II in Politics and Poetics 273
Tarn, Nathaniel 108n4
Tate, James 188
Taylor, Charles 28
"The Teacher" 70, 125, 160, 197–198, 241
"Teaching the Vietnam War" 43
Tell Me Lies About Vietnam 89
"Temple Poem" 136
Tet Offensive 5, 180, 202, 233
Texas Tech University Press 134–135, 161
"Thank You for Your Service" 11n12, 218n27
"That Was Then, This Is Now: Reflections on the Late American War in Vietnam" 108n11, 205
"They Want Enough Rice" 37, 38
"'They Want Enough Rice': Reflections on the Late American War in Vietnam" 205, 206n10
The Things They Carried 26, 174
The 13th Valley 25
"The Three Soldiers" 6
Thunder's Mouth Press 125–134
"Time on Target" 122, 135, 171–172
"To Maynard on the Long Road Home" 262–263
"To P.T., a Poet, Who Holds That Good Poets Are Always Nice People (Even Robert Frost)" 108n7
"To the Asian Victors" 160
"To Those Who Have Gone Home Tired" (poem) 71–72, 123, 134, 157, 263

To Those Who Have Gone Home Tired: New & Selected Poems (book) 13, 61, 125–134, 139, 149, 198, 250–251, 255–256, 258–263
Tokyo Art School 112
Tokyo National University of Fine Arts and Music 112
Tonkin Gulf Incident 179
Tracking the Media: Interpretations of Mass Media Discourses in India and Pakistan 271
Trinh, Staff Sergeant 116
Trocano, Thomas 227n17
truth-telling 168, 176
"Truth-Telling and Literary Values in the Vietnam Novel" 168
"Tugboats on the Delaware" 42
"Turning Sixty" 136
"Twice Betrayed" 129, 135
"Twodot, Montana" 124

"Unaccustomed Mercies" (poem) 131, 157, 219
Unaccustomed Mercy: Soldier-Poets of the Vietnam War (book) 53, 134–135, 161
"The Uncanny" 79
Under Fire 72
"Unforgettable Face A and B" 109–119
"Unforgettable Face A 2008" **110**
"Unforgettable Face B 2008" **111**
U.S. Air Force Academy 7, 202
"The United States Screw and Bolt Company" 43–46, 55
University of Bergamo 7
University of Delhi 271
University of Illinois at Chicago Circle 3, 141, 224
University of Massachusetts-Boston 189
University of Massachusetts Press 162
University of Notre Dame Vietnam Reconciliation Conference (1993) 221
University of Strasbourg II 183
University of the Arts in Philadelphia 199–206
University of Wales 7
University of Washington 39
Unreconstructed: Poems Selected and New 188
Unthank, Victoria Christine 137n1

V Is for Vendetta 200
Van Devanter, Lynda 34, 44, 136, 146, 151
Van Winkle, Clint 10–11, 241–246, 273
"Variations on Squam Lake" 133
The Veteran 6
Veterans of Foreign Wars (VFW) 100
VFW *see* Veterans of Foreign Wars
Viet Cong flag 185
"Viet Nam" 160

"Viet Nam—February 1967" 114, 121, 124, 142
Vietcong guerrilla 116
Vietnam, a Television History 12n32, 152n1, 207
Vietnam Generation 37
Vietnam Generation (journal) 129
Vietnam Generation Inc. & Burning Cities Press 126–134
Vietnam-Perkasie: A Combat Marine Memoir 3, 8–9, 14–21, 55, 114, 142–143, 171–175, 182–183, 199–206
Vietnam Veterans Against the War (VVAW) 5, 159, 214
Vietnam Veterans Memorial 5–6, 27, 77–87
"The Vietnam War and the Academy" 40–41
Vietnam War Commemoration 7
The Vietnam War in American Stories, Songs, and Poems 56
Vietnam War Films 272
Vietnam War Literature: An Annotated Bibliography of Imaginative Works About Americans Fighting in Vietnam 137n5
Vietnam War Paintings 12n22
"A Vietnamese Bidding Farewell to the Remains of an American" 133
Virginia Quarterly Review 33
Visible Signs: New and Selected Poems 188
"Visiting My Parents' Grave" 264–265
Voices from Captivity: Interpreting the American POW Narrative 272
The VVA Veteran 33, 162
VVAW *see* Vietnam Veterans Against the War

"Waiting for the Fire" 43
Walden, Dan 178, 182
The Wall 5–6, 33; *see also* Vietnam Veterans Memorial
"The Wall" (Doug Anderson) 5, 77–87
"The Wall" (Yusef Komunyakaa) 77–87
Walzer, Michael 66–67
"Wanting" 123
Wantling, William 38, 42
War Baby 161
War, Literature & the Arts: An International Journal of the Humanities 7, 33, 138n14, 202, 271
"A Warning to My Students" 68, 127–128, 205, 217n14
Warrior Writers project 165
Warrior Writers workshop for veterans of the wars in Afghanistan and Iraq 164
Washington Post 33
Watchmen 200
"Water" 129

Watergate 16
Watts Riots 72
"The Way Light Bends" 130
Wayne, John 63, 241
wdehrhart.com 202
Weigl, Bruce 34, 90–91, 190
"Welcome Home" parade 64
Wertheimer, Eric 10, 241–243
West Point 10, 221–222, 272
West Side Story 194
Westmoreland, Gen. William 33, 102, 237
WHAM see *Winning Hearts and Minds: War Poems by Vietnam Veterans*
"What Better Way to Begin" 136
"What I Know About Myself" 68, 133
"What Keeps Me Going" 96, 129, 165
"What Makes a Man" 149
"What War Does" 102, 105
"What We're Buying" 130
"What You Gave Me" 130
"What's the Point of Poetry" 165
"When I Saw the Wild Rabbit" 193
When War Becomes Personal: Soldiers' Accounts from the Civil War to Iraq 271
"Where Beauty Is Found" 192–193
Whitman, Walt 53
"Who's Responsible?" 32, 39
"Why Didn't You Tell Me?" 163
"Why I Am Certain" 127
"Why I Don't Mind Rocking Leela to Sleep" 106
"Why the Kurds Die in the Mountains" 131
Wilhems-Universität Münster 183
Williams, Kayla 107
Williams, Tony 97*n*7, 272

Williams, William Carlos 54, 188
Willson, Brian 34
Willson, David A. 4, 31–48, 274
Wilson, Keith 38
Wimmer, Adi 41, 167, 169
Wind 125
Winning Hearts & Minds: War Poems by Vietnam Veterans 1, 7, 62, 114, 120–122, 125, 131, 134, 142, 156, 158–159, 161–162, 165, 271
Winter, Jay 72
Winter Bells 125–134, 203, 256
"Winter Bells" 130
Wolf, John 222
Wolff, Tobias 24
"Words for My Daughter" 106
Words for the Hour 53
"The World of HAMADA Chimei: Elegy and Humor in Prints and Sculptures" 109
World War I 20, 22–24, 52, 72, 99
World War II 6, 63, 83, 88, 99–100, 113, 126, 170, 173, 178–179
Worlds of Hurt: Reading the Literatures of Trauma 93, 169
Wounded Knee 212
Wounded Warriors offices, New York City 164

Yates, Charles L. 9, 207–218, 274
Yoshida, Hiroshi 118*n*4
Yugen 50

Zinky Boys: Soviet Voices from the Afghanistan War 74*n*35